The Ottomans and Eastern Europe

The Ottomans and Eastern Europe

Borders and Political Patronage in the Early Modern World

Michał Wasiucionek

I.B. TAURIS

LONDON • NEW YORK • OXFORD • NEW DELHI • SYDNEY

I.B. TAURIS
Bloomsbury Publishing Plc
50 Bedford Square, London, WC1B 3DP, UK
1385 Broadway, New York, NY 10018, USA

BLOOMSBURY, I.B. TAURIS and the I.B. Tauris logo
are trademarks of Bloomsbury Publishing Plc

First published in Great Britain 2019
Paperback edition first published 2021

Copyright © Michał Wasiucionek, 2021

Michał Wasiucionek has asserted his right under the Copyright,
Designs and Patents Act, 1988, to be identified as Author of this work.

Cover design: Adriana Brioso
Cover image Trachten-Kabinett von Siebenbürgen – Ein Vornehmer Böyar in der Wallachën.
(© Art Collection 4 / Alamy Stock Photo)

All rights reserved. No part of this publication may be reproduced or
transmitted in any form or by any means, electronic or mechanical,
including photocopying, recording, or any information storage or retrieval
system, without prior permission in writing from the publishers.

Bloomsbury Publishing Plc does not have any control over, or responsibility for,
any third-party websites referred to or in this book. All internet addresses given
in this book were correct at the time of going to press. The author and publisher
regret any inconvenience caused if addresses have changed or sites have
ceased to exist, but can accept no responsibility for any such changes.

A catalogue record for this book is available from the British Library.

A catalog record for this book is available from the Library of Congress.

ISBN: HB: 978-1-7883-1847-1
PB: 978-0-7556-3853-6
ePDF: 978-1-7883-1857-0
eBook: 978-1-7883-1858-7

Series: The Ottoman Empire and the World

Typeset by Integra Software Services Pvt. Ltd.

To find out more about our authors and books visit
www.bloomsbury.com and sign up for our newsletters.

Contents

List of Illustrations	vii
Acknowledgements	viii
A Note on Transliteration, Place-Names and Personal Names	x
Introduction	1
The problem of state and the allure of factionalism	3
Patronage, networks and arenas	10
The outline of the book	15
1 The Human Landscape of Seventeenth-Century Eastern Europe	19
Constructing seventeenth-century Eastern Europe	20
The anatomy of arenas: Three early modern elites and their political environment	26
The rise of the faction	37
Part One Mechanics of Cross-Border Patronage	
2 Building Bridges, Building Trust	43
Familial matters	45
Ethnic–regional solidarities	60
Brothers in arms	70
Adapting the toolkit	78
3 Flows, Exchanges and Conversions	81
Politics and military	83
The sinews of factional power: The flow of economic resources	93
Information, communication and manipulation	105
Letters and watermelons: Civility and patronage	111
Part Two Factional Macro-Politics	
4 Friends and Enemies	117
Matei Basarab and Vasile Lupu	120
A faction breaks apart	129
Köprülüs and Cantacuzinos	141

5	Annexing Moldavia	149
	Voyvodalık/Beylerbeylik	153
	'A faction that could not lose' and its defeat: Jan Zamoyski and Polish–Lithuanian annexation attempt of 1595–1600	160
	The king and the poet: Sobieski's failure in Moldavia	171
	Why did Moldavia and Wallachia survive?	179
6	Choosing Ottomans?	183
	Notes	191
	Bibliography	244
	Index	273

List of Illustrations

Map

1 Ottoman–Polish borderland and the Danubian principalities in the mid-seventeenth century — xii

Figures

2.1 Voivode Ştefan Tomşa II's (1611–15 and 1621–3) Cyrillic monogram, stylistically inspired by the Ottoman *tuğra* (SJAN–Iaşi, M-rea. Galata ii/4) — 52

2.2 The Albanian patronage network in the mid-seventeenth century — 68

3.1 The value of Wallachian (solid line) and Moldavian (dashed line) *harac* payments (1500–1828). Based on: Bogdan Murgescu, *România şi Europa: acumularea decalajelor economice 1500-2010* (Iaşi, 2010), p. 33 — 95

3.2 Circulation and conversion of resources within cross-border 'shadow *iltizam*': a theoretical model — 99

4.1 The factional polarization of Polish–Moldavian patronage networks between 1606 and 1616 — 134

6.1 Romanian and Ottoman inscriptions commemorating the construction of a fountain near the St Spiridon Monastery in Iaşi, 1766 — 182

Table

2.1 Köprülü Mehmed Pasha's appointees in Moldavia and Wallachia (1656–61) — 67

Acknowledgements

The present book underwent a rather long and winding evolution before making its way to print. It started out as a loose jumble of ideas included in the research proposal submitted for the doctoral programme at the European University Institute in Florence, which slowly transformed into a doctoral dissertation and, subsequently, into a book. At every step of my research I have benefitted enormously from intellectual, institutional and moral support of my friends and colleagues whom I would like to acknowledge here. In the first place, I would like to thank my adviser in Florence, Bartolomé Yun Casalilla, whose readiness to provide me with guidance and his extraordinary patience greatly helped me during my research. His insightful comments and incisive questions allowed me to make sense of what I wanted to say. I will remain always indebted to him for his constant support.

Throughout the years of my research, I have benefitted greatly from the institutional and financial support of numerous institutions. At the European University Institute, I have found a uniquely stimulating and friendly environment. I had a pleasure to discuss the development of my research with my colleagues and professors, particularly Luca Molà, Jorge Flores and Antonella Romano. Our meetings have always been intellectually challenging and their pointed criticisms opening my eyes to new concepts and solutions to the challenges I encountered on the way. My five-month stay as the invited lecturer at the Center for Comparative History and Political Studies in Perm, Russia, was not only a wonderful teaching experience, but also a chance to brainstorm with Margarita Zavadskaya, Aleksei Gilev, Aleksandr Reznik, Lyudmila Kuznetsova, Alissa Klots, Jesko Schmoller, Vsevolod Bederson, Irina Shevtsova and Maria Grigoreva. The echo of our discussions certainly rings throughout the present study. Last but not least, my dear colleagues at the New Europe College in Bucharest and the ERC project *Luxury, Fashion and Social Status in Early Modern Southeastern Europe* have not only stimulated me intellectually, but also exhibited enormous patience every time my work on the manuscript forced me to take my time off.

At different stages of the writing process, parts or the whole of the text had been read by Marian Coman, Radu Dipratu, Mukaram Hhana, Mariusz Kaczka,

Acknowledgements

Gábor Kármán, Dariusz Kołodziejczyk, Michael Müller, Radu G. Păun, Hedda Reindl-Kiel and Cristina Vintilă-Ghiṭulescu, whose insightful feedback and valuable comments allowed me to revise and reshape the book. I owe special thanks to Dariusz Kołodziejczyk, who was the first one to introduce me to the field of Ottoman studies back in my freshmen year at the University of Warsaw and has offered guidance and encouragement ever since. I would also like to express my deep gratitude to all those who provided me with intellectual and moral support throughout my research: Cristian Bobicescu, Robert Born, Günhan Börekçi, Ilona Czamańska, Paulina Dominik, Tetjana Grygorieva, Zhenya Khvalkov, Aleksandra Konarzewska, Natalia Królikowska-Jedlińska, Erica Mezzoli, Przemysław Mrówka, Viorel Panaite, Mária Pakucs, Liviu Pilat, Jennifer Poliakov-Zhorov, Michał Połczyński, Michał Przeperski, Silvana Rachieru, Nicoleta Roman, Paweł Rutkowski, Suzan Meryem Rosita, Maria Rybakova, Hacer Topaktaş-Üstüner, Anna Wojczyńska and Margarita Zavadskaya. Special thanks to my dear friend, Aleksandra Konarzewska, who was always there for me and kept my spirits up, providing much-needed moral support and her trademark sarcastic sense of humour. For this, I am deeply indebted to her.

Throughout my research, I benefitted greatly from the kind assistance from the staff of the libraries and archives I have worked in. I am particularly grateful to Mihai Mîrza from the Iaşi branch of Romanian National Archives (SJAN – Iaşi) for his eagerness to help and patience, and the staff at the archives in Bucharest. I would also like to extend my heartfelt thanks to the editors at I.B. Tauris and Bloomsbury, as well as the British Institute at Ankara for their help, encouragement and including the present book into the series on the Ottoman Empire and the world around it.

Finally, I would like to thank my parents and my brother Marcin. Despite the fact that my academic pursuits have meant long periods of absence, they were always there for me, providing me with their moral support and love. They helped me to weather the crises and shared moments of happiness. This study would never appear if it was not for your help. *Dziękuję!*

A Note on Transliteration, Place-Names and Personal Names

Throughout the early modern period, as well as nowadays, the inhabitants of Eastern Europe spoke a plethora of languages and put them in writing in several scripts. As a result, modern scholar faces the dilemma of choosing the system(s) of transliteration of non-Latin script, none of which is without its drawbacks. For the sake of clarity, I have opted to render Ottoman and Romanian terms and names according to the rules of modern Turkish and Romanian orthography. For Russian and Ukrainian, I have opted for a slightly modified system employed by the Harvard Ukrainian Research Institute. While this arrangement is by no means a watertight solution, I hope it will prove convenient enough for the reader.

Choosing in which language to render place-names constitutes an even more complex challenge. Apart from the multiethnic character of Eastern Europe in the early modern period, the political map of the region changed enormously since the period of the discussion, making each choice somewhat arbitrary and – in some instances – politically charged. In choosing variants of place-names employed in the text, my guiding idea was again that of clarity. Hence, I employ standard English equivalents whenever they are available. In the clear majority of cases where no such option is available, I have preferred to use the place-names from the period as to avoid confusion as to which polity a particular town or village belonged at the time; I mention the modern equivalent whenever a certain locale is mentioned for the first time. Finally, I took account of the ethno-linguistic situation on the ground, particularly in opting for Ukrainian rather than Polish place-names for heavily Orthodox regions of the Polish–Lithuanian Commonwealth.

Personal names are even more problematic in this regard. Many of the individuals who make their appearance on the pages of the present study were polyglot and used different variants of their names, displaying different aspects of identity depending on the audience they addressed. For instance, the members of the Movilă family, prominently featured in the present study, are known as *Movilăs*, *Mogiłas* or *Mohylas*, depending on the language of the source and national historiographic tradition. The same applies to many of magnate

A Note on Transliteration, Place-Names and Personal Names xi

families of Ruthenian origin and Orthodox faith. As a rule of thumb, I have used the form I considered as the best fit with the individual's relationship with political, confessional and ethno-linguistic communities. Hence, I opted for Ruthenian-Ukrainian form in the case of Orthodox magnates of Ruthenia and Ukraine, and for Romanian forms for lineages of Moldavian and Wallachian origins, such as Movilăs. Finally, royal names – as customary – are rendered in English.

The dates, unless specified otherwise, are provided according to the Gregorian calendar.

Map 1 Ottoman–Polish borderland and the Danubian principalities in the mid-seventeenth century.

Introduction

With each gloomy, chilly day of December 1639 spent in Istanbul, Romaszkiewicz grew increasingly frustrated with his Ottoman hosts.[1] As an envoy of the Polish king, he had been sent to the Sublime Porte with a seemingly straightforward task of making arrangements for the arrival of a grand embassy, scheduled for the following spring. However, he found himself stuck in the Ottoman capital for months, in vain demanding a farewell audience and letters for King Vladislav IV. For this delay he blamed the deputy grand vizier (*kaymakam*), Tabanıyassı Mehmed Pasha. The latter disingenuously argued that the prolonged stay in the Ottoman capital was beneficial for the diplomat, allowing him to get a better grasp of imperial affairs. Romaszkiewicz, in turn, was convinced that the real reason for Mehmed Pasha's foot-dragging was a conflict unfolding between the rulers of Moldavia and Wallachia, over seven hundred kilometres north of Istanbul. According to the envoy, the *kaymakam* was in cahoots with Moldavian voivode Vasile Lupu, whom he had appointed in November to the throne of Wallachia. However, the incumbent Wallachian ruler, Matei Basarab, refused to comply and readied his troops to resist the invaders. Mehmed Pasha tried to prevent the Polish–Lithuanian Commonwealth – the Porte's chief rival in the Danubian principalities – from intervening in the conflict by effectively detaining Romaszkiewicz in the Ottoman capital. To break the stranglehold, the latter appealed to the *kaymakam*'s enemies within the imperial establishment, but they were unable to provide him with any substantial help, leaving Romaszkiewicz with no choice but to wait until the events run their course.

However, the situation changed dramatically as soon as the news from Wallachia started pouring in, sending shockwaves through the Ottoman political landscape. Rather than the reports of an expected Moldavian victory, the couriers brought letters from Matei Basarab, who boasted about his decisive victory over his rival's army. Vasile Lupu barely managed to evade capture and with a small retinue sought Ottoman protection. The news emboldened the Wallachian voivode's patrons at the Porte, who immediately moved against Tabanıyassı Mehmed Pasha, accusing him of overstepping his authority and deceiving the sultan. Seeing his plans unravel, the *kaymakam* immediately summoned Romaszkiewicz, handed over the letters and bid the diplomat farewell.

Although Romaszkiewicz was eager to leave the city, his departure had to be postponed once again, this time due to a torrential storm that hit the Ottoman capital. Stuck in Istanbul for another day, the envoy decided to pay the *kaymakam* one more courtesy visit. However, by the time he arrived at the grandee's mansion, Mehmed Pasha was on his way out, summoned by Sultan Murad IV, and Romaszkiewicz was instructed to wait for his return. Mehmed Pasha never returned to his residence. Instead, the sultan's guards showed up at the gate, barged their way into the mansion and began sealing the palace and detaining members of the *kaymakam*'s household. In the resulting chaos, Romaszkiewicz was mistaken for one of the grandee's servants and had a difficult time explaining his status before being let go and returning – clearly shaken – to his quarters. Later that day he learned of Tabanıyassı Mehmed Pasha's arrest and prompt execution on the orders of Murad IV, as the grandee took the fall for the Moldavian–Wallachian conflict and its outcome.

While Mehmed Pasha's Wallachian venture failed, this was not due to the Polish–Lithuanian intervention that he had been trying to prevent. In fact, he was extraordinarily successful in isolating Romaszkiewicz, who languished ineffectually in the Ottoman capital and had no impact on the course of events. Instead, the decisive blow that cost the grandee his life and almost brought down his political network was another faction very much like his own, spanning between the imperial centre in Istanbul and the Danubian principalities and including both members of the Ottoman establishment and Greek Orthodox elites of the periphery. This episode is by no means unique, and similar cross-border factions appear throughout the seventeenth century. The same applied for the Polish–Lithuanian Commonwealth, where powerful magnates formed their own cross-border ties with the voivodes and boyars of Moldavia and Wallachia. As these factions clashed and grappled with each other, the political fault lines ran not along political boundaries in the region, but rather across them. The elites of the Ottoman Empire, Poland–Lithuania and the Danubian principalities focused more – it would seem – on bringing down personal and political enemies rather than pursuing geopolitical objectives, however defined. As this book will show, this was precisely the case. Political actors throughout the region established cross-border patronage ties as means to secure resources and power necessary to realize their own personal and factional ambitions

Introduction 3

by reaching out and co-opting allies beyond the pale. As the number of such patronage networks proliferated, they coalesced into an alternative geography of power in the region, very much at odds with our perception of political geography. This process not only had a profound impact on both the political culture of respective polities, but also on the geopolitical shape of the region in the early modern period.

The problem of state and the allure of factionalism

The last decade of the sixteenth century constitutes a major watershed in the history of Polish–Ottoman relations. In the preceding period, the dynastic complex of the Polish Crown and the Grand Duchy of Lithuania – from 1569 known as the Polish–Lithuanian Commonwealth – constituted arguably one of the Sublime Porte's least troublesome neighbours. The Jagiellonian kings of the sixteenth century strived to maintain amicable relations with the Ottoman Empire – a sentiment overwhelmingly supported by the nobility. Following the dynasty's extinction in 1572, the Sublime Porte played an instrumental role in denying the Habsburgs the Polish throne.[2] For their part, the Ottomans were also wary not to spoil amicable relations between the two powers. However, by the mid-1590s the relations began to sour, ushering a period of growing tensions and recurrent warfare, which consumed over a quarter of the following century.

Two major issues propelled this escalation. In the east, predatory raids by the Crimean Tatars against Polish–Lithuanian and Muscovite territories intensified, but at the same time were increasingly matched by the rise of Zaporozhian Cossacks. As the latter coalesced into a numerous and efficient fighting force, they began to target Ottoman territories along the Black Sea coast. Since both the Commonwealth and the Porte lacked resources and resolve to curb their subjects, the raiding economy of the steppe continued, frequently spiralling out of control and putting both polities on the collision course.[3] The success of the 1648 Cossack rebellion against the Commonwealth only complicated the matters as both Poland–Lithuania and the Ottomans found themselves dragged into the infighting between competing Zaporozhian leaders, each trying to establish his rule across both banks of the Dnieper River.

Further to the west, along the arc of the Carpathian Mountains, another contentious issue was the control of the Danubian principalities of Wallachia (*Eflâk*) and, particularly, Moldavia (*Boğdan, Karaboğdan*). The position of these polities, sandwiched between the two territorial behemoths, forced their rulers to juggle their allegiances in order to stay afloat in the stormy waters of regional politics. Although in the 1380s, the voivodes of Moldavia had become vassals of the Polish Crown and continued to swear oaths of fealty to the kings in the following period, by the sixteenth century it firmly entered – along with Wallachia – the Ottoman orbit, rendering Polish claims to suzerainty all but defunct. The Jagiellonian kings, wary not to provoke the Porte, did not challenge this new state of affairs, but at the same time never renounced their suzerain rights. When the opportunity presented itself during the Ottoman–Habsburg 'Long War', Polish–Lithuanian troops entered Moldavia and installed a new voivode as a Polish–Lithuanian vassal, thus opening a new chapter of rivalry between the two powers, in which the Danubian principalities constituted both the stage of military conflict and its coveted prize.

However, once the dust settled and the Karlowitz treaty of 1699 concluded what turned out to be the last Polish–Ottoman war, its provisions hardly justified the resources – manpower, war material and money – poured into the conflict. Although the Ottomans succeeded in fending off the Polish–Lithuanian challenge in Moldavia and Wallachia, and even managed to increase its control over the principalities by means of so-called 'Phanariot regime', the boundary demarcated in 1703 differed little from the one established in the previous centuries. Moreover, the conflict took its toll on both Poland–Lithuania and the Porte: while in the 1590s both polities constituted first-rank regional – and, in the Ottomans' case, global – players, a century later they were widely considered spent powers, fighting a rearguard battle against more aggressive Russia and the Habsburgs.

Often overshadowed by the Russo-Ottoman wars of the eighteenth and nineteenth centuries, the Ottoman–Polish rivalry of the preceding period has nonetheless garnered considerable scholarly attention.[4] Admittedly, the fact that most studies regarding the topic appeared in local languages has limited their circulation beyond the confines of national historiographies, leading to their relative compartmentalization and limiting dialogue between them. In effect, different strands of scholarship continue to remain out of step with each other, with concepts long discarded within one field – such as the notion of 'Ottoman decline' – still perpetuated in others.

However, irrespective of the sources they utilize and interpretations they offer, most scholars share a similar set of assumptions regarding the logic of early modern Eastern European politics. Central to this paradigm is the concept of the states as cohesive, unitary actors, led by 'collective mind of the government' and pursuing their own geopolitical interests, in competition with each other on the international stage. Within this model, the Sublime Porte, Poland–Lithuania and the Danubian principalities appear to us as 'billiard balls on a pool table': solid, homogeneous objects, which change their course upon bumping into each other, but with no impact on their internal structure.[5] The success or failure of any particular polity boils down to the international balance of power and the ability of those in charge to correctly define and successfully pursue the state's objectives. Polish–Ottoman struggles for the Danubian principalities would, therefore, emerge from geopolitical imperatives of both powers, each seeking to protect and expand its zone of influence in the region – a battle from which the Porte ultimately emerged victorious. As to the political elites of the region, the state-oriented perspective reduces them to mere tools of the government, their only distinguishing feature being the level of competence they displayed when performing their duties.

Placing the state as the central actor in the early modern Eastern Europe hinges on a set of unspoken assumptions regarding structures and practices of political life, shaped by our own familiarity with modern nation states. We tend to think of the world as divided into defined, discrete units that act as political 'containers' setting territorial limits on the political activity of its inhabitants. Contact with the world beyond the pale occurs within a different realm, one of international politics, which remains the sole preserve of national governments.[6] The distinction between a territorially bounded sphere of domestic politics, accessible to non-state actors, and a separate, states-only world of international affairs, makes up the geography of power that scholars addressing seventeenth-century Eastern Europe have usually taken for granted.[7]

However, once we scratch the surface, these assumptions become problematic. The 'inside–outside' dichotomy underpinning this model is not a given. Instead, its existence hinges on state institutions themselves, which, by means of border policing, disciplinary measures and the activity of a specialized ministry of foreign affairs, discourage and suppress cross-border ties they consider illegitimate.[8] Thus, the maintenance of territorial sovereignty and the state's monopoly to interact with the outside world on a political level requires considerable resources and a degree of autonomy from other social forces.

Early modern polities lacked both. The wave of revisionist scholarship, in the making since the 1980s, has increasingly undermined the monolithic vision of premodern states.[9] As these critiques point out, early modern rulers possessed neither resources nor political will to seal off their domains from the world beyond the pale.[10] Political life unfolded within the context of what André Holenstein aptly described as *societas civilis cum imperio*, whereby 'society was transfused by a multitude of power relations of political and public character, and political power was at the same time always rooted in specific social situations'.[11] With overlapping jurisdictions, primacy of personal ties over impersonal institutions, and multiple political centres, early modern political world was characterized by porous boundaries and criss-crossing networks of power. Discussing the Ottoman case, Dariusz Kołodziejczyk pointed out that it is difficult to even establish what constituted the 'inside' and 'outside' of the 'well-protected domains'.[12] This undermines both the assumption that the geography of power in the early modern world was not dissimilar from the modern one, and the very notion of the state's agency.

Even against the backdrop of the early modern world in general, Eastern Europe seems to be a particularly awkward fit for a state-centred approach. Throughout the period, the region suffered from what we may call 'a low density of stateness', with state institutions lacking effective means to govern their own subjects. In the words of Orest Subtelny, this weakness was so pronounced that Eastern European polities hardly qualify as states:

> With weak rulers, minuscule armies, handfuls of officials, and complete decentralization, seventeenth-century Eastern Europe was in effect a region of stateless societies. [T]o argue that these East European polities were states in the modern or, indeed, in any sense of the word is simply misleading. Nor does calling them weak states solve the problem, for that appellation assumes that power rested, albeit insecurely or incompletely, in a specific type of political organization which, [...] was functionally non-existent in the region.[13]

Although Subtelny's claim of Eastern Europe's 'statelessness' is obviously exaggerated, it is clear that polities so diffuse we may discuss their very existence were unable to act either as monolithic actors or even as political containers, imposing limits on their own elites. Indeed, even a cursory survey shows a plethora of officials, dignitaries and individuals engaged in the conduct of Polish–Ottoman–Moldavian affairs, often working at cross-purposes.

At the first glance, this hardly applies to the Ottoman Empire, which Subtelny places squarely among foreign absolutist powers that succeeded in subduing local nobilities of the region. By the mid-sixteenth century, the Ottoman Empire reached a considerable level of centralization, relying ideologically on the sultans' claims to universal empire, while institutionally on political slavery, efficient bureaucracy and one of the most formidable militaries of the early modern world. In this sense, it could hardly be more different from rudimentary system of governance in the Danubian principalities, or Poland–Lithuania, whose assertive nobility limited royal power through privileges and representative

Introduction

assemblies. However, once we shift our focus away from the institutional scaffolding towards practices of political life, the differences largely dissipate. Just as among Polish–Lithuanian nobles or Moldavian–Wallachian boyars, Ottomans political endeavours in the region fell victim to factional squabbles, personal rivalries and outright sabotage.

Trying to reconcile this apparent lack of coordination with the assumed centrality of state interest forces a modern historian into an unenviable position of an arbiter in political conflicts of the past. To salvage the notion of a coherent state policy, they must take sides, deciding – based on fragmentary and often partisan evidence – whose actions furthered the state's purported goals, as well as those who stood in the way. In other words, the statist paradigm forces us to identify statesmen and spoilsports.

Seen through this lens, the seventeenth century would appear as a period when spoil sportsmanship ran rampant and true statesmanship was in short supply. In modern scholarship, this has been often described in terms of a parallel decline of Poland–Lithuania, the Ottoman Empire and the Danubian principalities. As generations of scholars argued, in the late sixteenth century, the high standards of competence and moral probity that had allowed these polities to flourish started to give way to widespread cronyism, corruption and incompetence. Engaged in petty squabbles, the elites of the seventeenth century lost sight of state interests, thus contributing to an inevitable decline, which reached its nadir in the eighteenth century.[14]

First formulated by sixteenth- and seventeenth-century moralists, who contrasted the mores of their own times with idealized virtues of yore, the narrative of moral decline was subsequently adopted among modern scholars. However, as it has been increasingly pointed out, there is little evidence to support it, and we find a number of capable individuals within the ranks of Ottoman officials, Polish–Lithuanian nobles and Moldavian–Wallachian boyars throughout the seventeenth century. Moreover, recent decades brought a major revision of the period as a whole: no longer perceived as an era of decline, the seventeenth and eighteenth centuries constituted a period of crisis and transformation in respective polities, which reshaped existing institutions and saw new patterns of political life emerging across the region. This suggests that the problem lies not with the seventeenth-century elites themselves, but with our expectations regarding their political behaviour. We should instead approach them on their own terms, with political power and authority highly personalized affairs, instead of forcing them onto a Procrustean bed of state-centred lens.[15]

The present book aims to accomplish precisely that, providing a reinterpretation of the political dynamics between the Sublime Porte, Poland–Lithuania and the Danubian principalities during the seventeenth century. As I argue, once we shift our attention away from the state towards individual actors, we discover an alternative geography of power in the region. Rather than conforming to the territorial limits of their respective polities, seventeenth-century elites reached out beyond the pale, forming patronage ties and factional networks that bound together individuals of different creeds, identities and political allegiances in pursuit of their own political interests. These cross-border alliances presented them with a viable alternative mechanism of procuring political, military and economic resources, which they could subsequently deploy to gain a competitive edge over their rivals. As such ties grew in number and importance, they amalgamated into an alternative, network-based geography of power, with profound effect both on the political culture in the region and the political map of Eastern Europe of the seventeenth century. Most importantly, the survival of Moldavia and Wallachia as distinctive political entities within the Ottoman orbit was less the product of the balance of power between Poland–Lithuania and the Porte than the outcome of cross-border factional rivalries and alliances, governed by different rules and imperatives than those of the states. Thus, to make sense of historical developments of the region, this alternative geography must be taken into account.[16]

In arguing for the importance of cross-border patronage, it is not my intention to claim that the state and its institutions were entirely irrelevant to the broader developments in the region. On the contrary, in many respects it provided scaffolding that structured political life. It served political actors by bestowing an aura of legitimacy upon their actions, set the limits of political arenas, and provided a considerable share of money and manpower by means of taxation and military mobilization. As a result, many of the resources circulating through cross-border networks were harnessed from what we would call state institutions, and many of those partaking in these networks held state offices. However, it would be a mistake to interpret the relationship between state and cross-border patronage as parasitical or to reduce the latter to a mere footnote. While patronage networks often fed on state resources, the opposite was also true, as many actors deployed money, manpower and information they acquired from their allies on the other side of the border in discharging their official duties and mobilizing troops for war. Thus, cross-border patronage should be understood as co-existing with rather than supplanting altogether the political geography of polities and their institutions. From the perspective of individual

Introduction 9

actors, both constituted avenues providing access to political resources, shaping their political strategies. As I will demonstrate throughout the study, though, factional concerns rather than state interest were the overarching factor that shaped the political landscape between Poland–Lithuania, the Ottoman Empire and the Danubian principalities.

In approaching this topic, I do not intend to provide a full account of patronage and factionalism in Eastern European politics, nor do I venture to provide a continuous narrative of Polish–Ottoman–Moldavian relations between the end of the sixteenth and the beginning of the eighteenth century. Either would be impossible tasks within the limits of the present study. Instead, I settle for a more modest goal of investigating the socio-political logic underpinning the emergence of cross-border patronage, the patterns of connectivity it produced, and the impact it had on geopolitics and political culture of early modern Eastern Europe. The focus on mechanisms means that the present study does not seek to provide a unitary narrative of individual factions' rise and fall, but rather offers a series of 'snapshots' elucidating particular features of the political environment they produced. As a result, several events and developments that had impact on geopolitics of the region, such as the emergence of Cossackdom, or the ecclesiastical ties that bound Poland–Lithuania, Ottoman lands and the Danubian principalities, have been left out of the analysis, unless crucial for understanding Polish–Ottoman–Moldavian relations.

Scholars have long recognized the role of patronage and factionalism in the political history of the Ottoman Empire, Poland–Lithuania and the Danubian principalities.[17] At least since the 1970s, studies have highlighted the growing importance of patron–client ties as a defining feature of seventeenth-century politics in the region. Authors have – either implicitly or explicitly – overwhelmingly kept their analyses within the bounds of a single polity, without considering the changes in other polities of the region. However, the devolution of power away from the royal centre and formal institutions towards patronage networks led by members of the elite seems to have occurred across the board at roughly the same time. This general 'rise of the faction' reduced rulers from the paramount arbiters in political affairs to mere faction leaders, struggling for hegemony in their respective political arenas. In turn, Moldavian–Wallachian boyars, Ottoman grandees and Polish–Lithuanian magnates increasingly accumulated power and privatized state resources, becoming the effective masters of their political environment.

While numerically inferior to the dense webs of patron–client relations within respective political arenas, cross-border bonds nonetheless had an outsize impact on the political landscape, offering actors access to resources they would otherwise be unable to acquire. However, their role in the political trajectory of the region has been largely obscured by the tacit assumption that factional politics occupy a subordinate position vis-à-vis state interests. Even if the phenomenon attracts any attention among scholars, it quickly becomes clear that the existing paradigm lacks the vocabulary to describe it, and particular instances of cross-border patronage have been treated as isolated incidents rather than pieces of a larger puzzle.[18] Only in recent years, a number of studies have successfully adopted a more comprehensive approach to the topic, demonstrating both the persistent importance of the phenomenon itself and methodological advantages such perspective has to offer.[19] Thus, the revision has long been overdue, as noted by Palmira Brummett, who pointed out that Ottoman historiography needs 'a paradigm, based on those commonly employed for the "classical," medieval, and modern worlds, which takes connectivity for granted and applies it to the Ottoman Empire'.[20] A unified approach towards Eastern European cross-border patronage presents such an opportunity, while at the same time elucidating the logic driving the Porte's presence in early modern Eastern Europe.

Patronage, networks and arenas

The task of approaching this network-based political geography requires us to recalibrate our conceptual tools and shift our focus away from the state as the central unit of analysis. This is by no means to suggest that formal institutions, territoriality were irrelevant. On the contrary, what we tend to associate with the state – formal institutions, legal framework and legitimacy – had a profound impact on the operation of cross-border patronage. Access to resources by means of office-holding played a central role in the political life, and as such cannot be simply written out from the analysis. However, individuals with such an access were not merely servants of the state, but also political actors, utilizing their position to pursue their own ambitions of wealth, power and career advancement. Thus, it is incumbent not so much to take the state out of the equation, but rather to disaggregate it to make room for alternative forms of political organization. In order to do this, I rely on three key notions: patronage, social networks and socio-political arenas.

Since its introduction into the vocabulary of historians and social scientists in the 1960s, the concept of patronage has been widely applied across a variety of disciplines. In the process, it acquired chameleon-like qualities, coming in

Introduction 11

different shapes and flavours. Most scholars rely on a metaphor of a 'lopsided friendship' – a dyadic, particularistic relationship between two social actors of unequal social status.[21] Although couched in the rhetoric of friendship and personal affinity, it is instrumental at its core, with both parties privy to the arrangement interested in obtaining resources that would otherwise remain out of their reach.[22] The exchange of resources within a patron–client dyad, however, does not follow the logic of commodity economy but instead subscribes to the Maussian logic of gift. Rather than constituting a one-off transaction, patronage remains open-ended, and in numerous instances could extend beyond a single generation.[23] The bond was maintained by a constant state of indebtedness, with the 'balance sheet' of the dyad kept in a constant state of disequilibrium.[24] However, once such perceived equilibrium is achieved and the exchange of resources ceases, both sides part ways and the relationship itself withers away.

Identifying patron and client within the dyad is where the relative consensus dissipates. Since the Polish–Lithuanian, Moldavian–Wallachian and Ottoman political actors partook in a variety of different social hierarchies, it is impossible to assume a one-to-one correspondence between formal hierarchies and the relative standing of partners within a dyad. Trying to establish whether, say, the Palatine of Ruthenia held a higher position than the *beylerbey* of Özü, would miss the point.[25] In order to identify the hierarchy within a dyad, scholars frequently resort to examining the type of resources each party brings to the relationship, patrons providing protection and material rewards in exchange for the client's loyalty.[26] However, I consider this distinction at the same time too vague and too restrictive. First, rather than a resource in its own right, loyalty constituted a precondition for the bond to coalesce and was expected from both the patron and his client. Moreover, as I will demonstrate in the course of the present study, various types of resources, such as money and material goods, flowed in both directions, providing the relationship with much-needed flexibility. Thus, the only way to distinguish a patron from his subordinate is to examine their behaviour and rhetoric within the dyad itself. This praxeological approach allows us not only to handle multiple social and political hierarchies, but also to address individual dyads in their own right while placing them within a larger social context.

Another important – and often ignored – aspect of patronage is its cultural framing and norms of behaviour. While the instrumental character of 'lopsided friendship' would suggest that the rhetoric of emotional affinity was a mere sham, this was clearly not the case. Patrons and clients alike had to conform to mutually accepted norms of interaction, which reinforced the hierarchy, but also maintained the honour of their partners intact. A failure to do so could put the whole arrangement in peril.[27] At the same time, long and frequent experience of successful cooperation carried the potential of reshaping the world view of patrons and clients alike, leading them to perceive patronage as a primary problem-solving mechanism and to an '"uncontested acceptance" (*doxa*) of clientelistic politics'.[28]

By its very nature, a patron–client dyad belongs to the realm of micro-politics, and in isolation could hardly produce a significant impact on regional politics. This issue of different scales poses distinct challenges.[29] First, large-scale patronage networks of the seventeenth century were more than a sum of their parts, but rather systems encompassing hundreds of individuals, spread across vast expanses of the Ottoman Empire, Poland–Lithuania and the Danubian principalities, operating under the constraints of slow and unreliable communications. Under such circumstances, direct contact between patron and his clients was often out of question, creating the demand for brokers that would provide a measure of coordination and trust between otherwise disconnected sectors of the network.[30] Although these brokers did not contribute their own resources, they performed crucial role in making patronage network viable. This was particularly important given that, in many instances, large-scale clienteles shared little more than their attachment to a single patron, increasing the risk of intra-factional struggle.

The second element in the methodological scaffolding is the concept of socio-political networks. As a concept that stresses connectivity and relational character of social interaction, they provide an approach suited not only for reconstructing cross-border patronage, but also a variety of other forms of social and political life. Its methodological flexibility has borne considerable fruit in discussion of state and state formation, envisaged as a 'coordinated and territorially bounded network of agencies exercising political power'.[31] Therefore, approaching political relations as a bundle of networks allows us to put formal institutions and patronage networks on an equal footing, thus removing the assumed hegemony of the state so prevalent in existing scholarship. The wealth of sociological and historical studies employing social network analysis provides us with a fine-tuned conceptual apparatus which can be readily applied to the subject at hand. Particularly, the notion of social capital, understood as 'a person's location in a structure of relationships', helps us to understand and address particular advantages of cross-border patronage.[32] However, this does not mean that thinking in network-based terms is free of its shortcomings and limitations.

Introduction   13

First, it is crucial to keep in mind that social networks are a tool we use to trace a phenomenon rather than the phenomenon itself. While a graph depicting ties between individual members of seventeenth-century elites gives the impression of constant contact and stability, factional cooperation was by no means continuous. Instead, it materialized in the form of isolated instances of exchanges and communication, which – if frequent enough – allow us to identify long-term alliances. As a result, the patronage network of an Ottoman grandee or a Moldavian boyar was by no means a tangible, static system, but rather a set of flows and circuits, owing its existence to the circulation of resources.[33] Ideally, a comprehensive list of such exchanges would provide us with a relatively complete set of data lending itself to standardization and quantitative analysis. However, this is obviously not the case: much of factional business was conducted orally, leaving us with no paper trail to follow, and the extant sources are fragmentary and imprecise. As a result, rather than a strict application of the social network analysis statistical apparatus, we are forced to treat the networks as a descriptive tool.

Secondly, the continuous character of social networks poses a perennial problem of 'boundary specification'. Delimiting the object of study is inevitably arbitrary, posing a double risk. On the one hand, adopting too-inclusive criteria of selection can easily lead to an explosive growth in the number of individuals and connections one has to take into account. Obviously, mapping *all* social ties is an impossibility and runs the risk of burying relevant information under a heap of superfluous data. Not all connections an Ottoman official maintained were of equal importance, and it is to be expected that he would have more frequent contact with people in his immediate vicinity. This does not necessarily mean, however, that such connections were of greater or equal importance as those with his clients away from the capital. In contrast, settling for restrictive criteria runs the risk of excluding connections vital to understanding of political dynamics in the region.

To avoid both pitfalls, I decided to fix my vantage point in the Danubian principalities and identify instances of cross-border patronage that bound local boyars to their counterparts at the Sublime Porte and in the Commonwealth. In the next step, I proceeded 'outward', taking into consideration other actors relevant for the topic at hand. While focusing on Moldavia and Wallachia – a political and economic backwater – may not seem the most obvious choice, the peripheral perspective they offer has distinct advantages. On the one hand, since the resources at disposal of the boyar elite were meagre in comparison with Polish–Lithuanian magnates or Ottoman grandees, local political life was more sensitive to the instances of cross-border patronage, making them easier to identify. Moreover, since the Danubian principalities constituted a contested space between the Commonwealth and the Porte, it is possible to use Polish–Moldavian factionalism as a 'control group' to elucidate particularities of Ottoman presence in the region.

Finally, as Claire Lemercier rightly pointed out, it is easy to overstate the importance of social networks, while ignoring other aspects of social life that cannot be described in relational terms. This is particularly the case factors such as cultural norms or individual agency.[34] Looking at seventeenth-century politics through the lens of social network analysis, it is easy to forget that the space Ottoman, Polish–Lithuanian and Moldavian elites inhabited was not a boundless, undifferentiated political landscape, devoid of political, religious and social boundaries. Even if not impermeable, these fault lines certainly mattered, shaping behaviour and posing obstacles to unrestricted flow of resources. In fact, the fragmentation of political landscape was a precondition for the emergence of the phenomenon at hand. For the cross-border patronage networks to exist, there had to be borders in the first place.

In order to account for different environments in which Eastern European elites operated, I utilize the notion of *socio-political* arenas. As employed by Frederick G. Bailey, the arena constitutes a social space, in which political actors compete for resources, the competition itself being regulated by a particular set of rules.[35] These included intersubjective personnel rules, dictating who could partake in the competition, as well as institutions and norms regarding behaviour, constraints and opportunities within the arena. Resources, embedded in the arena and mobilized via political networks, constituted the coveted prize of political and social rivalry. Needless to say, these rules differed significantly across political environments. Entering Ottoman establishment entailed – with some exceptions – embracing Islam or being born a Muslim; in turn, the personnel rules of Polish–Lithuanian arena made it an exclusive preserve of the nobility, leaving commoners and foreigners outside the competition. Personnel rules in the Danubian principalities were more inclusive, but they also barred Muslims and a variety of different categories from participating in local political life.

Introducing the notion of arenas into the framework provides us with several advantages. First, it allows us to accommodate non-relational features of political and social life without falling back on the idea of the state as a coherent entity. In contrast with the latter, arena does not carry the same essentialist undertones, instead conveying an image of a more nebulous political space with porous

Introduction 15

boundaries. At the same time, it is better suited to describe the structure of early modern politics, whereby actors partook in a number of smaller, encapsulated arenas, connected but nonetheless autonomous from state-level political dynamics. These smaller pockets of political life could operate according to different sets of rules, further restricting the circle of those allowed to enter. This was the case both in the Ottoman provinces and at the imperial centre, where the distinction took a physical form in restricting the access to the inner palace (*enderun*) for those serving in the 'outer' administration.[36]

The existence of multiple political arenas, each with a different set of personnel rules and norms governing competition for resources, posed a serious obstacle to actors' ability to move between different political environments. While not impossible, such mobility required much more than moving from one geographical location to another. In most instances, it entailed radical steps, such as religious conversion, and carried considerable risks of confiscation of property, permanent exclusion from one's native socio-political environment or even death. This sufficed to discourage most political actors from crossing over unless forced to do so by circumstances. At the same time, resources embedded in other arenas, if mobilized and deployed, could provide a competitive edge in political competition. These two factors – the advantage such resources could provide and the actors' inability to access them directly – provided the main thrust for the development of cross-border patronage. By expanding their networks beyond individual political arenas and forming alliances beyond the pale, Ottoman grandees, Polish–Lithuanian nobles and Moldavian–Wallachian boyars were able to create a complex system of mobilization, circulation and conversion of otherwise inaccessible resources, harnessing them for their own political goals.

The outline of the book

In order to elucidate different aspects of the cross-border patronage and its impact on Ottoman presence in the seventeenth-century Eastern Europe, the present study is divided into an introductory chapter and two main parts. Chapter 1 provides a general survey of the human and political context that led to the emergence of cross-border patronage in the seventeenth century. For the sake of clarity and to familiarize the reader with the region, the chapter largely relies on the state-oriented perspective, providing an account on the historical origins of the seventeenth-century political landscape of Eastern Europe. Thus, it touches upon two major aspects: on the one hand, the geopolitical order that took shape in the region, and on the other hand, the structure of Ottoman, Moldavian–Wallachian and Polish–Lithuanian socio-political arenas in which individual actors operated. Finally, in the concluding section of the chapter, I discuss the general 'rise of the faction' in this period, emphasizing parallels and similarities throughout the region.

With the wider background established, Part One approaches cross-border patronage at a micro-scale, focusing on mechanics that allowed for establishing and maintaining such cooperation. Chapter 2 discusses the tools the elites employed to build a viable cross-border faction and provide it with trust and cohesion. To overcome challenges posed by distance, unreliable communication and deficit of trust, Ottoman grandees and their Eastern European counterparts, creatively adapted their toolkits of faction-building in order to ensure loyalty and cooperation within their networks. Their determination to make such connections viable highlights the importance of patronage resources cross-border patronage provided. Chapter 3 examines both the character of these resources and the ways in which they circulated throughout the networks, constituting in the process a complex mechanism of transfer and conversion of different types of capital.

Part Two shifts the focus away from the mechanics of cross-border patronage relations towards their impact on the region's political life. Chapter 4 demonstrates, on the basis of three cases, that conflicts usually interpreted by scholars as driven by 'state interests' were in fact fuelled by personal and factional competition that spanned across multiple arenas. In the process, not only did patronage ties play a crucial role in procuring and transferring political resources, but at the same time harmonized the conflicts across the political boundaries. As a result, a conflict that originated in Moldavia or Wallachia could easily upset political balance at the Sublime Porte or in the Commonwealth, as actors prioritized factional agendas over purported 'state interest'.

Chapter 5 focuses on one of the most striking developments in regional politics during the seventeenth century, namely the political survival of Moldavia and Wallachia as distinct political entities. Although this period witnessed several attempts by either the Ottomans or Poland–Lithuania to introduce direct administration in the Danubian principalities, both Moldavia and Wallachia retained their political structures despite their apparent political and military weakness. While all scholars attributed both the inception and ultimate failure of incorporation plans through the lens of geopolitical rivalry and balance of power in the region, I argue that the explanation lies with cross-border factionalism, which undermined cooperation within the arenas, while strengthening alliances between them. However, the style and efficiency of Polish–Lithuanian and Ottoman patronage proved unequal for the Moldavian and Wallachian boyars, affecting the course of the seventeenth-century political struggle in the region. Conclusion brings together different threads running throughout the book, discussing the role of cross-border patronage in deciding the final outcome of seventeenth-century Polish–Ottoman rivalry in the region. As I argue, since the trajectory of regional politics was driven by factional concerns rather than state interest, the results of the conflict cannot be boiled down to the balance of power between the Porte and the Commonwealth. Instead, different styles of patronage played a crucial role in swaying Moldavian–Wallachian boyars in favour of the Porte.

Both the Ottoman Empire and particularly Poland–Lithuania have been often depicted in historiography as failures, rooted in the inability of their elites to adapt to new circumstances and produce institutions necessary for the political survival of the state. However, as I argue, the survival of the state was by no means the ultimate goal for Polish–Lithuanian, Ottoman or Moldavian–Wallachian elites, whose eyes were set on their own social and political reproduction and a political system that would allow them to thrive. Although these interests could align perfectly in many instances with those of the state, this could not be taken for granted, especially if alternative routes to procure necessary resources – such as cross-border patronage networks – were available. In that sense, Eastern European elites were not that different from their counterparts elsewhere, although particularities of the region meant that the gap between factional interests and matters of state survival put the Sublime Porte, the Polish–Lithuanian Commonwealth and the Danubian principalities at a particular disadvantage when they faced mounting challenge from their rivals.

1

The Human Landscape of Seventeenth-Century Eastern Europe

Travelling from the Polish–Lithuanian trade hub of L'viv to Istanbul in the seventeenth century entailed not only crossing long distances, poor and frequently dangerous roads, and adverse weather conditions, but also straddling an extremely diverse human landscape with a plethora of languages, religious creeds and political systems. This diversity, a product of converging influences from all around Europe and western Asia, simultaneously fragmented the region and bound it together. On the one hand, this heterogeneity manifested in the lack of a commonly accepted lingua franca that would facilitate exchange between the disparate elites in the way Latin or the triad of Ottoman Turkish, Persian and Arabic did in Western Europe and the Middle East, respectively. While this by no means precluded dialogue, the lack of a common language limited the local elites' ability to communicate with each other across cultural boundaries. On the other hand, the same multiplicity of intersecting boundaries and allegiances could bring otherwise disparate groups together. Since religious boundaries did not align with political ones, all Eastern European polities contained sizeable religious minorities, forcing them to develop ways to accommodate religious diversity among their subjects, while at the same time providing a fertile ground for cross-border ties.

These and other features of Eastern Europe's socio-political landscape had a profound impact on the options available for Ottoman grandees and their Polish–Lithuanian and Moldavian–Wallachian counterparts, who tried to expand their influence beyond the confines of their own arenas. Thus, to understand the role of cross-border patronage in the region, we must address the socio-political environment that allowed it to emerge and thrive throughout the early modern period. This included both the geopolitics writ large and the domestic political structures of the Ottoman Empire, Poland–Lithuania and the Danubian principalities. Although each exhibited particularities and internal dynamics of their own, together they underpinned the rise of factions and the development of cross-border patronage in the region.

Each of the three sections of the present chapter addresses a different key facet of this political environment. The first section sketches the geopolitical order of the region and its developments prior to the seventeenth century. In doing so, it reverts temporarily to the state-oriented perspective to provide a relatively concise picture of the political landscape in which the cross-border patronage relations emerged and flourished. Subsequently, I shift my focus towards the internal structures of individual arenas, presenting their structural features and political culture of their participants. Finally, the third section of the chapter shows how, despite wildly different institutional arrangements, we are able to identify a common trajectory in the region, consisting of a weakening monarchical power and ascendant factions based on patronage ties, which increasingly took over as key political players.

Constructing seventeenth-century Eastern Europe

Much of the seventeenth-century Eastern European political order had its roots in two significant developments of the mid-fourteenth century. First, the demise of the Golden Horde as the hegemonic power in the Black Sea steppe created a power vacuum, opening the region to expansion by neighbouring powers and facilitating the emergence of new local polities. Second, the Ottoman ascendancy to the status of a regional and, subsequently, global power unified Southeastern Europe under the banner of the sultans. Under the influence of these dual pressures, by the sixteenth century the political map of the region crystallized into a form it would retain throughout much of the early modern period.

The waning of the Golden Horde's power brought about by the economic downturn, demographic crisis and dynastic infighting caused it to unravel and break up into a number of minor khanates vying for dominance in the region.[1] The internal crisis paved the way for new contenders seeking to benefit from the empire's unravelling. In the scramble for the Golden Horde's legacy that ensued Poland, Lithuania, Muscovy, Hungary and the Ottomans initially emerged as major contenders.[2] By the later sixteenth century, however, the Ottoman conquest of Hungary (1526–41) and Polish–Lithuanian union reduced this number to three first-rank powers: Poland–Lithuania, the Sublime Porte and Muscovy–Russia. The latter would ultimately emerge victorious from the struggle over Eastern Europe in the eighteenth and nineteenth centuries, but

Human Landscape of 17th-Century Eastern Europe   21

until Peter the Great's reign (1682–1725), its influence along the Black Sea coast was limited. Located in the far north of the region and wary of Ottoman power, the Muscovite elites pursued a strategy of containment rather than expansion, relying on a series of fortified lines erected along the steppe frontier against Tatar raids.[3] Hence, throughout the seventeenth century, the struggle for control of the territories between the Carpathians and the Black Sea steppe unfolded between the Polish–Lithuanian Commonwealth and the Sublime Porte.

Into the steppe: Polish–Lithuanian expansion towards the Black Sea

Polish – and later Polish–Lithuanian – expansion towards the Black Sea dated back to the 1340s when King Casimir the Great (1333–70) made his bid to southwestern Ruthenian lands of Halyč and Podolia, in competition with Lithuanian and Hungarian rulers.[4] The conflict with Grand Duchy of Lithuania was resolved through a dynastic union under the Jagiellonian dynasty (1386), which by 1569 evolved into a composite monarchy known as the Polish–Lithuanian Commonwealth. These developments not only increased Polish–Lithuanian political clout, but also paved the way for colonization of the fertile lands and put important towns L'viv and Kam'janec' – important hubs of oriental trade – under royal authority. This process concluded in 1569, when the Ukrainian palatinates of Volhynia, Kyiv and Braclav were transferred from under Lithuanian authority to that of the Polish Crown. From then on, the latter assumed full responsibility for the Commonwealth's southeastern policy, while the Grand Duchy focused on diplomatic relations with Muscovy.

While the consolidation of Polish rule in southwestern Ruthenia created ample opportunities, it also posed new challenges. The vast and sparsely populated territories of Ukraine constituted a traditional slave-hunting ground that was fuelling the raiding economy of the Crimean Khanate. The only vestige of the Golden Horde to survive past mid-sixteenth century, the Khanate had been established in the 1420s by the Giray dynasty, who were descendants of Chinggis Khan, and, in the course of the 1470s, became a satellite of the Ottoman Empire.[5] Because of their Sunni creed, prestigious Chinggisid pedigree and military resources they wielded, the Giray khans enjoyed a distinct position within the wider Ottoman world, far superior to that of Moldavian, Wallachian and even Transylvanian rulers. The relations between the khans and the Porte were not always cordial, as the Tatar elites often resented Ottoman involvement and tried to conduct an independent policy in the region.[6] Nonetheless, the association with the Porte provided much-needed protection against the Khanate's more powerful Christian neighbours in exchange for Tatars' participation in Ottoman campaigns.[7] This largely symbiotic relationship also encouraged the development of Crimean raiding economy, based on slave-raiding expeditions to Polish–Lithuanian and Muscovite territories. In the seventeenth century, when the colonization efforts in the Ukraine pushed the frontier of settlement to the southeast, the raiding intensified and the Black Sea region became one of the primary sources of slaves sold on the Ottoman market.[8] The scale of this trade is difficult to determine, but the estimates suggest it amounted to over two million people – a figure comparable to those of the Atlantic 'Middle Passage'.[9] Tatar slave-raiding constituted a perennial source of tension in Polish–Ottoman relations throughout the seventeenth century, but diplomatic interventions in Istanbul had little impact. Thus, in order to avoid major incursions, Polish monarchs resorted to 'gifts', offered annually to the khan; however, low-scale raiding continued unabated, and whole sectors of regional economy relied on the cycle of slave-raiding and ransoming of captives.[10]

Crimean Tatars were not the only ones to engage in the raiding economy. The vast extent of Polish–Lithuanian steppe frontier and its sparse population meant that royal control remained largely nominal, and the region offered a haven to those willing to escape the authority of officials and noble landholders. This floating population began to band together for self-defence purposes, gradually coalescing into a loose military Cossack organization known as the Zaporozhian Host, organized as a political–military fraternity commanded by elected leaders. As the Cossacks' numbers and military proficiency increased, they began to launch their own raids against the Crimean Khanate and Ottoman territories along the Black Sea coast, pillaging as far as the suburbs of Istanbul.[11]

Polish–Lithuanian authorities never managed to develop a coherent policy towards the Cossacks and oscillated between accommodation and repression. On the one hand, the Host constituted the pool of a skilled and cheap fighting force, and the Cossack Register created in the 1570s aimed to put them on the royal payroll. However, the number of registered Cossacks was but a fraction of those claiming such status. Ad hoc recruitment for military campaigns only aggravated the Cossacks, whose service for the Commonwealth did not translate into privileges they coveted. At the same time, there were considerable pressures to suppress the Zaporozhian Host altogether. The havoc wreaked by Cossack raids against the Ottoman and the Crimean lands ran the risk of sparking a full-scale war against the Porte – a prospect that the nobility tried to avoid at all cost. Moreover, the Polish–Lithuanian elites were contemptuous towards the Cossacks, whom they saw as a mob of fugitive serfs threatening the established social order. The failure to accommodate Cossack demands led to a series of revolts and repressions, which culminated in a massive uprising of 1648. Led by Bohdan Xmel'nyc'kyj, the revolt crippled the Commonwealth and sparked a series of wars that continued until the end of the seventeenth century, drawing all Eastern European powers into what Brian Davies aptly called a 'Ukrainian quagmire'.[12]

Further west, the Polish expansion into southwestern Ruthenia put the Crown in contact with the Danubian principalities of Moldavia and Wallachia, which had emerged in the first half of the fourteenth century along the eastern and southern slopes of the Carpathian Mountains. While the circumstances of their formation remain at the centre of a heated scholarly debate, the main impulse came from the decline of the Golden Horde's authority in the region, which opened up the land for emigration of Romanian-speaking Orthodox elites from Hungarian Transylvania. Eventually, two nuclei emerged on the slopes of the Carpathian arc, which gradually expanded their reach, subduing rival centres in the process. While clear majority of Romanian scholars have assumed that the process of territorial state formation concluded in the fourteenth century, Marian Coman has recently demonstrated that the process was far from over. Instead, the authority of the voivodes was limited politically and geographically, and the authority they exercised hinged on patronage ties rather than administrative structures.[13] Only in the sixteenth century, under the Ottoman influence, did the process of consolidation conclude and the voivodes succeeded in co-opting the local elites.

From their appearance in the Eastern European landscape, Moldavia and Wallachia found themselves surrounded by more powerful neighbours. While in Wallachia the interactions with the Polish Crown were incidental and short-lived, Moldavian voivodes established a lasting bond with their northern neighbour and early on declared themselves Polish vassals. This decision not only reflected Moldavia's ties to southwestern Ruthenia, but also aimed at using the Crown as a counterweight against Hungarian encroachments.[14] In 1387, Voivode Petru I appeared before the king, and swore an oath to provide him with assistance and counsel; his successors renewed the bond of vassalage throughout the fifteenth century.[15] Polish suzerainty was not particularly onerous and the voivodes retained considerable autonomy in pursuing their own objectives.[16] However, in the second half of the century, the Ottoman expansion began to erode the Crown's influence in the principality. The bond of vassalage was renewed for the last time in 1485, and in subsequent years the relationship all but withered away.[17] An attempt to bring Moldavia back

24   *The Ottomans and Eastern Europe*

to the fold, undertaken by King John Albert in 1497, ended in a military debacle, effectively putting an end to the principality's status as a Polish vassal. However, Polish rulers never abandoned their rights, trying to exert influence in Moldavia and leaving open the possibility of reasserting their claims in more opportune circumstances.[18]

A global empire in the Black Sea region: Ottoman expansion

As the Golden Horde entered a period of decline, another Muslim power was ascending. Emerging from a small *beylik* in northwestern Anatolia, the Ottomans managed to establish a bridgehead in Europe by 1354 and used it as a springboard for further expansion in the Balkans. With no formidable opponent in the region, Ottomans quickly became a dominant force and, with the conquest of the Bulgarian tsardoms of Tărnovo and Vidin, reached the immediate vicinity of Wallachian lands. From the last decades of the fourteenth century until the 1460s, the principality gradually entered the Ottoman orbit, with its rulers becoming tributaries of the Porte.[19] Moldavian voivodes followed suit. In 1456 Petru Aron (1455–7) gave in to Sultan Mehmed II's ultimatum and agreed to pay tribute (*harac*) to the sultan's treasury.[20] Under Mehmed's successor, Bayezid II (1481–1512), Ottomans consolidated their positions in the region, seizing the commercial hubs of Akkerman and Kiliye and effectively transforming the Black Sea into an 'Ottoman lake'.[21] Furthermore, the demise of the Kingdom of Hungary (1526–41) removed a potential counterweight to the Porte's growing power. Thus, in 1538 a punitive campaign led by Sultan Süleyman led to the annexation of the Bucak region, firmly establishing Ottoman control over the Danubian principalities.[22]

Ottoman suzerainty proved more intrusive than Moldavia's relatively loose relationship with the Polish Crown. In their new role as Ottoman tributaries, Moldavian and Wallachian voivodes were obliged to pay an annual tribute (*harac*) and perform a number of military and political duties.[23] Initially, these obligations were not particularly onerous, but as time passed, the relations between the Danubian principalities and the Sublime Porte shifted decidedly in the latter's favour. In the second half of the sixteenth century, the amount of tribute paid by the voivodes skyrocketed, bringing them to the brink of insolvency and prompting a general rebellion against the Ottomans.[24] The Porte increasingly became involved in the matters of succession in the principalities, largely due to the competition for the throne and factional strife within the principalities.[25] The constant threat posed by the presence of numerous pretenders in the imperial capital forced the rulers to maintain their agents at the Porte (*capuchehaias*), responsible for managing day-to-day affairs and fending off potential challengers.[26]

The debate on the relationship between the Sublime Porte and the Danubian principalities has focused on the juridical status of the latter. A particularly heated controversy has surrounded the existence of capitulations (*'ahdnames*), which – it has been argued – would prove that the Ottomans recognized the autonomous status of Moldavia and Wallachia.[27] While I will discuss the details of this debate in the following chapters, this 'hunt for capitulations' bore little fruit. Instead, as Viorel Panaite noted, it seems that the Ottomans exercised their suzerainty according to customary practices and considered the Danubian principalities an integral part of the 'well-protected domains', and their voivodes as tax-collectors (*haracgüzar*) appointed by the sultan.[28]

Along the shores of the Black Sea and in the Danubian principalities, the Porte pursued a defensive strategy that belied their image as a polity bound on conquest and expansion. Following the conquest of Genoese and Venetian colonies which gave them full control of the sea, the Ottomans made no sustained push further into the steppe.[29] This comes as no surprise given that the sparsely populated territory hardly constituted an attractive target. Among Ottoman soldiers, northern campaigns were wildly unpopular, as the harsh conditions and cold were not offset by the prospects of booty.[30] The disgruntlement of Janissaries forced to participate in Osman II's campaign against Poland–Lithuania in 1621 was largely responsible for their rebellion and regicide the following year.[31] Therefore, the Porte was content to maintain a fortified rim guarding entry to the Black Sea, while leaving the conduct of steppe affairs to the Crimean khans. It was only in the second half of the seventeenth century that the Ottomans, disconcerted by the growing power of Muscovy, adopted a more aggressive policy in the region.

To defend its possessions in the region, the Porte relied on the Girays and the governors of two provinces (*eyalets*) established in Kefe (Caffa) and Özü (modern Očakiv in Ukraine). The latter, formed at the end of the sixteenth century, comprised territories from the Danube Delta to the mouth of Boh River in the north and was intended as a defensive line against Cossack raids. While the eponymous fortress was the official administrative centre of the province, few Ottoman officials wanted to reside in a remote stronghold, and instead stayed in Silistre just across the river from Wallachia. From this advantageous location, they not only defended the region against the Cossacks, but also monitored Moldavian and Wallachian voivodes.[32]

By the end of the sixteenth century, the Sublime Porte established a relatively coherent and efficient administrative–military system, allowing it to maintain its domination in the Black Sea region and the Danubian principalities. However, this control was by no means uncontested, leading to a series of conflicts and wars with the Commonwealth. The existing tensions, produced by the steppe raiding economy and competing claims to the Danubian principalities, were further exacerbated by the fact that on several occasions in the seventeenth century, Moldavian voivodes acted simultaneously as Ottoman tributaries and Polish vassals.[33] Even during the periods of peace between the Porte and Poland–Lithuania the dispute over the status of the Danubian principalities brewed under the surface. At the same time, the same tensions could empower lesser actors, offering them possibilities to juggle allegiances and call on a mightier ally in times of need.

The anatomy of arenas: Three early modern elites and their political environment

The Ottoman Empire

To many contemporaries and modern historians, the Ottoman Empire appeared as the state of unmitigated despotism, its institutions geared for war and conquest. For Polish–Lithuanian nobles, jealously guarding their cherished liberties, the empire built around the sultan's extended household and administered by his slaves seemed like the antithesis of an ideal political system embodied in the Commonwealth. This sentiment permeates the description by Krzysztof Zbaraski, the Polish–Lithuanian ambassador to the Porte in 1622–3:

> There are – as have always been – only two orders in Turkey, although they include more ranks and categories. The first [order] is the ruler himself; the other are his slaves. To the ruler belongs the *absolutum dominium* and he is, as if a deity on Earth, the source of all the fortunes and misfortunes that befall this nation.[34]

While long dominant in historiography, the vision of the Ottoman Empire as an unmitigated despotism has undergone a sea change in recent decades. The most important shift in this respect was the rejection of the decline paradigm, which saw the reign of Sultan Süleyman (1520–66) as the peak of Ottoman fortunes, followed by a protracted decline that demoted the once-powerful empire to the status of 'sick man of Europe'.[35] In contrast, the newer scholarship has revisited

Human Landscape of 17th-Century Eastern Europe   27

the seventeenth and eighteenth centuries, seeing them not as a downward spiral, but rather as a period of crisis and adaptation that allowed the empire to survive. This trend found its fullest expression in Baki Tezcan's notion of 'the Second Ottoman Empire', which presented the 'post-classical' polity not as a shadow of its former self, but rather an entity qualitatively different from what it had been in the earlier period.[36]

What is in a name? To answer this question, it is necessary to look back to the political and social evolution of the empire. Following its emergence in the fourteenth century, the Ottoman polity underwent numerous transformations, the most consequential being its centralization during the reign of Mehmed II. Material resources that the ruler acquired through territorial expansion and economic integration, as well as the sultan's prestige as the conqueror of Constantinople, allowed him to consolidate sultanic authority and reshape the imperial elite. Entrenched aristocratic clans, such as the Çandarlıs, and powerful frontier *bey*s were pushed aside in favour of sultan's slaves; the prebendal *timar* system expanded, along with the Janissary corps. Increased revenue extracted from tax-paying population (*reâya*) provided the sultan with the means to maintain a growing military–administrative class (*askeri*). At the apex of power, the principle of unigeniture and the practice of fratricide aimed to preserve the cohesion of the dynasty and secure the sultan's position as the uncontested head of the patrimonial state.[37]

By the second half of the sixteenth century, however, the system began to unravel.[38] As Baki Tezcan argues, the key factor was the economic shift towards monetized economy and accompanying social transformations.[39] In order to tap new sources of wealth, the imperial revenue-raising apparatus, based on dues in kind collected by *timar*-holders, had to be overhauled. In effect, starting from the late sixteenth century, the *timar*s were gradually phased out and replaced with tax-farming contracts auctioned to the highest bidder under the *iltizam* system.[40] These economic changes had unintended consequences, as they empowered new social actors, who made their way into the *askeri* ranks.[41] The influx of these 'outsiders' (*ecnebi*) not only undermined the existing boundary between *reâya* and *askeri*, but also increased the competition within elite ranks. Moreover, the monetization of economy empowered the Islamic legal scholars (*ulema*), whose legal expertise became indispensable in the sphere the imperial governance.[42]

These sweeping changes – the monetization of Ottoman economy, the changing character of the *askeri* class and the political ascendancy of the *ulema* – gradually limited sultanic authority. Following Mehmed III's ascension

28 *The Ottomans and Eastern Europe*

in 1595, the practice of fratricide effectively lapsed, depriving the rulers of military charisma they had enjoyed, and shifting the pattern of succession towards primogeniture.[43] The new rules of succession further curbed the ruler's position, providing a potential opposition with a possibility to replace the sultan with another member of the dynasty. In effect, the year 1622 witnessed the first regicide in Ottoman history, and until the end of the seventeenth century, most sultans were forcibly removed from the throne.

Rebellion became an increasingly frequent occurrence in Ottoman political life. *Kapıkulu* troops, the mainstay of the sultan's patrimonial household, underwent a significant change following the breakdown of boundaries between *askeri* and *reʿaya*. While previously the Janissary corps had consisted of handpicked slaves levied from among the Christian population of the empire through the *devşirme* system, the influx of free-born Muslims not only bloated the corps' size, but also changed its character. As their members engaged in trade and tax collection, the Janissaries transformed into an influential pressure group, ready to protect their financial interests against any encroachments by the ruler or other members of the elite, even by means of an armed revolt.[44]

The standing army was not the only one to employ rebellion as a political tool, and other groups within the elite soon followed. As Karen Barkey pointed out, the Porte had acted as a 'grand scheduler' with regard to the elites: by shuffling appointments according to differential schedules, it prevented individual officials from entrenching themselves in their positions and ensured control over the ruling class.[45] In the sixteenth century, this rotation was an attractive opportunity for the members of central and provincial elites, as *timar*-holders often willingly gave up their prebends, hoping to receive bigger allotments in the future.[46] However, by the end of the century, the fortunes of provincial cavalrymen took a turn for the worse. On the one hand, the *ecnebis* and individuals from the imperial centre took over higher ranks in provincial administration, blocking the careers of the provincial *askeri*.[47] On the other, as the fiscal administration transitioned to the *iltizam* system, the number of *timar*s decreased and competition intensified. By the seventeenth century, the practice of renouncing *timar*s virtually ceased, as *sipahi* came to see the rotation as a threat rather than an opportunity.

As *timar*-holders clung to their shrinking sources of revenue, their superiors were not much better off. The competition for offices among governors (*sancakbeys*) and governors-general (*beylerbeys*) gained momentum, contributing to the accelerating pace of rotation and longer periods out of office. This took a toll on the *ümera*'s finances, as they were expected to maintain 'well-

Human Landscape of 17th-Century Eastern Europe   29

outfitted households' and provide troops for campaigns.[48] Thus, to supplement their revenue and meet the demands, the governors increasingly engaged in a variety of economic activities, including trade, lending and tax-farming.[49]

Caught in the fierce competition, Ottoman provincial officials increasingly resorted to rebellion to retain their posts. This took place against the background of the militarization of Ottoman countryside, providing governors-turned-rebels with a ready pool of mercenaries, recruited in thousands by *celali* warlords. In many respects, these mercenary armies became 'rebels without a cause', roaming the countryside and trying to force their way into the ranks of the *askeri*.[50] Commanders dispatched to restore order quickly began to employ similar recruitment strategies and formed *sekban* armies of their own. Once disbanded, the mercenaries turned to banditry, disrupting economic life and displacing rural population. The havoc wreaked by the *celalis* converged with a series of demographic and environmental upheavals, plunging Anatolia into turmoil by the end of the sixteenth century.[51]

In response to this crisis, the Ottoman authorities adopted a flexible and lenient approach towards the rebels, bargaining with their leaders and oscillating between repression and co-optation into the system of governance. In effect, a revolt against the Porte was no longer a point of no return and became a stage in negotiations between the imperial centre and the rebels.[52] In effect, a rebel could become a respected Ottoman official overnight, with some individuals crossing this boundary on multiple occasions.

Thus, the Ottoman Empire of the seventeenth century was a polity in flux, as deep-cutting social and economic transformations restructured the political arena of the empire. As the patrimonial model of Süleyman's 'classical period' gradually gave way to the new socio-political order, many institutions entered a period of crisis or even decline. However, their demise did not signify a general decline of the empire, but rather an often painful and tumultuous adjustment to new conditions and challenges. Thus, for all the crises that the empire faced, the seventeenth century is better seen not as a time of decay, but rather one of adaptation.

Poland–Lithuania

At the beginning of July 1569, after much wrangling and dramatic turns of events, the Union of Lublin transformed the long-lasting dynastic union between the Polish Crown and the Grand Duchy of Lithuania into a polity known as the Polish–Lithuanian Commonwealth. While composite monarchies were commonplace in early modern Europe, the institutional trajectory of Poland–Lithuania produced a model so peculiar as to make many scholars doubt whether it is even comparable with other polities of the period.[53] This distinct political system had been in the making since the late fourteenth century, shaped by the complex dynamics within the dynastic union and the accumulation of privileges by numerous nobility, the latter estimated at 6 to 8 per cent of total population.[54] These factors produced the Commonwealth's most characteristic features, including the nobility's vast privileges and a monopoly on power, vibrant parliamentary life, elective monarchy and the consolidation of the 'second serfdom'.

The middle decades of the sixteenth century constituted a significant watershed in these developments. This period witnessed an unprecedented boom in the Baltic grain trade, which greatly benefitted the nobility and triggered the development of a market-oriented manorial economy.[55] Boosted by the revenues from the trade, Polish middle gentry launched a political offensive against a narrow elite concentrated at the royal court. The nobles called for an 'execution of the law', that is, the enforcement of the laws often ignored by the elite of powerholders. While rooted in a legalist and restorative rhetoric, the demands of this executionist movement involved a wide array of topics, including reclamation of alienated parts of the royal domain, religious tolerance, and the union between the Polish Crown and the Grand Duchy of Lithuania. Most importantly, they marked the political emancipation of the gentry and its growing role within the political system. While these demands initially met with hostility of the rulers, in the early 1560 the last Jagiellonian king, Sigismund II Augustus (1548–72) embraced the movement and pushed through both internal reforms and the issue of Polish–Lithuanian union. Most institutions of the Grand Duchy were brought in line with the Polish ones, thus preparing the ground for the act of 1569. From then on, Lithuania and the Crown would share the same elective monarch and a representative assembly (*Sejm*), while retaining their own distinct hierarchies, militaries and exchequers.

Sigismund Augustus's death and the end of the Jagiellonian dynasty in July 1572 tested these arrangements, while at the same time paved way to a fully fledged elective monarchy. Participating in the election became the right of every nobleman, and the king-elect was obliged to guarantee the foundations of the political order and conform to the restrictions and commitments imposed by the nobility. Should he violate the privileges, the nobles could invoke their right to withdraw their obedience and even resist the monarch by military means.[56] Although the ruler retained the exclusive right to appoint officials,

Human Landscape of 17th-Century Eastern Europe 31

his ability to handpick his supporters was limited by the established custom of lifelong tenure in office. Thus, kings often found themselves stuck with their predecessors' appointees, with whom they were not always on good terms. Moreover, the seventeenth century witnessed a crisis of trust between the kings and their subjects, who suspected the former of plotting to destroy the cherished political system and institute a dreaded *absolutum dominium*.[57]

For the Polish–Lithuanian nobles, the *Sejm* was the Commonwealth's crown jewel and a living embodiment of the *monarchia mixta* political system. The king was legally obliged to summon it at least every two years, although the political imperatives led to much more frequent sessions. The institution, consisting of the monarch himself, high-ranking officials with a seat in the Senate, and the Chamber of Deputies elected by local dietines (*sejmiki*), was the lynchpin of the political system. As the central representative body, it had broad legislative and juridical powers and decided on a variety of matters from taxation and war to minute personal grievances. The decision-making process relied on consensus-building since all bills had to be passed without voiced opposition. This requirement put a premium on bargaining and compromise, but it also made the proceedings cumbersome, making it easy to disrupt or undo the whole legislative process. Despite obvious procedural bottlenecks, in the first half of the seventeenth century the *Sejm* fulfilled its decision-making function quite efficiently. However, the turmoil of the mid-seventeenth century and the growing factionalization of the political scene caused the institutional crisis to take root. Starting in the second half of the century, the practice of *liberum veto* (blocking the proceedings by a single dissenting voice) increasingly paralysed the body, a process that culminated in the first half of the eighteenth century.[58]

With the *Sejm* increasingly unable to pass legislation and approve taxes, decision-making shifted towards provincial dietines, which constituted the backbone of the local political life and the main stage for most nobles. The local assemblies fulfilled numerous functions, including electing deputies to the *Sejm* and judicial tribunals, passing local regulations and deciding on the matters of taxation. This institutional devolution allowed the Commonwealth's political system to face immediate challenges, but at the same time fostered the sense of regionalism and led to a 'crater-like' structure of power, with authority dispersed both institutionally and geographically.[59] Neither the rudimentary administrative infrastructure nor the woefully underdeveloped fiscal apparatus was able to act as a centripetal force, and the lack coordination between individual bodies constituted a constant concern.[60]

Territories adjacent to Moldavian and Ottoman territories – the palatinates (*województwa*) of Ruthenia, Podolia, Braclav, Kyiv and Volhynia – had their own institutional and social peculiarities that set them apart from the rest of the Commonwealth. The process of their incorporation into the Polish Crown occurred in two distinct phases. Ruthenia and Podolia were annexed during the initial phases of the kingdom's expansion towards the Black Sea in the mid-fourteenth and early fifteenth centuries. In turn, Volhynia, Braclav and Kyiv had been possessions of the Grand Duchy of Lithuania until 1569, when King Sigismund Augustus ceded them to the Crown in order to break the Lithuanian magnates' resistance against the Union of Lublin.

The political and social makeup of the palatinates reflected these different trajectories. By the late sixteenth century, Podolia and especially Ruthenia had been part of the Crown for over two centuries and their socio-political life did not diverge significantly from the kingdom's central provinces. The nobility used Polish and Latin in official correspondence and daily life, and Polish noble lineages entered the local elite as early as the fourteenth century. With a strong and assertive middle gentry, well-versed in the intricacies of Polish political system, the local political life in Ruthenia differed little from the conditions in the core provinces of the Crown.

In this respect, the Ukrainian palatinates provided a stark contrast, and only began a protracted process of political integration. Local nobilities in Volhynia, Braclav and Kyiv were far less numerous (merely 1 per cent of the population) and predominantly Greek Orthodox; Ruthenian remained the official language of the chancellery, and the Second Lithuanian Statute continued as the law of the land.[61] This Ruthenian–Lithuanian heritage proved as durable in shaping the noble estate itself. Although the reforms of the 1560s attempted to mould a single, legally equal elite along Polish models, in fact they lumped together three distinct strata: princes (*knjazi*), lords (*pany*) and dependent boyars.[62] The *knjazi* lineages, who claimed descent from Ruthenian and Lithuanian dynasties, managed to retain their titles and political hegemony, despite the protests of a more egalitarian-minded Polish nobility.[63] Thus, by the beginning of the seventeenth century, the easternmost palatinates were only slowly adjusting to the political culture of the Crown.[64] Although the Cossack uprising of 1648 accelerated this process, the sense of regionalism persisted at least until the end of the century.[65]

The Union of Lublin triggered a massive surge in the population of the region, encouraged by colonization efforts by old and new landholders, which pushed the frontier settlement into the steppe. Massive latifundia emerged; for instance, *Knjaz'* Kostjantyn-Vasyl' Ostroz'kyj controlled over 80 towns and 2,760 villages,

Human Landscape of 17th-Century Eastern Europe   33

making him one of the greatest landowners not only in the Commonwealth but the early modern world.[66] However, fundamental constraints limited the revenues from these vast holdings. Serf labour was scarce and many fugitive subjects were running away to join the Cossacks or escape feudal obligations. The pool of available workforce was also continuously depleted by Tatar slave-raiding, forcing the nobles to maintain large military contingents to repel the raiders. Finally, there was no suitable commercial outlet that would make the export of grain profitable. In effect, the Ukrainian lands did not experience the development of a manorial economy that characterized the Vistula basin further west.[67] Instead, the landowners drew their revenue from cattle ranching, as well as excise dues and tithes. However, even if the region was not an economic powerhouse, the sheer scale of the holdings owned by local magnates provided them with enough revenue to secure a prominent position in the political and social life of the Commonwealth and the whole region.

Along with political and social differences, the dominant creed also set the Ukrainian territories apart from other palatinates of the Polish Crown (although not the Grand Duchy). The population of the region was overwhelmingly Orthodox, creating tensions with the Catholic rulers and church hierarchy. While the Confederation of Warsaw (1573) guaranteed the nobles religious freedom, the act did not specify the means to enforce it and any attempts to rectify the situation were obstructed by the Catholic bishops. At the same time, many local magnates who had acted as patrons of the Orthodox Church converted to Roman Catholicism to improve their position at the court. Although this wave of Catholicization did not reach lower ranks of the nobility until the second half of the seventeenth century,[68] the profound crisis of the Church led Orthodox hierarchs to accept papal authority. The Union of Brest', concluded in October 1596, split the Orthodox community in two and was overwhelmingly rejected by the faithful.[69] The conflict between the camps dominated the political scene and further escalated the tensions in the region.

Finally, Tatar slave-raiding expeditions posed a constant threat. According to the estimates by Maurycy Horn, only in the first half of the seventeenth century, at least seventy-five raids took place, but the actual figures are probably much higher.[70] The Crown's minuscule standing army of 2,000 men, thinly spread along a thousand-kilometre border, was unable to protect the region or stop the haemorrhaging of the population. This led to a massive militarization of the region, as local landowners assembled their own armies, which frequently reached considerable size. Although the size of these private troops is unclear, it is nonetheless obvious that they vastly outnumbered the royal forces.[71] Thus, the military accumulation provided local magnates with another valuable resource, which they could deploy to protect their own estates or pursue their political agendas.

Danubian principalities

Although the formation of Moldavia and Wallachia as distinct political entities occurred independently of each other and according to different schedules, they produced similar institutional and social arrangements which justify their joint treatment. Although the principalities' emergence onto the historical stage owed much to their initial ties with the Kingdom of Hungary, their political structures and means of legitimacy drew on Byzantine rather than Hungarian traditions. At the apex of the political hierarchy stood the voivode, who adopted the posture of an Orthodox autocrat.[72] In practice, however, the rulers exercised authority together with the local boyar elite, who held considerable influence in the princely council (*sfatul domnesc*).[73] Although primarily a judicial and advisory body, the council nonetheless partook in the decision-making process, serving as a link between the court and the countryside.

Until the end of the sixteenth century, the thrones of Moldavia and Wallachia remained in the hands of local dynasties – Bogdăneşti-Muşatini and Basarabi, respectively. While the dynastic pedigree was a precondition for ascending the throne, the highly irregular pattern of succession led to frequent conflicts within the extended dynasty. By the beginning of the seventeenth century, however, this dynastic principle had largely withered away. In the seventeenth century rulers increasingly came from among the boyar class or Orthodox elites of Istanbul, often fabricating dynastic lineage to enhance their legitimacy. This oversupply of potential rulers was further complicated by the growing role the Sublime Porte played in appointing and confirming the voivodes. In effect, starting from the mid-sixteenth century, the ever-growing number of pretenders flocked to Istanbul, leading to an increasing instability of voivodal tenure and accelerating the pace of turnover. On average, a seventeenth-century Moldavian ruler remained on the throne for mere three years, and his Wallachian counterpart – a mere year longer. Some rulers – such as Matei Basarab (1632–54) and Constantin Brâncoveanu (1688–1714) in Wallachia, and Vasile Lupu (1634–53) in Moldavia – were able to hold to power for much longer, but all operated under a constant threat of deposition and execution.

The origins and nature of the boyar class have been at the centre of heated historiographical debate, with scholars arguing for either control over landed property or office-holding as the defining criteria for membership.[74] However, until the mid-eighteenth century, when a series of reforms reshaped the status of boyars was a matter of social recognition rather than formalized criteria. The threshold for entry into the ranks of the elite was ownership of landed property, control over serf workforce, genealogy and office-holding, the latter becoming the decisive criterion over time.[75] In effect, throughout the seventeenth century, the boundaries of the boyar class remained fuzzy, making it relatively easy for outsiders to integrate themselves into the local elite, by way of appointment to office, acquisition of land in the principality and marriage.

The second half of the sixteenth and seventeenth centuries marked a period of major political and social reconfiguration in the Danubian principalities. First, the Ottoman fiscal pressure contributed to the consolidation of administrative structures, as rulers sought to meet the demands of the Porte. While in the course of the fifteenth century the voivodes' control of peripheral regions was limited, the need to raise the *harac* provided an impulse to expand revenue-raising apparatus and raise the fiscal burden.[76] Secondly, the unintended consequence of this growing demand for financial resources was a rapid transition towards monetized economy in order to meet fiscal demands.[77] This forced monetization disrupted peasant communities and self-contained boyar estates, forcing them to engage in the market economy.

Social structures adapted to the new economic realities, changing the way in which the boyars defined themselves. Gradually, office-holding overshadowed other criteria as the primary signifier of privileged social status, to the extent that the notions of 'boyar' and 'office-holder' became effectively synonymous.[78] The new generation of boyars embraced the economic changes, engaging in profitable cattle-ranching and grain trade. They also enjoyed greater control over manpower, since the burden of taxation forced many village communities to accept their tutelage. The elite also made a major push towards stabilizing and increasing the unfree labour, restricting the serfs' freedom of movement. Although the Moldavian–Wallachian iteration of serfdom never reached the cohesiveness on par with that in Poland–Lithuania, it nonetheless provided the local elite with stable economic basis.[79]

This transformation had far-reaching cultural implications. According to Petre Panaitescu, in the late sixteenth and seventeenth centuries a new cultural idiom emerged among the elite, which abandoned traditional Slavonic high culture upheld by the princely circles and the Orthodox Church, instead establishing a new literary and historiographical tradition in Romanian vernacular composed by the boyar themselves.[80] While some members of the elite tried to defend the position of Slavonic and develop it into a more flexible medium, by the mid-century Romanian established itself as the dominant literary tradition.

The transformation of Moldavian and Wallachian economies and the structural changes within the boyar class were intimately bound to another crucial phenomenon of the seventeenth century. Starting from the second half of the sixteenth century, the principalities witnessed a growing wave of immigration from the territories south of the Danube. These newcomers, described in Romanian historiography as 'Greco-Levantines' or 'pre-Phanariots', came to Moldavia and Wallachia, either on their own or accompanied the voivodes appointed by the Porte. Taking advantage of their financial resources and close ties with the rulers, they managed to secure positions in the administrative hierarchy, pushing away local competitors. Gradually, these families managed to integrate themselves into the local elite by means of marriages and land acquisition.[81] The takeover of offices and land by the newcomers led to a backlash by disenfranchised local boyars, who frequently resorted to violence against perceived interlopers, with only limited success.[82]

The impact of the 'Greco-Levantine' influx into the ranks of boyars had tremendous consequences and played a crucial role in the formation of cross-border patronage relations. As Radu Păun pointed out, for prominent families of 'Greco-Levantine' stock – such as Rusets, Carageas or Asanis – their integration into the local elite did not mean relinquishing their sources of social and political power in the imperial centre. Instead, they became 'multipositioned social actors, in the sense that they acted in several arenas at the same time'.[83] Entrenched in the Moldavian–Wallachian and Ottoman political arenas, they frequently acted as brokers facilitating cross-border patronage ties between the Danubian principalities and the imperial capital.

Thus, throughout the seventeenth century, Moldavian and Wallachian elites experienced a period of rapid transformation that created new possibilities, but also posed new challenges. Driven by fiscal demands, the shift from traditional economic patterns to a monetary economy provided the boyar class with new sources of revenue and incentivized the expansion of serfdom. The overhaul of the revenue-raising apparatus and territorial consolidation also transformed the boyars' access to offices into the crucial component of their elite status. At the same time, the growing competition within the elite, the influx of Greco-Levantines and the rapid turnover at the throne increased political instability and provided an incentive to build up factional structures as a problem-solving mechanism.

The rise of the faction

Early modern Ottoman, Polish–Lithuanian and Moldavian–Wallachian elites operated in different political environments, each with a distinct set of rules, opportunities and constraints. What could these disparate arenas have in common as to warrant their inclusion within the same model? Admittedly, putting them on an equal footing may seem like a fool's errand. However, once we look at the developments in political practice and the distribution of power within the elite, we can identify common trends. This is best illustrated by comparing three statements by specialists in Polish-Lithuanian, Ottoman and Romanian history:

> The Polish political elite was closely tied to the magnates, who secured either for themselves or for their protégés all of the key offices in the province [...] Perhaps one should not regard the Polish king as head of state so much as the head of his own faction, more or less equal to others.[84]
>
> The sultans' powers became dispersed and contested. Instead of a state understood as one imperial household, power shifted among elite households divided by factional rivalries. Sultans periodically tried to revive the warrior-ruler role as late as the reign of Mustafa II (r. 1695–1703), in his case with disastrous results.[85]
>
> [W]e find numerous boyars at the helm of their clientele. [...] They were described by their contemporaries as 'holders' of the country, its 'alphas and omegas', but also as 'the sources of all evil' of the age; they threw their support behind one voivode or another, depending on their kinship ties and personal interest. Only rarely did they face execution for their part in schemes against the rulers [...] more often, the rulers tried to get rid of them by means of poison, but with little success.[86]

These descriptions, formulated independently of each other, bring to light a common thread that runs throughout the seventeenth-century history of the region. Political power shifted away from the rulers towards members of the elite at the helm of their own patronage networks. This devolution of power and political resources, which we can call 'the rise of the faction', signified a shared trajectory of political evolution, despite obvious institutional differences between the arenas.

The main feature of this general trend was a growing reliance on patron–client ties for recruitment into the officialdom and subsequent career advancement. Gaining access to offices and positions of power constituted a valuable resource and a scarce one to that. As the seventeenth century progressed, it became even more difficult, as the growing competition outstripped the supply of coveted posts. This phenomenon was most visible among Ottoman officials, where the influx of *ecnebi* exceeded the capacity of the administration to accommodate the interests and aspirations of the military class. Even when the traditional system of recruitment, the child levy (*devşirme*) lapsed, the problem of too many candidates competing for too few positions remained unresolved.[87] The similar process took place in Moldavia and Wallachia, where the immigration of Greco-Levantines increased competition for a limited number of posts. The situation differed somewhat in the case of Poland–Lithuania, where the noble estate did not experience such challenges. However, the limited number of offices available and the sheer size of the noble estate made the struggle for offices similar in ferocity, a problem further compounded by the lifelong tenure of incumbents.

To remain in power, high-ranking officials began to expand their patronage networks by co-opting ambitious upstarts, who hoped the grandees' backing would provide them with a competitive edge in their own careers. This trend led to the establishment of *kapıs* – grandee households, modelled after the household of the sultan himself, bound to their leaders by intricate webs of kinship, political slavery and patronage. These extended political edifices were decidedly goal oriented and meant to increase their heads' influence within the administration and further careers of their subordinates. By the end of the seventeenth century, the system had proven so successful that it overshadowed other channels of recruitment into the Ottoman officialdom.[88]

In Poland–Lithuania, the pattern differed somewhat due to the Commonwealth's decentralized structure and the crucial role of representative assemblies. Nonetheless, the underlying logic was similar. Although the magnates enjoyed a far more secure position than their Moldavian–Wallachian and Ottoman counterparts, they had to maintain constant presence at local assemblies to secure local support for their political ventures. This they accomplished by captivating local opinion leaders, which in turn influenced the noble grassroots.[89] From the clients' point of view, their association with a powerful magnate offered access to the royal court and perspectives of appointment to official posts. Although most lower-rank positions did not account for much in terms of authority or economic gain, they allowed their holders to distinguish themselves from the mass of nobility and were thus coveted by aspiring individuals.

Economic interests converged with political ones. Seventeenth-century Eastern Europe witnessed many economic and social upheavals, depleting the elites' wealth. In the Ottoman Empire, the system of rotation, meant to accommodate the interest of multiple claimants, increased its pace: the tenures became shorter, while periods out of office extended in length.[90] This placed a considerable burden on the members of the elite, expected to maintain and finance their households even out of the rotation. As the expenses mounted and competition increased, a series of wars, rebellions, and environmental and demographic crises reduced the traditional sources of revenue.[91] In Poland–Lithuania and the Danubian principalities, the economic downturn and the havoc wreaked by multiple wars left many nobles and boyars destitute, forcing them to seek relief and protection of local potentates.

In effect, patronage networks became sprawling machines of revenue-raising and redistribution. Among the Ottoman officialdom, the growing cost of political competition incurred by members of the elite increased their involvement with economic activity, most notably by means of tax-farming, as a means to finance their political households.[92] *Iltizam* contracts provided a flexible mechanism for financing the political household, whereby a grandee could delegate his clients to collect taxes on the ground or approach provincial notables to act as his agents. In this manner, factional and tax-farming networks reinforced each other, binding peripheral elites to the imperial centre.[93]

For Polish–Lithuanian nobility and Moldavian–Wallachian boyars, tax collection did not offer such rewards as for their Ottoman counterparts. The Commonwealth's haphazard and inefficient revenue-raising system repeatedly failed to collect expected sums. In turn, onerous tax burden and widespread evasion in Moldavia and Wallachia put tax collectors at risk of paying the difference from their own pockets.[94] However, office-holding provided opportunities for enrichment through fees and exactions from the population. Instead, Polish–Lithuanian magnates used their extensive landholdings to expand their political influence by leasing their own estates, or royal lands they controlled, to their noble clients, in a manner not dissimilar from the Ottoman grandees' use of *iltizam*.[95]

Finally, another facet of the rise of the faction concerned military affairs. This phenomenon operated on two levels. On the one hand, military commanders used their position to promote their clients to officer posts and to curry the favour of the rank-and-file.[96] As competing factions began to penetrate military units, the army became politicized, with soldiers taking the side of their patrons in the periods of political conflicts. On the other hand, the seventeenth century saw faction leaders recruit their own troops outside the existing system.[97] The conflicts and turmoil of the late sixteenth and seventeenth centuries produced a ready pool of military men seeking employment, which they found on the payroll of local potentates. With a fighting force of their own, Ottoman grandees and Polish–Lithuanian magnates could leverage their troops to secure appointments, intimidate opposition or resist central authorities.[98]

This political, financial and military build-up of factions shifted the balance of power within individual arenas, enhancing the position of high-ranking officials at the expense of monarchs and central institutions. Unable to break the stranglehold, the rulers entered the political fray, building their patronage networks and competing for resources with other faction leaders, creating their own favourites and raising stakes in the competition. The result was a growing crisis of coordination between individual factions, often disrupting political and military ventures.

It would be easy to interpret these developments as evidence of declining standards of service by the self-serving elites. However, the reality seems to have been far more complex. While the expansion patronage networks privatized a growing share of resources embedded in the political arenas and disrupted administrative hierarchies, the members of factions did not seek to subvert the political system. In fact, patronage networks played a central role in key areas of governance, such as revenue-raising and military mobilization.[99] Nonetheless, their political objectives did not necessarily align with what we would call state interest, and the resources they controlled could just as easily be turned against central authorities.

Thus, in spite of the indelible differences existing between Ottoman, Polish–Lithuanian and Moldavian–Wallachian political arenas, we can discern a common pattern of factional build-up and privatization of resources during the seventeenth century. Rather than a sign of decline, the expansion of patronage networks took place in response to challenges posed by new circumstances, providing Eastern European elites with a problem-solving mechanism in an increasingly competitive and volatile environment. Cumulatively, these changes had a transformative influence on the patterns of political life, shifting the balance of power between the ruler and the elite and contributing to growing privatization of resources and administrative functions. In the following part, I will address how this factional build-up manifested itself in a cross-border context.

Part One

Mechanics of Cross-Border Patronage

2

Building Bridges, Building Trust

Trust underpins the lion's share of human interaction. It facilitates cooperation, reduces the risks inherent in joint ventures and enables social actors to anticipate the behaviour of their partners. The higher the stakes, the more crucial trust between partners becomes. In this respect, factional politics was definitely a high-stakes game, as its participants continuously ran the risk of losing property, wealth and life, making trust a primary concern.

In the competitive, back stabbing environment of seventeenth-century Eastern Europe, trust was hard to come by. Members of the elite usually competed for limited resources and were eager to bring down their rivals through subversion or sabotage. Vast distances and poor communications only exacerbated these risks, making it hard for officials to control the situation. This constant threat is best illustrated by what Günhan Börekçi dubbed 'the grand vizier's dilemma'.[1] For a grand vizier, leaving Istanbul to lead a campaign carried considerable risk of removal, since his enemies at the Porte could exploit his absence to discredit him in the eyes of the sultan and seize power themselves. Nor did delegating military command remove the threat entirely: should the appointee achieve a major victory, he could leverage his prestige to take the incumbent's place.

To shore up their position, grandees relied on clients, strategically placed within the ranks of the officialdom and responsible for fending off competition. In this sense, seventeenth-century patronage relations were *trust networks*, where 'members' relations to each other put major long-term collective enterprises at risk to the malfeasance, mistakes or failures of other network members'.[2] However, the reliance on patron–client bonds merely deflected the problem of trust rather than solved it, since the clients could just as easily defect if it suited their interests. Thus, to ensure the viability of their political edifice, prospective faction-builders had to develop bonding mechanisms that would ensure loyalty and reduce the inherent risks.

Ideally, the faction-builders would be able to recruit their partners from among a tightly knit group of acquaintances, with whom they shared a long track record of successful cooperation. This favoured closing factional ranks, since 'closed networks – that is to say networks in which people are connected such that behavior goes unnoticed – create an advantage by decreasing the risks that would otherwise inhibit trust'.[3] However, closure came at a price, imposing narrow limits on the faction's ability to grow and expand its power base. Thus, a viable strategy required striking a balance between closure and brokerage, 'coordinating people between whom it would be valuable, but risky, to trust'.[4]

The necessity of reconciling these two imperatives led members of the elite to develop bonding mechanisms intended to integrate new members and reduce the risk of defection. The exact contents of those toolkits of faction-building, as I choose to call them, varied considerably from one arena to another, depending on socio-political institutions, established practices and cultural idioms shared by respective elites. For instance, the system of political slavery, a basic building block of Ottoman political households, had no parallel either in Poland–Lithuania or in the Danubian principalities, where personal freedom was a prerequisite for participation in political life. For all their differences, however, the efforts and tools employed served the same purpose of building a cohesive political machine.

Thinking about faction-building in terms of toolkits has the advantage of highlighting the pragmatic approaches of the early modern elites. As Jane Hathaway pointed out, no Ottoman official tried to establish a homogeneous system held together by a single bonding mechanism.[5] Individual grandees accumulated their networks gradually throughout their careers, co-opting prospective clients when opportunities presented themselves. Thus, the structure of factions was more akin to bricolage, comprising a variety of social ties, formed on an ad hoc basis and employing multiple bonding mechanisms.

On the spectrum between closure and brokerage, cross-border patronage tilted heavily towards the latter, providing access to otherwise unavailable resources. While this feature made cooperation attractive, it also exacerbated trust issues. Apart from inhabiting different geographical locations, Ottoman grandees, Polish–Lithuanian nobles and Moldavian–Wallachian boyars lived in different socio-political and cultural environments. Their social worlds intersected sporadically, and face-to-face contact was infrequent. There was no reliable reputational mechanism in place to reduce the risk of malfeasance. Rules governing different arenas also rendered many established tools of faction-building incompatible with the requirements of cross-border patronage. Thus, to construct an efficient political machine, seventeenth-century elites had to innovate, calibrating their faction-building tools and coming up with alternative bonding mechanisms. The fact that they went to considerable lengths in doing so testifies to the importance they attached to reaching out beyond the pale.

Familial matters

Early modern politics revolved around family. Thinking in terms of a multigenerational patrimonial lineage was ubiquitous, and the imperatives of its biological and social reproduction shaped social practices and political strategies.[6] Family members constituted a ready pool of recruits for political enterprises, and marriages served to construct and cement alliances. This applied equally to Ottoman, Polish–Lithuanian and Moldavian–Wallachian elites, although how these ties operated varied according to legal, social and cultural norms dictated by their environment.

In Poland–Lithuania and the Danubian principalities, the dominant practice of partible inheritance was among the most important features shaping familial strategies. The requirement to divide the property among all heirs posed a serious risk to the stability of the lineage's material and political position in the long run. In Moldavia and Wallachia, the practice of dividing boyar estates led to recurrent waves of fragmentation and consolidation that continued throughout the early modern period and caused a fall of many grand boyar families.[7] In Poland–Lithuania, magnate families tried to avoid this risk by establishing entails (*ordynacje*), meant to bypass customary norms and safeguard landholdings for future generations.[8] However, despite this relative instability, the material and political status of these elites were far more secure than that of their Ottoman counterparts.

The Ottoman model of familial relations followed a different pattern, rooted in Hanafi legal tradition and influenced by the blueprint provided by the sultanic household. Like their Christian counterparts, the Muslim elite used the system of pious foundations (*vakfs*) to bypass inheritance regulations and avoid the dispersal of family's economic resources.[9] However, their ability to pass their wealth to descendants was severely limited by their status of sultan's slaves (*kul*) that formed the backbone of the group's collective identity and political power. In effect, their property could be subject to confiscation (*müsadere*) at any moment.[10] While this practice was applied less frequently in the seventeenth century and often failed to identify all grandee's possessions, it still put the

Ottoman elite in a more precarious position than that of their Polish–Lithuanian and Moldavian–Wallachian counterparts.[11]

What set the Ottomans apart from other elites in the region was the ubiquity of political slavery as a faction-building tool. The model set by the dynastic household following a well-established Islamic tradition was replicated in a fractal-like manner, with Ottoman officials establishing their own *kapıs*.[12] Rather than constituting an abased underclass, slaves were integrated into family structures, with the bond tying them to their master operating as a form of surrogate kinship.[13] In some instances, it was the slaves rather than biological offspring that inherited leadership within the household after their master passed away.[14] In fact, the widespread practice of concubinage and harem slavery meant that the distinction between family and slaves remained blurred to the point of being indistinguishable.

As the seventeenth century progressed, the nexus between familial and political life grew in importance, particularly within the sultanic household itself. The transfer of the harem to the Topkapı Palace and the end of princely appointments to provincial posts brought all members of the dynasty under a single roof and reshaped relations within the family.[15] The most important consequence of this process was the political ascendancy of queen mothers (*valide sultan*), who assumed important political roles, including the regency on their minor sons' behalf.[16] In effect, *valide sultans* and other prominent members of the harem became influential political brokers in their own right, extending their patronage networks beyond the confines of the palace and into the ranks of imperial administration. Moreover, the sultans tried to reclaim the political ground lost to grandee households by marrying off female members of the dynasty to prominent officials.[17] Marital alliances were by no means restricted to the imperial centre: in Egypt, for instance, the need to safeguard factional cohesion led to a practice of 'inheriting wives', whereby a new household head would marry the widow of his deceased predecessor.[18]

As a bonding mechanism, familial ties offered prospective faction-builders several advantages. Deeply embedded in and reinforced by widely accepted social, cultural and legal norms, they facilitated establishing long-lasting bonds, thus reducing the risk of potential defection. However, the very same advantages they offered turned into considerable obstacles in a cross-border context. Differences of creed and social status between Polish–Lithuanian, Moldavian–Wallachian and Ottoman elites meant that establishing such ties required either interfaith marriages or conversion. This ran against the very foundations of the social order, meant to protect the moral communities against apostasy and religious miscegenation. Thus, both customary norms and religious law left few options available to faction-builders to expand their networks and limited the political role of those who decided to cross over. Still, this did not discourage actors seeking a competitive edge from engaging in such ventures.

Converts and cross-border politics: Biological kinship and its limitations

The obstacles in deploying familial ties as a faction-building tool are best illustrated by the circulation of converts between the Danubian principalities and the Ottoman Empire. By the late sixteenth century, Moldavian–Wallachian elites seem to have come to terms with the prospect of individual conversions to Islam.[19] While the sources are unforthcoming on the matter, there was a steady trickle of Moldavian and Wallachian boyars moving, either on their own accord or involuntarily, to the Ottoman core provinces, where they embraced Islam. However, these conversions meant forfeiting all landed estates and exclusion from the political life of the principalities. In some instances, such converts were even purged from collective memory. This radical break with the converts' social background and identity not only hurt them economically, but also undid the familial patrimony and social status they had inherited from their ancestors and were supposed to pass over to the next generation. In effect, few boyars embraced Islam unless forced to do so by circumstances.

The career of Apostol – Kürd Salman Çavuş – epitomizes a typical trajectory of such individuals. In November 1594, he was serving as the Wallachian agent in Istanbul, when the incumbent voivode, Michael the Brave (1593–1601) started his rebellion against the Porte. Stranded in the Ottoman capital and suspected of knowing about the revolt in advance, Apostol decided to convert and enter the ranks of the *askeri*.[20] He reappears in Wallachian sources in 1631 under a Muslim name Kürd Salman Çavuş, trying to reclaim gypsy slaves who had belonged to his father. However, his request was denied by the voivode and princely council on the grounds that since he had 'rejected the [Christian] law', he no longer had a legitimate claim to his father's property.[21] Ultimately, he managed to assert his rights only after his conversion back to the Orthodox faith.[22]

In fact, it seems that most boyars who decided to convert to Islam later returned to the Danubian principalities and the Orthodox faith of their ancestors.[23] This suggests not only that their attachment to the new faith was rather weak, but also that they found the opportunities they enjoyed as Muslims disappointing. Few secured official appointments and had any impact on the

Ottoman political scene. For boyars, conversion offered an uncertain future and a certain loss of their family's patrimony; for voivodes and pretenders, embracing Islam was a recognition of defeat and an end to their ambitions.[24] Reverting to Orthodox creed only reduced their options: while they could feel relatively safe among local boyars, at the same time – as *zimmi*s and apostates – they had to lay low and not attract the unwanted attention of Ottoman authorities. In effect, such converts had little influence over political affairs and little potential as clients.

There was one major exception to the pattern of converts' irrelevance in cross-border politics throughout the period under discussion. In 1591, the fortunes of Wallachian voivode Mihnea II (1577–83 and 1585–91) took a turn for the worse in the face of growing financial burden and stiff competition for the throne. Moreover, his chief representative in Istanbul, *Ban* Iane Cantacuzino, undermined the ruler's position, intending to replace him with his candidate. With dim prospects to retain the throne, Mihnea left for the Ottoman capital and embraced Islam 'to have a better life'.[25] Following his conversion, already as Mehmed Bey and supported by the grand vizier, he secured an appointment as the *sancakbey* of Niğbolu (Nikopolis), just across the Danube from his former domains.[26] The conversion also allowed him to escape financial woes and the Venetian *bailo* complained that he refused to honour the debts he had incurred as the ruler of Wallachia.[27]

While Mihnea converted, the former voivode's natural son, Radu, was sent away to the Venetian territories, where he was supposed to obtain education and establish political ties under the tutelage of the Brutti merchant family.[28] The choice was by no means accidental given that the Bruttis had extensive ties with both the Wallachian dynasty and Grand Vizier Koca Sinan Pasha and were favourably disposed towards Mihnea II and his offspring.[29] The young Wallachian's sojourn in the *Serenissima* was cut short, though, by the outbreak of rebellion in the Danubian principalities in November 1594. Sensing the opportunity to put his eight-year-old son on the throne, Mehmed Bey recalled Radu to Istanbul.[30] Upon his son's arrival, the *sancakbey* immediately threw himself into the fray, lobbying with senior officials in favour of his son.[31] It is worth noting that in doing so, Mehmed Bey went against the line adopted by the subsequent grand viziers, Ferhad Pasha and Koca Sinan Pasha, who at this time attempted to introduce direct Ottoman administration in Wallachia and Moldavia. He also reached out to the Polish–Lithuanian authorities, requesting permission to hire soldiers in the Commonwealth and promising 'gifts and rewards for the soldiers that would serve his son in Wallachia'.[32]

Despite all the efforts he made until his death in 1601, Mehmed Bey was unable to install his son in Wallachia, even though Radu Mihnea was officially appointed by the Porte in 1596 and 1601. However, his authority remained purely nominal as long as the incumbent Michael the Brave had the means to resist any change on the throne. After the voivode's death, the principality became engulfed in a three-way struggle for power between Radu Şerban, Polish-backed Simion Movilă and Radu Mihnea, which the latter was unable to tilt in his favour.[33] He managed to capture the throne only in 1611, a full decade after his father passed away. In the following years, he managed to enhance his position, ruling both in Wallachia (1611–16 and 1620–3) and Moldavia (1616–18 and 1623–6), becoming one of the most consequential voivodes of the seventeenth century.

At first glance, Radu Mihnea's success in 1611 had little to do with his father's support. However, Mehmed Bey's assistance came at a critical juncture, providing his young son with a political capital necessary to begin his campaign. The Ottoman *sancakbey*'s determination in promoting Radu Mihnea's bid for the throne put the latter in touch with important members of the imperial elite and the Orthodox community in Istanbul. While unsuccessful until much after Mehmed Bey's death, these attempts made the teenage pretender a known quality at the Porte and thus a safe bet for Ottoman officials in 1611.[34] It is hard to imagine that the young voivode would be able to secure similar level of support were it not for his father.

Interestingly, Mehmed Bey's Muslim offspring were far less successful and remained in the shadow of their Christian half-brother. None seems to have secured any significant posts in the imperial administration, either central or provincial. When Radu Mihnea finally ascended the Wallachian throne, his brothers took up residence at his court, disconcerting the boyars, disgruntled by the favours the ruler granted to his Muslim kin.[35] Eventually, two of them converted to Christianity and entered a Moldavian monastery as monks.[36] Mustafa, the only one to remain a Muslim, lived until at least 1636 in Silistre, residing in a house constructed by Mehmed Bey.[37]

Mehmed Bey's uniqueness as a politically influential convert of Moldavian–Wallachian stock demonstrates the inherent weakness of kinship ties as a faction-building strategy in a cross-border context. For the bond to be viable, many pieces of the puzzle had to fall into place. This was hard to accomplish, given that most conversions of the principalities' ruling class were conjectural in nature rather than a part of any long-term strategy. In the case of Mihnea II–Mehmed Bey, a number of factors played to his and his son's advantage. The status of a former voivode spared him the slow advancement through official ranks, while the appointment as the *sancakbey* of Niğbolu placed him in a favourable position to promote his sons interests. Finally, the upheaval of 1594 also worked to his advantage, allowing him to promote Radu Mihnea as a viable candidate. Even under these circumstances, however, it took over a decade before the expected results materialized. In the volatile tug-of-war between cross-border factions, familial ties proved too cumbersome to constitute a reliable faction-building tool alone.

Raising and housing a client: Household recruitment as a cross-border strategy

Rather than trying to construct a cross-border network from scratch, it was more convenient to identify potential patrons and clients on the other side of the religious and political divide. To do so, some Ottoman grandees recruited Christian clients, whom they integrated into the household and subsequently promoted to the throne. Istanbul constituted a large reservoir of prospective clients, as pretenders flocked to the imperial capital in the hope of securing the appointment.[38] In that manner, the inclusion into the *kapı* and physical proximity within the household were intended to construct a surrogate form of kinship.[39]

Unfortunately, estimating the extent of this phenomenon is extremely difficult. References to Moldavian and Wallachian pretenders living in the Ottoman grandees' households for extended periods provide a useful, albeit imperfect, indicator of such arrangements. Estimating the scale of such arrangements is virtually impossible, although the extant sources clearly underreport the scale of such alliances. Within the universe of Istanbul politics, Moldavian and Wallachian pretenders occupied a lowly position, well below Ottoman officials and foreign diplomats. Their relative unimportance meant that, unless they succeeded in securing the throne, their actions were usually ignored by diplomatic and local sources. Thus, the examples presented below aim to demonstrate the pattern of connectivity rather than its magnitude.

Reporting on the appointment of Moldavian voivode Ştefan Tomşa II in November 1611, French ambassador Achille de Harlay de Sancy claimed that *Kaymakam* Gürcü Mehmed Pasha orchestrated the nomination. According to the diplomat, the new voivode had been the grandee's long-time protégé and used to live in Mehmed Pasha's residence before his appointment.[40] The close bond between the future voivode and the Ottoman grandee is confirmed by other sources and survived for decades. According to Krzysztof Zbaraski, Gürcü Mehmed Pasha called Ştefan Tomşa II and Kantemir Mirza his sons, while they reciprocated 'describing the vizier as their father'.[41]

Tomşa's attachment to a single household, however, is somewhat undercut by his participation in the war against the Safavids, which allowed him to establish an alternative set of patronage relations with the future grand vizier, Nasuh Pasha. Once on the Moldavian throne, Tomşa remained loyal to the Sublime Porte and, personally, to his Ottoman patrons. In turn, three grand viziers – Nasuh Pasha, Öküz Kara Mehmed Pasha and Gürcü Mehmed Pasha – steadfastly supported their client despite recurrent boyar revolts and Polish–Lithuanian diplomatic pressure to remove the controversial voivode.[42]

The career of a Wallachian pretender and voivode, Mihnea III (1658–9) sheds more light on how physical proximity within the household translated into a cross-border patronage bond. A long-time resident of the Ottoman capital, Mihnea based his bid on the throne on the spurious claim of dynastic origin and, more importantly, his powerful protectors, Gürcü Ken'an Pasha and Burnaz Atike Sultan.[43] Mihnea entered Ken'an Pasha's *kapı* at a young age, serving as a page and obtaining education in letters and religious sciences befitting a member of the Ottoman elite. His membership in the household spanned decades and continued after Ken'an Pasha's death in 1652. Moreover, through the grandee's wife, Atike Sultan, the pretender managed to establish a bond with *valide sultan* Hatice Turhan.[44] The robust patronage network allowed Mihnea to make a successful bid for the throne in 1658, which was not only supported politically but also bankrolled by Atike Sultan, who contributed 140,000 *akçe* for this purpose.[45] That the Ottoman princess was ready to pay for her client's bid suggests that she saw it as an investment, although one that ultimately did not pay off: the following year, Mihnea III rebelled against the Porte and was replaced on the throne with a protégé of Köprülü Mehmed Pasha.[46]

Although Ştefan Tomşa II remained loyal to the Porte throughout his reign, while Mihnea III took up arms against the Ottomans soon after securing the throne, their careers share some common features. While entrenched in imperial power networks, both voivodes failed to establish a secure power base in the principalities. Ştefan Tomşa II's reign in Moldavia was plagued by recurrent boyar revolts and Polish–Lithuanian military interventions, forcing him to rely on mercenary troops and individuals of obscure origin.[47] Similarly, Mihnea III encountered a vehement opposition of the local elite, and only by massacring Wallachian leaders in July 1659 he was able to enhance his position.[48] Their weak grip on power is also implied by their constant efforts to appropriate dynastic legitimacy, religious ceremonies and – in Ştefan Tomşa's case – Ottoman symbols (see Figure 2.1).[49]

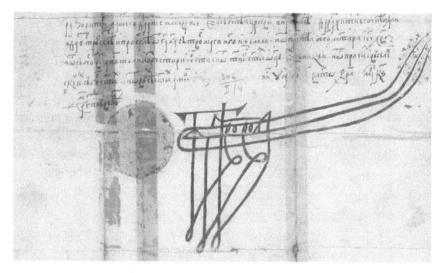

Figure 2.1 Voivode Ştefan Tomşa II's (1611–15 and 1621–3) Cyrillic monogram, stylistically inspired by the Ottoman *tuğra* (SJAN-Iaşi, M-rea. Galata ii/4).

The inherent weakness of Ştefan Tomşa and Mihnea III's position in the principalities was in many respects a flip side of the mechanisms that allowed them to secure the throne in the first place. The need to remain in physical proximity of their patrons' residence in Istanbul alienated them from the Moldavian–Wallachian political arena and the local elite. It comes as no surprise that Mihnea III had no landholdings in the principality and likely never visited Wallachia before his appointment. Ştefan Tomşa II, in turn, inherited relatively modest estates in southern Moldavia, but he spent most of his adult life abroad and never held any official rank in the principality.[50] While well-integrated into the imperial patronage networks, both Mihnea III and Ştefan Tomşa were comparatively ill-equipped to bridge the gap between Ottoman and Moldavian–Wallachian political arenas.

Marriage as a faction-building tool: Cross-border marital networks of the Movilă dynasty

In comparison, the divide separating the boyars from Polish–Lithuanian nobility seemed easier to cross. Unlike in the Ottoman case, straddling from one arena to another did not require conversion, making it easier for individuals to form familial bonds across the political boundary. Particularly in the first half of the seventeenth century, this was facilitated by the multi-confessional character of the Polish–Lithuanian noble estate and a venerable tradition of marriages across confessional lines. By the 1620s, almost a third of noble families in the palatinates of Braclav and Kyiv were confessionally mixed, and the overwhelming majority was Greek Orthodox.[51] Thus, from the religious standpoint, nothing stood in the way of Moldavian and Wallachian elites hoping to establish familial ties with their northern neighbours.

It was rather the matter of social status than that of religion that stood in the way of intermarriages between the boyars and Polish–Lithuanian nobles. The latter looked down on their Moldavian–Wallachian counterparts, whom they considered little more than peasants. This sentiment is illustrated by Hieronim Ossoliński, who stated that 'there are no nobles in Moldavia, since all there are equal and accustomed to the fact that one day you may be herding goats, only to become a grand lord overnight'.[52] As such, they hardly constituted a suitable match for the upper echelons of the nobility, except for those who had managed to secure Polish–Lithuanian noble status or ascend the Moldavian throne.

In developing their marital alliances, the Movilă dynasty that ruled Moldavia between 1595 and 1611,[53] was by far the most successful. The family had established itself at the top of the political elite in the principalities in the course of the 1570s and 1580s.[54] However, the volatile nature of Moldavian politics at this juncture, marred by heated conflict and rapid turnover at the throne, meant that in the last decades of the sixteenth century, Ieremia Movilă and his brothers, Simion and Gheorghe, were forced to seek refuge in the Polish–Lithuanian Commonwealth. During their exile in 1579–82, they came into contact with Crown grand chancellor and Crown grand *hetman*, Jan Zamoyski, who would become their future patron.[55]

For Zamoyski, establishing ties with Moldavian émigrés at this time constituted an important addition to his rapidly growing faction; for Movilăs, the bond offered means to secure their livelihood in exile and garner support for their return to the principality. To achieve this, though, the Movilăs had to meet the requirements of *ius indigenatus*, which restricted landholding to Polish–Lithuanian nobility. Obtaining the status of *indigena* was no easy feat since by the late sixteenth century wrested control of the process from the monarch, delegating it to the *Sejm*. A complex and arduous process put in place required a recommendation from a provincial dietine before submitting the motion to the central representative assembly.[56] Zamoyski's influence among the nobility greatly facilitated the Moldavians' efforts, and in 1593 the *Sejm* granted the *indigena* privileges to Ieremia Movilă and another boyar, Luca Stroici.[57] The chancellor's role in the process was reflected in the crest

54 *The Ottomans and Eastern Europe*

adopted by Movilă, who included the heraldic symbol of his patron, thus establishing a link of fictive kinship.[58]

Ieremia Movilă and Luca Stroici's inclusion into the ranks of Polish–Lithuanian nobility constituted a watershed for the Moldavian émigré community in the Commonwealth. Until 1593 Ieremia had been but one among the relatively undifferentiated group of high-ranking boyars seeking a safe haven in Poland–Lithuania. However, the patronage ties established with Zamoyski quickly made him the uncontested leader and principal broker between the powerful magnate and other émigrés.[59] This paved the way for Ieremia Movilă's enthronement as the ruler of Moldavia in September 1595, enabled by Zamoyski's military intervention in the principality. In the following years, more naturalizations followed, not only bringing the principality's elite closer to Poland–Lithuania, but also solidifying the position of Ieremia Movilă and Jan Zamoyski as principal distributors of crucial political resources.[60]

After the year 1600, Ieremia Movilă and his family began to increasingly rely on marital ties to mobilize Polish–Lithuanian support. This came at a critical juncture: in September that year, Zamoyski intervened again in Moldavia to shore up Ieremia Movilă's control of the principality. Although in military terms the campaign was a success, it also created fissures within the faction, to the extent that Zamoyski considered replacing Movilă with a more malleable voivode. Under these circumstances, the chancellor approached Prince Myxajlo Vyšnevec'kyj (Wiśniowiecki), a Ukrainian magnate and Zamoyski's ally, with an offer to marry Ieremia Movilă's eldest daughter, Regina–Chiajna. Vyšnevec'kyj responded enthusiastically, but the marriage was postponed until the prospective bride reached suitable age.[61] Negotiations resumed two years later. Both parties swiftly reached an agreement, and the wedding took place on 25 May 1603. Recognizing Zamoyski's role in the affair, both Vyšnevec'kyj and Movilă invited the chancellor as a guest of honour.[62]

While the initiative belonged to Zamoyski, each party had a vested political interest in concluding the marriage. For Zamoyski, the union gave a prospect of consolidating his faction and strengthening the bond with Vyšnevec'kyj, whose patronage network was among the largest in the Ukraine. The latter not only enhanced his prestige by marrying into a ruling family in Moldavia, but also received Regina's lavish dowry, giving him much-needed financial relief.[63] Ieremia Movilă, in turn, was able to mend fences with the chancellor, whose support was crucial for the voivode's political survival. Moreover, Zamoyski's advanced age and deteriorating health prompted Movilă to search a new patron, who would replace his long-time partner. Vyšnevec'kyj, as one of largest landowners in the region, an experienced soldier and a scion of a powerful lineage with impeccable Orthodox credentials constituted a viable option in this respect.

The marriage established a blueprint employed in the following years. In February 1606, Ieremia's second daughter, Maria, married Stefan Potocki, the *Starosta* of Felin.[64] Although the Potockis were relative upstarts, they already had managed to establish their hegemony in the Palatinate of Podolia. Ieremia's new son-in-law alone controlled fifteen towns and over a hundred villages in the immediate vicinity of the Moldavian border.[65] Thus, he was able to provide the voivode with military assistance on a moment's notice, greatly improving the Movilă's position in regional politics. The marital strategy initiated by Ieremia continued after his death in August 1606, when his widow Elizabeta Lozonschi took over the management of familial affairs. In April 1616 yet another wedding took place, this time between Elizabeta's third daughter, Caterina, and Prince Samijlo Korec'kyj.[66] Through skilful management of familial affairs, the Movilăs succeeded in assembling a powerful political bloc along the principality's northern border.

In the course of the decade that followed Ieremia Movilă's death, his sons-in-law repeatedly intervened in Moldavian affairs, supporting the cause of their relatives against rival dynastic claims and Ottoman-backed Ştefan Tomşa II. Although ultimately unsuccessful in securing the throne, they nonetheless kept the Movilăs' dynastic ambitions alive until 1616. That year, the last expedition undertaken by Vyšnevec'kyj and Korec'kyj ended in a total defeat and effectively buried any hopes to restore Ieremia's descendants to the Moldavian throne. Elizabeta and her sons were taken captive by the Ottoman troops and subsequently converted to Islam.[67]

The debacle of 1616 put an end to the family's quest for the Moldavian throne. However, it did not spell the end of the Movilăs' matrimonial alliances with Polish–Lithuanian elites. In 1620, Ieremia and Elizabeta's youngest daughter, Ana, married the Castellan of Sieradz, Maksymilian Przerębski.[68] Throughout her life, she concluded three more marriages, all her spouses hailing from prominent Polish–Lithuanian families. Similarly, her sister Maria remarried after Stefan Potocki passed away in 1631. Her second husband was the Palatine of Sandomierz, Mikołaj Firlej, the scion of a distinguished senatorial lineage.

At first glance, these marriages seem to have followed the pattern set by Ieremia Movilă and his wife. However, upon a closer examination, we detect a shift away from Moldavian affairs. Marital alliances with Vyšnevec'kyj, Potocki and Korec'kyj had exhibited a clear geographical focus on the Commonwealth's southeast, adjacent to Moldavia. After 1616, in turn, the scope shifted decidedly towards the Crown's central regions. The sole exception to this rule was Ana's fourth husband, Stanisław Rewera Potocki. Even in the latter case, Moldavian affairs did not constitute the motive for the marriage: the couple married only in 1659, long after the Movilăs' chances to retake the throne withered away. Instead, Potocki was more interested in Ana's dowry and the land she inherited from her three previous spouses. The reason for this shift is clear: with no male descendants after 1616, Ieremia Movilă's offspring lost any chance to retake the principality. No longer having a vested interest in Moldavia, the sisters integrated themselves into the social world of the Polish–Lithuanian elite, largely abandoning ties to their place of origin.

Reviving the model: Miron Barnovschi and the appropriation of Movilăs' heritage

The debacle of 1616 did not mark the end of the Movilăs' political heritage. The success that Jan Zamoyski and Ieremia Movilă had achieved at the beginning of the century inspired the next generation eager to replicate the model. Maksymilian Przerębski, the Castellan of Sieradz who had married Ana in 1620, entered the protracted legal battle over the family's Polish–Lithuanian estates. Although his main area of political activity remained on the western borders of the Crown, the struggle over inheritance prompted him to involve himself in the region. This overlapped with the ascendancy of Movilă's relative, Miron Barnovschi, who in January 1626 became the voivode of Moldavia.[69]

Barnovschi, despite his blood ties with Movilăs, was not a member of their political circle.[70] Instead, in the 1610s, he sided with their nemesis, Ştefan Tomşa II, universally despised in the Commonwealth. Moreover, Polish sources accused Barnovschi of allying himself with Tatars and participating in their predatory raids.[71] In particular, the boyar cultivated his friendship with Kantemir Mirza, an ambitious Tatar aristocrat, who managed to establish himself as the leader of the Bucak Tatars and attain virtual independence from the Crimean khans.[72] Barnovschi's association with some of the Commonwealth's most notorious adversaries made him an unlikely heir to the Movilăs' legacy, and it comes as no surprise that he was described as a 'scoundrel' by Polish authors.

Once in power, however, Miron Barnovschi (1626–9) carried out a volte-face, embracing his maternal descent from the dynasty and recreating the system of alliances in Poland–Lithuania.[73] In Przerębski, he found an enthusiastic ally, ready to provide him with necessary political support. In many respects, both he and Barnovschi reproduced the model that Zamoyski and Ieremia

Movilă had employed over three decades prior. The Polish magnate assisted the voivode in securing the status of *indigena* in 1628, and Barnovschi's crest reflected Przerębski's contribution.[74] French ambassador in Istanbul, Philippe Harlay de Césy, even reported spurious rumours that Barnovschi was married to Przerębski's daughter.[75] Finally, when in 1629 the Ottomans forced Barnovschi to flee Moldavia, Przerębski supported his client's efforts to organize a Polish–Lithuanian intervention in the principality.[76]

That Przerębski and Barnovschi's followed the path trailblazed by Jan Zamoyski and Ieremia Movilă at the beginning of the seventeenth century demonstrates the potential both Polish–Lithuanian magnates and Moldavian boyars saw in kinship as a reliable faction-building tool. Although the fact that Barnovschi had no offspring prevented him from establishing a network of marital alliances on par with that of Movilăs', he was able to use his blood ties to whitewash his past and reinvent himself as a pro-Polish ruler, with Przerębski's assistance. While in the early 1620s Polish nobles had seen the voivode as a 'scoundrel', by the end of the decade he became a respectable heir to Movilăs' political legacy.[77]

The Caterina affair: Marriage, religion and faction in the Moldavian–Ottoman context

Whereas in Polish–Moldavian relations marital alliances revolved around the questions of social status, in the case of Ottoman elites, confessional differences came to the fore. While Hanafi law permitted Muslim men to take non-Muslim wives, the fear of religious miscegenation among the boyars meant that such unions would lead to social and political ostracism within the principality. The challenges did not discourage some members of the elite, though. The second marriage of Moldavian voivode Vasile Lupu demonstrates that those seeking to strengthen their bond with the Muslim elite came up with creative ways to overcome the obstacles.

In September 1639, *Bailo* Alvise Contarini informed the Venetian authorities of a short but heated controversy that engulfed the Ottoman officialdom. At its heart was the planned wedding of a recently widowed Moldavian voivode. According to the diplomat:

> [Vasile Lupu] brought a new bride from Circassia, from a distinguished family, and of exquisite beauty. On the way back to Moldavia [she] was detained by the Pasha of Silistre, since, according to the laws of the country, Circassian women, as Muslims, are not allowed to marry Christians.[78]

The controversy soon escalated, since Vasile Lupu was reportedly preparing to reclaim his bride by force, should *Beylerbey* Halil Pasha refuse to release her.[79] Ultimately, the conflict was resolved by *Kaymakam* Tabanıyassı Mehmed Pasha, who forced the governor to release Lupu's second wife, known as Caterina Cercheza ('the Circassian'). According to the Venetian diplomat, the *kaymakam* was bribed by the Moldavian voivode to rule in his favour, prompting Contarini to remark that in the Ottoman Empire 'even the stipulations of law have no power against the lust for gold'.[80]

While Contarini presents a straightforward and seemingly convincing interpretation of the events, his account relies on the assumption that Caterina was, indeed, a Muslim. However, this was not the case. Other accounts, whose authors had more direct access to the events and Caterina herself, leave no doubt that she was a Christian throughout her life. Moreover, it seems that everyone involved in the affair was aware of this fact, including Halil Pasha himself. Niccolò Barsi, a Luccan monk who accompanied the bride from Bahçesaray on her way to Moldavia, informs us that the *beylerbey*'s claims were only a pretext to detain the Moldavian mission. The Ottoman official personally encouraged the bride to convert, but she rebuffed him and – to drive her point home – ostentatiously consumed pork in public.[81] Similarly, Evliya Çelebi, who met Caterina during his sojourn in Moldavia, emphasizes that she was a Christian throughout her life.[82]

If the dispute over Caterina's creed was merely a smokescreen, why did the marriage trigger such a controversy among Ottoman officials? Barsi claimed that Halil Pasha, smitten by the bride's beauty, tried to claim her for himself.[83] However, it seems that Caterina's singular importance stemmed not from her physical beauty, but rather her kinship ties. For a woman from peripheral Circassia, Vasile Lupu's future wife was surprisingly well-connected among Ottoman grandees. Evliya Çelebi, describing his encounter with Caterina in 1659, remarks that she was a niece of Derviş Mehmed Pasha, the *beylerbey* of Damascus and the future grand vizier.[84] Barsi, in turn, informs us that the Moldavian entourage was well received in Bahçesaray because Caterina's unnamed sister was Khan Bahadur Giray's spouse.[85] Finally, in 1653 Paul of Aleppo identifies Şirin Bey, the leader of the most important aristocratic clan in the Crimean Khanate, as Vasile Lupu's brother-in-law, a bond established through the voivode's marriage with Caterina.[86] Thus, marrying Caterina allowed Vasile Lupu to tap into a powerful kinship network that spanned from Circassia to the Ottoman centre and the Crimean Khanate.

However, the bride's family was itself divided on the matter. While Bahadur Giray gave his blessing to the projected marriage and provided his sister-in-law with a military escort, Derviş Mehmed Pasha vehemently opposed the union and tried to derail Vasile Lupu's plans.[87] As a high-ranking member of the imperial elite and Caterina's uncle, his opinion carried considerable weight. It is likely that he was responsible for spreading rumours regarding the bride's Muslim identity, which would go a long way to obstruct the marriage. While no contemporary source explains this divergence of opinions, a glimpse at factional ties within the Ottoman officialdom allows us to understand the motives of those involved in the dispute.

In the course of the 1630s, Vasile Lupu embarked on an ambitious dynastic project of taking control of both Moldavia and Wallachia. To achieve this goal, he formed a strong bond with the grand vizier and, later, *kaymakam*, Tabanıyassı Mehmed Pasha, reinforced by common ethnic–regional origin, which I will discuss in the following section. However, apart from political support at the Porte, taking control of Wallachia required military assistance from the Crimean khan, who wielded the most formidable military resources in the region. The projected alliance seems to have been the main reason for Vasile Lupu's marriage with Caterina, and the warm welcome she received at the Crimean court was a proof of Bahadur Giray's willingness to enter the alliance. This Crimean connection did not escape the attention of some contemporaries, who saw it as Lupu's main reason for his second marriage.[88] Reframing the marriage as a faction-building venture also explains Tabanıyassı Mehmed Pasha's decision to disregard Halil Pasha's protests. Rather than as an impartial umpire, the *kaymakam* intervened in favour of his client, Vasile Lupu, whose plans he fully supported.

The opposing camp, including the *beylerbey* of Özü and Derviş Mehmed Pasha, subscribed to a similar factional logic. Caterina's uncle had cooperated with Tabanıyassı Mehmed Pasha at the beginning of his career and even served as the grandee's *kethüda*.[89] By 1639, however, the two grandees parted ways and Derviş Mehmed Pasha defected to Tabanıyassı's sworn enemy, Silahdar Mustafa Pasha.[90] The latter's patronage network included Halil Pasha, the *beylerbey* who detained Caterina, and Matei Basarab, whom Vasile Lupu wanted to replace on the Wallachian throne.[91] A marital alliance with the khan would greatly enhance the Moldavian ruler's position and – indirectly – shift the balance within the Ottoman political arena. Thus, it should come as no surprise that Derviş Mehmed Pasha and his allies did all in their power to prevent that from happening. Although they failed in this respect, the resolve they showed during the conflict played an important role in the escalating conflict between the factions, discussed in more detail in the following chapters.

The convoluted controversy over Caterina brings to light both the limitations of cross-border marital alliances, and the determination and creativity of those involved to overcome them. That Vasile Lupu went to considerable lengths to establish a familial bond with Bahadur Giray demonstrates how attractive marriages could be in promoting factional interests and providing trust to the network. At the same time, the fierce resistance staged by Silahdar Mustafa Pasha's partisans makes clear that they considered the alliance a major threat to the balance of power.

Ethnic–regional solidarities

In a pioneering study published in 1974, Metin Kunt provided a major revision of the established notions regarding the role of ethnic–regional ties among Ottoman officials.[92] Whereas it had been assumed that the process of recruitment erased the *kuls'* identities, moulding them into a homogeneous class of sultan's servants, Kunt demonstrated that such bonds retained their importance in day-to-day politics of the empire. Ottoman officials continued to speak their native languages, sport customary attire and maintain contact with their communities.

While this certainly imbued the imperial elite with a multicultural flavour, more important for everyday politics were the solidarities that brought together officials of the same ethnic–regional background. In the seventeenth century, as the spatial and social mobility within the empire increased, these *cins* solidarities became a crucial faction-building tool. They facilitated integration of new members of the elite, brought together patrons and clients, and provided trust necessary for the patronage networks to work.[93] On a broader scale, they also contributed to the emergence of two adversarial blocs of 'easterners' coming from the Caucasus and 'westerners' hailing predominantly from Bosnia and Albania.[94] In this sense, the seventeenth century constituted the high water mark of ethnic identities within the imperial elite. Their role subsequently declined with the rise of civilian bureaucracy (*kalemiyye*), recruited from among free-born Muslims, and the phasing out of *devşirme* levy.[95] According to Baki Tezcan, these transformations redrew social boundaries in favour of religious criteria, leading individuals to 'lose touch with some of the collectives he or she had been affiliating with and come to essentialize that one particular facet of his or her identity', including their ethnic or regional communities.[96]

Arbănaș/Arnavud: Defining Albanian in cross-border networks

Apart from the ebbs and flows of ethnic–regional solidarities, the influence of individual groups within Ottoman officialdom was also in flux. Among the 'westerner' bloc, Bosnians, who had been a dominant group in the second half of the sixteenth century, were increasingly overshadowed by officials of Albanian origin. While the cause of this shift is unclear, some scholars theorized that the custom of *besa* ('word of honour') played a role in reducing the risk of defection.[97] Imperial service also offered an attractive opportunity for local families to acquire wealth and influence, proven by their willingness to participate in *devşirme* levies.[98] Even though the Islamization process made considerable inroads among Albanians, the sense of their distinctiveness persisted. In the eighteenth century, Ottoman officials preferred to refer even to Muslim members of the group by their ethnonym rather than to their confessional identity.[99]

It is important to remember that, for all their reliance on ethnic–regional ties, Ottoman grandees did not intend to build a homogeneous 'Albanian' faction, but instead took advantage of the existing solidarities as a means to pursue their own political goals. Thus, there was never a national or ethnic political bloc within the Ottoman officialdom; instead, ethnic–regional solidarities were woven into the broader fabric of political alliances.[100] They constituted a tool to reach out and integrate new members into the faction or reinforce the existing alliances. However, this role was by no means restricted to the Ottoman political arena, and reliance on shared origin came to play an essential role in the development of cross-border patronage.

In contrast to the Ottoman officialdom, no 'easterner'/'westerner' dichotomy arose within the Moldavian–Wallachian ruling class. While some families originating from the Caucasus found their way into the boyar elite, they played no autonomous role as a coherent bloc in Moldavian and Wallachian political life.[101] Instead, the opposition between local lineages (*pământeni*) and newcomers from the Ottoman lands, collectively described as 'Greeks' or 'Greco-Levantines', constituted the main axis of differentiation. Although the use of ethnonyms would suggest that ethnic or linguistic criteria were decisive, the distinction was more a product of social changes and political competition. The influx of newcomers from the Ottoman provinces, either as merchants or members of princely entourages, threatened the position of established boyar families.[102] The rivalry for political and economic resources led to a construction of a new set of social boundaries. As Bogdan Murgescu pointed out:

The distinction between an 'indigene' (*pământean*) and 'non-indigene' was based not solely on ethno-linguistic criteria but included geographical, political and 'moral' criteria. The ambiguity was exploited by the boyars, allowing them to exclude or assimilate those they deemed undesirable.[103]

This is not to say that there was no linguistic or ethnic basis for the dichotomy.[104] Still, its primarily political purpose blurred the relationship between ethnic–regional categories and the term since accusations of 'being Greek' were meant to discredit political opponents and exclude them from the arena rather than indicate their ethnic affiliation.[105] In effect, the boundaries were constantly contested and redrawn, as boyars mobilized different facets of their identity to suit immediate circumstances and their political interests. Sometimes, this led to paradoxical outcomes. For instance, in April 1633 Lupu Coci – future voivode under the name Vasile Lupu – participated in a rebellion against Moldavian incumbent Alexandru Iliaş, accusing the latter of promoting Greeks over local boyars.[106] However, when the leaders lost control of the crowd and a fully fledged anti-Greek pogrom broke out, Lupu – born to a family of 'Greco-Levantine' descent – was himself severely beaten by the mob, who deemed that 'he was a Greek too'.[107]

From this perspective, the distinction between 'Greeks' and local boyars is a rather unhelpful one in examining ethnic–regional solidarities. The seventeenth-century notion of *pământean* was effectively an 'empty' category, constructed in opposition to the Greek 'Other'. In turn, the latter was a blanket term encompassing all newcomers, which contained a variety of individuals of various ethnic origins and different walks of life.[108] Since early modern Moldavian and Wallachian boyars left few ego documents that would reflect their self-identification, it is in many respects nigh impossible to determine whether the 'Greek' label reflected the individual's ethnic identity or was merely as a political slur.

Fortunately, not all labels utilized in the Danubian principalities during this period fit neatly into the binomial opposition between 'Greeks' and 'locals', and thus seem more attuned to ethnic–regional origins of individual boyars. Therefore, they provide us with more insight into their role as a faction-building tool. Arguably the most important among them is the term *arbănaş* ('Albanian'), used to describe several prominent figures of the seventeenth-century Moldavian–Wallachian political life.[109] The way authors of this period deploy this category diverges from blanket notions of 'Greeks' and 'locals' described above. Unlike the latter terms, it seems devoid of value judgement, instead being invoked to explain why certain individuals banded together in their political ventures. Also, the term is usually associated with *neam*, meaning people or lineage, suggesting that for Moldavians and Wallachians it had similar ethnic–regional connotations as the Ottoman *cins*.

To what extent does the Romanian term *arbănaș* correspond with Ottoman *Arnavud*? The exact contents of each term are difficult to ascertain, and scholars have been split in identifying either ethnicity or place of origin as a decisive factor.[110] Since we have no official population records, it is next to impossible to identify the localities in which most Ottoman officials and Moldavian–Wallachian boyars were born or grew up. However, it would be a mistake to assume that in case of relatively small, interconnected groups, such as patronage networks, labels such as 'Albanian' necessarily reflected a definite set of linguistic or geographic criteria. Given the fluid and multifaceted nature of early modern identities, invoking ethnic–regional identity was subject to constant renegotiation, as actors 'used them for their own advantage when they needed'.[111] Thus, the litmus test for the claims to Albanian identity was its recognition by their partners.[112] Therefore, rather than trying to unpack the contents of the labels *arbănaș* and *Arnavud*, it is sufficient to examine whether their usage in the Danubian principalities and the Ottoman Empire aligned with one another. In short, to establish a rough equivalence between the two terms, a more feasible strategy is to examine whether Moldavian–Wallachian and Ottoman sources applied these labels to the same individuals rather than to analyse what exactly they understood under respective terms.

In Moldavia, the most important figure described as an Albanian was Vasile Lupu (1634–53), whose political longevity and outsized ambitions garnered the attention of his contemporaries and modern historians alike. His career as a boyar and the voivode shows the flexible and multifaceted character of early modern identity, and he is referred to interchangeably as a Moldavian, an Albanian and a Greek, often by the same source. While individual scholars attempted to 'nationalise' the voivode as a Romanian,[113] the overwhelming consensus has accepted Franz Babinger's conclusions that the future voivode was born in the village of Arbanasi near Razgrad in northwestern Bulgaria.[114] At the same time, contemporary sources trace the origin of his family to numerous locales across the Balkan Peninsula, from Epirus to Macedonia to the banks of the Danube.[115] However, they are unanimous in identifying the voivode as being of Albanian origin.[116] Most importantly, however, he is identified as such by an Ottoman author, Evliya Çelebi. The peripatetic traveller visited Moldavia during the reign of Vasile's son, Ștefaniță (1659–61) and took some time to describe the palace built by the voivode, approvingly commenting that the 'Albanian infidel'

64 *The Ottomans and Eastern Europe*

had exquisite taste.[117] That both Ottoman and Moldavian sources describe the voivode as an *Arnavud/arbănaş* suggests that both elites applied the terms in a similar manner, allowing us to see them as rough synonyms. This paves the way for us to retrace the ethnic–regional solidarities in the context of cross-border patronage.

Retracing Albanian networks: First generation

Not only the references to Albanian identity indicate similar concepts in Moldavian–Wallachian and Ottoman sources, but they also usually appear in the context of political alliances and patronage relations. Moldavian chroniclers Miron Costin and Ion Neculce emphasize the voivode's background not at random, but rather to explain patron–client ties he formed with other political actors in Moldavia and beyond. According to Miron Costin, Vasile Lupu's Albanian origin was the central factor in promoting another boyar and future voivode, Gheorghe Ghica:

> Voivode Vasile brought [Gheorghe Ghica] to the court, since he was Albanian, of the same origin as him. He subsequently served on lower posts, eventually becoming the *Vornic* of Lower Moldavia. Vasile trusted him and upon seeing that he was skilled in all matters and trustworthy, as a *capuchehaia* should be, sent him to serve as his *capuchehaia* at the Porte.[118]

We know even less about Gheorghe Ghica's origins than about those of Vasile Lupu. Some scholars, relying on the information provided by Moldavian chronicles, suggest a locality of Köprü as the boyar's place of birth.[119] However, this theory is based on spurious evidence, and a more reliable tradition places the origins of the family in the vicinity of Ioannina in Epirus.[120] Still, just as in Vasile Lupu's case, the sources refer to him as an Albanian and identify Ghica's background as the critical factor in his political career.[121]

Under Vasile Lupu, Gheorghe Ghica quickly rose through the ranks of the local elite, securing a high-ranking office as the *vornic* of Upper Moldavia.[122] Although this put him at the apex of Moldavian administrative hierarchy, he rarely appears in documents issued by the voivodes, and his landed estates remained surprisingly meagre.[123] It seems that he spent much time away from the principality, serving for extended periods as Vasile Lupu's *capuchehaia* in Istanbul. His performance in this capacity apparently won him high praise among his contemporaries. In 1653, Voivode Gheorghe Ştefan (1653–8), who came to power at the helm of the rebellion against Vasile Lupu, decided to

Building Bridges, Building Trust 65

retain Ghica as his agent in the imperial capital, notwithstanding the latter's ties with the ousted ruler.[124] In order to ensure the boyar's loyalty, Gheorghe Ștefan initially detained his family, and subsequently arranged a marriage between his daughter and Ghica's son, Grigore. This scheme backfired in 1658, when Grand Vizier Köprülü Mehmed Pasha deposed Gheorghe Ștefan and appointed Gheorghe Ghica as the new ruler of Moldavia.

Miron Costin suggests that Mehmed Pasha chose Ghica on a whim and condemns the latter for failing to stand up for his ruler.[125] However, another Moldavian author, Ion Neculce, provides a different, and in many respects fascinating, account. Like other early modern boyar chroniclers, Neculce knew Costin's account and envisioned his own work as its continuation from the year 1661. At the same time, by way of introduction, he composed a collection of forty-two legends from the earlier period, using both written sources and oral tradition. Among those short stories, known as *A Collection of Stories* (*O samă de cuvinte*), we find a description of Gheorghe Ghica's career and the circumstances that led to his appointment to the throne.

Although Neculce retains the core of Costin's account, he takes his narrative in a different direction, focusing both on the voivode's youth and the circumstances of his appointment. According to Neculce, Ghica set out from his village in his teens, determined to seek a patron in the imperial capital. In his journey he was accompanied by a young Muslim boy, and the two grew fond of each other. Prior to their arrival to Istanbul, they made an oath that should either succeed, he will support the other. Subsequently, they parted ways and set out to find their suitable patrons.

Eventually, both achieved the success they were hoping for. The Muslim boy entered the household of a powerful grandee and, after a long career, made a name for himself as Köprülü Mehmed Pasha and managed to become the grand vizier. Subsequently, the audience granted to the Moldavian *capuchehaia* becomes a reunion of childhood friends:

> When [Ghica] was at the Porte with other boyars, the vizier recognised him, but Ghica did not recognise the vizier. Thus, Vizier Köprülü summoned his treasurer and ordered him in secret 'Do you see this old Moldavian boyar at the Divan? Take him and keep him in your quarters until the Divan concludes and later bring him to me in secret.' Upon being separated from other boyars, Ghica became frightened, not knowing what was happening. After the Divan concluded, they brought him to the vizier, and the vizier asked him who he is and where is he from, asking 'You know me, don't you?' Ghica replied where he is from, and that he does not know the grand vizier. Then Vizier Köprülü said

'Remember what we talked about then on the road?' and continued 'You forgot, but I have not, and I will make you the voivode in Moldavia'.[126]

Ghica initially protested, expressing loyalty to his ruler and pleading in his favour. The grand vizier agreed to postpone the appointment but, when Gheorghe Ştefan failed to conform to the orders, promptly replaced him with Ghica.

The story of childhood friends meeting after decades at the apex of power seems too good to be true and certainly was. Although some scholars took this story at face value, it is certain that both Neculce and his oral sources took considerable liberties in embellishing the events. Many details, such as the age of the protagonists, or the origins of Mehmed Pasha's sobriquet (which Neculce derives from the island of Cyprus), are blatantly wrong.[127] However, it would be a mistake to dismiss the whole account, since its very existence suggests a strong personal and political bond between the grand vizier and the voivode that intrigued contemporaries.[128]

Another Moldavian source provides further insight into the matter. During his second reign in Moldavia (1711–16), Voivode Nicolae Mavrocordat (Greek Mavrokordatos) commissioned a scribe in his chancellery, Axinte *Uricariul*, to produce an official compilation of Moldavian and Wallachian chronicles. In composing this work, Axinte added little new information, but a rare original fragment of *The Parallel Chronicle of Moldavia and Wallachia* addresses the relationship between Gheorghe Ghica and the grand vizier. The section, covering the events in Wallachia between 1659 and 1664, was based, according to the author, on an eyewitness account of a certain *Comis* Iştoc, who served the voivode's son, Grigore. It comprises a description of the conspiracy between an influential boyar, *Postelnic* Constantin Cantacuzino, and Grigore Ghica to replace the latter's father at the Wallachian throne. The whole affair was sponsored by Panagiotis Nikoussios, the Grand Dragoman of the Porte and one of the most important brokers in the Köprülüs' circle.[129] The most significant obstacle to the plan, according to this account, was that '[Gheorghe] Ghica was very dear to the grand vizier *since they were both Albanians*' [emphasis mine – M.W.].[130]

That ethnic–regional solidarity would play a role in Köprülü Mehmed Pasha's ties with the Moldavian boyar is by no means surprising. The grand vizier's Albanian background was frequently mentioned in the sources.[131] Although it seems that Mehmed Pasha was the third generation of his family to serve in the imperial administration, ethnic–regional bonds played a crucial role in his career.[132] Starting from the 1620s, the list of his patrons included Grand Vizier

Kemankeş Kara Mustafa Pasha (who promoted him to the position of *mirahor*), Kasım Ağa (who recommended him as the grand vizier) and another 'westerner', Hüsrev Pasha.[133] Thus, the grand vizier was no stranger to using ethnic–regional solidarity as a faction-building tool, and it seems plausible to argue that they played a role in promoting Gheorghe Ghica to the thrones of Moldavia (1658–9) and Wallachia (1659–60).[134]

Indeed, Köprülü's appointees to Moldavia and Wallachia form a homogeneous familial and ethnic–regional group. During his six-year tenure as the grand vizier, Mehmed Pasha granted the throne five times to four individuals. In January 1658, he installed Gheorghe Ghica in Moldavia and Mihnea III in Wallachia. The latter's rebellion led to a new reshuffling: Ghica was transferred to Wallachia, while in his stead Köprülü appointed Ştefaniţă Lupu (1659–61), Vasile Lupu's son. Finally, when Gheorghe Ghica failed to meet the expectations, he was replaced by his son, Grigore, as the new ruler of Wallachia (1660–4 and 1672–4) (see Table 2.1).

What becomes immediately clear is that Köprülü Mehmed Pasha's appointees constituted a very narrow and exclusive circle, bound by familial and ethnic–regional solidarity not only between themselves, but also with the grand vizier and his household. The only non-Albanian in this group, Mihnea III, owed his throne to the support of another *kapı*, led by Atike Sultan, with possible involvement of queen mother, Hatice Turhan. His appointment was likely a product of a power-sharing agreement between these households but quickly unravelled after Mihnea III's rebellion and his expulsion from the principality.[135] This paved the way for the 'Albanian' bloc of Köprülüs, Lupus and Ghicas to total domination of the Ottoman Empire and the Danubian principalities. The degree to which these three families managed to monopolize the political scene is even more striking when we take into consideration that Vasile Lupu and Gheorghe Ghica continued to exert power, acting as their sons' representatives at the Porte.

Table 2.1 Köprülü Mehmed Pasha's Appointees in Moldavia and Wallachia (1656–61)

Appointee	Principality	Year	Origin
Gheorghe Ghica	Moldavia	1658	Albanian
Mihnea III	Wallachia	1658	*Kapı* of Burnaz Atike Sultan
Gheorghe Ghica	Wallachia	1659	Albanian
Ştefaniţă Lupu	Moldavia	1659	Son of Albanian Vasile Lupu
Grigore Ghica	Wallachia	1660	Son of Albanian Gheorghe Ghica

Köprülü Mehmed Pasha's grand vizierate was a period when this Albanian network reached the peak of its power and cohesion, but by no means encompassed the whole period of its existence. In fact, it seems that its origins reached as far back in time as the 1630s and Vasile Lupu's early reign in Moldavia (Figure 2.2). During the second half of the decade, the Moldavian voivode embarked on an ambitious plan to establish his family in both Danubian principalities and enlisted assistance of former grand vizier Tabanıyassı Mehmed Pasha. The grandee was a *devşirme* graduate born in Drama, who early in his career managed to secure a powerful patron in Chief Black Eunuch Hacı Mustafa Agha.[136] This *intisap* relation gave a huge boost for Mehmed Pasha, who was dispatched (as his first provincial appointment) to Egypt and subsequently served for five years as Murad IV's grand vizier. In the late 1630s, he also established close ties with Kemankeş Kara Mustafa Pasha. As contemporaries inform us, the cornerstone of cooperation between the grandees was their shared Albanian origin.[137] At the same time,

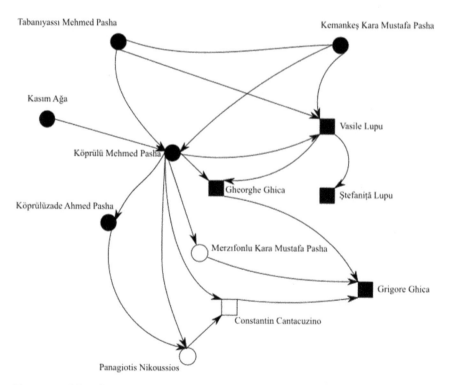

Figure 2.2 The Albanian patronage network in the mid-seventeenth century. Circles indicate Ottoman officials, while squares indicate members of Moldavian–Wallachian elite. Black shapes indicate individuals of Albanian origin; white indicates actors of other ethnicities. Arrows indicate the flow of patronage.

Mehmed Pasha ardently supported Vasile Lupu's attempts to take control of Wallachia, while Gheorghe Ghica, another fellow Albanian, coordinated their efforts in his capacity as the Moldavian *capuchehaia*.[138] Following Tabanıyassı's death, Kara Mustafa Pasha took over, playing a crucial role in protecting Vasile Lupu after the demise of his ally. Thus, it is safe to say that the 'Albanian' cross-border network, which monopolized power under Köprülü Mehmed Pasha, had been active for at least two decades prior to his appointment as the grand vizier.

Generational change and the waning of ethnic-regional solidarities

The Albanian network's activity did not begin with Köprülü Mehmed Pasha's emergence as the grand vizier, nor did it cease when he passed away in September 1661. His son and successor, Köprülüzade Ahmed Pasha, continued his father's strategy, although with a lesser consistency. This was largely due to the passing away of the faction's 'old guard', and a shift in the character of ties that bound individual members. Within a couple of months of Köprülü Mehmed Pasha's death, Vasile Lupu and his son, Ştefaniţă, passed away, followed in 1667 by Gheorghe Ghica. The new generation, which grew up in an environment different from that of their fathers, had a weaker attachment to ethnic–regional identities.[139] Tellingly, references to the common origin of the first-generation members of the faction subside at the point of generational change, and are overshadowed by different patterns of connectivity. For instance, the career of Grigore Ghica suggests that his rise was propelled not so much by ethnic–regional solidarity, but rather by the patronage of Grand Dragoman Panagiotis Nikoussios.[140] At the same time, the Danubian principalities plunged into a bitter factional struggle, which accelerated turnover of the voivodes. The career of another voivode, Gheorghe Duca, suggests the continued viability of the system, although under changed circumstances and through somewhat different means. According to an anonymous Moldavian author:

> Voivode Duca was from the Greek land of Rumelia. He came to this country as a small boy, and Voivode Vasile brought him to the court, where he served several voivodes, eventually becoming a grand boyar.[141]

Duca's career was in many respects a carbon copy of Gheorghe Ghica's route to the throne, and so was his background. According to Anton Maria del Chiaro, a Florentine secretary at the Wallachian court, Duca was 'of the Greek rite and of Albanian origin, born in a village called Policcani'.[142] Other sources similarly indicate the voivode's Albanian origin.[143] The family retained a strong attachment to the region and supported a burgeoning Epirote community in Moldavia.[144]

70   *The Ottomans and Eastern Europe*

Under Köprülüzade Ahmed Pasha, Gheorghe Duca became one of the faction's most important members in the Danubian principalities. However, despite his origins, ethnic–regional identity was not invoked in the sources to explain his rise to power. Instead, his web of alliances was based primarily on his personal ties with the grand vizier and Grand Dragoman of the Porte, Panagiotis Nikoussios, a crucial broker within the Köprülü faction.[145] His position was further buttressed by a marital alliance he concluded with an influential Ruset family.[146] The Ottoman grandee and Nikoussios steadfastly supported the voivode and reportedly intervened to save his life on two separate occasions. Following Ahmed Pasha's death, Duca was able to ingratiate himself with Kara Mustafa Pasha, and ascended the Moldavian throne one more time, in 1678. His services were additionally rewarded in 1681 when he began his short-lived tenure as the Cossack *Het'man* of Ottoman-controlled Ukraine.[147] Thus, despite hailing from a similar background as that of Gheorghe Ghica, Duca and his partners relied more on personal acquaintance and marital alliances than ethnic–regional solidarities. As more viable avenues for providing trust became available, the role of the latter diminished in the factional calculus of power.

The Ottoman–Moldavian–Wallachian network based on shared Albanian origin of its members is remarkable for its longevity. It crystallized from a set of interpersonal bonds in the 1630s, reached its high-water mark under Köprülü Mehmed Pasha and survived, albeit in a somewhat diminished form until the second siege of Vienna. Its resilience in a volatile political landscape demonstrates two essential issues in cross-border patronage. On the one hand, it confirms the importance of ethnic–regional solidarities as a faction-building tool able to provide trust necessary to make the network work. On the other, it testifies to the importance of cross-border patronage itself, showcasing the effort put by individual grandees and boyars to construct a viable political system and maintain it against all odds.

Brothers in arms

The seventeenth century was a time of war. Following a costly and inconclusive 'Long War' (1593–1606) against the Habsburgs, the Ottoman Empire became embroiled in a series of conflicts against the Safavids, Venice and Poland–Lithuania. The Commonwealth faced similar challenges, and protracted wars against Muscovy and Sweden brought it to the brink of collapse in the 1650s.

Moreover, both powers had to deal with multiple armed revolts, which stretched thin their military resources and forced them to expand their armies.

From a faction-builder's perspective, the military build-up and extended campaigns offered fertile grounds for recruitment, further facilitated by the existing chain of command. In comparison with the sixteenth century, this period witnessed political emancipation of the military, and soldiers became an increasingly influential pressure group in their own right.[148] The increased demand for manpower opened up the ranks for new social strata, who sought either employment or privileged status. Taken together, these developments offered a ready pool of potential clients. While by no means all instances of military service translated into patron–client ties, those that did provide an insight into patterns of connectivity at the time of military conflict.

Ştefan Tomşa II: A *sekban* on the Moldavian throne

In the Ottoman Empire, the crucial shift took place in the last decades of the sixteenth and seventeenth centuries, triggered by the rise of *sekban* mercenary troops. A set of demographic, environmental and economic factors led many peasants to abandon their land, creating a floating population of gun-wielding part-time soldiers, constantly oscillating between military service and banditry.[149] Provincial governors quickly tapped this new source of cheap and expendable military force, mobilizing *sekban*s for imperial campaigns or rebellion against the Porte. As Baki Tezcan pointed out, the phenomenon first took shape in Syria but soon spilled over to neighbouring regions.[150] The militarization of the countryside and demographic pressure, combined with the growing disgruntlement of provincial governors, *timar*-holders and jobless *sekban*s coalesced into a tinderbox, which exploded in the *celali* rebellions and the collapse of political order.[151] Only with utmost difficulty was the Porte able to regain control, but low-level banditry continued to plague the empire for decades to come.

The *celali* rebellions wreaked havoc and caused massive economic and demographic losses in the empire's core provinces. At the same time, they had a transformative effect on Ottoman political culture and the way the Porte interacted with the imperial periphery. *Celali* warlords and their mercenary armies were in many respects 'rebels without a cause', seeking inclusion into the imperial system rather than its destruction.[152] Central authorities adopted a flexible approach to bandit leaders and recalcitrant officials, bargaining with them rather than launching a full-scale crackdown.[153] In their turn, commanders tasked with suppressing the unrest quickly adopted rebels' tactics and began recruiting their own *sekban* armies.

In this respect, Nasuh Pasha, an ambitious grandee and an influential, albeit polarizing figure, was one of the pioneers. A *devşirme* recruit of Albanian origin, he ascended through the ranks with the help of powerful patrons, Safiye Sultan and Chief Black Eunuch Hacı Mustafa Agha.[154] During his service in Anatolia, he also married a daughter of local Kurdish notable, Mir Şeref Bey, thus establishing a substantial power base in the region.[155] However, his initial performance as a commander was lacklustre, and when his conflict with another Ottoman official ended in the latter's murder, rumours of Nasuh's pending execution began to spread. However, the grandee managed to recoup his losses by recruiting a massive *sekban* army, which by May 1609 reached around 7,000 soldiers.[156]

Among them was probably a future Moldavian voivode, Ştefan Tomşa II. As I have mentioned, French ambassador de Sancy claimed in 1611 that the voivode had been living in the residence of Gürcü Mehmed Pasha and secured the appointment thanks to the grandee's political support. However, from the correspondence between Hungarian officials we learn that 'since Moldavian Voivode Ştefan had campaigned for a couple of years against the *kızılbaş* (*kazulok*), the Turkish emperor made him the voivode and gave him [a daughter] of a distinguished and wealthy Greek as a wife'.[157] This remark refers to the Ottoman war against the Safavids, which broke out in 1603 and continued with varying intensity until 1612. This begs the question, when and in what capacity could a Moldavian pretender participate in this conflict?

Upon his arrival to the Ottoman capital, Ştefan Tomşa II had enjoyed a long career as a soldier of fortune. According to contemporary accounts, he served in an infantry unit in Poland–Lithuania during Livonian wars (1578–81), subsequently enlisting to the French army in the war against Spain, where he spent some time in captivity.[158] After a short stint in Habsburg service, the future voivode arrived in Istanbul around 1601, where he threw himself into the political fray, trying to secure the Moldavian throne. Tomşa appeared as a serious contender in 1607, trying to take advantage of the succession struggle in the principality, but ultimately had to postpone his plans.[159] Following this failed attempt he disappeared from the sources to resurface only in late 1611 and reassert his claim, this time successfully.

The knowledge that the Moldavian voivode resided in the palace of Gürcü Mehmed Pasha for an extended period allows us to estimate the period of his service on the Safavid front. Throughout this period, the grandee resided in Istanbul and performed his duties as the *kaymakam*. Thus, to fight at the Safavid

Building Bridges, Building Trust

front, the voivode had to enlist under the command of a different grandee. Given the lull in Ottoman activity on the Safavid front in the preceding period, when imperial troops focused on the pacification of the countryside, it stands to reason that the future voivode would join the campaign when the Porte launched a new offensive against Shah Abbas's troops in 1608–11. This corresponds neatly with the surge of recruitment by Nasuh Pasha, who was unlikely to be particularly picky about his troops' confessional identity and would certainly appreciate an experienced soldier.

Tomşa's participation in Anatolian campaigns led to a wave of accusations and rumours, alleging that he was 'a Turk' and a Janissary.[160] However, it is unlikely: there is no indication in the sources of his conversion to Islam, a prerequisite for joining the corps. Thus, it stands to reason that he served as a *sekban* mercenary. Since mercenary troops were cheap and disposable, there were virtually no restrictions regarding religious creed or social status, and we find Christian mercenary units on the Ottoman payroll during the Long War.[161] If Tomşa was indeed a mercenary, this would further support the argument of his association with Nasuh Pasha, the largest *sekban* employer in Ottoman establishment at this point.

The events surrounding Tomşa's appointment in November 1611 seem to confirm this. While diplomatic sources credit Gürcü Mehmed Pasha with orchestrating the nomination, the main reason for this seems to have been Nasuh Pasha's absence from the capital.[162] However, it is unlikely that the *kaymakam* acted without taking the grand vizier's opinion into account. After Nasuh Pasha returned to the Ottoman capital and took over the reins of power, he steadfastly supported the voivode despite mounting boyar opposition and Polish–Lithuanian diplomatic pressure.[163] It is hard to believe that he would defend someone else's nominee so vehemently. Moreover, the three grandees – Nasuh Pasha, Gürcü Mehmed Pasha and Öküz Mehmed Pasha – had the same patron, *Kızlar Ağası* Hacı Mustafa Agha, and likely cooperated with each other until Nasuh Pasha's falling out with the next chief black eunuch that led to the grand vizier's execution.[164] Thus, it stands to reason that Ştefan Tomşa II was a candidate of the whole faction rather than just of an individual grandee.

While scholars have assumed that the rise of *sekban* armies weakened patron-client ties, given the transactional character of the bond between mercenaries and their employer, the close relationship between Ştefan Tomşa and Nasuh Pasha suggests a more nuanced approach.[165] More inclusive than *kapıkulu* troops, the mercenary units could serve as a meeting ground for individuals coming from different walks of life. Although a clear majority of such ties dissolved

74 *The Ottomans and Eastern Europe*

once the troops concluded their service, there is no reason to doubt that their commanders would promote their more capable subordinates, transforming military service into political capital. In Ştefan Tomşa II, it seems, Nasuh Pasha and his allies found a perfect candidate to expand their faction, and his military service strengthened the bond between them.

A rebel voivode and his Ottoman patron: Matei Basarab and the political culture of the *celali* age

While serving the Porte on the battlefield could produce solidarity, so could rebellion. The changing political culture of the *celali* age, with its emphasis on bargaining and accommodation, reverberated in the Danubian principalities. In some instances, this repertoire was not only similar to that employed by rebel leaders in Anatolia, but also involved the same protagonists, who encouraged their prospective clients to rebel and assured them of their support at the Porte. In the case of Abaza Mehmed Pasha, his political network in the Danubian principalities was forged by rebellion against the imperial centre.

Abaza Mehmed Pasha was one of the most formidable figures in the Ottoman political scene of the early seventeenth century. An 'easterner' from the Caucasus, he entered the political scene as a treasurer of another *celali* leader, Canpoladoğlu Ali Pasha.[166] After the warlord's defeat, victorious Halil Pasha integrated Mehmed Pasha into his household and promoted him to a series of governorships in Anatolia. The turning point came in May 1622, when a Janissary revolt in Istanbul resulted in the regicide of Sultan Osman II. At this point Abaza Mehmed Pasha declared himself the sultan's avenger and launched a campaign targeting Janissaries across Anatolia.[167] This set the central authorities into a panic, especially given that the rebel governor's battle cry garnered considerable support even in the capital.[168] What followed was a series of inconclusive campaigns, interrupted by similarly inconclusive attempts at negotiations and reconciliation with the rebel grandee. Only in 1628, the forces led by the new grand vizier Hüsrev Pasha managed to finally put down the rebellion and force Abaza Mehmed Pasha to surrender. Tellingly, the maverick grandee went unpunished. Instead, Murad IV received him with full honours, pardoned the former governor and promptly appointed him as the *beylerbey* of Bosnia and, later, Özü–Silistre. In doing so, the sultan attempted to harness the grandee's talent in raising and financing *sekban* troops, while at the same time to cut him off from his power base in Anatolia.[169]

Building Bridges, Building Trust 75

By the time Abaza Mehmed arrived in Silistre, the political situation in the Danubian principalities reached boiling point. The incumbent rulers of Moldavia and Wallachia, Alexandru Iliaş and Leon Tomşa, respectively, were facing the fierce opposition of the boyars, who accused them of excessive taxation and filling offices with their hangers-on. In Wallachia, where the opposition concentrated in the western region of Oltenia, in 1630 boyars revolted against the ruler and sought refuge in Transylvania, lukewarmly supported by Prince György Rákóczy.[170] Trying to defuse the situation, Leon Tomşa attempted rapprochement, partially giving in to the boyars' demands.[171] These concessions managed to convince most rebels, and their ranks dwindled, leaving a small group of hardliners under the leadership of *Aga* Matei of Brâncoveni.[172] Failure of a campaign meant to oust Leon Tomşa in 1631 furthered sapped their morale, and by early 1632 it seemed that the rebellion would soon die out.

Despite him being a scion of one of the wealthiest Wallachian lineages, Matei's career prior to 1632 was a lacklustre one. For over two decades, the only title he held was that of a cup-bearer (*paharnic*), a minor and insignificant office, usually granted only to young boyars entering Wallachian political life. In 1628, he was appointed as the grand *aga* and entrusted with the command of the infantry, but even this was an office low in the administrative hierarchy.[173] As a boyar, he stayed largely aloof from the Bucharest court and resided in his estates in Oltenia. His decision to join the rebellion was dictated largely by a personal grievance against one of Leon Tomşa's favourites.[174] In the initial phase of the revolt, he played second fiddle and ascended to the leadership only after more prominent boyars reconciled with the voivode.

As the Wallachian revolt seemed to be reaching an anticlimactic end, the arrival of Abaza Mehmed Pasha to Silistre changed the situation drastically. According to the Wallachian chronicle, the *beylerbey*

> upon seeing how the Greek voivodes from Constantinople destroy and impoverish the country, decided to summon *Aga* Matei from Transylvania and put him on the throne, so that this unfortunate country would get some relief and peace. Thus, he sent a priest from Niğbolu, Ignatie the Serb, calling [Matei] to come [to Wallachia] to be the voivode by the will of the pasha.[175]

Sources differ whether Abaza Mehmed Pasha or the rebel boyars initiated the contacts.[176] Still, the grandee enthusiastically embraced Matei's cause, encouraging him to take control of the principality. In doing so, Abaza Mehmed Pasha was overstepping his authority and went against explicit orders from the

Porte. While Leon Tomşa was dismissed in Istanbul during the summer of 1632, Radu Iliaş, incumbent Moldavian voivode's son, was appointed in his stead.

Despite the pressure from the imperial capital, Abaza Mehmed Pasha persisted in the supporting Matei, who in the meantime entered the principality and staked his bid for the throne. However, rather than advancing to Bucharest, the voivode and his army first went to Niğbolu to meet the *beylerbey*.[177] There a ceremony of appointment took place, whereby Mehmed Pasha bestowed upon his client a robe of honour and provided him with additional troops for the upcoming campaign. Only then Matei entered the Wallachian capital and, in the battle on the outskirts of the city, defeated the Moldavian–Ottoman army sent to enthrone Radu Iliaş.[178]

Defying the Porte was a gamble for Abaza Mehmed Pasha, and the incumbent grand vizier, Tabanıyassı Mehmed Pasha, repeatedly threatened the maverick grandee with death in case should he not abandon Matei.[179] However, the governor did not budge, and his client's victory on the battlefield greatly strengthened his bargaining position vis-à-vis the Porte. Eventually, a messenger arrived from the capital, recognizing the voivode on the condition that Matei would personally go to Istanbul to kiss the sultan's robes. After consulting with his Ottoman patron, who assured him of his support, the Wallachian voivode proceeded with a great entourage to the imperial capital. There, Radu Iliaş's supporters launched a last-ditch attempt to reverse the decision. Moldavian *capuchehaia* – and father-in-law of Radu Iliaş – Curt Çelebi rallied the support of Tabanıyassı Mehmed Pasha, 'bringing to the vizier Greeks and Greek and Turkish women to complain how they lost their husbands, brothers, and sons in the war waged by Matei'.[180] The stalemate continued for a month before Murad IV's direct intervention eventually tilted the balance in favour of the Wallachian voivode, known in historiography as Matei Basarab (1632–54). His relationship with Abaza Mehmed Pasha continued, and Moldavian chronicler Miron Costin did not hesitate to call the voivode the grandee's *çırak*, an apprentice or client.[181]

Why did Abaza Mehmed Pasha risk so much in throwing his weight behind Matei, whom he had never met before? Although Wallachian chronicles claim he took pity on the population overtaxed by Leon Tomşa and his entourage, it is unlikely that the grandee, who spent most of his career roving the Anatolian countryside with his army, would be that concerned about the plight of Wallachian taxpayers. However, if we look at the events through the prism of Abaza Mehmed's past, it becomes clear to what extent his and Matei's strategy replicated the grandee's own political experience in Anatolia. With the skilful balancing of patronage ties and armed resistance against the centre, both Abaza

Mehmed Pasha and his Wallachian client pursued a new pattern of politics that emerged during the *celali* rebellions.

In this context, the motives behind *beylerbey*'s support for Matei become understandable. During his career as both a governor and a rebel, Abaza Mehmed Pasha had made numerous enemies in the Ottoman establishment. Even if they failed to secure his execution at this point, they would gladly welcome his fall. To buttress his position, the grandee thus needed a strong power base, but his position as the *beylerbey* of Özü initially offered little in this respect. Having spent all his career in Anatolia, Abaza Mehmed Pasha was an outsider to the region and lacked familiarity with local politics.[182] From this perspective, the Wallachian rebellion was a godsend, allowing him to identify potential allies and support them against the Porte. Subsequently, he could use his official capacity and political expertise to cobble his power base from among those disgruntled with the policy of the Sublime Porte.

Interestingly, Matei Basarab's successful bid for the throne encouraged another attempt to capture the throne with Abaza Mehmed Pasha's support. In April 1633, Alexandru Iliaş, Moldavian voivode and the father of Matei Basarab's rival, was overthrown by a boyar revolt.[183] Once victorious, the rebels quickly moved to elect a new ruler, overwhelmingly deciding to summon Miron Barnovschi who, after having lost the throne in 1629, resided in his Polish–Lithuanian estates.[184] The former voivode decided to take up the offer and rushed to Iaşi.[185] Upon his arrival, he reached out to Matei Basarab and Abaza Mehmed Pasha, requesting their assistance in obtaining Ottoman recognition. Assured of their support, he proceeded with a great boyar entourage to Rusçuk, where he met the *beylerbey* and discussed the details of his bid and future cooperation.[186] Encouraged by Abaza Mehmed Pasha, the voivode and his Moldavian supporters arrived to Istanbul in late June 1633. However, as it turned out, Barnovschi miscalculated and was immediately thrown in prison and promptly executed on the orders of Grand Vizier Tabanıyassı Mehmed Pasha. After several days of imprisonment, the boyars who had accompanied the unfortunate pretender could elect a new voivode, opting for Moise Movilă (1630–1 and 1633–4).[187]

Both contemporaries and modern scholars disagree on the motives behind Barnovschi's execution. Some argued that autocratic Murad IV had been displeased with the boyars' initiative to elect their own ruler, which seems unlikely.[188] Others suggested that the Porte was suspicious of Barnovschi's pro-Polish leanings and long residence in the Commonwealth.[189] However, in this respect, Moise Movilă hardly differed from the executed voivode. He was a Polish *indigena*, and during the so-called 'Abaza Pasha War' (1633–4) fed Polish–Lithuanian commanders with intelligence and ultimately fled to the Commonwealth.[190] Finally, Miron Costin attributes the voivode's death to a conspiracy between the grand vizier and Lupu Coci, who wanted to ascend the throne himself.[191] All these factors certainly could have an impact on the decision to execute Barnovschi. However, the fact that the boyars could elect his replacement suggests that the main concern was the voivode's association with Abaza Mehmed Pasha, who had become by this point the focus of Moldavian and Wallachian opposition against the Porte. Barnovschi's success in Moldavia, replicating that of Matei Basarab, would make the grandee an uncontested hegemon in the Danubian principalities. It seems that Tabanıyassı Mehmed Pasha, who lobbied for the maverick governor's execution in 1632 and would eventually succeed in 1634, tried to forestall Abaza's rise.

Although Ştefan Tomşa II and Matei Basarab's rise to power differed significantly, their careers were a product changing patterns of political life, triggered by the *celali* rebellions and the growing role of mercenary troops. For Tomşa, the growing scale of *sekban* recruitment facilitated his entry into military ranks and the establishment of patronage ties with a future grand vizier. In turn, the emergent political culture of the seventeenth century, based on a combination of rebellion, bargaining and patronage, allowed Matei to ascend the throne and establish himself as one of the longest-ruling voivodes in this period. Although their career patterns differed, both can thus be considered *celali* voivodes, their success enabled by the transformations the Ottoman Empire was undergoing in the *celali* age.

Adapting the toolkit

The toolkits applied by Ottoman, Moldavian–Wallachian and Polish–Lithuanian elites in building their cross-border networks were not particularly novel or more encompassing than those they used in their home arenas. Marriage, kinship, military service, ethnic–regional solidarities – all these tools were lock, stock and barrel of factional politics. However, in deploying them, individual actors showed considerable creativity, which allowed them to overcome legal restrictions and establish new alliances beyond the pale. The controversy surrounding Vasile Lupu's marriage with Caterina shows both the complex political and legal environment in which they had to navigate, but also their determination to make their political edifice viable.

Ottoman officials trying to establish their factional presence in the Danubian principalities found their traditional toolkit inapplicable. The absence of provincial administration similar to that in the core provinces of the empire and the Christian creed of the local elite meant that they could not simply recruit mamluks, find prospective clients in the Janissary corps or dispatch members of their households. As was the case with many political arenas across the empire, there were also significant obstacles in the form of the collective identity of the peripheral elite, which limited access for outsiders, forcing households from the imperial centre to seek alliances with local powerholders and play according to local rules.[192] However, as shown in the case of the Albanian patronage network that survived for the better part of the century, once established, these alliances could continue beyond a single lifespan.

In comparison, Polish–Lithuanian magnates trying to establish their influence in Moldavia and Wallachia faced fewer obstacles. Shared religious identity facilitated marital relations, and the presence of naturalized boyars within Moldavian elite eased cooperation. However, we do not get the impression that they outnumbered the ties between the boyars and Ottoman grandees. Although Romanian scholars have generally assumed that money was all that mattered in securing the appointment, the ubiquity of trust-building and faction-building mechanisms tells a different story. In spite of rapid turnover, imperial officials and their Moldavian–Wallachian counterparts sought to establish strong bonds with each other, going beyond simple corruption. That they were willing to do so betrays that they considered such cross-border ties important for their broader political designs.

3

Flows, Exchanges and Conversions

Establishing a viable faction was not an art for art's sake. Faction-builders embarked on this arduous task to further their political goals and procure necessary resources. Thus, whereas patronage networks frequently appear to us as static webs of alliances, their very existence and operation depended on a constant flow of resources mobilized, transferred and deployed by their members to gain an edge over competitors. In this sense, early modern faction constituted a complex mechanism relying on resource flows to generate capital. Thus, it conformed to the model proposed by Nan Lin:

> When certain goods are deliberately mobilized for a purposive action, they become capital. Capital is an investment of resources intended to generate returns. Thus, it is tailored by the actor to meet an organization's demand. In return, the actor may be rewarded with social (reputation), economic (wealth), or political (power) resources. [...] Through social ties and networking, actors gain additional resources of direct and indirect ties.[1]

No single type of capital dominated either factional politics in general or cross-border patronage. Maintaining political influence required more than just amassing a web of political alliances. A successful faction-builder also required economic resources and military power to shore up his position, and access to information to coordinate between disparate segments of the network and respond to external threats. Moreover, not every resource acquired through patronage networks could be immediately deployed in the political arena; in many instances, it had to be converted first into a different type of resource. For example, money did not necessarily translate into an increased political clout but had to be procured to enhance prestige or recruit a fighting force. The same resource could also vary in importance depending on whether it was utilized in Poland–Lithuania, the Danubian principalities or the Ottoman central arena. As Bartolomé Yun Casalilla pointed out, we should think of early modern elite households – and factions – as systems of not only procurement and transfer, but also conversion of different types of resources among their members.[2]

Examining the exchanges and conversion of resources within cross-border factions is no easy task. Insiders left behind little written evidence: communication between members seems to have been conducted orally, and most of the written records were either deliberately destroyed or withered away through the centuries. Thus, most of extant information comes from outsiders, such as diplomats or historians, whose knowledge of the factions' inner workings was often limited. In effect, they frequently relied on hearsay and gossip, producing vague or unreliable accounts. For instance, it is a well-nigh hopeless task to identify precise information regarding money flows between Ottoman officials and their Moldavian–Wallachian clients, except that 'great sums' of money changed hands. In other cases, we are merely able to identify a single instance of exchange within an alliance that spanned several decades. Frequently, it is difficult even to establish what sort of resources flowed through the network, as the only indication of patron–client relationship is an off-hand remark that two actors were long-time friends. Despite these truly homeopathic doses of information, it is nonetheless clear that exchange of resources in cross-border patronage was widespread, and the instances we learn about are but a tip of an iceberg.

The second challenge concerns methodology and the relationship between patronage and formal political institutions. While constituting alternative systems of resource flows and agencies, patronage networks and state institutions were by no means contradictory and mutually exclusive. On the contrary, the resources constantly shifted between the two circuits. The exercise of power and authority was a highly personalized affair, and the distinction between public and private remained blurred. Factional resources were frequently deployed for ventures mandated by the political centre, while patronage relations were crucial for 'muddling through' and mobilizing formal institutions for political goals. Given that patrons and clients were simultaneously high-ranking officials, it is difficult to disentangle the two systems and identify underlying rationales. For instance, during the tenure of Köprülü viziers, interests of state and faction aligned to the point of being virtually indistinguishable. Nonetheless, we are able to identify fissures between these two types of power networks, particularly in the periods of conflict that pitted two cross-border factions against one another.

This chapter addresses the patterns of resource flows and their conversion within cross-border patronage between Ottoman officials, Moldavian–Wallachian boyars and Polish–Lithuanian nobility, in four key areas. In the first section, I address the matters of power, influence and political support, crucial for political survival and career advancement. These political resources tied in with the patrons' ability to provide a fighting force to protect factional interests and defeat political adversaries. In their capacities as commanders of standing armies and as military employers, Ottoman grandees and Polish–Lithuanian magnates were able to mobilize troops on a massive scale and deploy them in support of their Moldavian and Wallachian clients. In the second section, I move to examine the economic and financial flows within cross-border factions. Economic exploitation of the Danubian principalities by the corrupt and rapacious Ottoman elite has long been the trope in Romanian scholarship, and an epitome of the 'Turkish yoke'. However, as I argue, it would be a mistake to consider these payments as simple bribes or a product of extortion; instead, they provided financial resources necessary for maintaining cross-border factions and were by no means one-sided. Moreover, economic realities in Poland–Lithuania and the Ottoman Empire produced divergent attitudes towards resources of the Danubian principalities, resulting in different styles of cross-border patronage. In the third section, I shift my attention to the complex role of patronage in the procurement of information and control of communication channels. Slow communications and difficulties in acquiring and verifying reports made information a scarce and valuable resource. Not only could early access tilt the political balance; a reliable patronage network in control of communication flows allowed to manage its dissemination and spin the news. Finally, the last section addresses a diverse array of objects that circulated between members of the factions, ranging from luxury garments, through watermelons, to simple courtesy letters. While some of those objects were valuable, others were not, and their importance stemmed from their status as personal gifts rather than their monetary value. Nonetheless, they played a crucial role in holding the faction together, signalling continued interest in joint endeavours, emphasizing the affective character of the bond and reinforcing factional cohesion. These various circuits weaved together a complicated and multifaceted fabric of cross-border patronage relations and underpinned the political system in the region.

Politics and military

For most contemporary observers and modern historians, the sphere of political and military competition constituted the hallmark of cross-border patronage. In effect, sources duly note instances of political cooperation and protection, which furthered individuals' careers and fended off competitors. However, this factional dimension is often lost in modern historiography, overshadowed by scholars' efforts to identify state agency. Once we look at the pattern of appointments and actors involved, however, it becomes clear that there was surprisingly little consistency and the decision-making process engaged a wider array of actors than institutional arrangements and official prescriptions dictated. In the context in which personal ties overshadowed formal hierarchies, cross-border patronage provided the way of lubricating the wheels of administration and mobilizing both political and military resources.

Influence peddling: Cross-border patronage and decision-making process

In theory, the authority to appoint Moldavian and Wallachian rulers rested with only a handful of people. In the first place, the sultan himself, and the grand vizier as his deputy were at liberty to nominate and dismiss the voivodes, as well as staff the imperial administration. In the Danubian principalities, local rulers acted at the interface between Moldavian–Wallachian and Ottoman political systems and appointed officials within their domains. This seemingly clear-cut system was undercut by competing claims of the Polish court. Polish–Lithuanian diplomats insisted that the right to nominate Moldavia rulers belonged to the king, whose appointee would receive Ottoman confirmation. At the same time, concessions were made to accommodate dynastic ambitions of the Movilă family.[3] Even after the period of polyvassalage came to a close, Polish–Lithuanian diplomats demanded that Moldavian voivodes should be subject to royal approval and exhibit commitment to maintaining peace between two empires. Needless to say, the king was also at liberty to handpick officials in Poland–Lithuania, although this prerogative was limited by the custom of lifelong tenure in office. Thus, in theory, only five people at the time (sultan, grand vizier, Polish king and voivodes) claimed the authority to promote officials and grant them political favours.

Obviously, this neat schema in no way reflected realities on the ground. A variety of Ottoman, Polish–Lithuanian and Moldavian–Wallachian political actors partook in the decision-making process, trying to influence the appointments in the region. These included magnates, key officials, palace favourites and female members of the dynasty, all trying to install their allies on crucial posts. In effect, the actual political process turned formal hierarchies upside down, as rulers and grand viziers found themselves playing second fiddle to the actual movers and shakers of regional politics.

Flows, Exchanges, Conversions 85

Illustrative in this respect is an exchange of letters between King Vladislav IV and Crown Grand *Hetman* Stanisław Koniecpolski in the fall of 1634. Following a short 'Abaza Pasha War' of 1633–4, the king hoped to use the ongoing negotiations to enhance his influence in Moldavia and promote his candidate to the throne. He set his eyes on Nicolae Catargi, an influential boyar active during the peace talks.[4] In a letter to Koniecpolski, he instructed the *hetman* to promote Catargi's cause by all means possible and relay his orders to the negotiators.[5]

Koniecpolski, who had his own candidate to the Moldavian throne in the person of Moise Movilă, did not comply. In his response to the king, he declared his unwavering loyalty, but insisted on sending an envoy to Vladislav to explain the monarch 'what sort of a man [Catargi] is'.[6] Unfortunately, we do not know the contents of the mission, but it succeeded in bringing the king back in line. Five days later, Vladislav abandoned the idea and sided with Koniecpolski's plans:

> With regard to Catargi [...] not only do we not want him anywhere in the vicinity of our lands, but we do not want him even to be mentioned in our talks with the Porte. [...] We have no doubt that the Cupbearer of Braclav [Jakub Zieliński, who conducted the negotiations – M.W.] will follow your instructions and see to it that, in case he encounters resistance to the candidature of Moise [Movilă], he would promote by all means necessary either his brother, Ion, or [Iancu] Costin.[7]

It comes as no surprise that all candidates listed in the letter were Koniecpolski's clients and that the *hetman* attended to their interests by discouraging Vladislav from alternative solutions.

In the Ottoman Empire, the disconnection between the formal hierarchies and actual influence was no less pronounced. Ottoman political theory promoted a vision of an intimate bond between the sultan and the grand vizier as the backbone of governance and the link between the sphere of the inner household (*enderun*) and administrative apparatus (*birun*). This vertical relationship between the ruler and his deputy was meant to limit factional interference and secure the grand vizier's control over imperial administration. However, the changes of the late sixteenth and seventeenth centuries undermined this model, empowering alternative political centres and blurring the boundaries between the two spheres of Ottoman politics.[8] The sultans' efforts to reassert control over officialdom through favourites, eunuchs and female members of the dynasty only deepened this trend.

This realignment in Ottoman politics was not lost on Moldavian and Wallachian elites, who recognized the crisis of the grand vizierate in the first half of the seventeenth century and the emergence of new political actors. Miron

Costin perfectly captured this shift when discussing the state of affairs at the Porte in the 1630s:

> Under Sultan Murad, all matters in the empire were handled by two men, who were Murad's favourites (*musaipi*). The first one was silahdar – the Sword-bearer, who carries the sultan's sword and mace; the other was *Kızlar Ağası*, who manages the imperial household and oversees the sultan's women. These two men oversaw all imperial affairs, while the vizierate was very weak in comparison. They say that whenever the grand vizier happened to meet any of them, he kissed his robes.[9]

For Moldavian and Wallachian elites, this diffusion of power offered new possibilities, increasing the number of potential patrons in the Ottoman establishment. Rather than trying to curry the favour of the sultan and the grand vizier, voivodes and pretenders attached themselves to different powerholders at the Porte. As the cohesion of imperial elite unravelled under the pressure of factionalism, it provided new options and incentives for cross-border cooperation.

A glimpse at the network of Wallachian voivode Matei Basarab illustrates these new circumstances. As shown in the previous chapter, Matei Basarab captured the throne as a rebel voivode supported by Abaza Mehmed Pasha. However, this alliance ended abruptly, when the Ottoman official was executed in 1634, becoming the scapegoat for the Polish–Ottoman war. His death forced Matei to seek a new patron, who would be able to provide much-needed assistance against his rival, Vasile Lupu. Throughout the 1630s, Matei managed to cobble together a heterogeneous set of patron–client ties, spanning across different branches of imperial administration. Among his allies we find an interpreter of the Porte Zülfikar Efendi, Murad IV's favourite Silahdar Mustafa Pasha, and a bureaucrat from the financial department, Ruznameci Ibrahim Efendi.[10] Their influence did not stem directly from the offices they held, but rather from the new configuration of power and the changes that the imperial political arena was undergoing since the late sixteenth century.

The role of Ruznameci Ibrahim Efendi as both Matei Basarab's patron and the head of financial administration is particularly instructive in this respect. A native of Mostar, he climbed the ranks of financial bureaucracy in the 1620s and 1630s, taking the reins of financial administration on Murad IV's behalf.[11] To some extent, his prominent position in Ottoman politics reflected a general trend of the emancipation of financial bureaucracy underway since the late sixteenth century.[12] However, it was the context of Sultan Murad IV's reign

Flows, Exchanges, Conversions

that made Ibrahim Efendi indispensable. In the earlier decades, *kapıkulu* corps emerged as a powerful pressure group with vested economic interests.[13] As the revolt in May 1622 and the regicide of Osman II had demonstrated, ignoring their demands could cost the ruler his throne and his life. Murad IV faced a similar crisis in 1632 when soldiers' unrest wreaked havoc in the capital. The revolt was eventually suppressed, but placating the troops remained a constant concern and Ibrahim Efendi's main duty. It seems that he succeeded in managing this difficult task successfully and reportedly promised the sultan that 'as long as I'm alive, fear not the sipahis or Janissaries'.[14] The bond between him and Murad IV went beyond that of a ruler and his official. Ibrahim Efendi became one of the sultan's most powerful *musahibs*, nicknamed in some sources 'little emperor' (*küçük hünkar*).[15] According to Giovanni Battista Ballarino, when the bureaucrat fell ill in January 1637, the sultan visited him on a daily basis and expressly ordered the *şeyh ül-Islam* and the *kaymakam* to follow suit, effectively putting all decisions at the Porte on hold.[16] Ibrahim Efendi's death during the Baghdad campaign was the cause of the sultan's great grief.[17] At the same time, it produced a major realignment in the patronage system, whereby Silahdar Mustafa Pasha emerged as Murad IV's most influential favourite and took over some of the deceased official's duties.[18]

The sultan was not the only one to mourn Ibrahim Efendi's demise.[19] According to a Venetian report, the official had been a patron of Matei Basarab, and his death forced the Wallachian voivode to seek a new ally at the Porte. Therefore, he dispatched a mission to Istanbul to identify potential patrons. Once in the capital, the envoys were approached by Silahdar Mustafa Pasha who 'offered to replace the late Ruznameci as the protector of the prince and his lands'.[20] The offer was readily accepted, and the grandee provided the voivode with substantial assistance against Vasile Lupu and his Ottoman allies.

While sources provide little detail on the relationship between Ibrahim Efendi and Matei Basarab, there is no doubt that the latter relied heavily on the grandee's protection. As a rebel voivode and an associate of Abaza Mehmed Pasha, Matei Basarab was in a precarious position and repeatedly faced the threat of being ousted from the throne. In this context, becoming a client of the sultan's favourite was a matter of political survival. Sources remain silent on what Matei Basarab offered in return. However, in the light of Ibrahim Efendi's double role as the sultan's favourite and the manager of imperial financial affairs, it is likely that a threefold increase in the amount of Wallachian *harac* – anomalous in the seventeenth century – and its temporary redirection towards the Inner Treasury (*hazine-i enderun*) was part of the arrangement.

88   *The Ottomans and Eastern Europe*

While I address the flow of economic resources in the following section, this connection points to the ways formal institutions and patronage networks intersected and the conversion of different types of capital. The Wallachian *harac* traditionally accrued to the outer treasury (*hazine-i amire*), managed by the *başdefterdar*. However, in 1639 Matei Basarab claimed that he was paying three times as much as his predecessors and that the money entered *hazine-i enderun*.[21] This shift confounded Romanian historians, who suspected either a mistake or a conflation of tribute with other obligations.[22] Seen from the institutional perspective, the transfer made little sense. Given Ibrahim Efendi's control over the outer treasury and his political clout, one would expect his opposition to this alienation of revenue. However, once we take into consideration that Ibrahim Efendi was not only a bureaucrat in the financial department but also a favourite of Murad IV, a likely explanation emerges.

Unlike other Ottoman patrons involved with cross-border patronage, the career of Ibrahim Efendi depended on his ability to manage the imperial finances and meet the demands of the *kapıkulu* corps. Ultimately, however, it was not his financial acumen but Murad IV's favour that allowed him to play an outsized role in imperial politics. Thus, his primary concern was accommodating the sultan's interest rather than just balancing the accounts. From this standpoint, the increase of *harac* offered by Matei Basarab eased Ibrahim Efendi's task and provided a strong argument in favour of retaining the voivode in office. At the same time, for Murad IV, redirecting the stream of revenue to the inner treasury made perfect sense given the context of his reign. Having asserted his power only in 1632 and determined to curb the influence of grandee household, the sultan had every reason to wrest economic resources from the imperial establishment and consolidate them in the inner treasury.[23] Given the close association between the sultan and Ibrahim Efendi, it seems that the latter supported Murad IV's efforts to reassert his power and carried out his programme.

This model suggests a complex interaction between administrative hierarchies, political factionalism and economic resources. Patronage relations between the sultan, Ibrahim Efendi and the Wallachian voivode followed – to an extent – the established administrative hierarchies but their character seems to reflect factional considerations. Ibrahim Efendi was able to use his financial acumen to become Murad IV's *musahib*. This provided him with considerable political resources that he used to protect Matei Basarab against rival factions. In exchange, Matei provided economic resources in the form of an increased *harac* that Ibrahim Efendi converted back into political capital, allowing him to maintain his position within the sultan's circle. Thus, what seems to be a simple case of administrative adjustment turns out to be a patronage-driven system of transfer and conversion of resources between the Porte and Wallachia.

While the ties between Moldavian–Wallachian voivodes and their Ottoman patrons feature most prominently in the sources, the emerging networks of patronage encompassed boyar elites as well, particularly in the second half of the seventeenth century. Their involvement in cross-border patronage triggered an inversion in the balance of power between boyars and voivodes, a process well illustrated by the activity of *Postelnic* Constantin Cantacuzino and his descendants in Wallachia. Member of a prominent family of Greek origin, Constantin became in the course of the 1650s and 1660s one of the most influential political figures in the principality.[24] Acting as an important patron in the Wallachian political arena, he also reached out to Ottoman officialdom, where he established bonds of friendship with Köprülü Mehmed Pasha and the grand dragoman of the Porte, Panagiotis Nikoussios.[25] This allowed him to become a virtual kingmaker in Wallachia, and in 1660 he approached Grigore Ghica with an offer to promote him to the Wallachian throne, on condition that he would defer to Cantacuzino's judgement. Grigore, an ambitious forty-year-old impatiently waiting to succeed his father, agreed. The letter Ghica wrote to his ally leaves no doubt about the power relations between them:

> Since you have left, I have been as if mute and deaf, and without any solace [...] I am unwilling to go beyond what you say, and I will offer you no advice. I leave all matters to you, and you should proceed as you see fit [...] I lay all my trust in you and invest all my faith in you since you and I are one.[26]

The scheme succeeded, and according to Wallachian sources, it was allegedly Constantin Cantacuzino who personally recommended Grigore Ghica to Köprülü Mehmed Pasha.[27] In the following years, the *Postelnic* acquired considerable influence over Wallachian politics. However, his relationship with the voivode turned sour as the latter tried to free himself from the boyar's tutelage. The conflict culminated in 1663 when Grigore Ghica along with the boyar's enemies orchestrated his arrest and subsequent execution.[28]

The murder of Cantacuzino triggered a factional conflict that extended for decades but did not restore the balance of power between the voivode and the Wallachian elite. On the contrary, most Wallachian voivodes in subsequent decades were non-entities, acting as little more than ciphers for faction leaders. Despite the backlash, Cantacuzinos managed to retain their influence, largely due to support offered to them by Merzifonlu Kara Mustafa Pasha, who shielded them from repressions following the *postelnic*'s execution and, in his capacity as *kaymakam* and later grand vizier, promoted pro-Cantacuzino candidates to the throne.[29] Illustrative of this inversion was the reign of Antonie of Popeşti (1669–72). The voivode was a boyar of modest substance, appointed by Kara Mustafa Pasha at the behest of the Cantacuzinos; the latter took three-quarters of seats in the new princely council and used their position to launch a crackdown on their opponents.[30] According to chronicler Radu Popescu, Antonie's dependence on the faction leaders was so great that he had to rely on their allowance to buy food for his court.[31]

This inversion of political balance has led Romanian scholars to engage in a debate over the seventeenth century as the period of 'boyar regime' (*regim boieresc*) as opposed to autocratic rule along post-Byzantine models.[32] Whether such a regime existed or not continues to be a contentious topic, the critics arguing that boyar class did not act as a coherent group, nor did the change in power balance produce new institutional arrangements.[33] However, focusing on cross-border patronage as a political tool allows us to understand how this change took place. By reaching out to Polish–Lithuanian and Ottoman patrons, Moldavian–Wallachian faction leaders accessed political resources sufficient to overpower hostile rulers and establish themselves at the apex of their respective arenas. The success of cross-border patronage in mobilizing political capital induced other participants to follow suit and created a bandwagon effect that levelled the playing field for Moldavian–Wallachian elites.

Factional politics and military power

Despite the role political influence played in cross-border patronage, a simple administrative fiat did not suffice to enforce a favourable decision and had to be backed up by military action. This was particularly important for the Danubian principalities, whose troops proved woefully insufficient in size and quality. Except for the 1593–1601 period, Moldavian and Wallachian armies were widely considered undisciplined, untrained and prone to flee the battlefield. As such, they rarely could offer any effective resistance to either Ottoman or Polish–Lithuanian troops and were usually relegated to auxiliary duties. Thus, securing military support from either the Porte or the Commonwealth constituted a decisive factor in tilting the political balance in the Danubian principalities. In mobilizing the means to wage war, cross-border patronage again played a crucial role.

Flows, Exchanges, Conversions 91

Although usually treated as an extension of state policy, Polish–Lithuanian and Ottoman war-making in the region was effectively a public–private partnership, since much of mobilization and military command relied on patronage networks within the standing army or privately employed troops. This fits the pattern of early modern military affairs in general, heavily reliant on military entrepreneurship.[34] This was particularly true for Poland–Lithuania, whose underdeveloped fiscal system allowed for a minuscule standing army of only 1,500–5,000 men in the first half of the seventeenth century. While the *hetman*s, who wielded command of royal troops, became arguably the most powerful officials in the Commonwealth, they were constantly forced to co-opt local magnates and their private troops, as well as negotiate with their own soldiers to prevent desertion and mutiny.[35] To overcome these challenges, they leaned heavily on patronage networks among soldiers and nobility. At the same time, individual magnates wielded enough military power to launch their own campaigns into Moldavia without looking to the *hetman's* consent.[36] While contested by some contemporaries as detrimental to the Commonwealth, private military interventions abroad were not unanimously condemned. During the *Sejm* of 1613, fresh after Stefan Potocki's disastrous campaign in Moldavia, the magnate's supporters demanded that the king pay ransom for the unfortunate magnate or exchange him for a Polish-held fortress of Hotin.[37] Moreover, Lithuanian magnate Janusz Radziwiłł defended Potocki's actions, arguing that it would be unjust to condemn nobles for seeking military glory.[38]

This private–public nexus in mobilizing military resources becomes clear once we examine Polish–Lithuanian interventions in Moldavia between 1595 and 1620. Of six campaigns undertaken in this period, three had at least some royal sanction, and have been interpreted in modern scholarship as state-sponsored ventures. In turn, the other three (1607, 1612 and 1615–16) have been condemned as private expeditions driven by local magnates' irresponsible adventurism.[39] Once we look at the composition of the armies, however, the distinction dissipates. 'State' expeditionary forces led by Jan Zamoyski in 1595 and 1600 included a quarter of privately employed troops; most of the high-ranking officers were also Zamoyski's clients.[40] The share of private troops was even greater in 1620 and the constant squabbles over the chain of command greatly contributed to the debacle of the campaign.[41] Conversely, private campaigns of 1607–08 included units on the royal payroll. Only in 1615 Princes Korec'kyj and Vyšnevec'kyj seem to have led a purely private contingent into Moldavia. However, as I will show in Chapter 4, this divergence was a direct result of their conflict with *Hetman* Stanisław Żółkiewski and his cross-border faction. Even then, the two magnates were able to assemble an army of 12,000 soldiers that proved to be a match for Moldavian and Ottoman troops for almost a year.

Despite a far more efficient fiscal system and a larger standing army, Ottoman officials faced similar problems. 'To obey, but not act' reigned supreme, and commanders in the field often dragged their feet or simply ignored orders issued by their superiors and political rivals. For instance, in 1658 Fazlı Ahmed Pasha, tasked with installing Mihnea III in Wallachia, was not particularly eager to follow the orders. He advanced so slowly that it took his army almost three weeks to cover 140 kilometres from Yergöğü (Giurgiu) to Târgoviște, despite lack of any resistance.[42] Ahmed Pasha was subsequently executed for what was a clear act of sabotage directed against Köprülü Mehmed Pasha's plans.[43] However, not all officials had Köprülü's influence and resolve to punish recalcitrant officials. Abaza Mehmed Pasha's actions discussed in the previous chapter went unpunished, despite his open defiance. In enforcing orders and mobilizing military resources, patronage was the principal tool to avoid red tape and political subterfuge.

Negotiations and bargaining were particularly important in securing Crimean military support. While Tatar troops were crucial for projecting Ottoman power in the Black Sea region, the khans' distinct status provided them with considerable leverage. Thus, Ottoman authorities had to coax the Crimean rulers, and even then, it remained uncertain if the khan would comply with the demands. For instance, when Grand Vizier Koca Sinan Pasha enlisted Ghazi Giray II's help in the annexation plans, he was forced to appoint the khan's nephew as the *beylerbey* of Moldavia.[44] However, Ghazi Giray jumped ship as soon as Polish–Lithuanian counteroffer proved more attractive. While few seventeenth-century khans went that far, many paid only lip service to the Ottoman demands. The contingent provided by Mehmed Giray IV in 1658 was of little assistance to the Moldavian ruler since, as Miron Costin noted wryly, 'there were only three hundred of them, and not only did they not fight, but they were nowhere to be found when the fighting started'.[45]

In his book on social capital, Ronald Burt quipped that 'formal relations are about who is to blame. Informal relations are about who gets it done'.[46] Moldavian–Wallachian, Polish–Lithuanian and Ottoman elites of the early modern period would certainly agree. Procuring political and military resources was a messy process, involving 'muddling through' and building personal bonds rather than relying on formal hierarchies and procedures. The role of patronage becomes even more pronounced once we turn our attention to the flow of economic resources.

The sinews of factional power: The flow of economic resources

Leading a faction was an expensive venture. Members of the household had to be clothed and fed; clients rewarded with gifts and sources of revenue; maintaining a lifestyle befitting the high-ranking social and political status was also necessary. This put a considerable strain on the patron's finances and could potentially lead him into a crippling debt. However, as expensive as this could turn out, factional structures also provided means for increasing revenue of their members. Large cross-border networks made them particularly well-suited for harnessing potential sources of wealth and moving them between the arenas. In this section, I will address the mechanisms of economic flows that underpinned cross-border factionalism and their place within the larger logic of factional politics.

Factional payoffs: Ottomans, Moldavians and 'shadow *iltizam*'

In discussions over the Ottoman impact on Moldavian–Wallachian history, few topics have attracted as much attention as the Sublime Porte's financial demands. For modern Romanian scholars, the economic exploitation of the Danubian principalities became the hallmark of the 'Turkish yoke' and the main cause of the principalities' underdevelopment. This perspective overlaps with the one of Ottoman 'moral decline', putting the blame for the increasing outflow of money from Moldavia and Wallachia on the demoralization among Ottoman officials. According to one scholar:

> The onset of the Ottoman decline that started in the last quarter of the sixteenth century, and particularly the corruption and abuse of power, led to the rising price – material and moral – paid by non-Muslims [in the Danubian principalities – M.W.] to maintain their religious identity and political organization.[47]

Indeed, during the late sixteenth and again in the seventeenth centuries, the outflow of money from the Danubian principalities increased, and much of it ended up in Ottoman grandees' pockets. Such payments came to constitute a considerable share of the voivodes' expenditure, putting a strain on their finances.[48] However, moral judgement aside, explaining these developments through moral decline fails to capture their underlying logic and is in many respects a circular argument with no explanatory power. Moreover, the amount of money disbursed to the Ottoman officials was not the only thing that changed; the channels utilized for this purpose changed as well. To address these issues,

94   *The Ottomans and Eastern Europe*

we should thus look past the unhelpful narrative of moral decline and to the rise of cross-border patronage and the shifting Ottoman political order.

As I have mentioned in Chapter 1, the payment of *harac* by the voivodes constituted the lynchpin of their status as Ottoman tributaries and tax collectors (*haracgüzar*).[49] In line with the stipulations of Hanafi *ius gentium*, such payments constituted a legal obligation of non-Muslim subjects (*zimmis*) in the 'Abode of Islam' (*dar al-Islam*) and the symbolic expression of their subordinate position.[50] Apart from their legal and symbolic significance, these remittances also constituted a major channel for monetary transfers between the Danubian principalities and the Porte. Other obligations, most importantly customary gifts to the sultan and high-ranking Ottoman officials (*pişkeş*) and the duty to provision Istanbul and imperial troops, complemented the payment of *harac*.[51]

Until the mid-sixteenth century, the amount of *harac* due annually was relatively modest, and its financial role remained secondary to its symbolic role as a sign of submission. However, starting from 1538, the financial burden skyrocketed. While in 1541 the voivodes of Wallachia were expected to contribute annually a little over a million *akçe*, by 1574–83 their obligations increased sixfold. The Moldavian tribute was smaller but registered a similar growth from 10,000 ducats (or 600,000 *akçe*) in 1538 to over 60,000 in the last quarter of the century.[52] The debasement of *akçe* in 1585–6 eroded the value of the tribute in real terms, but even the reduced demand stretched the limits of the principalities' financial capabilities. The pressure to raise additional revenue provided an impulse to overhaul Moldavian and Wallachian fiscal system, and by the end of the sixteenth century, the inhabitants of the principalities paid two to four times more per capita in taxes than anywhere elsewhere in the Ottoman Empire.[53]

As Mihai Maxim pointed out, the *harac* increases originated from the fierce competition for the throne, deficits in the imperial treasury and the consolidation of Ottoman control over the principalities.[54] As numerous pretenders strove to outbid each other, they began to borrow heavily from Ottoman creditors. The voivodes' turnover increased exponentially, further exacerbating the principalities' financial woes. By the early 1590s the burden of debt reached staggering 110–120 million *akçe* for Moldavia and over 700 million for Wallachia, far outstripping the voivodes' ability to meet the payments.[55] Eventually, in November 1594 the whole system went down in flames when voivodes Michael the Brave and Aron massacred dozens of their Ottoman creditors in what amounted to a particularly gruesome default, and the rebellion against the Porte that followed brought the flow of *harac* to a halt. When the payments resumed, the annual sum was scaled down to a more manageable level to 30,000–35,000 ducats (equivalent to 3.6–4.2 million of debased *akçe*) and remained relatively stagnant throughout the seventeenth century (see Figure 3.1).[56] Only in 1632 did the Wallachian *harac* increase, most likely due to the specific circumstances surrounding Matei Basarab's rise to power and his relationship with Ibrahim Efendi.

It is unsurprising that, in the aftermath of a revolt caused by the growing financial burden, the Porte would reduce its financial demands. What *is* surprising is that *harac* remained relatively stagnant throughout the rest of the century, despite the fact that all factors that had driven the increases of the late sixteenth century – competition for the throne, financial woes of the imperial treasury and allegedly rampant corruption of Ottoman officials – remained in place. Instead, a growing share of the cash flows was redirected towards customary gifts (*pişkeş*) and informal payments, which outstripped the *harac* as the largest category of remittances.[57] While in the earlier period the value of such gifts had been largely symbolic, by the end of the seventeenth century they constituted as much as a quarter of total expenditure of the Wallachian treasury.[58] Thus, the beginning of the seventeenth century saw a general reconfiguration of financial ties between the Danubian principalities and the imperial centre rather than a simple rehashing of an established pattern.

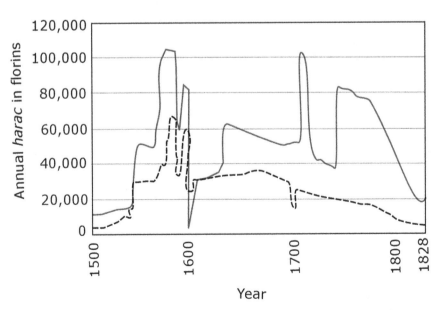

Figure 3.1 The value of Wallachian (solid line) and Moldavian (dashed line) *harac* payments (1500–1828).

The question of why the Moldavian–Wallachian *harac* remained stagnant throughout the century has garnered relatively little attention among scholars. According to Tahsin Gemil, who addressed this issue in the 1970s, the traumatic memory of the revolt of 1594 and the risk of Polish–Lithuanian or Habsburg intervention discouraged the Porte from increasing the principalities' fiscal burden.[59] However, this explanation leaves a number of questions unresolved. First, not only did the amount *harac* not grow but actually failed to keep up with inflation, with little effort to stabilize its real value despite constant deficits in the imperial treasury.[60] Secondly, if the fear of rebellion prevented the Ottoman officials from increasing the amount of tribute, why did the value of *pişkeş* payments increase during the same period? Finally, the amount of *harac* demanded from Dubrovnik, where no such geopolitical threats were present, also stagnated during the seventeenth century.[61] Thus, the explanation rooted in regional geopolitics falls short of addressing the phenomenon. However, once we approach the topic through the lens of cross-border patronage and Ottoman political landscape, the underlying logic of this shift becomes clearer.

The devolution of power and the growth of political household not only increased the grandees' political influence, but also posed new challenges. Maintaining a 'well-outfitted household' was an expensive affair, forcing Ottoman officials to seek new sources of revenue. This financial and political pressure induced some members of the elite to engage in commerce and moneylending. Under the Köprülüs, the land regime instituted in newly conquered provinces of Crete, western Transylvania and Podolia was tailored to benefit the grand vizier's household.[62] However, it was tax-farming (*iltizam*) that provided the most popular means to procure economic resources for grandees' political activity.[63]

During the seventeenth century, the Ottoman revenue-raising system witnessed a sea change, as the prebendal *timar* system was gradually phased out in favour of a tax-farming *iltizam* system based on competitive bidding. While the system had existed since the mid-fifteenth century, it gained momentum with the monetization of the imperial economy and the emergence of new sources of revenue.[64] Succinctly put, within this arrangement, the right to collect fiscal revenue from a particular source was auctioned off to the highest bidder on a short-term contract in exchange for down payment and annual remittances to the treasury, while the tax-farmer (*mültezim*) was entitled to pocket surplus revenue.[65]

Ottoman grandees quickly grasped the advantages of tax-farming and became major investors in *iltizam* contracts. The hierarchical structure of patronage networks made them well-suited for the purposes of tax collection, as the heads of the households were able to distribute shares of the contract among their clients or associates who would subsequently collect the taxes on the ground, or co-opt local notables in the provinces.[66] In effect, the relationship between *kapıs* and tax-farming became a symbiotic one, allowing Ottoman grandees to finance their political activity, while also relieving the fiscal administration from the burdens associated with tax collection. Thus, by the end of the seventeenth century, *iltizam* arrangements came to constitute the financial backbone of the 'rise of faction' in the Ottoman Empire.

The development of an *iltizam*-based fiscal system triggered a commodification of offices associated with tax collection. For instance, the Ecumenical Patriarchate, transformed into an *iltizam* in the second half of the fifteenth century, attracted the Orthodox financial elite of the imperial capital, transforming the patriarchal seat into a predominantly financial institution open to competitive bidding.[67] This drove the price of appointment up and contributed to the high turnover at the apex of the Orthodox ecclesiastical hierarchy.

The position of Moldavian and Wallachian voivodes as Ottoman tax collectors (*haracgüzars*) was not unlike that of other *mültezims* and was subject to similar pressures, particularly in the second half of the sixteenth century.[68] In exchange for an appointment fee and annual payment of *harac*, the voivodes gained control of the principalities' fiscal apparatus, which they could use to recoup their initial investment and turn out a profit. Fierce rivalry for the throne encouraged competitive bidding, resulting in the rise in the amount of *harac* and growing debts accumulated by Moldavian and Wallachian rulers. This created what can be described as an investment bubble that crashed in the revolt of 1594.

At first glance, the stability of *harac* in the seventeenth century marks a departure from the system of competitive bidding. However, once we look at other *mukataas* across the Ottoman Empire, we find similar developments within the *iltizam* system. As Murat Çizakça pointed out in his survey of the institution, we can identify numerous 'frozen' *iltizams*, where the sums remitted to the imperial treasury remained stable or even decreased despite an apparent rise in their tax base.[69] Unsurprisingly, most of these *mukataas* were in the hands of high-ranking officials and bureaucrats. In such instances, the *mültezims* utilized their political resources and position within the imperial administration to prevent a reassessment of their tax-farms, thus increasing the net profit drawn from the contracts. The number of 'frozen' tax-farms increased over time, illustrating how grandee households were able to deploy their political leverage to maximize their revenue.

Against this background, the seventeenth-century stagnation of *harac* and the growing value of gifts present themselves in a new light. For Ottoman grandees seeking to fund their households, the Danubian principalities constituted an attractive source of revenue they could harness to gain an edge in the political struggle at the Porte. However, the dual character of the voivode's position as an Ottoman tax collector and an Orthodox ruler meant that Muslim officials were unable to take control of the principalities' revenue-raising apparatus directly.[70] By investing their political resources in cross-border patronage and promoting Christian clients to positions of power, Ottoman officials were able to circumvent this obstacle and redirect the monetary flows to their own factions in what amounted to a 'shadow *iltizam*'.

Whereas at its core *iltizam* contracts remained an economic transaction between the state, *mültezim* and the latter's business partners,[71] the 'shadow *iltizam*' encompassed not only a financial arrangement but also a political bond. The Ottoman grandees' inability to secure direct control over Moldavian–Wallachian resources provided them with a strong incentive to cooperate and exchange resources with the local elites. On the one hand, Moldavian and Wallachian rulers controlled access to financial resources of the principalities but lacked the political pull to secure their position on the throne; on the other hand, Ottoman officials had sufficient political resources to provide a modicum of stability and fend off contenders but had no means to tap monetary resources they coveted. Cross-border patronage and side payments in the form of gifts bridged this gap. The economic resources thus harnessed were subsequently used to finance factional structures, thus converting the economic capital into the political one (see Figure 3.2).

From this perspective, the transformation of *pişkeş* from a symbolic expression of subordination into the most important circuit of financial transfers becomes understandable. By repurposing the established institution, Moldavian and Wallachian rulers were able to short-circuit the monetary flows and privatize them within the faction in exchange for political resources required for their political survival. For the same reason, receiving payments directly from their clients constituted an attractive alternative for Ottoman grandees, who thus gained direct control of means to fund their political enterprises and household structures, even if formally they remained outside of the arrangement between the Porte and the voivodes.

Thinking about Moldavian and Wallachian financial ties to the Porte as akin to *iltizam* allows us also to understand the stagnation of *harac* coinciding with the growing value of *pişkeş* gifts. In the case of *iltizam*, since a *mültezim* realized

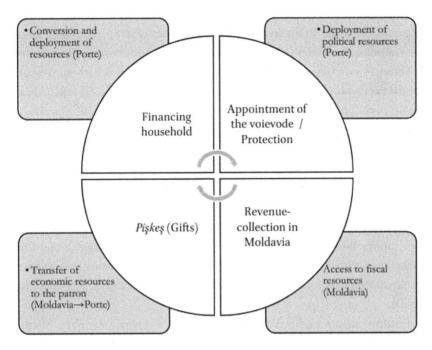

Figure 3.2 Circulation and conversion of resources within cross-border 'shadow iltizam': a theoretical model.

his profit by pocketing surplus revenue from the *mukataa*, he could increase his share either by forcing the taxpayers to pay more or trying to reduce the amount due to the imperial treasury. The same applied for the Danubian principalities, and, as the events of 1593–1601 had shown, the demands of both the treasury and Ottoman patrons could outstrip the principalities' ability to pay. The resulting trade-off, which increased the revenue of political households at the expense of the imperial treasury, subscribed to the new political logic of the seventeenth century. As the sultanic authority diminished in favour of grandee households, so did the role of the central treasury, and its share in the revenue from Moldavia and Wallachia decreased. In effect, the structure of the seventeenth-century cash flows coalesced into a new system, more privatized and better suited to the factional logic of the seventeenth century.

It is difficult to establish the amount of money flowing through such privatized channels. However, the sums involved had to be considerable. Only in the second half of 1639, two Ottoman grandees, Tabanıyassı Mehmed Pasha and Silahdar Mustafa Pasha, allegedly received 86,000 florins, or over 10 million *akçe*, from their Moldavian and Wallachian clients. It is difficult to establish whether these claims corresponded to reality,[72] but available documents for the reign of Constantin Brâncoveanu confirm large sums being distributed among the Wallachian voivode's Ottoman patrons.[73] The distribution of gifts (*plocoane*) to Ottoman officials consumed a significant share of the Wallachian treasury's annual expenditure, fluctuating between 8 and 27 per cent of total expenses, and the list of recipients amounted to 'who's who' of the imperial political scene.[74]

One could argue that these arrangements amounted to little more than corruption and extortion by Ottoman officials. However, it seems that establishing such channels of 'shadow *iltizam*' was seen as an investment rather than a bribe. Moldavians and Wallachians took the initiative and actively sought Ottoman patrons, offering them friendship and revenue for their protection.[75] In turn, some patrons, such as Burnaz Atike Sultan, were willing to invest their own money into the bid of their client.[76] These instances suggest that those engaging in cross-border patronage expected that their investment of economic resources would pay off in the future, either in terms of financial gain or political capital.

Unfortunately, we know little about other ways in which members of cross-border patronage networks mobilized economic resources. However, there are some indications that Ottoman grandees enabled their Moldavian clients to maximize their profits, going as far as allowing for war profiteering. One of the most interesting instances of such arrangements took place in 1672 when the Porte launched a full-scale campaign against Poland–Lithuania. The march of an army estimated at 80,000 men, led by Sultan Mehmed IV and Grand Vizier Köprülüzade Ahmed Pasha, posed considerable challenges in terms of logistics and provisioning.[77] The task of providing foodstuffs fell on Moldavian voivode Gheorghe Duca, who had been a long-time client of the grand vizier. While a daunting task, it also provided a business opportunity, as the troops spent over 150 million *akçe* on foodstuffs alone.[78] As Bogdan Murgescu pointed out, the voivode monopolized the provisioning and drew a hard bargain, selling foodstuffs to Ottoman soldiers at inflated prices.[79] It seems that the grand vizier, who received lavish gifts from Duca during the campaign, was aware of the situation and enabled Duca's scheme. It was only when disgruntled soldiers and local boyars appealed to directly the sultan that the voivode's plan backfired. According to Ion Neculce, Mehmed IV immediately ordered Duca's execution, but Köprülüzade Ahmed Pasha managed to convince the ruler not only to spare the Moldavian's life, but also to delay his dismissal.[80] The grand vizier managed to install his client again in 1674 as the ruler of Wallachia, which shows that he did not mind his actions during the Kam'janec' campaign.

Such instances of diverting revenue – directly or indirectly – from state coffers have usually been interpreted as the symptom of the moral decline of Ottoman officials and outright extortion of the Moldavian–Wallachian voivodes. However, such interpretations do not consider the flip side of the phenomenon described above. During the period under discussion, factions took over a considerable share of duties we associate with the state: they handled considerable share of tax collection and played a large role in mobilizing troops for military campaigns. Thus, although this 'privatization' changed the balance of power and the factions incurred 'operational costs', it does not mean that the revenues were 'lost' in pashas' pockets. At the same time, factions proved efficient mechanisms of moving the economic resources across the imperial space. This was particularly important in the context of cross-border patronage, which allowed Moldavian–Wallachian and Ottoman elites to short-circuit official channels and secure factional control over the stream of revenue. Each side of the exchange gained something in this arrangement: Ottoman officials obtained money to maintain and expand their households, while their clients in the principalities ensured their patrons' continued support at the Porte.

Seeking land: Polish–Lithuanian approach to cross-border resources

Cash flows also feature prominently in Polish–Moldavian patronage networks. Several magnates involved in Moldavian affairs reputedly received regular payments from their clients south of the border. On some occasions, these revenues triggered heated debates during *Sejms* proceedings, as their recipients were accused of prioritizing their private interests over the common good. In 1597, the clients of grand Crown *hetman* and chancellor had to defend their patron against such accusations during the *Sejm*:

> In the Chamber of Deputies [*izba poselska*], the first to take the floor in the morning was Sir Uhrowiecki, the *Starosta* of Chełm. In his reply to the *Podkomorzy* of Sandomierz, he insisted that, contrary to what the latter had said the previous day, the Crown *Hetman* does not take any gifts from the Moldavian voivode [...]. [*Podkomorzy*] had argued that it would be better if the Commonwealth rather than private individuals would receive these payments.[81]

Despite Uhrowiecki's protests, other sources also refer to the money received annually by Jan Zamoyski from his Moldavian client, Ieremia Movilă. A careful observer of the Polish–Lithuanian political scene, *Nunzio* Claudio Rangoni discussed the matter at length in his 1604 report. According to him, Movilă was

102   *The Ottomans and Eastern Europe*

sending his patron numerous gifts, cattle and money in exchange for support for him and his brother, Simion. However, as Rangoni claims, Simion Movilă's failure to establish his rule in Wallachia greatly saddened the chancellor, since he would receive double the amount received from Moldavia.[82] Although there are few references to cash payments in Zamoyski's correspondence, the cattle delivered to him by Movilă's agents appears frequently in the letters they exchanged.[83]

Zamoyski was not the only one whose financial ties with Moldavian voivodes found their ways into parliamentary proceedings. During the first *Sejm* of 1613, similar accusations were raised against Stefan Potocki, the *Starosta* of Felin. A wealthy magnate and brother-in-law of Voivode Constantin Movilă had launched in summer 1612 an invasion of Moldavia, trying to put his relative back on the throne. The campaign resulted in a crushing defeat, and the unfortunate commander found himself in the Yedikule prison. During the debates, his supporters lobbied the deputies to ransom him, going as far as to propose ceding the fortress of Hotin. However, these proposals met with powerful opposition. Jan Swoszowski, an experienced deputy close to Potocki's enemies, retorted that Potocki embarked on a campaign without official consent and had made a fortune of *złotys* on Moldavian cattle trade and received tens of thousands of *złotys* from the voivodes. Thus, not only the Commonwealth's treasury should not pay the ransom, but the magnate's property should be confiscated.[84] Two decades later, Moise Movilă similarly offered *Hetman* Stanisław Koniecpolski cattle, wine and a thousand *złotys* in exchange for his support.[85]

In comparison with huge sums circulating between the Ottoman centre and the Danubian principalities, Polish–Moldavian exchanges seem modest in value and haphazard. It is likely that, given the cost of military mobilization and the constant shortages of cash faced by the Movilăs, their Polish–Lithuanian patrons actually registered a net loss. However, this does not mean that their cross-border patronage strategies did not take economic resources into account. Instead, it seems that, in contrast to Ottoman grandees, Polish–Lithuanian magnates were more interested in arable land rather than ready cash.

This interest in acquiring landed property in Moldavia can be seen in a confusing episode from 1611, when Moldavian envoys, Nestor Ureche and Costea Băcioc, filed a complaint against Stefan Potocki, accusing him of seizing and censoring their instructions, removing all issues that affected his interests. While I will focus more on the political aspect of these events in the following chapter, one of the fragments erased by the magnate involved his landholdings:

Flows, Exchanges, Conversions 103

Citizens of the Polish Crown have occupied many lands in Moldavia, greatly oppressing the poor subjects [of the voivode]. Thus, the envoys shall demand from His Majesty the appointment of a commission to resolve those matters. The *Starosta* of Felin removed this point since it concerned his estates.[86]

According to boyars' complaint, Potocki occupied a swath of land within Moldavian borders and set out to colonize it with serfs, without any legal claims. On the surface, this was a recent development and it should come as no surprise that Constantin Movilă would file a protest. However, this was not the case. First, other fragments censored by the Polish magnate show that he was acting in collusion with the voivode and his clan against the mounting disgruntlement of the boyars. Secondly, since 1609 Potocki and his brothers had been involved in the Polish–Lithuanian campaign against Muscovy, leaving Stefan with little opportunity to establish a territorial foothold in Moldavia.[87] It seems that Potocki took control of the land after his first intervention in the principality (1607–08), and enjoyed tacit support of his brother-in-law, despite boyars' protests. However, in October 1611, as Constantin Movilă's position at the Porte deteriorated, he could no longer afford to alienate the local elite and was compelled to include the matter in the instructions for his envoys. Potocki's land grab was not unique, and other Moldavian voivodes complained that 'the citizens of the Polish borderland are so eager to engage in land-grabbing that they do this without any recourse to justice or appeal to the courts'.[88] The nobility's focus on land becomes even clearer in the context of Polish–Lithuanian plans to annex Moldavia, discussed in Chapter 5, where the issue of redistributing land occupied a central spot in the unfolding debates.

This role of land as the key economic resource in cross-border patronage had both economic and cultural origins. In contrast to the Ottoman Empire, the reliance on serf labour in agriculture and the underdevelopment of industry meant that Polish–Lithuanian economy was monetized to a limited extent. While the Baltic grain boom of the sixteenth and early seventeenth centuries brought large amounts of bullion into the country, most continued into the Ottoman lands to cover eastern trade deficit.[89] These economic constraints meant that the level of monetization remained low and the monetary circulation limited. A series of military disasters in the second half of the seventeenth century further added to these constraints and reduced the extent of market economy.

However, the attachment to land was not merely a matter of economic structure, but also tied in with the social and cultural self-definition of nobility. Starting from the sixteenth century, the ideal of landowner-*cum*-knight began to take root, becoming the model for the Polish–Lithuanian elite. Land-owning constituted not only a crucial aspect of the noble habitus and a principal means of securing livelihood, but also a prerequisite for full participation in political life and access to coveted offices.[90] Landless nobles were treated with contempt and usually excluded from dietine proceedings. In turn, for magnates, acquiring landed estates constituted an important part of faction-building strategies, allowing them to expand their territorial reach and maintain growing clienteles.[91] This stood in stark contrast with the Ottoman elite, which (with few exceptions of *mülk* lands) did not enjoy similar property rights and thus attached significantly less importance to this type of economic resources.

Interestingly, Polish–Lithuanian nobility was aware that their focus on landholding and serf labour as a source of subsistence and self-definition was in many ways similar to that of Moldavian and Wallachian boyars. This became apparent in 1672 when the Ottoman invasion led to the annexation of Podolia. Still shocked by the events, the local nobility tried to negotiate with the imperial officials to retain their landholdings and serfs. This struggle was recorded in an unsophisticated verse by Stanisław Makowiecki, a local nobleman who partook in the negotiations:

> The nobles inquire about their villages,
> Let's stay in them without worries
> [The vizier] replied: "You're free to remain
> Keep what you have, what's to your liking
> But as for serfs, you will not keep them."
> Makowiecki replies: "How can we survive
> If we lose our peasants?
> For, they live on our land,
> Clearly, the Turks do not know about this."
> The interpreter responds: Your words are in vain,
> As you don't know their laws.
> This would be against their law
> If the serfs would remain under your hand
> The vizier says: Their pleas are of no use
> As the Emperor would not allow it
> In Moldavia, they have the treaties
> But here, the fortress was taken by the sword.[92]

The similarities in Polish–Lithuanian and Moldavian–Wallachian elites' attachment to landholding as a crucial economic and social resource did not necessarily facilitate cross-border patronage. The focus on land as the primary economic resource put Polish–Moldavian networks at a relative disadvantage

Flows, Exchanges, Conversions

compared with those linking the Danubian principalities with the Ottoman Empire. Unlike money, land constitutes a fixed resource that cannot be easily divided, moved or multiplied. Thus, in the long run, Moldavian boyars and their Polish patrons would have competed for a limited amount of economic resources that could not be transferred from one arena to another without redrawing the political boundaries in the region. In turn, the Ottoman officials, operating within the context of a monetized economy and unencumbered by the cultural link between landholding and elite identity, had at their disposal a more flexible mechanism based on liquid cash, better suited to the requirements of cross-border patronage. As I will show in the following chapters, this difference had a profound effect on the outcome of Polish–Ottoman rivalry.

Information, communication and manipulation

While less tangible than economic or political resources, information played a crucial role in the factional world of early modern Eastern Europe. In the age before modern time–space compression set in, procuring reliable information and communicating across vast distance constituted was an arduous, time-consuming task, but one crucial for successful participation in social, economic and political life. The credibility of sources was often in doubt, and informants often relied on street gossip; the channels of communication were prone to breakdowns and leaks.

These limitations made access to information a crucial resource for successful factional competition. Early access to news provided an edge over rivals and could prove decisive in the scramble for resources and offices. This meant that placing clients at crucial nodes of information gathering remained a crucial preoccupation for faction-builders. However, control over information and communication was not merely a matter of procuring reliable news, but also allowed grandees to manipulate their contents or their flow, withhold them or manage their dissemination for the factional benefit.[93] In this sense, the political communication produced 'a corridor of power', which could be utilized to further actors' goals or bring down their rivals.[94] This procurement and dissemination of information occurred on two different levels, which corresponded to the Venetian notions of *communicazione* and *pubblicazione*. The former described the flow of information within the political institutions (or patronage networks), kept secret from outsiders, while the latter meant dissemination of information to the wider public.[95]

Ottoman, Moldavian–Wallachian and Polish–Lithuanian elites embraced different concepts regarding the ideal model of political communication, which affected the ways the information circulated within the arenas. According to the Ottoman political theory, the backbone of the whole system was the intimate bond between the sultan and his grand vizier, who would act as the ruler's stand-in in all administrative matters of the imperial administration.[96] This dependence of the sultan on his deputy was remedied by the flow of petitions (*arz*) from the subjects, which played a central role in mandated the ruler's legitimacy as an upholder of justice and rectifier of officials' oppression of the population. In turn, Polish–Lithuanian nobility fashioned a different model of political communication, emphasizing the importance of the open flow of information and decrying any attempts to keep communication secret. Always suspicious of king's motives and 'practices', and seeing the liberty to speak their mind as a civic virtue, the nobles demanded scrutiny over royal council's proceedings and protested attempts to restrict access to vital pieces of information. These demands only increased in the mid-seventeenth century, when the crisis of trust between the court and the nobles led the latter to call for further measures to prevent royal conspiracies.[97]

However, it should come as no wonder in the cut-throat context of factional rivalry that keeping communication within the network secret and learning adversaries' secrets remained a constant preoccupation. This largely explains the relative dearth of sources on cross-border patronage, since most letters concerning delicate matters were burned after reading. Moreover, much of communication was conducted orally through trusted clients, further limiting our knowledge about the factions' inner workings. At the same time, seizure of correspondence and opening of letters was a common practice. As Ion Neculce informs us, the voivode of Moldavia, Constantin Duca, employed a certain Nicolae Deport, whose main task was opening intercepted letters and informing the ruler about their contents.[98] Polish–Lithuanian diplomats in Istanbul constantly complained about their correspondence being seized by the voivodes, and its contents divulged to their Ottoman patrons.[99]

This was particularly important since Moldavian and Wallachian voivodes were important information brokers in the region. As Ottoman appointees, they were expected to gather intelligence on Polish–Lithuanian, Muscovite and Crimean developments on behalf of Ottoman authorities.[100] At the same time, they also passed information in the opposite direction, informing Polish–Lithuanian magnates of recent events at the Porte and the Crimean Khanate.[101] There are numerous indications that the Moldavian and Wallachian

Flows, Exchanges, Conversions

information-gathering systems were efficient; for instance, it seems that the Porte first learned about the conclusion of the peace of Ryswick in 1697 from Constantin Brâncoveanu rather than from any of European ambassadors in Istanbul.[102] This intelligence network provided voivodes with considerable informational resources that they could deploy for the purposes of their factional interests.

Ottoman grandees and Polish–Lithuanian magnates did not hesitate to use Moldavian and Wallachian clients for information-gathering purposes, sometimes addressing delicate political matters. These endeavours posed considerable risks. For instance, in 1666, Köprülü Ahmed Pasha's client Gheorghe Duca was removed from the throne and nearly lost his life when one of such schemes backfired:

> The reason for the dismissal was the following. By that time, the Crimean Khan Selim Giray [the chronicler's mistake, Mehmed IV Giray was the khan at this point – M.W.] came under suspicion of betraying the empire. Thus, Köprülü Ahmed Pasha, who at this time was the grand vizier and participated in the siege of a fortress in Crete, instructed Duca to write a letter to the Khan to learn if he was harbouring evil thoughts against the Porte. Thus, Duca followed the instructions and wrote to Selim Giray words of friendship, calling him the emperor and disclosing many secrets in his letter.[103]

However, the letter was intercepted by the Ottoman governor of Özü, who sent them to the sultan's court. The sultan and Kara Mustafa Pasha, who acted as the *Kaymakam* of the Imperial Stirrup (*kaymakam-ı rikab-ı hümayun*), immediately ordered Duca to be removed from the throne. Only Ahmed Pasha's intervention saved the unfortunate voivode from losing his life.

The importance of factional channels of communication had far-reaching implications for political events. For instance, in November 1639, the Porte issued a series of orders, which mandated the removal of Matei Basarab from the Wallachian throne and the appointment of Vasile Lupu in his stead. However, as Hasan Vecihi mentioned, the *çavuş* tasked with informing Matei of his removal from power was accompanied by a certain Tatar Süleyman, a client of Silahdar Mustafa Pasha.[104] In their secret rendezvous, the latter encouraged voivode not to abandon the throne, but instead confront Ottoman forces, promising the political support of the sultan's favourite. These assurances clearly emboldened Matei, who refused to comply and mobilized his troops. At the same time, in order to break the stranglehold that Vasile Lupu's allies held over communication, the Wallachian voivode channelled his correspondence through his patron, thus allowing him to spin the news and sway Murad IV's opinion.[105]

108   *The Ottomans and Eastern Europe*

While communication within the faction was crucial for the success of political ventures, selective *pubblicazione* also provided ample opportunities. This was the strategy employed by Derviş Mehmed Pasha and his allies to prevent the marriage between Vasile Lupu and Caterina. The lack of access to the channels of communication and information flowing through Moldavian–Ottoman factional networks constituted a constant problem for Polish–Lithuanian officials. Jerzy Kruszyński, sent in 1636 to demand the removal of Vasile Lupu from the throne, learned this the hard way. From the very outset, the diplomat encountered difficulties, as his sojourn in Iaşi was beset by the hostility of the voivode and quarrels over ceremonial.[106] Once in the imperial capital, Kruszyński was stonewalled by Lupu's Ottoman allies and spent fifteen weeks trying to secure an audience with the sultan, while Moldavian agents spread gossip putting Kruszyński's diplomatic status in doubt. The reports he sent to the royal court were intercepted by Vasile Lupu; ultimately, he was put under the custody of Moldavian *capuchehaias* and prohibited from any contact with Poland–Lithuania.[107] Despite these ordeals, Kruszyński was leaving Istanbul convinced of the success of his mission and the imminent removal of Vasile Lupu from power. The meeting with Ken'an Pasha, the *beylerbey* of Özü, dispelled these hopes. While Ken'an Pasha was no friend of the Moldavian voivode, he informed the envoy that the orders received from the Porte made no mention regarding the issue.[108] As a result of collusion between Vasile Lupu and his supporters, the Polish–Lithuanian efforts came to naught, and the Moldavian voivode's position remained unchallenged.

However, arguably the most elaborate scheme involving cross-border patronage took place at the Polish–Lithuanian *Sejm* of 1597. The political climate of the Commonwealth suggested that the proceedings would be far from smooth. The most polarizing issue was the ecclesiastical Union of Brest' from October 1596, which subordinated the Orthodox hierarchy in Poland–Lithuania to the papal authority. While its conclusion had been supported by the Orthodox hierarchy and the royal court, it encountered vehement opposition among the population, led by powerful magnate Prince Kostjantyn-Vasyl' Ostroz'kyj.

The confessional dispute was not the only challenge to the prince's position. He was also engulfed in a major factional conflict with the Grand Crown Chancellor and *Hetman* Jan Zamoyski. Since the 1570s, Zamoyski had been building his own political and economic system in southern and southeastern provinces of the Commonwealth, amassing enormous landholdings and political influence. This expansion impinged on the Ostroz'kyjs' political turf in Volhynia and Ukrainian palatinates. While initially both tried to maintain

Flows, Exchanges, Conversions

peaceful relations, a set of political and economic issues eventually put the two magnates on the collision course.[109] In this confrontation, several factors put Zamoyski at a disadvantage. While his rise through the ranks of nobility was meteoric, he lacked Ostroz'kyj's distinguished lineage and deep roots in the local political scene. Moreover, his relations with King Sigismund III were hostile, since the monarch successively chipped away the chancellor's political influence by denying his clients' appointments and encouraging them to abandon their patron.

In such an adverse political climate, Zamoyski designed a strategy meant not only to defend his position but to humiliate his enemies in the process. At the centre of this plan was Nikeforos Parasios, the *protosynkellos* of the Ecumenical Patriarchate, who led the anti-unionist counter-synod in Brest' and was crucial in galvanizing the Orthodox opposition against the Union. Active in the Danubian principalities since the early 1590s, Nikeforos was a high-profile figure in local political and ecclesiastical life, with ties to both Moldavian voivodes and the Ottoman court.[110] He also played a role as an intermediary between the imperial authorities and Jan Zamoyski during the latter's intervention in the principality.

In spring 1596, Nikeforos was arrested while trying to cross the Polish–Moldavian border to participate in the upcoming synod. He managed to escape from the prison in Hotin and find sanctuary in the estates of his ally, Prince Kostjantyn-Vasyl' Ostroz'kyj. Ieremia Movilă immediately demanded that the fugitive be handed over to Moldavian authorities and requested Zamoyski's intervention in the matter.[111] Nonetheless, Ostroz'kyj's protection allowed the Greek *protosynkellos* to retain his freedom and arrive in Brest' for the synod held in October 1596. As the highest-ranking churchman in attendance, Nikeforos led a counter-synod that rejected the union with Rome and excommunicated the unionist camp. Under growing pressure from Zamoyski and the king, Ostroz'kyj eventually gave in and promised to bring Nikeforos to the upcoming *Sejm* to respond to the charges.

The charges against the *protosynkellos* were grave indeed, including lying about his official capacity, spying on behalf of Koca Sinan Pasha and the *valide sultan*, driving Moldavian treasury into enormous debt, entering Poland–Lithuania without royal permission and scheming to replace the Moldavian voivode. Also, accusations of sodomy were brought up, involving intercourse with a small boy.[112] Apart from Parasios, a certain Jani, Ostroz'kyj's servant, also stood trial for trying to smuggle Nikeforos's incriminating letters out of the Commonwealth.

As Tomasz Kempa pointed out, many contemporaries considered the trial a farce and suspected Zamoyski had fabricated the evidence.[113] The chancellor, an experienced parliamentarian and an expert in shaping his public image, took great pains to maintain factional control over the proceedings and evidence. Mikołaj Zebrzydowski, one of Zamoyski's closest allies, presided the tribunal, while the bulk of the evidence was provided by the envoys of Ieremia Movilă. During the public audience with the king, the envoys swore their loyalty to the Commonwealth and publicly demanded justice to be served, explicitly drawing the connection between Nikeforos and Ostroz'kyj.[114] During the trial, Zebrzydowski coached the Moldavians regarding their statements, clearly under Zamoyski's direction. Members of the chancellor's faction had a hand in producing material evidence as well: the letters incriminating Nikeforos and Jani were 'discovered' by another of Zamoyski's clients.[115] According to contemporary observers, the whole trial served not to convict Nikeforos, but rather to discredit Ostroz'kyj.

Ultimately, the tribunal failed to issue a verdict and the trial was put on hold, never to resume. For Zamoyski this constituted a major success, nonetheless. The proceedings provided a public stage to launch an attack against his main adversary, associating Ostroz'kyj with a presumed Ottoman spy and casting doubt on his integrity. Moreover, since Nikeforos was not acquitted, the chancellor detained the *protosynkellos* in the castle of Marienburg (today Malbork), where he remained until his death in 1602, despite Ostroz'kyj's appeals.[116] This outcome suited Zamoyski, who was able to strike a blow against his adversary's prestige and retain Nikeforos as leverage for years to come.

Discussing the influence of the Ottoman 'Mediterranean faction' in the late sixteenth century, Emrah Safa Gürkan noted:

> Trying to read the decision-making process and strategy formulation independent from the realities of factional rivalries would be to overlook the corporate interests at the heart of Ottoman politics. Those who shaped policy were a far cry from disinterested officials, formulating strategy as a result of careful and objective calculations of long-term strategic objectives.[117]

This holds true for Ottoman presence in Eastern Europe, as well. Imperial elites, just like their Polish–Lithuanian and Moldavian–Wallachian counterparts, operated within limits imposed by slow communication and distance, which made access to information difficult and troublesome. However, while posing considerable challenges, it also provided ample opportunities. Taking control of communication channels through cross-border patronage allowed for spinning

Flows, Exchanges, Conversions

the news and their selective dissemination. As a result, central authorities usually operated on the basis of biased information filtered through factional interests of those involved.

Letters and watermelons: Civility and patronage

In August 1646, Łukasz Miaskowski, an important figure in the palatinate of Podolia, received a letter from the Moldavian governor of Soroca, Ştefan. The boyar thanked Miaskowski for his support and wished him to stay in good health. At the same time, he discussed a matter of an unusual shipment that accompanied the letter:

> As for watermelons [...] due to great heat this year, they have turned flabby, but I send you a hundred of the best I've been able to find, along with forty melons. Although the fruits are somewhat modest and bland, I humbly ask you to accept them, Sire, as a gift from your friend and servant.[118]

This was not the only time that Miaskowski received watermelons as a gift from Moldavian officials. Sometime earlier, his servant, Wojkuszycki, informed him that another shipment from Soroca arrived in Hotin as a gift of friendship from the governor.[119]

While we may see these gifts as somewhat at odds with massive sums of money, troops and information circulating through cross-border patronage networks in the region, such seemingly trivial items were an important component of factional politics. Although their monetary value was relatively modest, their main role rested in the symbolic aspect of their exchange, increasingly recognized by modern scholarship.[120] In the political world reliant on personal ties and affective rhetoric, personalized gifts and kind words constituted not only a token of friendship but also an important tool for establishing and maintaining political alliances.[121]

The contents of such exchanges and direction of the flows varied wildly within and across the arenas. Sometimes the objects involved may seem pedestrian. As Hedda Reindl-Kiel has shown, large allotments of foodstuffs from the palace kitchens distributed daily among the members of the sultanic household were meant primarily for redistribution among their dependents, thus reinforcing the vertical bonds tying them to their patrons.[122] However, the importance of some gifts was considerable enough as to warrant their inclusion on the pages of the chronicles of the period. For instance, Wallachian author Radu Popescu mentions that a lavish personal gift initiated the lasting bond between the Cantacuzino family and Merzifonlu Kara Mustafa Pasha that largely defined the relationship between Wallachia and the Porte in the 1670s and 1680s. According to Popescu, when Mustafa Pasha arrived in Bucharest in 1660 to oversee the change on the throne, Şerban Cantacuzino approached him with a gift of a beautiful horse and harness. The grandee was happy with the mount and, as the Wallachian boyar claimed, this exchange initiated the long period of cooperation between the two households, culminating in Şerban's appointment to the throne in 1678.[123]

These exchanges served a double purpose. On the one hand, such personalized gifts gave credence to the affective rhetoric of friendship that permeated cross-border patronage. While there is a tendency to dismiss the claims to friendship as a mere window dressing, they were treated with utmost seriousness by contemporaries. As Urszula Augustyniak pointed out, gift-giving enhanced the prestige of clients, since it set them apart from paid servants, even if at times their actual position was not so much different.[124] On the other hand, offering gifts to one's patrons and clients was a principal means of keeping the channels of communication open and expressing continued interest in political cooperation. For instance, following his first deposition in 1615, Ştefan Tomşa II fell on hard times: not only was he removed from the throne, but his possessions were confiscated by Ottoman authorities. His sole consolation was a gold-embroidered *kaftan* presented to him by his patron, Gürcü Mehmed Pasha, which testified to the grandee's continued willingness to cooperate with the voivode.[125] Indeed, in 1621 Mehmed Pasha's support allowed Tomşa to return to the throne, despite several years spent out of power. In this sense, civilities and personal gifts, while more modest than massive resources discussed above, were crucial for maintaining political cohesion of the faction.

That these exchanges' importance as tokens of friendship outweighed their monetary value is best illustrated in the exchange of letters within cross-border factions. Given that their members were scattered across vast distances, there were few opportunities for face-to-face interaction between patrons and clients, making the exchange of correspondence a surrogate means to provide the much-needed personal connection. Particularly informative in this respect are the letters sent by the Moldavian grand *logofăt* (chancellor), Luca Stroici, to Jan Zamoyski. Within Zamoyski–Movilă faction, Stroici occupied a special position. Awarded Polish noble title together with Ieremia Movilă, he was the only boyar who enjoyed direct access the Crown chancellor and made considerable effort to uphold this bond.[126] His letters to Zamoyski only sporadically touch on any specific matters but are replete with wishes of good health, declarations

Flows, Exchanges, Conversions

of friendship and assurances of unwavering loyalty.[127] Stroici never missed a chance to address his patron, and in some periods seems to have been writing a letter every two days. Anxious that this constant barrage of correspondence may annoy Zamoyski, he asked forgiveness, but phrased his apology in a way that would assure him of Stroici's determination to serve his protector:

> I've heard that my frequent letters became tiresome for you since I do not pass any opportunity to address you in writing, my lord. I do this being eager to perform any services for you, which I offer so often to you; now as well, I wish you to remain in good health, hoping that God will bestow it upon you for a long time.[128]

Apart from expressions of loyalty, Stroici also played into Zamoyski's intellectual pursuits and seems to have promised the chancellor a manuscript on Moldavian history, further ingratiating himself with his patron.[129] Even if this constant flow of correspondence could be annoying at times, it was nonetheless an auspicious omen for Zamoyski, ensuring him of Stroici's continued interest in maintaining the bond.

This strategy was perfected by another boyar with strong ties to the Polish–Lithuanian establishment. Miron Costin, one of the most important political figures in late-seventeenth-century Moldavia, had spent his childhood in Poland–Lithuania and acquired education in the Jesuit college of Bar before returning to the principality and rising through the ranks of local officialdom. Fluent in Polish and Latin, which he combined with literary talents and skill in managing cross-border ties, he harnessed his oeuvre to ingratiate himself with Polish–Lithuanian patrons. As a result, his two works in Polish, known as *Polish Poem* and *Polish Chronicle*, were dedicated, respectively, to King John III Sobieski (1674–96) and one of his closest associates, Marek Matczyński, with whom Costin exchanged numerous letters.[130]

From this standpoint, it becomes clear that civilities and personalized gifts constituted an important component of cross-border patronage strategies, acting as a catalyst that facilitated establishment and upkeep of patronage ties. In the absence of day-to-day interaction between the members of the faction, these small favours and expressions of gratitude played a crucial role in keeping the channels of exchange open. At the same time, individual goods could be converted into different types of capital, even if hard evidence is lacking. For instance, while a relatively humble commodity, the watermelons that Miaskowski received could be repurposed to gain political capital on the dietines. While opinion leaders among local nobility formed relatively stable bonds with magnate factions, many of the rank-and-file participants were mobilized through one-off transactions and flocked to the assemblies to participate in social events rather than to pursue political ambitions.[131] In order to sway their opinion, magnates held numerous feasts, providing ample quantities of food and spirits. Within such context, watermelons, rarely encountered on Polish–Lithuanian tables, would constitute a somewhat exotic good and an advantage in ensuring support of lesser nobles. While we cannot be sure, if Miaskowski's watermelons served such a political purpose, this possibility further underscores the role of seemingly trivial objects circulating through patronage networks in the region.

Part Two

Factional Macro-Politics

4

Friends and Enemies

Although the discussion in the previous chapters focused on internal structures of cross-border factionalism, patronage networks obviously did not operate in isolation. Their existence and advantages they provided to their members stemmed directly from the constant competition with other political groups, struggling to secure control over resources. This was no different with regard to Polish–Lithuanian, Ottoman and Moldavian–Wallachian actors of the seventeenth century, as they grappled and scrambled to secure their hegemony and bring down potential rivals. As the struggle intensified, it brought about a series of political crises that reverberated beyond the sphere of purely factional politics.

However, this factional component of regional politics has been underplayed in the scholarship, as historians struggled to identify geopolitical foundation at the heart of individuals' actions, assuming that service to the state and the ruler *ought to* provide the basis for decision-making among the elites.[1] Hence, in cases when such a rationale seemed lacking, the blame was put on the venality of individuals that failed to live up to the ideals of state service. As political cohesion within the arenas fragmented with the rise of factionalism and few decisions went uncontested, the impression we get is one of failing moral standards of the elites, ready to sacrifice the interests of the polity in favour of personal gain.

If we look at the sources, this standpoint does not seem unwarranted. Powerholders in the Ottoman Empire, Poland–Lithuania and the Danubian principalities presented themselves as willing to rectify the ills of the age, curb in quarrels within administrative ranks and overcome the resistance of their venal and self-serving peers. Thus, the legitimizing tools employed by early modern political actors converged with the state-centric viewpoint of modern scholarship, trying to separate private interests from those of the polity.

However, such a distinction would be arbitrary at best, effectively misconstruing the realities on the ground. The principle of working for the common weal, either as a loyal servant of the sultan or as an exemplar of civic virtue, undoubtedly played a role both in decision-making and in self-representation strategies of the elites. As Michael Braddick pointed out with regard to early modern England, the 'authority of an individual performing an office depended on the presentation of a self that conferred natural authority on them – they presented a front which represented an abstract political authority rather than their individual will'.[2] Polish–Lithuanian, Ottoman and Moldavian–Wallachian elites were no different in this respect, as they constantly strove to present their actions as conforming to culturally defined concepts of virtue and faithful service.

Patronage, despite being bread and butter of seventeenth-century politics, did not fit easily with these ideal standards. As a result, it remained something of a dirty secret among Eastern European elites, with those involved in such practices trying to obscure its role in decision-making and political struggle. For instance, Koca Sinan Pasha, a five-time grand vizier and one of the most influential patrons of his time, took the pains to convince Murad III that he did not engage in factional politics and had few followers of his own, a statement at odds with the realities on the ground.[3] When justifying their actions, virtually all participants in early modern politics utilized the rhetoric of loyal service and selfless statecraft, rather than discussing their actions through personal and factional interests. The latter was reserved for political adversaries, whose ulterior motives they tried to discredit.

This mechanism of legitimizing factional interests by invoking ideals of service and duty found its way into historical sources. As the political field fragmented into competing factions, so did the historiography of the period. Many authors, bound through patronage to particular groups, produced accounts intended to appropriate the title of moral paragons for their political allies and denigrate their adversaries. This phenomenon became particularly salient in Wallachia, where both boyar factions – the Cantacuzinos and the Băleanu–Leurdeanu bloc – produced their own account of the principality's history. In Poland–Lithuania, heated discussions at the noble assemblies similarly pitched competing factions against one another, each claiming to act for the common good. That those engaged in patronage were often reluctant to bring it up to justify their actions leads to a somewhat paradoxical situation: the authors closest to the events are frequently the least reliable in elucidating the role of factionalism in their political ventures.

However, as I shall demonstrate in the present chapter, cross-border patronage was central to political developments in the triangle of Poland–Lithuania, the

Porte and the Danubian principalities. While in all three cases their factional component has been considered secondary to broader geopolitical considerations, they were, in fact, a product of competition for resources between and within patronage networks. The latter is particularly important, since patronage-based factions were 'quasi-groups' rather than homogeneous structures, and encompassed numerous cliques bound vertically to the patron, but with no horizontal ties between them.[4] In effect, once the vertical bond was severed, for instance upon the patron's death, the faction could descend into an internal competition between different groups, ultimately leading to the disintegration of the whole political edifice. As I will show, it is a testimony to the strength of cross-border ties that, should such decomposition occur, the fault lines frequently straddled boundaries of individual arenas rather than aligned with them.

In order to show the dynamics of such conflicts, the present chapter focuses on three instances of such inter- and intra-factional clashes in the seventeenth century. In the first section, I address one the competition that defined Ottoman–Moldavian–Wallachian relations for much of the 1630s. The rivalry between Voivodes Vasile Lupu and Matei Basarab defined most of this period, inducing the members of the Ottoman top brass to pick their sides. Although the conflict originated in the Danubian principalities, the proliferation of cross-border patronage networks meant that they reached its climax at the imperial centre in the dramatic events of December 1639. In the following part, I shift my attention to examine how such factions broke up into competing segments, once the death of their founders created a vacuum of power at the top. Jan Zamoyski's military interventions in Moldavia and the enthronement of his client, Ieremia Movilă, created a relatively stable system of patronage based on the cooperation between the two. However, following their deaths in 1605–06, the faction suffered a succession crisis and broke up into two competing camps, supporting different branches of the Movilă dynasty and vying for influence in both Poland–Lithuania and Moldavia. Ultimately, their rivalry led to the collapse of the Commonwealth's influence in the principality by 1611–16. Finally, the third case study tackles more muted, but still relevant, tensions within the Köprülü patronage network in the third quarter of the century. While the Köprülüs managed to establish themselves as hegemons in the Ottoman political arena, they also suffered from growing tensions within their ranks. Although the competition between Köprülüzade Ahmed Pasha and his deputy Merzifonlu Kara Mustafa Pasha did not lead to an open rupture within the faction, the competition between their clients in Moldavia and Wallachia seriously disrupted the political life in the principalities.

Matei Basarab and Vasile Lupu

In many respects, the middle decades of the seventeenth century can be considered a high water mark of Moldavian and Wallachian fortunes. The reigns of Matei Basarab (1632–54) and Vasile Lupu (1634–53), respectively, ushered in an unprecedented period of political stability, in stark contrast to the rapid turnover of the earlier period. Both voivodes exhibited considerable skill in ensuring their political survival and their long reigns set the stage for an economic and cultural revival. At the same time, however, the two rulers remained openly hostile to each other, and their rivalry shaped the political developments in the region that culminated in a series of open military conflicts. In the process, both voivodes repeatedly enlisted their allies' support, both within the region and at the Sublime Porte.

The prominence of both Lupu and Matei in Romanian history has resulted in numerous studies devoted to their reigns and political conflicts. Trying to identify the origins of their rivalry, scholars have generally focused on the local political scene and the voivodes' geopolitical orientations. Within this model, Matei Basarab – a scion of the local elite, who ascended the throne as a rebel – is depicted as a champion of the boyars willing to cast off the 'Turkish yoke' with support from Christian powers. In contrast, Vasile Lupu is presented as an ambitious newcomer of Albanian origin, who owed his throne to the Porte and represented a 'pro-Ottoman' orientation throughout much of his reign.[5] The Moldavian voivode's association with Ottomans and his non-Romanian origin coloured much of scholars' opinions on the conflict that unfolded between the two since his affiliation with the Porte appeared as incongruous with the national aspirations of Moldavians and Wallachians.[6] As a result, attempts to rehabilitate Vasile Lupu, undertaken by historians, have focused either on 'nationalizing' him or presenting his ties to the Porte as purely instrumental and conjectural.[7]

Arguably, Vasile Lupu enjoyed strong support at the Porte as he tried to fulfil his political objectives, most notably in his numerous attempts to oust Matei from Wallachia and establish himself as the ruler of both principalities. However, as I have pointed in Chapter 2, this does not mean that he pursued a consistent pro-Ottoman policy, nor that Matei Basarab's actions allow us to describe him as an adversary of the empire. Although Matei's standing at the Porte was weaker, his path to the throne was made possible by the very transformation of the imperial political culture of the *celali* age. His first Ottoman patron, Abaza Mehmed Pasha, was far more consequential for securing the voivode's reign than his Christian ally, Transylvanian prince György Rákóczy I (1630–48).[8] Moreover,

Friends and Enemies 121

as the following survey demonstrates, many high-ranking officials within the Ottoman establishment continued to lend their support to Matei Basarab against Vasile Lupu. Thus, the dynamics of this conflict go beyond a simple dichotomy between pro-Christian and pro-Ottoman attitudes of either voivode, putting the role of factional connections on display.

Already upon the appointment of Vasile Lupu in 1634, there had been some bad blood between him and Matei Basarab. The origins of this hostility are not entirely clear, although sources suggest that Lupu's machinations at the Porte had been instrumental in the execution of Miron Barnovschi, Matei's prospective ally.[9] Vasile Lupu also granted refuge to some prominent enemies of the Wallachian ruler. Among them, the most notable were Catargis, influential Wallachian boyars of Greek origin who had supported their kin Radu Ilias against Matei Basarab in 1632. Once in Moldavia, they became important members of Vasile Lupu's circle, rising to key positions within local officialdom and pushing the voivode towards a confrontation with Matei Basarab.[10] They also rejected all attempts at reconciliation with their Wallachian adversary. Already in the summer of 1634, Nicolae Catargi approached Murtaza Pasha, trying to sway the official against Matei Basarab, seemingly acting with Lupu's consent.[11] With their strong position among Orthodox notables of the imperial capital, the Catargis' support constituted a boon for the Moldavian voivodes in the years that followed.

Soon, the tensions escalated further. In May 1635, when Matei was touring the western provinces of the principality, the Moldavian voivode amassed troops at the border, planning to launch an attack against his rival. Forewarned of the impending danger, the Wallachian ruler returned in haste to Târgoviște and mobilized his soldiers, causing Lupu to give up his plans, at least temporarily.[12] It is clear that Vasile Lupu acted not only on the Catargis' behest but pursued a more ambitious goal of installing his family in both principalities. Much ink has been spilled concerning these plans, with scholars interpreting them as stemming from the personal ambition of the voivode, struggle for national unity or even plans to restore an Orthodox empire in Southeastern Europe.[13] However, the most recent precedent in this respect was the reign of Radu Mihnea, who during his last reign in Moldavia (1623–6) managed to install his son, Alexandru, on the Wallachian throne.[14] Voivode Alexandru Ilias pursued a similar scheme in 1632 when he unsuccessfully supported Radu Ilias against Matei Basarab. Thus, rather than the dynastic project of Vasile Lupu, what is interesting is the strategy pursued by each voivode to tilt the balance in his favour.

Matei Basarab's alliance with the Transylvanian prince, concluded in March 1635 and renewed on numerous occasions in the following years, and care taken by the voivode to ingratiate himself with Polish–Lithuanian diplomats constituted the basis for interpreting his position as a pro-Christian one, in contrast to the pro-Ottoman stance of his rival. However, such a depiction ignores several patron–client ties that bound the Wallachian voivode to Ottoman establishment. Among them, we find Zülfikar Agha, a Hungarian renegade and an experienced dragoman with strong ties to the Transylvanian prince and his Istanbul-based agents.[15] However, the voivode's principal supporter at the Porte at this point seems to have been Ruznameci Ibrahim Efendi, who acted as Sultan Murad IV's favourite and chief financial officer.[16] Following the execution of Abaza Mehmed Pasha, Matei Basarab's first Ottoman patron, in the aftermath of 1633–4 Polish–Ottoman war, Ibrahim Efendi took over as the main protector of the Wallachian ruler's interests at the Porte. He is identified as such in December 1637 and continued in this role until his death.[17]

That such high-ranking official lent their assistance to Matei Basarab makes it clear that Ottoman officials did not act in unison during the unfolding conflict between him and Vasile Lupu. Rather than rallying around the Moldavian voivode, the grandees were split on the matter, pursuing their own factional interests. Contemporaries seem to have recognized this more clearly than modern historians. In his chronicle, Miron Costin depicts imperial establishment in this period as split between two major factions led by the chief black eunuch (*kızlar ağası*) and Silahdar Mustafa Pasha. According to him, while Vasile Lupu associated himself with the former, Matei became a client of Mustafa Pasha.[18] Costin's account, as well as other sources, conveys a picture of two evenly matched camps within the Ottoman officialdom rather than one of unanimous support for Vasile Lupu at the Porte.

At the same time, what Costin describes as a stable configuration of Ottoman and Moldavian–Wallachian political scene was, in fact, a fluid and ever-changing set of alliances. As early as August 1636, Jerzy Kruszyński reported on the expected appointment of Radu Iliaş to the Moldavian throne that the pretender 'thanked his promoter and a great favourite of the emperor, Silahdar [Mustafa] Pasha'.[19] Soon afterwards, the grandee seems to have briefly weighed in his support for Vasile Lupu.[20] Mustafa Pasha's vacillating position seems to indicate his initial difficulties in finding a suitable client that would allow him to establish a foothold in Moldavia and Wallachia, particularly since other grandees actively sought clients among the pretenders scrambling for Ottoman support.

Friends and Enemies   123

The year 1637 witnessed a further escalation of the conflict as another key figure – Tabanıyassı Mehmed Pasha – directly intervened in the conflict. This official of Albanian origin and a fellow countryman of Vasile Lupu had begun his career in the *kapı* of the Chief Black Eunuch Hacı Mustafa Agha.[21] The latter seemed to have great plans for his client, and in 1628 Mehmed Pasha received the governorship of Egypt as his first provincial appointment. When his tenure ended four years later, the *beylerbey* returned to Istanbul and was swiftly appointed by Murad IV to the grand vizierate. While there are some indications that he established the patron–client bond relatively early into his tenure, his involvement in Moldavian–Wallachian affairs is hard to reconstruct, as he spent most of his grand vizierate leading imperial troops against the Safavids. However, in February 1637, a failure to relieve the fortress of Revan and a mutiny among Janissary corps led to his dismissal and return to Istanbul. Soon after his arrival in the capital, Mehmed Pasha was appointed to a provincial post as the *beylerbey* of Özü, which allowed him to intervene directly in the affairs in the Danubian principalities and the Black Sea coast.

Despite his demotion, Mehmed Pasha did not fall out of favour with Murad IV. His new appointment came with an important task of pacifying the steppe fringes of the empire. A long-simmering conflict between the Giray khans and Tatar aristocrat Kantemir Mirza, who had secured a near-independent position in the Bucak came to a head when Inayet Giray moved his troops against the recalcitrant chieftain.[22] Ottoman authorities decided to utilize the opportunity to remove both powerholders, replacing Khan Inayet Giray and executing Kantemir. As the new governor, Tabanıyassı Mehmed Pasha was appointed to lead a mop-up operation. Leaving the imperial capital in August 1637, Mehmed Pasha was in good spirits, and according to the Venetian *bailo* 'he was undisturbed by the past demotion, as he could double all that he had lost'.[23] Subsequent events show that he planned to accomplish this in collusion with Vasile Lupu. According to Miron Costin, Tabanıyassı Mehmed Pasha even requested the appointment to the *eyalet* himself, hoping to assist his Moldavian client.[24]

Both Moldavian and Wallachian voivodes were summoned to bring their troops to the *beylerbey*'s camp and assist in the operations against the Tatars. Vasile Lupu swiftly dispatched his soldiers, accompanied by his son, Ion, and the Catargis. Matei Basarab, in turn, suspected that the governor had ulterior motives and the order was a ruse to lure him into the military camp, where he would be executed and replaced with Lupu's son, a plan confirmed by Ottoman sources.[25] Thus, he refused to comply and amassed his troops to confront the looming invasion. However, Mehmed Pasha, unwilling to risk a military encounter and

124 *The Ottomans and Eastern Europe*

potential complications, postponed his plans once again, focusing on Tatar affairs instead, much to Lupu's dismay.[26]

The events of the abortive 1637 campaign and Ruznameci Ibrahim Efendi's death reshuffled the political alliances in the region and at the Porte. On the one hand, the events consolidated the bond between Vasile Lupu and Tabanıyassı Mehmed Pasha, who from thereon took a more active role in promoting his client's dynastic ambitions. At the same time, the death of Ibrahim Efendi deprived Matei Basarab of his main Ottoman protector, leaving him vulnerable and forcing him to seek a new patron among the imperial officialdom. Thus, he immediately dispatched a mission to approach grandees willing to offer their support. According to Alvise Contarini, 'Silahdar [Mustafa Pasha] offered to replace the late Ruznameci in looking after the prince and the province'.[27] This corresponded with the Mustafa Pasha's wider strategy to consolidate his power as Murad IV's *musahib*.[28]

Thus, by late 1637, the factional lines increasingly hardened, setting the stage for an open confrontation. In his attempts to oust Matei Basarab, Vasile Lupu was supported by Tabanıyassı Mehmed Pasha, Chief Black Eunuch Idris Agha, as well as Janissary agha and future grand vizier Kemankeş Kara Mustafa Pasha. Against this influential coalition, the Wallachian ruler could count on Zülfikar Agha and Silahdar Mustafa Pasha, as well as the latter's political allies, including Nasuhpaşazade Hüseyin Pasha, Derviş Mehmed Pasha and the governor of Damascus Osman Pasha, among others.[29] This factional build-up eliminated the middle ground and limited other pretenders' chances to secure an appointment. Leon Tomşa, who tried to secure support at the Porte, suffered torture and humiliation, paraded through the streets of Istanbul seated backward on a donkey and with canine intestines hung around his neck.[30] Scared by this punishment, other potential claimants laid low, waiting for a more opportune moment.

Despite a lull in the conflict caused by Murad IV's Baghdad campaign, the factional build-up continued. In the summer of 1639, the issue of marriage between Vasile Lupu and Caterina, the sister-in-law of Khan Bahadur Giray, discussed in Chapter 2, triggered yet another confrontation between the two blocs. While Silahdar Mustafa Pasha and his supporters were unable to prevent the marriage from taking place, the controversy showed the determination of both camps to gain the upper hand in the Danubian principalities and served as a harbinger of the showdown later that year.

On 2 November 1639, *Kaymakam* Tabanıyassı Mehmed Pasha dispatched a set of orders to the voivodes and governors of adjacent provinces.[31] In them, he declared the dismissal of Matei Basarab and ordered him to step down without resistance. He was to be replaced by Vasile Lupu, while his son, Ion, was to receive the Moldavian throne. Given Ion Lupu's youth and frail health, this arrangement would mean Vasile Lupu's effective rule in both principalities; Lupu adopted the title of 'the voivode of Moldavia and Wallachia' and intended to retain power in Moldavia as well.[32] Moreover, Mehmed Pasha instructed the governor of Özü and Khan Bahadur Giray to provide troops necessary to effectuate the change. At the same time, Vasile Lupu dispatched his Albanian client, Gheorghe Ghica, as a *capuchehaia* in Istanbul, undoubtedly to coordinate the effort.[33]

The attempt to remove Matei Basarab had been in the making for some time in utmost secrecy, catching the Venetian *bailo* by surprise.[34] However, Silahdar Mustafa Pasha and his faction were ready to counteract. The same mission sent to deliver to Wallachian voivode news of his dismissal included a certain Tatar Süleyman, a member of the grandee's household. In a secret conversation with Matei, Süleyman urged the deposed ruler to prepare for military resistance, assuring him of Mustafa Pasha's continued backing and suggesting to address a petition to the sultan.[35]

This declaration of support emboldened Matei, who refused to vacate the throne and immediately mobilized the troops to oppose the Moldavian army. At the same time, he and his boyars dispatched a petition (*arz*) to sway the opinion of the sultan.[36] The petition betrays an intimate knowledge of Ottoman rhetoric and political culture. Rather than challenging the decision itself, Matei and his supporters fashioned the Wallachian voivode as a loyal servant of the Porte, juxtaposing him to Vasile Lupu, whose actions brought oppression upon the sultan's subjects.[37] This was a clever political strategy since it struck at the heart of Ottoman legitimacy, namely the role of the sultan as the upholder of justice and protector of *reâya* against oppression. Tellingly, the petition was sent to Silahdar Mustafa Pasha so as not to be intercepted by Lupu's Ottoman allies.

Simultaneously with the political struggle at the Porte, military operations began in the Danubian principalities. In late November, Vasile Lupu entered Wallachia at the helm of Moldavian–Tatar army, slowly advancing towards Târgoviște. However, he proved a rather mediocre commander and in early December was surprised by Matei's forces near the village of Ojogeni. The battle ended in the Wallachian's decisive victory, and Vasile Lupu barely managed to flee the battlefield accompanied by five soldiers, seeking Ottoman protection in the town of İbrail (Brăila).[38] Within a single day, the situation changed completely, making Vasile Lupu vulnerable and giving initiative to Matei Basarab and

126   *The Ottomans and Eastern Europe*

Silahdar Mustafa Pasha, who were now able to retaliate against the Moldavian voivode and Tabanıyassı Mehmed Pasha.

Matei Basarab immediately dispatched another petition to Silahdar Mustafa Pasha, along with the news of the victory at Ojogeni. The petition reiterated accusations against Vasile Lupu and presented Matei's actions as an attempt to protect Murad IV's subjects.[39] Once the news reached Istanbul, it sent shockwaves across the Ottoman political scene and sent the imperial officials into a frenzy.[40] If we are to believe the account by Miron Costin, the moment of presenting the *arz* to the sultan, orchestrated by Mustafa Pasha and Wallachian agents, involved a significant element of political stagecraft:

> The man [sent by Matei] with the letters, knew how to proceed and waited until the emperor went to the countryside to stroll and hunt. Then, he put his horse in a gallop in front of the emperor to attract his attention. Seeing him in haste, the emperor ordered to stop and summon the man, asking him where he came from. The man responded that he comes from Wallachia with letters to the emperor, to inform him about the great spillage of blood and destruction Voivode Vasile brought upon the country when he came with his army against voivode Matei. Immediately, the emperor demanded to see the letters and read the petition with complaints against Vasile, which mentioned that Vasile boasted that he received diplomas from the vizier to rule in both Moldavia and Wallachia.[41]

Interestingly, the *arz* does not mention Tabanıyassı Mehmed Pasha, focusing solely on Vasile Lupu's actions in Moldavia. However, all sources agree that the unfortunate *kaymakam* became the main target of attack by Matei's Ottoman allies. Silahdar Mustafa Pasha insisted that Mehmed Pasha had betrayed the sultan's trust by claiming that the change on the throne would be unopposed and acting without the ruler's consent.[42] On the same day, he managed to secure the dismissal and imprisonment of his rival, who was swiftly executed in Yedikule and his possessions subject to confiscation. The post of *kaymakam* was now taken by Deli Hüseyin Pasha, one of Silahdar Mustafa's allies.

Having dealt with Mehmed Pasha, the victorious faction moved to consolidate their gains. Matei Basarab was quickly confirmed as the voivode of Wallachia, and a new set of orders instructed authorities in İbrail to apprehend Vasile Lupu.[43] Forewarned about the impending arrest, Vasile Lupu managed to evade capture, fleeing in nothing but a nightgown and slippers.[44] Once in his principality, he made a desperate appeal to Stanisław Koniecpolski, with whom he had been in hostile relations. The *hetman* briefed the king about the mission of Nicolae Catargi and Grigore Ureche 'the gist of their mission was that, having lost any

Friends and Enemies 127

hope in Turkish support, the voivode declares himself ready to enter under the protection of His Majesty, and forever renounces his claim to Wallachia.[45]

While Lupu's desperate measures seemed to indicate his imminent removal from power, the political situation changed once again. By March 1640, Wojciech Miaskowski, the Polish–Lithuanian ambassador who crossed Moldavia on his way to Istanbul, reported that Vasile Lupu managed to regain Ottoman favour and was openly hostile towards the diplomat, working in collusion with imperial officials.[46] Given that mere two months earlier the Moldavian ruler had been ready to accept Polish–Lithuanian suzerainty, this recovery was startling. What changed during this short period? The answer brings to light inherent limitations posed by slow communication, biological accidents and even bad luck.

At the height of the conflict in December 1639, not all Vasile Lupu's patrons were present in Istanbul. Among the absentees, the most important one was undoubtedly Grand Vizier Kemankeş Kara Mustafa Pasha. The grandee of Albanian origin and an ally of Tabanıyassı Mehmed Pasha had served as the agha of Janissaries prior to his promotion to the grand vizierate during the siege of Baghdad. Following the conquest of the city, he remained in the borderland to negotiate a peace treaty with the Safavids, which delayed his return to Istanbul. Thus, when the conflict reached its critical phase, Mustafa Pasha was two weeks away from the imperial capital, reaching the city only at the beginning of January the following year. The absence from the imperial centre prevented him from weighing in on the conflict at a critical juncture. This window of opportunity was enough for Silahdar Mustafa Pasha to execute Tabanıyassı Mehmed Pasha and order the arrest of Vasile Lupu. However, once in the capital, the grand vizier managed to shore up the position of the Moldavian ruler and check Silahdar Mustafa Pasha's influence.[47]

His task was further facilitated by the death of Murad IV in February 1640. The sultan's demise and the accession of his brother Ibrahim not only removed a strong personality at the centre of Ottoman politics, but also reduced the influence of Silahdar Mustafa Pasha, whose power had hinged on his intimate bond with the late sultan. Once the change on the throne took place, his political clout collapsed. Almost immediately Kara Mustafa Pasha moved to marginalize the former *musahib*, appointing him as the *beylerbey* of Temeşvar and later ordering his execution.[48] These unexpected circumstances coalesced, resulting in the anti-climactic resolution of the conflict between Vasile Lupu and Matei Basarab. While the conflict had originated in the Danubian principalities, in the end, two Ottoman grandees – Tabanıyassı Mehmed Pasha and Silahdar Mustafa Pasha – were the only ones to take the fall. Vasile Lupu hoped to resume

128 *The Ottomans and Eastern Europe*

his plans to oust his Wallachian nemesis in cooperation with the grand vizier, but Kara Mustafa Pasha exhibited a more hesitant approach, which annoyed the voivode.[49] However, the hesitation shown by the grandee was not entirely unwarranted, since he increasingly lost ground within the Ottoman arena in favour of a new court faction associated with Sultan Ibrahim, eventually leading to the grand vizier's execution in January 1644.[50] It is no accident that starting from 1643, Vasile Lupu increasingly abandoned his hostile attitude towards Poland–Lithuania and Matei Basarab, with whom he reached a rapprochement the following year, meant to bring an end to the hostilities.[51]

The story of the factional conflict that engulfed Ottoman and Moldavian–Wallachian political arenas in the late 1630s offers us three important observations. First, if seen from the perspective of either the Porte or the Danubian principalities, the events seem to make little sense. Geopolitical considerations are prominent in their absence and the there is little evidence to argue that, in choosing sides, Ottoman officials were concerned about the balance of power in the region. Nor does the allegedly 'pro-Christian' stance of Matei Basarab seem to play a role in mobilizing support for Vasile Lupu. Instead, what we see are two cross-border factions vying for power in the Danubian principalities and the Ottoman centre. While scholars explained away these preferences as a result of rampant corruption among imperial officialdom, the main concern was the competition between factions.[52] Indeed, money changed hands, but the gist of the conflict laid elsewhere. Establishing factional control over Moldavia and Wallachia entered the calculus of power for Ottoman officials, and their competition drove the events throughout the conflict.

Secondly, while most seventeenth-century sources – both European and Ottoman – provide similar accounts of the unfolding conflict, one Ottoman chronicle constitutes an interesting departure in this respect. Hasan Vecihi, a bureaucrat of Crimean origin, who spent much of his career as a seal-bearer of Kemankeş Kara Mustafa Pasha and as such had intimate knowledge of the events, would seem like the most authoritative source of information on the matter. However, this is not the case. According to him, while Silahdar Mustafa Pasha cooperated with Matei Basarab in exchange for money he received from the voivode, Tabanıyassı's motives were different. The *kaymakam* allegedly did not support Vasile Lupu at all. On the contrary, his goal was to remove *both* him and Matei, who had snubbed him by failing to show him appropriate respect during his tenure as the governor of Özü.[53] Vecihi's account is written from an obviously partisan perspective, a fact that did not escape the attention of later historians. Mustafa Naima, while citing Vecihi's interpretation, ultimately discards it

Friends and Enemies 129

in favour of the alternative version he deems more plausible.[54] Nonetheless, the effort Vecihi took to erase any references to Tabanıyassı Mehmed Pasha's cooperation with Vasile Lupu shows that, despite being relatively widespread, cross-border factionalism remained an embarrassing secret.

Finally, the rapid shifts in power in December 1639 and January 1640 remind us of considerable risks and vulnerability of early modern politics to factors beyond the control of their participants. Many things could go wrong, and many did. In the span of three months, the balance of power shifted back and forth, bringing each faction on the verge of victory and the brink of absolute defeat. While the first reversal can be blamed on Vasile Lupu's military ineptitude, it was the unexpected death of Murad IV and the arrival of Kemankeş Kara Mustafa Pasha that denied Silahdar Mustafa Pasha a decisive victory and brought about his sudden downfall. This serves a reminder that no amount of meticulous preparation could remove the inherent risks of factional conflict.

A faction breaks apart

At no point in the seventeenth century did Polish–Lithuanian elites come as close to establishing their hegemony in the Danubian principalities as during the reign of the Movilă dynasty between 1595 and 1611. Following a military intervention in autumn 1595 and Ieremia Movilă's accession, the new voivode accepted King Sigismund III as his suzerain, acquired landed estates in the Crown, and relied heavily on Polish assistance to retain the throne and pass it to his descendants. However, his main bond with the Commonwealth was factional rather than institutional. Movilă's rise to power was orchestrated by his Polish–Lithuanian patron, Jan Zamoyski, and the relationship between the two continued to form the core of Polish–Moldavian nexus.[55] While, as I will show in the following chapter, their cooperation went through a period of crisis, it nonetheless provided a measure of political stability in Moldavia and constituted a lynchpin of Polish–Lithuanian influence in the principality. Once both Jan Zamoyski and Ieremia Movilă passed away in 1605–06, the struggle to replace them at the apex of their faction tore the patronage network apart, triggering a succession conflict that divided the political edifice into two competing segments and allowing Ottoman grandees to reassert their control of the principality within five years.

Succession was always a difficult moment in factional politics, further aggravated by the fact that neither Zamoyski nor Movilă left a strong candidate

130 *The Ottomans and Eastern Europe*

to take over the mantle. By the time of his death on 3 June 1605, the chancellor's only son, Tomasz, was only eleven years old, and therefore unable to assert control of the factional affairs. In order to secure the political and economic foundations of his family's power, in his will Zamoyski established a joint custody over his offspring, appointing his five closest associates to act as legal guardians: the bishop of Kulm Jerzy Zamoyski, Crown Field *Hetman* Stanisław Żółkiewski, Palatines of Cracow and Lublin, Mikołaj Zebrzydowski and Marek Sobieski, as well as Mikołaj Uhrowiecki.[56] Although the system was meant to provide stability until Tomasz reached adulthood, cracks began to appear soon. Marek Sobieski passed away in November the same year, while Uhrowiecki quickly found himself marginalized by his more powerful colleagues. The dwindling number of guardians produced further divisions, as the rift between Żółkiewski and Zebrzydowski began to grow. Both had been among Jan Zamoyski's most trusted and influential lieutenants and hoped to replace him at the helm of his political edifice. Whereas Zebrzydowski engaged in a total opposition against King Sigismund III and pushed for open confrontation, eventually plunging the Commonwealth into a civil war (1606–08), Żółkiewski sided with the monarch, although his conciliatory stance drew criticism from both sides.[57] By 1608, Zamoyski's faction in its original form was no more.[58]

Zamoyski's death and the ensuing competition between his associates sent ripples across the southeastern provinces of the Crown. While most of the local nobility stayed aloof from the events of the civil war, the late chancellor's extensive landholdings and factional structures in the region caused a major reshuffling of the local political scene. Although Stanisław Żółkiewski, with his control of the army and influence in the local dietines, seemed like a natural political heir, his position was by no means uncontested, as other magnates, such as the Potockis and Vyšnevec'kyjs moved to fill the power vacuum.[59] These competing claims posed a serious challenge to Żółkiewski's ambitions, particularly since his apparent lack of tact, arrogance and irascibility did him no favours.[60]

At the time when the conflict in Poland–Lithuania was reaching new heights, Ieremia Movilă's death in June 1606 created similar problems in Moldavia, triggering a fierce competition between potential successors. At first glance, the late voivode's eldest son, Constantin, seemed like the most natural choice. During his reign, Ieremia Movilă put considerable effort to transform his personal rule into a hereditary one, obtaining a diploma from Sigismund III in this respect.[61] The marital union between Constantin's sister, Maria, and Stefan Potocki was another step in this direction, strengthening the family's bond with Polish–Lithuanian elite after Zamoyski's death. Nonetheless, the prospect of

Constantin succeeding his father encountered vehement opposition among the boyars. Its causes are not entirely clear, some scholars emphasizing that Ieremia's son was in his teens and lacked necessarily political experience, while others suggesting a pro-Ottoman shift among the boyars.[62] However, none of these explanations seems satisfactory. Later events showed that Constantin's age was not the opposition's main concern, and we find no indications of an anti-Polish backlash. In fact, many of Constantin's opponents seem to have retained strong bonds with Poland–Lithuania and even fled the principality when Ştefan Tomşa II took power in 1611.

Instead, the focal point of the conflict seems to be a domestic one, specifically, the future position of Constantin's mother, Elizabeta Lozonschi, and her kin. During her husband's reign, Elizabeta became an influential and polarizing figure, using her position to further her clan's interests.[63] Benefitting from her protection, the Lozonschis aggressively accumulated political and economic resources, intimidating other boyars and forcibly seizing their estates.[64] Given Constantin's young age, Elizabeta was likely to step in as a de facto regent for her son, which would give the reviled Lozonschi clan even more power.

To prevent this, the boyars had to come up with an alternative candidate to the throne. They found him in Constantin's paternal uncle, Simion Movilă. Simion had remained in the shadow of his older brother throughout his life. Ieremia promoted his sibling's interests and managed to install him, with Zamoyski's help, as the ruler of Wallachia in October 1600. However, Simion was unable to retain the throne, as his preference for Moldavian boyars and heavy-handed treatment of local lineages, culminating in the conflict with the influential Buzescu brothers, quickly alienated the Wallachian elite.[65] Forced out of the principality, he made several attempts to return to power, none successful in the long term. From the boyars' perspective, his lack of direct ties to the Lozonschis constituted a particularly important asset, and Simion was elected as Ieremia's successor.[66]

Ottoman authorities quickly recognized the new voivode, but the election sparked protests of the Polish–Lithuanian court, opposing the election and Ottoman confirmation since they infringed the royal prerogative to appoint Moldavian rulers, as well as the hereditary rights of Ieremia's offspring.[67] Ultimately, the king conceded and accepted the new voivode on the condition that this precedent would not violate the rights of Constantin, who would succeed Simion on the throne.[68] While the king was anxious to uphold his prerogatives and prestige, the general preference for Ieremia Movilă's branch was not only a matter of royal legalism. In July 1605, Sigismund III instructed his ambassador to Istanbul to consult the members of the Potocki family to learn 'from the *Starosta* of Kam'janec' and his brothers whom they would like as the voivode'.[69] There is no doubt that Stefan Potocki, soon to become Ieremia's son-in-law, and his brothers supported the interest of Constantin over those of Simion. Thus, the king's stance on Moldavian succession originated not only from his concern with royal prerogative but deferred to the interests of the magnate family.

Why Sigismund III did so is understandable in the light of Potockis' political career in this period. Stefan Potocki and his brothers registered a meteoric rise to prominence during the last decades of the sixteenth century, owing primarily to their distinguished military careers and skilful political manoeuvring. While they initially attached themselves to the faction of Jan Zamoyski, they subsequently crossed over to the royal camp and adopted an increasingly hostile attitude towards their erstwhile patron.[70] Soon, they became one of the pillars of the royal political camp and translated royal favour into their strong position in the Palatinate of Podolia.[71] During the civil war of 1606–08, they provided unequivocal support for Sigismund III and actively participated in the military operations. It is therefore clear that they were in a position to take over the management of Moldavian affairs following Jan Zamoyski's death and enjoyed royal favour in doing so. This, in effect, provided them and their Moldavian clients – Constantin and the Lozonschis – with a considerable edge over the boyar opposition.

The reign of Simion Movilă constituted but a short interlude in the escalating dynastic conflict. The voivode died suddenly in September 1607, and many suspected that he was poisoned by Elizabeta to pave the way to the throne for his thirteen-year-old son.[72] The opposition did not die out but instead coalesced around the candidature of Simion's eldest son, Mihăilaş, and his mother Marghita–Melania.[73] Both candidates were of roughly the same age, further suggesting that Constantin's youth was not the central issue. Fighting broke out between supporters of each branch, resulting in Mihăilaş's victory and Constantin's escape to Poland–Lithuania, where he appealed for help to Stefan Potocki and Myxajlo Vyšnevec'kyj.[74] The king, for whom the Potockis provided much-needed support during the civil war, gave his permission to organize an expedition and provided 1,500 troops to install Constantin on the throne.[75] In December 1607, the magnates entered Moldavia and ousted Mihăilaş, bringing the Lozonschi clan back to power.[76] The ousted voivode tried to cobble up a Wallachian–Ottoman coalition to mount a counterattack, but his sudden sickness and death cut these plans short.[77]

Friends and Enemies 133

While this new round of dynastic conflict has been described as a clash between pro-Polish and pro-Ottoman tendencies within the Moldavian elite, there is little evidence to support this interpretation.[78] While the details on the factions' composition are murky, many boyars with strong ties to Poland–Lithuania threw their support in favour of Mihăilaș. For instance, Vasile Stroici, who commanded the voivode's troops, was himself a Polish *indigena* married to a noblewoman from Podolia, and it seems implausible to consider him programmatically opposed to the principality's continued association with the Commonwealth.[79] Moreover, following the defeat and subsequent demise of Mihăilaș, Marghita and Simion Movilă's remaining offspring sought refuge in Poland–Lithuania, under the protection of Field Crown *Hetman* Stanisław Żółkiewski. The latter assigned the exiles his estate in Džadyliv.[80] Therefore, the gist of the conflict were not divergent geopolitical orientations, but rather a more personal competition between opposing factional camps.

By January 1608, the cross-border Potocki–Lozonschi faction established its hegemony in the principality. With Constantin Movilă on the throne, his mother took over the management of Moldavian affairs and continued to promote her clan's interests. Potocki was also handsomely rewarded for his efforts in money and land. The voivode's maternal uncle, Vasile Lozonschi, became a particularly reviled figure.[81] According to the boyars, he roamed the countryside with an armed entourage and intimidated the local elite. In a complaint to Sigismund III, boyars claimed:

> Spoiled by the support from his kin and bad upbringing, he committed all kinds of evil deeds, fearing neither God nor honest people. He has committed many rapes, murders, and seized villages from the poor folk. He has six hundred men under his command, who are the worst riff-raff, and he persecuted the poor folk by quartering them in houses of the poor people of the principality [...]. Many senior men reproached them for his misdeeds, but he paid them no heed, hurling further insults instead. Finally, when the Bishop of Roman chastised him, Lozonschi beat him up with up with a mace, knocking out his teeth.[82]

However, the position of Lozonschi–Potocki faction in Polish–Moldavian relations was by no means uncontested, as their opponents set up a rival patronage network, supporting the dynastic claims of Simion's offspring. That the family of Mihăilaș found refuge at the court of Stanisław Żółkiewski was indicative of this process, and the *hetman* would become the focal point for Moldavian boyars trying to oust Lozonschis from power.

Żółkiewski had many reasons to throw down the gauntlet, as he was locked in a fierce struggle against the Potocki family. The latter, profiting from the king's trust, moved to curb the *hetman*'s influence at the dietines, the court and the army. With time, the hostility only escalated and eventually reached its boiling point during the Polish–Lithuanian intervention in Muscovy during the Time of Troubles (1609–11), when the Potockis openly challenged Żółkiewski's command and undermined his political position.[83] In this context, it comes as no surprise that the latter retaliated against his adversaries' political interests in Moldavia. Thus, he increasingly threw his weight in favour of Simion Movilă's offspring and boyar opposition against the Lozonschi clan (see Figure 4.1).

This parallel rivalry provided the background to a confusing episode in October 1611. Since the year's beginning, the position of Constantin Movilă began to deteriorate, and the Ottoman authorities increasingly sought to replace the voivode in favour of Ştefan Tomşa II. To counter the threat and secure Polish–Lithuanian help, two high-ranking boyars – Nestor Ureche and Costea Băcioc – were sent to alert the *Sejm* of the imminent Ottoman intervention and secure help of the Commonwealth. However, Stefan Potocki intercepted the embassy and removed

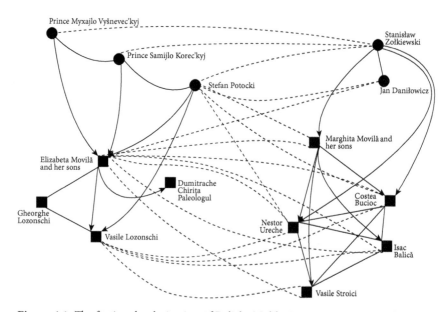

Figure 4.1 The factional polarization of Polish–Moldavian patronage networks between 1606 and 1616. Circles represent actors hailing from the Polish–Lithuanian political arena, while squares represent those active in Moldavian arena. Solid lines indicate alliances (with arrows indicating the flow of patronage), whereas dashed lines represent conflicts between the actors.

Friends and Enemies 135

from their instructions several issues he deemed undesirable. Following their arrival at the court, Ureche and Băcioc tried to reconstruct the original contents of their instructions, allowing us to analyse what the magnate tried to suppress.

As I have mentioned, some excised fragments concerned Stefan Potocki's economic interests and his seizure of land in the principality. However, most of censored content was political in nature, and the magnate's interventions made little to no sense on the surface. Most importantly, Potocki took issue with the very scope of the mission – a plea to the king to provide Movilă with troops to oppose the looming Ottoman invasion:

> A point that used to be here instructed us to request from His Majesty a powerful and mighty protector of Moldavia, and we were to demand an appointment of the Palatine of Kyiv [Stanisław Żółkiewski – M.W.]; the *Starosta* of Felin erased this point [...] Having received our instruction, we were told to insist that His Majesty and the Commonwealth send troops on the border as quickly as possible, since the threat is imminent. The *Starosta* banned us from spreading such rumours and mentioning them to the king, claiming that they are false claims invented by boyars, who want to bring the Palatine of Kyiv [to power].[84]

Potocki's act of censorship in this matter is particularly confusing and seemingly goes against the interests of his brother-in-law. Ottoman preparations to oust Constantin from Moldavia were underway, and his position had been deteriorating for a while. Less than two months later, the imperial army entered the principality and installed Ștefan Tomșa II. Thus, it would seem that Potocki's actions were self-defeating and the magnate was in denial about the imminent danger to his interests.

However, his other interventions in the text suggest that Potocki continued to support the interests of Constantin Movilă and his familial clan. Apart from official instructions, the envoys carried a set of letters from the boyars, which focused on the abuses suffered at the hands of the voivode's kinsmen. At the centre of these complaints was the behaviour of Vasile Lozonschi and his violent crimes against other members of the elite. While Elizabeta initially expressed concerns about the accusations and ordered her brother to be detained, he was forewarned by other kin and managed to evade arrest. Thus, the boyars decided to ask the king to act and mete out justice. Elizabeta, fearing for her brother's life, changed her mind and turned against Lozonschi's accusers:

> They decided to remove Ureche, Balică and Băcioc, either by poison, slander or violence. Lozonschi hired some Cossacks to kill the boyars, but they managed to intercept his letters. Moreover, the Lozonschis were afraid that Lord Palatine

[Żółkiewski] would arrive at the helm of his troops and punish Vasile. Thus, they approached the *Starosta* of Felin during the *Sejm*, pleading with him to prevent the appointment as [the protector of Moldavia]. Instead, they encouraged Potocki to assume this role himself. He agreed to these requests, even if during the princely council [in Moldavia] a decision was taken in favour of the Palatine of Kyiv. The *Starosta* thwarted these plans and falsely informed the king that no peril loomed over Moldavia, and all such news were invented by the boyars.[85]

Thus, by underplaying the Ottoman threat, Potocki acted in collusion with his Moldavian kin rather than against them. Instead of being concerned with Polish–Lithuanian influence in the principality, the *Starosta* and Lozonschis saw the rival boyar faction and the prospective assignment of Żółkiewski to Moldavia as greater threats to their interests than the Ottomans, going as far as to deny the plans of the Sublime Porte. Factional politics were thus a far greater concern than regional geopolitics.

Other details surrounding the mission are similarly puzzling. The crucial task of securing Polish–Lithuanian support was entrusted to Nestor Ureche and Costea Băcioc, two boyars that the Lozonschis tried to kill. Both, along with Isac Balică, were among the wealthiest members of the Moldavian elite and crucial figures within the Movilăs' familial–political system.[86] At the same time, the proposal to request Stanisław Żółkiewski's appointment had been agreed upon at Constantin Movilă's princely council, despite subsequent attempts by the voivode and his kin to prevent it from happening. Thus, rather than a unified front on the eve of Ottoman invasion, the Moldavian elite sent contradictory messages that ultimately cost Movilă his throne.

The insistence of boyars to appoint the *hetman* as the 'protector of Moldavia' and the Lozonschis' vehement, albeit clandestine, opposition show that the dispute was not limited to Moldavian politics. The relative stability of Constantin Movilă's reign had allowed the Lozonschis, in cahoots with Stefan Potocki, to establish their hegemony and suppress boyar dissent. However, by 1611 their grip on power weakened and Constantin could no longer afford to alienate the opposition. Thus, the original contents of the instructions should be read as a lip service paid to boyar demands, who saw the appointment of Żółkiewski, the redress of abuses and the appointment of Ureche and Băcioc as a way to break the stranglehold of Lozonschi–Potocki faction. However, the voivode and his clan, although forced declare their support for the demands, were unwilling to relinquish their positions and tried to prevent the grievances from reaching the king, enlisting the help of Stefan Potocki.

Friends and Enemies   137

While the documents leave out Żółkiewski's direct involvement with the opposition, the *hetman* seems to have cooperated with the boyars behind the scenes. He undoubtedly had a political interest in gaining control over Moldavian affairs and reducing the political clout of his sworn enemy. The most important piece of information regarding his role in the conflict is the participation of Hieronim Otwinowski, a distinguished diplomat with considerable expertise in Ottoman affairs. Along with his service to the Commonwealth, he was also Żółkiewski's client, deeply involved in the *hetman's* political designs for Moldavia. According to the boyars, it was Otwinowski who informed Żółkiewski of their arrest and the seizure of letters, who in turn passed the news to the king.[87]

The whole dispute over instructions became moot less than two months later when Constantin Movilă was forced to flee the principality to his exile in Poland–Lithuania. Despite this setback, the conflict did not abate in the following years but escalated further. While Polish scholarship generally depicts Żółkiewski as a selfless statesman in contrast to his adventurist adversaries, this does not seem to be the case.[88] The evidence suggests that he was not against restoring the Movilăs to power by force of arms; instead, his main concern was to promote his own client to the throne and prevent Constantin Movilă's in-laws from succeeding in their plans.

This attitude materialized the following year when Stefan Potocki undertook the first attempt to oust Ștefan Tomșa and restore his brother-in-law to power. Much to Żółkiewski's chagrin, who preferred to see his own candidate, Gavril, Potocki secured Sigismund III's tacit support and participation of royal troops in the planned invasion. In his capacity as the *hetman*, Żółkiewski found himself forced to participate in the preparations, but clashed repeatedly with the magnate and continued to criticize him in the letters to his allies.[89] The campaign ended in a crushing defeat at the battle of Cornul lui Sas (July 1612): Constantin Movilă perished trying to flee the battlefield, while Potocki was taken captive and transported to Istanbul.[90] Following the battle, Żółkiewski refused to provide any assistance to defeated troops, and instead opted to conclude a treaty with victorious Tomșa. While his behaviour has been interpreted in terms of the *hetman's* unwillingness to risk a conflict with the Porte, it seems that Żółkiewski actually welcomed Potocki's defeat. His supporters at the first *Sejm* of 1613 opposed any proposals to ransom the captive magnate, and Żółkiewski himself and his Moldavian allies tried to promote the *hetman's* protégé, Gavril Movilă, as the new voivode of Moldavia.[91]

The final showdown between the two factions took place in 1615. In summer, a large-scale boyar revolt broke out in Moldavia, with the rebels seeking to

138   *The Ottomans and Eastern Europe*

oust the incumbent Ștefan Tomșa. The outbreak was quickly suppressed, but it put onto display the voivode's widespread unpopularity among the elite and rekindled the hopes of Elizabeta Movilă to regain the throne for her offspring. She enlisted the help of Princes Myxajlo Vyšnevec'kyj and Samijlo Korec'kyj, who mobilized an army of around 12,000 people, and in November 1615 led their men into the principality and installed Alexandru Movilă, Ieremia's second son, as the new ruler.[92] However, the reception they received from the boyars was lukewarm at best, as many would rather see Gavril Movilă as their new voivode.[93] Although Vyšnevec'kyj died two months into the campaign, allegedly killed by an Orthodox priest who gave him a poisoned communion bread, Korec'kyj managed to hold out until August before being forced to surrender to Ottoman troops.

The campaign was not sanctioned by the king, but the princes' initial success won them considerable support among the nobility. Żółkiewski in turn, from the outset adopted a hostile attitude, denying them any military support and even preventing private reinforcements to cross over to Moldavia.[94] At the same time, he tried to sway the public opinion against the venture, depicting the campaign as a result of Elizabeta's scheming and even as divine punishment:

> I hoped that we could enjoy some peace, but as God's punishment for our sins a new conflagration has broken out because of Elizabeta, late Ieremia's widow, and others, who assist her in her plans. Upon hearing about a revolt in Moldavia, she began to conspire to put her son, named Alexandru, a child of ten or eleven years, on the throne, and she recruited, along with her friends, a great number of men of the worst riff-raff.[95]

Żółkiewski's allies followed suit. Jan Daniłowicz, the palatine of Ruthenia, issued a number of circular letters to the local nobility presenting the soldiers fighting in Moldavia as good-for-nothings and emphasizing the destruction they caused in the Commonwealth.[96] At the same time, the *hetman* himself insisted that supporting Alexandru Movilă would lead to the annexation of the principality by the Ottomans.[97] However, this propagandistic effort failed to convince everyone, and the dietine of Halyč, bordering with Moldavia, cautiously praised the princes' military exploits.[98] Similarly, at the *Sejm* of 1616, many deputies lambasted the *hetman* for his unwillingness to support Korec'kyj's troops.

Apart from trying to derail the princes' campaign, Żółkiewski had his own designs regarding Moldavia, mobilizing his clients to secure the throne for Gavril Movilă. Rumours circulated that the *hetman* was preparing his own military expedition to install his protégé.[99] The pretender and his mother Marghita were

Friends and Enemies   139

sent to Istanbul along with Hieronim Otwinowski. Although the latter's mission was to prevent further Ottoman involvement, Korec'kyj's agents explicitly called him 'the *Hetman*'s creature and a schemer on behalf of Marghita'.[100] While most scholars interpreted Żółkiewski's actions as driven by state interests, this was not how contemporaries saw them.[101] Many considered that, by withholding any assistance to Korec'kyj, the magnate's main goal was to sabotage Alexandru Movilă and clear the way for Gavril:

> [Korec'kyj's actions] were inconvenient for the *Hetman* for two personal reasons, although they were good and very beneficial for our Commonwealth; if only the king offered his support and made an effort at the Porte, the Turkish emperor would have agreed for Movilă's offspring to ascend the Moldavian throne [...] Two following motives led the *Hetman* to undermine the princes. First, he was concerned about their good fortune; second, he has always been concerned about the profits he drew from Moldavia and hoped to secure even more when, after having caused the princes' defeat, he would install Gavril, whom he kept at his court.[102]

Żółkiewski and Daniłowicz tried to justify their actions, claiming that they could not act without permission of the king and the *Sejm*.[103] However, they largely failed to convince their opponents, especially when Żółkiewski publicly reiterated his support for Gavril's candidacy, thus indirectly confirming the accusations.[104]

Despite mounting criticism, the *hetman* continued to support his client and his diplomatic effort seemed to succeed. The Dutch ambassador in Istanbul took notice of Gavril's arrival to the imperial capital and expected his upcoming appointment to the throne.[105] However, the appointment did not take place, and it was only in 1618 when the pretender managed to become the voivode of Wallachia for an ephemeral reign of less than two years. From the principality, Gavril dispatched a letter, thanking his long-time patron for his support, but this did not change the fact that Żółkiewski's decade-long struggle for Moldavia failed to produce results the magnate hoped for.[106]

While he managed to derail the plans of his opponents and even promote Gavril to the position of power, Żółkiewski's partial victory came at a considerable cost. After a daring escape from Yedikule and swashbuckling adventures on the way back to the Commonwealth Korec'kyj became a popular hero for many nobles[107]; in turn, the *hetman* was widely blamed for the failure of 1615–16 campaign, which continued to plague him until his death in 1620. His authority among the magnates and in the army collapsed, as his command was constantly challenged by his subordinates. In 1618, a campaign against Tatar raiders ended in an embarrassing defeat, when commanders refused to follow Żółkiewski's orders and join his camp. This debacle drew a new wave of criticism against the octogenarian magnate accused of incompetence and senility.[108]

In a way, the conflict between Żółkiewski and Korec'kyj eventually led to the death of both, when the Crown army – this time in an official capacity – intervened in Moldavia in 1620. As scholars argue, the campaign, conceived as a pre-emptive strike against the Ottomans, was planned by Żółkiewski to restore the authority and prestige he had lost in 1616.[109] However, the campaign was plagued by constant squabbles and poor discipline, which led to a defeat in the battle of Țuțora, and the annihilation of the Polish army during its retreat north. Żółkiewski perished on the battlefield, while his second-in-command Stanisław Koniecpolski and Samijlo Korec'kyj fell into Ottoman hands. Koniecpolski eventually returned to Poland–Lithuania in 1623, but Korec'kyj did not survive his second imprisonment at Yedikule, strangled on the grand vizier's orders.

In her analysis of the 1615–16 campaign, Ilona Czamańska challenged the line of thought that saw the magnates' intervention as irresponsible adventurism, bringing attention to the rivalry between the Movilăs as a driving force behind the factional conflict.[110] However, the dynastic conflict was merely a piece of a larger puzzle that spanned Polish–Lithuanian and Moldavian political arenas. The deaths of Jan Zamoyski and Ieremia Movilă in 1605–06 created a political vacuum at the core of their cross-border network and triggered a prolonged competition for their political legacy. This rivalry eventually caused the faction to break up into distinct segments vying for power and resources in both Poland–Lithuania and Moldavia. However, instead of fragmenting along the boundaries of arenas, this decomposition ran across them. From the ashes of the Zamoyski–Movilă faction rose two cross-border patronage networks pitted against one another, supporting different members of the Movilă dynasty.

The rivalry between the Potocki–Lozonschi faction and their opponents eventually led to the collapse of Polish–Lithuanian influence in Moldavia but had little to do with geopolitical concerns. There seems to have been no ideological difference between either of the factions, and there is no evidence that backers of Simion and Mihăilaş were in any way more pro-Ottoman than members of the Lozonschi clan. Żółkiewski did not hesitate to conduct his own negotiations with the Porte, while at the same time trying to derail his political rivals' military campaign. Eventually, these events produced major geopolitical consequences and allowed the Porte to reassert its control over the principality, but these considerations played only a small role in the actions of those involved, taking a back seat to factional tug-of-war.

Köprülüs and Cantacuzinos

By the time of Köprülü Mehmed Pasha's appointment to the grand vizierate in September 1656, the Ottoman fortunes seemed to reach their nadir. The war against Venice for the island of Crete, begun in 1645, did not go as planned, and the loss of Bozcaada to the *Serenissima* constituted not only a strategic setback but also a profound embarrassment. The situation in the imperial capital was similarly grim: religious and political unrest engulfed Istanbul, while the Ottoman establishment itself was torn apart by the factional struggle that reached new heights, with grand viziers nominated and dismissed in quick succession. In effect, reinvigorating the institution increasingly became the proposed solution and a way out of the crisis.[111] This trend materialized in the appointment of the vigorous octogenarian Köprülü Mehmed Pasha and a strong mandate he received from Sultan Mehmed IV and his mother Hatice Turhan to restore order and suppress the opposition. In the following years, the grand vizier successfully cracked down on the opposition, broke the Venetian stranglehold on the Dardanelles and brought provincial powerholders back in line.[112] Mehmed Pasha's accomplishments allowed his son, Köprülüzade Fazıl Ahmed Pasha to succeed his father at the apex of Ottoman hierarchy and provided him with unprecedented security at the office, which he held until his death in 1676.

The 'Köprülü Restoration' (1656–83) was often depicted in historiography as a last-ditch effort to restore the Ottoman glory days of Süleyman's reign. However, these similarities were largely superficial. There was no return to the patrimonial and autocratic sultanate of the early sixteenth century. Unable to stabilize the political scene, the sultanic household effectively empowered one of the grandee *kapıs*, allowing it to take over the administrative apparatus and govern on the dynasty's behalf.[113] While the reign of Mehmed IV also saw the revival of the sultan's image as a mobile and active *ghazi*, aimed at restoring the prestige of the sultanate, it did not translate into the sphere of actual decision-making, controlled by the Köprülüs.[114] Thus, rather than a restoration of 'classical' institutions, the second half of the seventeenth century saw a negotiated surrender of the Ottoman ruler to the imperial grandees.

Upon taking over the reins of power in 1661, Köprülüzade Ahmed Pasha inherited a faction firmly entrenched at the apex of the political arena. His closest associate and brother-in-law, Merzifonlu Kara Mustafa Pasha became the grand admiral, while other members of the faction took over posts across the empire. Mehmed Pasha's purge of administration and the repressions following

142   *The Ottomans and Eastern Europe*

the Abaza Hasan Pasha revolt of 1658 crippled the opposition and decimated the ranks of potential challengers. This factional takeover extended to the Danubian principalities where, as I have shown in Chapter 2, Köprülü Mehmed Pasha appointed his fellow Albanians from the Ghica and Lupu families. Thus, one would expect that this hegemony would put an end to factional infighting that marred the Ottoman Empire in the precedent decade. In effect, the succession of three grand viziers – Köprülü Mehmed Pasha, Ahmed Pasha and Merzifonlu Kara Mustafa Pasha – has usually been depicted as harmonious and unproblematic.[115] However, when we look at this long period of factional dominance from the perspective of the Danubian principalities, we can see that cooperation within the household was not as smooth as one would expect. While the Köprülüs and their Moldavian–Wallachian clients successfully marginalized other groups, the internal rivalry between cliques created tensions within the faction. Although these conflicts never led to full-scale breakup of the network, they still had an impact on the political developments of the period.

The first cracks within the cross-border patronage system began to appear as early as the grand vizierate of Köprülü Mehmed Pasha. While the grandee managed to install his Albanian clients on both thrones, he failed to satisfy all expectations. In late 1659, Moldavian ruler Gheorghe Ghica was transferred to Wallachia to make room for Vasile Lupu's son, Ştefaniţă. According to Dimitrios Ramadanis, the voivode was reluctant to accept the change and conceded only at the behest of other members of the faction.[116] This new reshuffling did not account for the ambitions of Gheorghe's son, Grigore. Already in his thirties, the *beyzade* grew impatient and tried to secure the throne for himself. However, by late 1659 there was little room left for manoeuvre, as both thrones were already filled by the grand vizier's clients. Thus, to secure the coveted appointment, Grigore had no choice but to unseat one of the incumbents.

Ghica's ambitions disconcerted other members of the faction. By early 1660, Vasile Lupu, who represented the interests of his son in Istanbul, suspected Grigore of trying to replace Ştefaniţă in Moldavia.[117] Grigore vehemently denied the allegations and the conflict fizzled out soon. In turn, the ambitious *beyzade* shifted his attention, aiming to replace his father as the voivode of Wallachia. As I have mentioned earlier, to accomplish that, he enlisted support of *Postelnic* Constantin Cantacuzino and Grand Dragoman Panagiotis Nikoussios. Albeit Köprülü Mehmed Pasha had doubts concerning the voivode's removal, this new coalition proved sufficient to effectuate the change. In September 1660 Gheorghe was detained and transported to Istanbul, while his son took over as the new ruler in Bucharest.[118] However, the period of former voivode's disgrace was relatively brief, and he lived out his days in Istanbul, acting as Grigore's *capuchehaia*. Thus, Grigore's political ambitions created tensions within the network but ultimately failed to produce a lasting rupture.

He was not the only member of the faction to pursue his own political ambitions. Gheorghe Ghica's dismissal also marked the first foray by Kara Mustafa Pasha into Moldavian–Wallachian affairs. A son of Anatolian *sipahi* from the vicinity of Köprü, Mustafa Pasha grew up in Köprülü Mehmed Pasha's household and became the family's most important client, eventually succeeding Ahmed Pasha as the grand vizier. In his capacity as the *beylerbey* of Özü he arrived in Bucharest to install Gheorghe Ghica, but his sojourn in the city produced a lasting political bond. As I have mentioned, Şerban Cantacuzino offered him a fine horse, a gift that the grandee clearly appreciated.[119]

The patron–client relationship between Kara Mustafa Pasha and the boyar family was thus established, and their actions frequently put them at odds with other members of the faction. In contrast to his friendly attitude towards Cantacuzinos, Mustafa Pasha seemed to have clashed with other clients of the family. In March 1661, the grandee raided the Moldavian town of Galați and imprisoned three members of Ştefaniță Lupu's council. The boyars were released only after the direct intervention of Köprülü Mehmed Pasha.[120] While we are unable to determine the cause of the conflict, in the following years a pattern of Mustafa Pasha's disruptive behaviour exacerbated tensions within the faction.

The same year saw a series of changes in the faction, as the 'old guard' gradually passed away. This shift – which I have discussed in Chapter 2 – marked a restructuring of the networks and it was clear that the new generation took over.[121] Köprülüzade Ahmed Pasha succeeded his father as the grand vizier, and Kara Mustafa Pasha was promoted to the post of grand admiral. At the same time, Grand Dragoman Panagiotis Nikoussios assumed the crucial role of a broker between the imperial and Moldavian–Wallachian political arenas.[122] The transition was smooth, but it also carried the risk of conflict in the future between the household head and his second-in-command. When he was taking over the reins of power, Ahmed Pasha was only twenty-seven years old and it seemed likely that he would remain at the helm of the household and administration for decades. For ambitious Kara Mustafa Pasha, who was of almost the same age, this reduced his chances of ascending to the grand vizierate, which he coveted. Moreover, time worked against him, increasing the likelihood of Ahmed Pasha being succeeded by his younger sibling. Although loyal to the household, Kara Mustafa Pasha clearly tried to position himself as the heir apparent and establish his power base by promoting clients to administrative postings.[123]

Köprülü Ahmed Pasha's involvement in the war against Venice and the active lifestyle of Sultan Mehmed IV provided Mustafa Pasha with an opportunity to extend his reach. To remedy the difficulties created by the mobility of the sultanic court and Ahmed Pasha's presence at the front, top administrative offices underwent reorganization. Apart from Istanbul-based *kaymakam*, the Deputy of the Imperial Stirrup (*rikab-ı hümayun kaymakamı*) was to accompany the sultan during his hunting trips and acting as the liaison with the imperial administration. The office, held by Kara Mustafa Pasha, took precedence over its counterpart in the capital and allowed him to exercise considerable political influence.[124] The grandee was eager to benefit from his position, which increasingly led to breakdowns of communication and clashes with Köprülüzade Ahmed Pasha.[125]

The pattern of Kara Mustafa Pasha acting on his own and clashing with other members of the faction became particularly acute in the case of the Danubian principalities. This was prompted by the collapse of an alliance between Grigore Ghica and the Cantacuzinos in Wallachia. The voivode, who enjoyed the support of the grand vizier and Nikoussios, increasingly resented the influence of the boyar family and sided with their enemies among the Wallachian elite.[126] The matters came to a head when Ghica's allies imprisoned *Postelnic* Constantin Cantacuzino in the monastery of Snagov and killed him on 30 December 1663.[127] A full-scale campaign of repressions against his kin ensued, and the family had to seek refuge in the Ottoman Empire. Şerban Cantacuzino, who took over the leadership of the faction, stayed at the palace of Kara Mustafa Pasha, demonstrating that the *kaymakam* decided to support the family against the voivode.[128]

The conflict with Cantacuzinos and the support the latter enjoyed at the Porte clearly weakened Grigore Ghica's position and made him more inclined to seek rapprochement with the Habsburgs during the 1663–4 war.[129] During the campaign of 1664, the Wallachian and Moldavian forces were put under the command of the *beylerbey* of Buda, Hüseyin Pasha, who undertook the siege of Lewenz (modern Levice in Slovakia). However, during the fight the Wallachian troops retreated from the battlefield, contributing to the Ottoman defeat.[130] Blamed for the military setback and accused of conspiring with the Habsburg generals, Ghica failed to meet with the grand vizier and fled through Hungary to Vienna and subsequently to Venice.[131] Nonetheless, the Porte's response to this defection was surprisingly lenient. Panagiotis Nikoussios continued to support the voivode, while Ahmed Pasha himself issued explicit orders that Gheorghe Ghica was not to be harmed for his son's actions.[132] Moldavian ruler

Friends and Enemies 145

Istratie Dabija, whose troops had also abandoned Ottomans during the battle of Lewenz, received the grand vizier's pardon and retained the throne.[133] Ghica's flight seemed to mark yet another clash between Ahmed Pasha and Kara Mustafa. Whereas anti-Cantacuzino boyars hoped to secure the nomination for their candidate Dumitrașco Buzăianul, the *kaymakam* swiftly appointed Radu Leon, more sympathetic to the Cantacuzinos.[134] The decision was not consulted with Ahmed Pasha, drawing the grand vizier's ire.[135]

Mere two years later, the pattern repeated itself with regard to the Moldavian throne. In 1666, the incumbent voivode, Gheorghe Duca, sent a letter to the Crimean khan Mehmed Giray IV (1654–66), allegedly calling him *padişah* and implying his willingness to rebel against the Ottomans. As Moldavian sources inform us, he acted on behalf of the grand vizier, who doubted the khan's loyalty and instructed Duca to verify his suspicions.[136] However, the letters were intercepted by Ottoman authorities and sent to the sultan and Kara Mustafa Pasha. The latter, 'being an enemy of Duca' immediately replaced the voivode with Iliaș Alexandru (1666–8), while also ordering the execution of the deposed ruler. Only when Köprülü Ahmed Pasha stepped in and vouched for his client the execution order was rescinded.[137] The following year, Kara Mustafa Pasha installed Antonie of Popești as the voivode of Wallachia, effectively handing over the control of the principality to his Cantacuzino clients.[138]

As Özgün Yoldaşlar rightly pointed out, the tripartite division of power between the grand vizier and his two deputies, necessitated by the peripatetic sultan's hunting trips and the war against Venice put a strain on the decision-making process and political communication between different centres of power. The grand vizier was repeatedly caught off guard by the decisions taken by Kara Mustafa Pasha, and bringing Mehmed IV along for the Kam'janec' campaign in 1672 likely aimed to hold the administration together.[139] However, the recurrent pattern of disputes between Ahmed Pasha and his second-in-command over appointments in the Danubian principalities suggests that they were not only the result of misunderstandings. Kara Mustafa Pasha's consistent support for the Cantacuzinos and his hostility towards Duca and Ghica – clients of the grand vizier and grand dragoman – suggests that the grandee tried to profit from their patrons' absence to extend his patronage network. It is likely this intra-factional competition had fuelled rumours that the *kaymakam* was plotting against the grand vizier.[140]

Ahmed Pasha's actions following his return from Crete confirm this hypothesis. The restriction of Kara Mustafa Pasha's authority and a purge of his key clients were clearly meant as a warning to the ambitious grandee.[141] At

146 *The Ottomans and Eastern Europe*

the same time, Köprülü reversed the pro-Cantacuzino policy in the Danubian principalities. Encouraged by Nikoussios, he summoned Grigore Ghica from Venice.[142] When in 1672 the Cantacuzinos tried to secure the appointment of their partisan Gheorghe Drugănescu to succeed ineffectual Antonie of Popeşti, the grand vizier allegedly responded that 'if you want a stronger ruler, I will give you one with an iron fist' and nominated their sworn enemy, Ghica, as the new voivode.[143] Repressions against the Cantacuzinos ensued. The boyars were thrown into prison in Edirne, with Şerban the only one to evade capture. However, despite Kara Mustafa Pasha's efforts to rehabilitate his clients, Şerban and his closest associates were apprehended and temporarily exiled to Crete.[144] At the same time, Ahmed Pasha went to great lengths to back Grigore Ghica and Gheorghe Duca. In November 1673, when the defection of Wallachian troops contributed to a major Ottoman setback at Hotin, Ahmed Pasha readily accepted the voivode's explanations shifting the blame to Sarı Hüseyin Pasha's inept strategy and his rude treatment of Moldavian and Wallachian rulers.[145]

While by 1672 the fortunes of Kara Mustafa Pasha and the Cantacuzinos reached their all-time low, they were able to recoup their losses in the following years. Köprülüzade Ahmed Pasha's deteriorating health and the close relationship Mustafa Pasha had with Mehmed IV allowed him to rebuild his position within the administration. The prospect of Kara Mustafa Pasha's upcoming nomination to the grand vizierate caused the members of Köprülü faction to rally around him and helps to explain the continuity at the top of administrative–factional structure.[146] His assertion of control seems to have been facilitated by the passing away of Panagiotis Nikoussios, whose support for Grigore Ghica clashed with Kara Mustafa Pasha's interests.[147] At the same time, the Cantacuzinos' marital alliance with Gheorghe Duca and his appointment to the Wallachian throne in 1673 allowed the family to restore their political influence in the principality.[148] Köprülü Ahmed Pasha's death in November 1676 thus paved the way for Kara Mustafa Pasha and his allies to take control of both the Sublime Porte and the Danubian principalities. Emboldened by the promotion of their patron, the Cantacuzinos came under suspicion of trying to unseat Duca. The voivode responded by arresting members of the family, but he was forced to release them on the orders of the grand vizier.[149] Finally, in 1678 he was transferred to Moldavia, while the vacant throne was taken by Şerban Cantacuzino (1678–88), thus consolidating the position his family had achieved thanks to their alliance with the Ottoman grandee.

Unlike other factional disputes discussed in this chapter, the competition within Köprülüs' cross-border network did not produce a lasting rupture.

Friends and Enemies 147

However, this does not mean that it did not have larger ramifications. Rather than a homogeneous group acting in unison, even the most successful grandee household of the seventeenth century suffered from infighting between different cliques within their ranks, which extended beyond a single political arena. In supporting his clients in Moldavia and Wallachia, Kara Mustafa Pasha's interests clashed with those of Köprülü Ahmed Pasha, souring the relationship between them and creating an impression of a somewhat chaotic and contradictory policy. This rivalry at the apex of Ottoman hierarchy was exacerbated by the ongoing factional conflict in Wallachia, which pitted the grand vizier's clients against the powerful Cantacuzino family. In supporting their own men, Ahmed Pasha, Kara Mustafa Pasha and Panagiotis Nikoussios were ready to overlook serious issues, such as Grigore Ghica's defections from the battlefield and the resulting Ottoman defeats in major battles.

While different in details, the cases of cross-border factional conflicts discussed above follow the same underlying logic. Rather than selflessly pursuing what historians would interpret as a state interest, Ottoman, Polish–Lithuanian and Moldavian–Wallachian elites were deeply involved in factional struggles and ready to aid their partners beyond the pale. These factional interests were not necessarily disruptive: for instance, the Köprülüs' takeover of Ottoman administration aligned the interests of the household with those of the empire, improving coordination between different officials and reinvigorating military power of the Porte. Even in such instances, though, factional competition took priority over geopolitical concerns. This manifested most patently in the very survival of the Danubian principalities and the failure of Ottoman and Polish–Lithuanian annexation attempts in the seventeenth century.

5

Annexing Moldavia

That the Ottomans never conquered Moldavia and Wallachia has long been an axiom in Romanian historiography, and a matter of national pride.[1] Scholars repeatedly emphasized the distinct position of the Danubian principalities, arguing that the absence of direct imperial administration, *kadi* courts and mosques adorning the landscape placed the principalities outside the imperial space. Generations of scholars implied that this status of autonomy originated from 'capitulations' (*'ahdname*s) that the local elites had managed to wrest from the Porte, which spelled out their privileges and obligations as Ottoman tributaries.[2]

However, for such crucial documents, the purported capitulations have proven extremely elusive. The documents presented by Moldavian–Wallachian boyars to substantiate their claims during the Russian–Ottoman peace negotiations at Focşani in 1772, considered authentic by nineteenth-century historians, were debunked by Constantin Giurescu as forgeries compiled from several sources and tailored to suit the interests of the local elite.[3] This gave a renewed impulse for scholars to engage in a veritable hunt for capitulations in the Ottoman and European archives, but these efforts garnered relatively meagre results. Thus, in order to salvage the concept that the Ottomans recognized Moldavian and Wallachian status as separate states, historians argued that the diplomas of appointment (*berat*s) issued for the voivodes were in fact *'ahdname*s in disguise.[4] However, these documents fall short of providing a legal basis for the proposed distinct status of the Danubian principalities; instead, they demonstrate the composite character of Ottoman imperial governance.[5]

Research conducted by Viorel Panaite in recent decades changed the parameters of the discussion. Approaching Moldavia and Wallachia from the perspective of the Islamic *ius gentium*, he demonstrated the role of Hanafi legal theory and customary practices as the principal source of the arrangements between the Porte and the tributary princes. The Ottoman sultans considered both principalities an integral part of the 'well-protected domains', and insisted that the voivodes were their officials just like any other governor.[6] The status of the Danubian principalities relied on customary arrangements and evolved along with the balance of power between the voivodes and the Sublime Porte. No privileges or treaties fixed the juridical status of Moldavia and Wallachia in the long term, and the inhabitants of both principalities enjoyed a status similar to other *zimmis* inhabiting the Ottoman domains.[7]

This well-substantiated revisionist argument constitutes a welcome change in the debate, shifting the focus away from the largely futile search for '*ahdnames* and placing the status of the principalities within the wider context of Islamic legal theory and Ottoman practice. However, another important question remains: If the Danubian principalities were conquered by the Sublime Porte by the mid-sixteenth century, why did the latter never introduce direct imperial administration, instead relying only on local political institutions? Using Halil İnalcık's schematic model of the 'Ottoman methods of conquest', why was the first phase – forcing local rulers into submission – never followed by the second, the establishment of Ottoman provincial system of governance?[8]

Surprisingly for such a central topic for Moldavian and Wallachian history, few contributions directly addressed the issue directly. Particularly important in this respect is a thesis put forward by Petre P. Panaitescu in his 1947 study 'Why Did the Turks Never Conquer the Romanian Countries?'[9] The subsequent career of this contribution is somewhat puzzling. Panaitescu himself was a contradictory personality, whose established reputation as a rigorous and sober scholar of the Middle Ages and a specialist in Slavonic philology coincided with his active participation in the ultranationalist Iron Guard. The study itself was conceived as a historical essay only seven pages long, rather than an in-depth study of the topic. Nonetheless, it became the central point of reference for future generations of Romanian historians.

In his argument, Panaitescu went against the majority opinion that had attributed the survival of the Danubian principalities to their military effort. Instead, he proposed an explanation that took into account two major factors. First, the geographical position of Moldavia and Wallachia was peripheral to the grand strategy of the Ottoman Empire in Europe and its main axis of expansion towards Central Europe.[10] This off-centre position discouraged imperial authorities from spending military and financial resources on establishing direct control in the region; instead, by retaining local rulers and institutions, the Porte secured a bulwark against Poland–Lithuania and Muscovy without having to foot the bill. The second major factor was the profitability of existing arrangements and the superior efficiency of Romanian administration over the Ottoman one. However, his argument in this regard is a testimony to the climate of the 1930s and 1940s, mixing essentialism, Orientalist stereotypes and racial overtones:

> The Ottoman conquest and rule led to the complete exhaustion of the wealth of conquered provinces; it was exploitation, not management. The Turks never possessed the qualities of settlers or managers of economic affairs. [...] Ottoman sultans and the leaders of the empire were aware of this fact. They knew that if they had sent a pasha to Moldavia and Wallachia, the corrupt and dishonest Ottoman officials would soon cause the resources to dry up, scatter the wealth, and oppress to the local population. [...] Thus, it was in the interest of the empire to ensure that its breadbasket, without which the capital and the army would starve to death, was well-run, and this could be achieved only under Romanian administration.[11]

Obviously, Panaitescu's vision of Ottoman agricultural and administrative incompetence and the inherent superiority of Romanian skills in these areas is untenable and belongs to the history of historiography rather than current historical debates. However, for all the obsolescence of his argument, the connection Panaitescu drew between financial interests of the Porte and the continued existence of Moldavian–Wallachian institutions merits attention, even if its gist must be sought elsewhere.

Unfortunately, few attempts have been made in the following years to revise Panaitescu's arguments. The most encompassing alternative was put forward by Mihai Maxim, who shifted the focus back to geopolitical and military factors. According to the Romanian Ottomanist, Moldavia and Wallachia's position was not peripheral to the Ottoman expansion but should be considered as important as the route to Vienna.[12] Thus, it was rather the armed resistance of the voivodes and the geopolitical configuration in the region that discouraged the Porte from establishing direct control in the principalities. At the same time, he softens Panaitescu's argument of an alleged Ottoman administrative incompetence, arguing that the corruption engulfed the Porte only when it entered a period of decline. Rather, the system of indirect rule was profitable because the Ottomans were able to outsource administrative and military costs, thus reducing the expenditure of the imperial treasury.

Maxim envisioned his argument as a corrective to Panaitescu's arguments. However, his argument falls short of providing a plausible explanation for the survival of Moldavian and Wallachian political institutions. The number of military campaigns led by the sultans in the region, cited as the main argument for the Danubian principalities' importance in the Ottoman grand strategy, does not take into account the changing nature of Ottoman warfare and the changing position of the ruler within the system.[13] More importantly, there seems to have been no concerted effort by the Porte to do away with the principalities. Throughout the seventeenth century, there was a single attempt to introduce direct Ottoman administration. However, even this attempt, undertaken in direct response to the revolt of November 1594 in exceptional circumstances in the midst of the 'Long War' against the Habsburgs (1593–1606) and *celali* rebellions in Anatolia, was quickly abandoned. Throughout the seventeenth century, rumours of impending annexation spread among contemporaries on numerous occasions but there is no evidence that the Porte made any serious attempt to carry them through, despite far more favourable geopolitical situation and its military capacity to quash potential resistance.

The Porte was not the only one to attempt incorporation of the Danubian principalities; similar projects circulated among the Polish–Lithuanian nobility. They were put into motion on two separate occasions, but – just like the Ottoman ones – ended without reaching their goals. At the beginning of the period under discussion, Jan Zamoyski led two military interventions in direct competition with a parallel Ottoman effort. While he succeeded in installing his clients in Moldavia and Wallachia, he failed in his attempts to secure their integration into the Commonwealth. Decades later, the Danubian principalities became a target of King John III Sobieski's dynastic plans, but with even more modest results.

These abortive attempts have been usually explained through the prism of geopolitics and the relative balance of power between states in the region. However, this approach ignores that at no point the elites acted in unison to realize such ventures. On the contrary, it seems that Ottoman grandees and their Polish–Lithuanian counterparts engaged more in factional strife than in carrying through campaign objectives. In effect, these attempts to redraw the political map of the region fell apart, defeated by internal conflict rather than enemy forces. In all these failed attempts, cross-border patronage played a prominent role. On the one hand, by strengthening ties between the arenas, it weakened the bonds within them, making it more difficult to enforce cohesion during such ventures. At the same time, as a mechanism of resource procurement, it provided a viable alternative to territorial expansion for members of the elite. Finally, the attempts at a radical restructuring of political environment upset the status quo and produced winners and losers, pitting members of the same faction against each other. As a result, while facilitating coordination between the arenas, the web of cross-border patronage acted as a check on any attempts to integrate them.

Annexing Moldavia 153

Voyvodalık/Beylerbeylik

If we believe the diplomatic correspondence of the period, the perspective of replacing the Danubian principalities with provincial administration loomed large throughout the seventeenth century. Rumours of imminent appointment of *beylerbeys* circulated with astonishing frequency.[14] Scholars have shared the view that the existence of the two 'statelets' (*devletçikler*) was hanging by a thread and their survival throughout the early modern period was the product of skilful diplomatic effort and geopolitical configuration.[15]

What is surprising, however, is the discrepancy between the ubiquity of such rumours and the lack of hard evidence to indicate the Porte's resolve to implement the plan. Even when the Ottoman officials enjoyed near liberty to rearrange political relations in the region, no steps were taken in this respect. For instance, in 1660 Grand Vizier Köprülü Mehmed Pasha allegedly toyed with the idea of replacing Gheorghe Ghica with an Ottoman official, but was quickly dissuaded from doing so.[16] Fear of military resistance does not seem to be the issue; mere two years earlier, Ottoman troops were able to oust both voivodes and the prince of Transylvania while waging war against Venice and dealing with Abaza Hasan Pasha's rebellion in Anatolia. Thus, despite military superiority, the Ottoman authorities showed time and again their preference for cross-border patronage and reluctance to transform the principalities into *eyalets*.

To understand this conservative approach, we should turn to the single instance, when the Porte did try to introduce direct provincial administration. Revisiting this abortive venture of 1595 sheds light on the inherent limitations Ottoman grandees encountered while trying to restructure the relationship between the imperial centre and Moldavian–Wallachian periphery. Undertaken in the midst of the war against the Habsburgs, the project was shelved after a single campaign. The internal struggle for power between factions was just as instrumental in derailing the project as was the rebel voivodes' military resistance.

In 1593, border skirmishes between Habsburg and Ottoman troops on the Croatian border escalated into a full-scale war, dragging both empires into a thirteen-year-long and ultimately inconclusive struggle. The following year the Porte received another blow, when Transylvanian prince Zsigmond Báthory sided with Habsburg troops, soon followed by the voivodes of Moldavia and Wallachia, Aron (1591–2 and 1592–5) and Michael the Brave (1593–1601). The revolt caught the Porte off-guard, compounding to the already difficult military situation on the front.

The rebellion was also a personal embarrassment for the incumbent grand vizier, Koca Sinan Pasha, who had appointed Michael the Brave back in September 1593.[17] The grandee, already in his seventies, was an influential figure with a distinguished career and extensive power base. After rising through the ranks, he joined the faction of Sokollu Mehmed Pasha, who held sway over administration throughout the 1560s and 1570s. This alliance allowed him to secure the governorship of the wealthiest Ottoman possession, Egypt. In this position, he became enmeshed in a fierce struggle with other officials responsible for military operations in Yemen. After the latter were recalled to Istanbul, Sinan Pasha took over the command himself, successfully quashing the Zaydi resistance in the Yemeni hinterland.[18] In 1574, he engineered a successful establishment of Ottoman rule in Tunis. These accomplishments brought not only prestige but also political influence and wealth. By the end of the decade, he helmed the Indian Ocean faction within the imperial administration and invested heavily in spice trade passing through the Red Sea.[19] These patronage resources meant that he was well-poised to establish hegemony on par with that of Sokollu Mehmed Pasha.

However, the political context changed greatly following the death of Sokollu Mehmed Pasha in 1579. Sultan Murad III, who tried to reassert his control over administration and prevent the rise of another all-powerful vizier, constantly shuffled the grandees to maintain the balance of power between competing factions.[20] In effect, from his first appointment as the grand vizier in 1580 until his death in 1596, Sinan Pasha held the post on five different occasions alternating with his long-time enemies Ferhad Pasha and Lala Mustafa Pasha.[21] Personal hostility between the grandees and their unstable position in office fuelled factional build-up and mutual recriminations. Moreover, the growing number of clients within their households strained the capacity of the imperial institutions. To accommodate the interests of their own followers, grand viziers purged their predecessors' men and filled the posts with their associates. This uneasy balance unfolded against the background of growing disgruntlement in the army and fierce competition for *timars* between provincial cavalrymen.[22]

Moldavian–Wallachian rebellion of November 1594 posed a serious challenge to Sinan Pasha, since not only did the setback occur on his watch, but Michael the Brave had been his appointee. In response, he immediately carried out the appointment of two new voivodes, Ştefan the Deaf (*Surdul*) and Ştefan Bogdan, to replace the rebel voivodes in Moldavia and Wallachia respectively, and instructed border governors to provide required troops.[23] However, the campaign meant to force the principalities into submission ended in failure.[24]

The new defeat produced major changes among Ottoman officials, facilitated by the dynastic succession. Upon the accession of Mehmed III (1595–1603), Sinan Pasha was away from the capital, which put him at a disadvantage and permitted Ferhad Pasha to ingratiate himself with the new ruler and secure promotion to the post in February 1595.[25]

The new appointee was Koca Sinan Pasha's sworn enemy. According to Ibrahim Peçevi, their enmity dated back to 1582, when the two officials exchanged harsh words during the 1582 royal circumcision festival.[26] Soon after appointment, Ferhad Pasha ordered his adversary to leave the capital and immediately purged the officials associated with Sinan Pasha's faction. In total, fourteen governors were dismissed[27]; the changes included a new appointee to the throne of Moldavia brought by Ferhad Pasha from among his clients.[28] Thus, despite Sinan Pasha's failure, Ferhad Pasha initially preferred to stick to a tried solution rather than attempt a general overhaul of the principalities' position within the empire.

This changed at the end of April 1595, when the imperial council gathered to discuss the question whether the upcoming campaign should be directed against Habsburg forces in Hungary or Moldavian–Wallachian rebels. According to Mustafa Selâniki, the debate revealed considerable differences of opinion. Many officials abstained altogether or supported the Hungarian campaign, while the idea of moving against rebel voivodes found vociferous supporters in *Kapudan Pasha* Ciğalazade Sinan Pasha and particularly *Şeyh ül-Islam* Bostanzade Mehmed Efendi. The latter insisted that subduing domestic revolt took precedence over the war against the Habsburgs, and the grand vizier eagerly sided with this standpoint.[29]

Unlike the earlier attempts to restore order, the campaign against the Danubian principalities was not meant to install new voivodes but intended a general overhaul of Ottoman system of governance in the region. Moldavia and Wallachia were to be transformed into imperial provinces, each under the authority of a *beylerbey*. However, the new system administrative structure did not follow faithfully the pattern predominating at the imperial core. As Mihai Maxim pointed out, among appointees to the newly created provinces, we find no officials associated with the *timar* system. Instead, both Moldavia and Wallachia were to become *salyaneli* provinces along the lines of Egypt and several more distant Arab provinces, remitting the annual lump sum to the central treasury.[30]

This solution, according to the Romanian scholar, was meant as a concession to the local elite, guaranteeing that the dismantling of political institutions would not be accompanied by rearrangement of land ownership.

156 *The Ottomans and Eastern Europe*

However, a comparison with the evolution of Ottoman political economy in this period provides us with a more plausible explanation. By the end of the sixteenth century, the *timar* system was in disarray, and in 1600 only about 10 per cent of its beneficiaries performed active military duty.[31] As the fiscal system of the empire moved towards *iltizam*, even the extant prebends changed their nature, becoming both an investment and a reward for members of grandee households.[32] From this perspective, the institution of Moldavia and Wallachia as *salyaneli* provinces constituted a preferable option from a factional point of view, short-circuiting the flow of resources to the treasury and the faction.

Realizing this project was bound to create difficulties. Despite his efforts, Ferhad Pasha failed to purge Sinan Pasha's influence from the administration and the army. The deposed grandee, who remained in a virtual exile in Malkara, kept a web of his key clients in the administration, waiting for an opportune moment to return to power. Moreover, the *kaymakam* appointed for the time of the campaign, Damad Ibrahim Pasha, had political ambitions of his own. Thus, Ferhad Pasha's departure for the Wallachian campaign put him in considerable danger of being deposed at the behest of his adversaries.

These fears soon materialized, when Sinan Pasha and Damad Ibrahim Pasha joined forces to undermine the grand vizier. According to Mustafa Naima, the *kaymakam* deliberately neglected logistical preparations, while Koca Sinan Pasha mobilized his clients among the troops.[33] When the army was leaving the imperial capital, the fighting broke out between backers of Sinan Pasha and Ferhad Pasha, casting a shadow on the prospects of the campaign.[34] In the imperial palace, a campaign of slander began, accusing the grand vizier of cowardliness and a secret pact with the rebel voivodes. Bostanzade Mehmed Efendi joined the opposition, and by July 1595 Ferhad Pasha was removed from power before the actual campaign even started.[35] He tried to recoup his position by appealing to Safiye Sultan, but eventually, Sinan Pasha's pressure led to his execution in October.

After ascending the grand vizierate Sinan Pasha hijacked his predecessor's plan regarding the Danubian principalities, but the factional struggle took its toll on the troops. The changes at the apex of administrative hierarchy delayed the beginning of the military action and led to a decline in morale of the troops. A fitting expression of this confusion was the fact that the postings of the *beylerbeys* of Moldavia repeatedly changed hands before the campaign even started. Immediately after taking over the reins of power, Sinan Pasha removed Ca'fer Pasha, Ferhad Pasha's pick for the office. While Ca'fer was an experienced

Annexing Moldavia 157

official, who had distinguished himself during the 'Battle of the Torches' (1583) that gave the Ottomans control of Şirvan, he was also a lifelong associate of the grand vizier's sworn enemies.[36] Thus, Sinan swiftly replaced him with his own candidate, Ibrahim the *sancakbey* of Vize.[37]

However, the new appointee also failed to hold to what was still a virtual posting. To enlist the help of Crimean troops, the grand vizier had to accommodate Khan Ghazi Giray II's interests. The latter drove a hard bargain, initially demanding to place the principality under Giray dynasty.[38] Ultimately, a compromise was reached, whereby Ahmed Bey, the *sancakbey* of Bender and Ghazi Giray's nephew, would become the governor of Moldavia.[39]

These factional squabbles delayed the beginning of the invasion. Sinan Pasha's army entered the principality only in mid-August, and on its march towards Bucharest, it was surprised and defeated by Wallachian forces at Călugăreni. This defeat did not halt the march north, and the Ottoman troops occupied Bucharest and Târgovişte, but the morale was low. Sinan Pasha's position was endangered by Damad Ibrahim Pasha's influence at the Porte as the *kaymakam* tried to get rid of him the same way he had done with Ferhad Pasha. Ultimately, by October 1595 the imperial troops pulled out of Wallachia, suffering yet another defeat in the battle of Yergöğü (modern Giurgiu in Romania). The campaign meant to introduce provincial administration in Wallachia ended in total failure.

Matters were not going any better on the Moldavian throne where the burden of enforcing the annexation was on Ghazi Giray II's Tatar troops. By early September 1595, Jan Zamoyski entered the principality, installing Ieremia Movilă as the new voivode, thus launching a competing bid for hegemony in the region. The Crimean army, in turn, entered Moldavia only in October, giving Polish–Lithuanian troops enough time to entrench their positions. However, this perspective hardly sat well with the khan. Ghazi Giray II had political designs of his own and, although he agreed to support his nephew, he clearly did not welcome the prospect of greater Ottoman presence in the region. This provided an opportunity for Zamoyski, who after two days of inconclusive fighting at Țuțora (19–20 October 1595) convinced the khan to abandon the annexation plans in exchange for nine villages in southeastern Moldavia and a promise of annual gifts from the Commonwealth.[40] Zamoyski himself was surprised by how quickly he was able to reach an agreement.[41] Left with no other option, Ahmed Bey conceded; in the following years, he tried to secure the magnate's recommendation for a lifetime appointment as the *sancakbey* of Silistre.[42] Thus, by October 1595 the attempt to transform Moldavia and Wallachia into run-of-the-mill Ottoman provinces was in shambles.

158 *The Ottomans and Eastern Europe*

This failure led to the dismissal of Koca Sinan Pasha in November 1595, but the death of his replacement, Lala Mustafa Pasha, brought him back to power the following month. However, there was no return to the annexation plans. Instead, Sinan Pasha decided to back the proposal by Mehmed Bey, the former voivode of Wallachia and the governor of Niğbolu, who promoted his son as the new ruler of the principality. According to Selâniki, this idea was backed by an *arz* from the Wallachian population, undoubtedly orchestrated by the governor.[43] This marked a return to old arrangements, which was continued after Sinan Pasha's death in April 1596. The project of establishing a provincial administration in Moldavia and Wallachia was officially dead, never to be revived again in any meaningful way. By summer 1596 Sinan Pasha and his successor Damad Ibrahim Pasha managed to broker a precarious peace with Michael, thus securing the dangerously exposed flank in the war in Hungary.[44]

Romanian scholarship has unanimously emphasized the military exploits of Michael the Brave, who managed to halt Ottoman attempts to re-establish control in the region and briefly took control of Moldavia, Wallachia and Transylvania. While this is certainly true, we should also note that the Ottoman debacle was very much a result of factional strife within the ranks of imperial officialdom, which seemed more interested in fighting among themselves than make a concerted annexation attempt. The demise of Ferhad Pasha and appointment of Sinan Pasha caused serious delays and crippled Ottoman war machine on the eve of the invasion. Ghazi Giray II jumped ship as soon as he felt he could reach a better bargain with the Polish–Lithuanian authorities.

This factional strife helps us explain why the Ottomans never returned to these plans and why cross-border patronage provided an attractive alternative to outright annexation. The Porte certainly controlled sufficient military resources to implement provincial administration in Moldavia and Wallachia during the seventeenth century. The 1595 debacle took place in particularly difficult circumstances for the empire. It occurred at the time when the Porte was locked in an expensive and inconclusive conflict in Hungary, Anatolia suffered a collapse of social order and the principality of Wallachia experienced a period of resurgence of its military capacity. However, these unfavourable conditions were absent for much of the seventeenth century. In 1658, the Ottomans were able to quickly subdue the principalities while simultaneously dealing with Cretan war and a revolt in Anatolia. Thus, transforming Moldavia and Wallachia into regular provinces was well within reach of the Ottoman military capacities, if the imperial establishment would opt to do so.

However, this was not the case, and the fierce factional struggle suggests the reasons for this reluctance. Any attempt to establish provincial administration required considerable resources and carried no smaller risks for the grand vizier. Since it stood to reason that the positions in the new administration would go to his clients, the institutional rearrangement would upset the balance of power between the factions and trigger resistance of rival households. This was exactly the case in 1595 when the failed expedition and resulting factional struggle cost the life of one grand vizier and brought down his successor. Given these threats, it comes as no wonder that Ottoman grandees were reluctant to redraw the administrative map unless it gave them prospects of rewards large enough able to outweigh the risks involved.

The general preference of Ottoman establishment to continue the existing pattern throughout the seventeenth century suggests that the prospective gains were insufficient to warrant such attempts, and cross-border patronage constituted a viable alternative channel to procure necessary resources. It also required fewer resources and carried a lesser risk for the grandees. As the intended structure of the *eyalets* as *salyaneli* provinces demonstrates, the Ottoman officials were primarily interested in procuring cash revenue rather than expanding the *timar* system. To tap these resources, they did not need to take direct control of the sources of revenue, but just to ensure a steady flow of resources. This could be accomplished through putting Christian clients in positions of power. The eagerness of Sinan Pasha and his successors to distance themselves from the annexation attempt of 1595 suggests that they considered this arrangement sufficient to their factional interest.

The survival of Moldavia and Wallachia under indigenous institutions produced losers, though. Unlike the top echelons of Ottoman officials, their middle-rank clients were not directly involved in cash flows between the voivodes and the Porte, while the offices they were initially appointed to never materialized. Neither Ibrahim Bey nor Ahmed Bey managed to ascend administrative hierarchies following their short stints as would-be governors of Moldavia. In 1598 we find Ibrahim collecting taxes on wine in Edirne, as he clearly failed to secure another governorship.[45] Ahmed Bey managed to return to his post as the *sancakbey* of Bender, but his career stagnated as well. In short, the survival of Moldavia and Wallachia hit the lower ranks of Ottoman officialdom far more than it did their superiors and patrons. However, they lacked the political pull to defend their positions once their patrons opted not to introduce provincial administration in the Danubian principalities.

160   *The Ottomans and Eastern Europe*

While solid evidence is lacking, it is likely that the divergence between interests of upper and lower ranks of Ottoman establishment contributed to the widespread rumours about the imminent abolition of the principalities and the apparent lack of any steps to follow through with the plan by the Porte. The persistence of such news provides evidence that there were 'rumblings from below' by lower-rank officials, who would benefit financially and politically if additional administrative posts would have been added to the pool. These rumours were further amplified by European diplomats and pretenders to the thrones, creating a sense of urgency and impending doom. However, the grandees who profited from cross-border patronage were clearly not that invested in such initiatives, and their stance ultimately prevailed. In this sense, the survival of Moldavia and Wallachia resulted from financial and political concerns. However, this was not due to geopolitical considerations, nor the alleged lack of administrative skills among Ottoman officials. Rather, the main cause was the fragmentation of the imperial political scene and the availability of cross-border patronage as an alternative, less risky and ultimately more profitable arrangement, well-tailored to the needs of faction leaders wielding real power in the imperial centre.

'A faction that could not lose' and its defeat: Jan Zamoyski and Polish–Lithuanian annexation attempt of 1595–1600

The reign of Sigismund III Vasa in Poland–Lithuania (1587–1632) began in a context not dissimilar from that of Sultan Murad III's accession in Istanbul fourteen years earlier. Upon ascending the throne, both inherited administrations controlled by powerful ministers at the helm of vast and entrenched patronage networks. While both Sokollu Mehmed Pasha and Jan Zamoyski had been instrumental in their accession, their overarching influence put narrow limits on royal authority. Two episodes illustrate this balance of power. Upon meeting the grand vizier, Murad III almost kissed Sokollu's hand, and only a quick reaction of the latter prevented the faux pas.[46] Zamoyski was similarly nonplussed by the new ruler. He allegedly called a young and taciturn king a 'mute devil from Sweden' and showed Sigismund little respect.[47] While in no position to remove their all-powerful officials, Murad III and Sigismund III were unwilling to act as figureheads, and instead slowly but steadily tried to reassert their control of the system of governance and curb Sokollu and Zamoyski's influence.

Among his contemporaries, Jan Zamoyski was by all standards a towering figure. A scion of middle-gentry family and a man of broad intellectual horizons, he managed to catapult his family to the apex of the Polish–Lithuanian elite, combining considerable political talent with ruthlessness in pursuing his goals. Following his studies in Padua, he returned to the Commonwealth to become a secretary of King Sigismund II Augustus (1548–72), the last ruler of the Jagiellonian dynasty. Simultaneously, the ambitious upstart became one of the most vocal representatives of the gentry. By the mid-sixteenth century, this social group managed to emancipate itself from the influence of few powerful families holding positions in the royal council. The political ascendancy of the gentry in the form of so-called executionist movement, demanding enforcement of *Sejm* decisions and the recovery of royal domain alienated by the elite, gained the king's support and provided a springboard for the young nobleman. While not among the movement's first-rank leaders, Zamoyski managed to establish himself as a popular figure, playing an important role during the first two *interregna*.

The election of Transylvanian prince Stephen Báthory as the king of Poland (1576–86) constituted a major watershed in Zamoyski's career. The new monarch appreciated the nobleman's political acumen and his popularity among the gentry, quickly promoting him to high positions and making him his right-hand man. By 1576 Zamoyski received an appointment to the post of Crown vice-chancellor, and two years later took full control of the chancellery.[48] In 1581 the position of Crown grand *hetman* ensured his control of the royal military. According to Wojciech Tygielski, the chancellor effectively became Báthory's viceroy, utilizing his vast power to expand his estates, promote his clients and crack down on his adversaries.[49]

In doing so, Zamoyski was treading new path and reshaping Polish–Lithuanian political culture. Whereas the earlier generations of the country's elite relied primarily on their position in the royal council, the chancellor's political edifice was much more comprehensive and tapped various sources of political power. This strategy rested on four distinct but nonetheless interconnected pillars.[50] First, royal favour provided him with patronage resources necessary to rally support for Báthory's policy at the dietines. As Báthory's closest associate, his main task was mobilizing support for the king's policy and ensuring the nobility's consent to taxes necessary to finance the war against Muscovy (1579–82). Zamoyski's services were repaid through rapid promotion and the chancellor's control over appointments, which he used to expand his clientele and place his associates in key positions of power.

162   *The Ottomans and Eastern Europe*

The offices of grand chancellor and grand *hetman* offered the magnate vast discretionary powers and patronage resources. He exercised full control of the Crown chancellery and the documents issued in king's name, which gave him considerable leverage in domestic policy and effective control over diplomatic affairs.[51] Simultaneously, with the office of Crown *hetman,* he took not only command over royal troops, but also military jurisdiction, logistics, influence over appointments of officers, and diplomatic correspondence with the Sublime Porte and its satellites. These official duties came with ample power of patronage since it was necessary for any ambitious noble seeking position in the army or among royal secretaries to secure the support of the all-powerful magnate. Thus, it comes as no surprise that by the late 1580s both institutions were staffed almost exclusively by Zamoyski's clients. His influence included senatorial posts, with a coherent political bloc of officials owing their careers to the chancellor's backing.

This web of patronage was by no means restricted to the centre but also encompassed scores of clients in the provinces. Since the political system of the Commonwealth ascribed a crucial role to the provincial dietines, Zamoyski co-opted local opinion leaders to coax the rank-and-file into supporting his agenda. This web of political ties entrenched Zamoyski's position across the Commonwealth, although it was the strongest in the southeastern palatinates of the Crown, which reliably elected Zamoyski's supporters as deputies to the *Sejm*.[52]

Finally, the magnate set out to provide a sound economic foundation for his family's ascendancy. Although he inherited merely a couple of villages from his father, by 1586 he had established one of the largest landholdings in the Commonwealth, comprising over six hundred villages and numerous towns. The crown jewel of his domains was the town of Zamość, built according to the principles of an ideal Renaissance city and housing, apart from the founder's residence, a prestigious humanist academy he founded and maintained. The measure of Zamoyski's success is illustrated by the fact that the entail he established (*Ordynacja Zamojska*) survived until the communist land reform in 1944, providing a stable economic basis for the family's political position.[53]

This prudent strategy of political, military and economic accumulation materialized by the 1580s in a formidable political machine that Wojciech Tygielski called 'a faction that could not lose'.[54] Either directly or through his clients, Zamoyski had firm control of the Commonwealth's administrative apparatus, provincial dietines and political appointments. Thus, it comes as no surprise that he would see himself as a senior partner rather than a servant when 21-year-old Sigismund III arrived from Sweden to take the Polish throne. However, the latter had no intention to be Zamoyski's puppet, and the conflict between the two would soon dominate the political landscape of the Commonwealth.

The young monarch was unable to confront the chancellor openly. Instead, he sided with Zamoyski's adversaries and used his royal prerogatives to block the careers of the latter's clients.[55] This is well illustrated by the fact that Zamoyski, showered with appointments and land grants during Báthory's reign, did not receive a single village from Sigismund III. The ambitious magnate soon retaliated, and the tensions reached a boiling point at the *Sejm* of 1592. During the proceedings of what came to be known as the 'Inquisitorial *Sejm*', the king was effectively put on trial, accused of plotting with the Habsburgs to abdicate in their favour and leave for Sweden.[56] While no steps against the monarch were taken, Sigismund III nonetheless suffered a public humiliation while Zamoyski's supporters openly criticized him at the public forum. Although later the two sides publicly reconciled, the mutual hostility only grew and, from then on, the chancellor would become the focal point of opposition against the king, relying on the vast political capital he had accumulated in the 1580s. In turn, the king would continue to chip away Zamoyski's influence and build his own faction to match that of his adversary.

Following the Inquisitorial *Sejm*, the intensity of the conflict abated somewhat, as both Zamoyski and the king turned to other matters. The latter increasingly engaged in his succession to the Swedish throne, where the prospect of a devout Catholic ruler triggered a growing opposition of predominantly Protestant estates. Zamoyski, unwelcome at the court, turned his attention to the southeastern provinces of the Crown, the core of his political machine. Particularly important in this respect was the dietine of Vyšnja. Comprising the bulk of the Palatinate of Ruthenia, the dietine played an outsized political role in the region. Unlike other local dietines, dominated by magnate families, the palatinate had a politically active and relatively independent middle and upper gentry, whose opinion was often followed by other assemblies.[57] As such, the support of the dietine could not be taken for granted and had to be won by co-opting local opinion leaders. Zamoyski's faction had a strong presence in the region, and many local notables, such as Stanisław Żółkiewski, Jan Szczęsny Herburt and Jan Tomasz Drohojowski, were among the chancellor's close associates.[58] At the same time, the constant threat of Tatar predatory raids meant that many nobles of the region were choosing military careers, thus entering the purview of Zamoyski's political interests as the grand *hetman*. Therefore, for the magnate's political survival in his conflict with the king, retaining support of his Ruthenian clientele was of utmost importance.

164   *The Ottomans and Eastern Europe*

In the meantime, another conflict was in full swing just south of the Polish–Lithuanian border, where the Habsburg–Ottoman war spilled into the Danubian principalities. In November 1594, Moldavian voivode Aron, along with his Wallachian counterpart, rebelled against the Porte and joined Habsburg forces. While successful in repulsing the Ottoman counterattack, the voivode faced another threat from within the Christian ranks and was soon ousted by Ştefan Răzvan (1595), who seized the throne with Transylvanian backing.[59] These internal conflicts took place against the background of impending Ottoman invasion and volatile military situation, prompting the new ruler to plead for Polish–Lithuanian military assistance.

Despite pressure exercised by Habsburg and papal diplomats, the Commonwealth stayed aloof from the conflict, trying to maintain amicable relations with the Porte and suspecting ulterior motives in the project. Zamoyski, whose stance on the matter was decisive, was a long-time enemy of the dynasty and did not welcome the prospect of contributing Polish–Lithuanian troops to the war effort. Upon his departure for Sweden in 1594, the king had begrudgingly vested his adversary with extensive discretionary powers on the matter, and in summer 1595 the chancellor concentrated his troops near the Moldavian border to follow the course of events.[60] Thus, given the circumstances, the Polish–Lithuanian response to the conflict over Moldavia would be firmly under control of the king's chief adversary.[61]

The news of the Ottoman plan to introduce direct imperial administration in Moldavia – discussed in the previous section – prompted Zamoyski into action. On 26 August 1595, he consulted senators present in his army, who expressed their support for the idea of entering Moldavia and claiming it for the Commonwealth.[62] Securing their consent was not difficult given that the top echelons of the military were staffed almost exclusively by Zamoyski's clients and associates. In early September, the army of seven thousand men crossed the Dniester and entered Moldavia, forcing Ştefan Răzvan to flee and installing Zamoyski's client, Ieremia Movilă, as the new voivode.[63] The troops then advanced south towards Iaşi and, after occupying the city, moved to a more defensible position at Ţuţora to await Crimean troops.

As I have already mentioned, defending these gains turned out to be easier than Zamoyski had anticipated. After two days of inconclusive fighting, Khan Ghazi Giray II reached an agreement with the *hetman* and recognized Movilă as the new voivode, promising to support the latter at the Porte. With Movilă's position secured, Zamoyski returned to the Commonwealth to prepare for the upcoming *Sejm*, leaving part of his troops to protect Polish–Lithuanian position in the principality. The campaign was a resounding military and diplomatic success. In one swift move, the chancellor managed to re-establish Polish–Lithuanian claims to the principality and install his own candidate on the throne without alienating the Sublime Porte.

This new framework was reflected in two important documents. The first one, the instrument of peace issued by the khan, did not amount to an Ottoman *'ahdname*, but nonetheless recognized Zamoyski's actions in Moldavia and secured the throne for Ieremia Movilă.[64] However, even interesting document was the oath sworn by the new voivode, which regulated the relationship between him and the Polish Crown. While the oath was delivered orally, it was subsequently written down and signed by the boyars. It included several far-reaching provisions, which went beyond the voivode's recognition of Polish–Lithuanian suzerainty.[65]

The most important condition sworn by Ieremia Movilă was the promise to carry out the incorporation of Moldavia to the Polish–Lithuanian Commonwealth. The details of the arrangement are unknown, and there is considerable divergence of opinion what the future status of the principality would have been. While Constantin Rezachevici argued that Moldavia would become but one of the palatinates, Cristian Bobicescu suggested that its status would be more akin to that of the Polish Crown or the Grand Duchy of Lithuania, as one of the constitutive parts of the composite monarchy.[66] The phrasing of the document is unclear, but none of the interpretations seems entirely correct. On the one hand, it is clear that, following the incorporation, Moldavia would retain some institutional identity; however, the document also stated that it would become part of the Crown rather than enjoy the position of parity.[67] While the text exhibits some similarities to the Union of Lublin from 1569, it seems more likely that the future status of Moldavia would be similar to that of Royal Prussia, which retained its specific institutional arrangements and strong regionalism, while at the same time being an integral part of the Polish Crown.[68]

Another critical concession granted Moldavian boyars the right to acquire landed estates in Polish–Lithuanian territories and the permission for nobles to do the same in Moldavia. In many respects, the point mirrored similar arrangements included in the act of Union of Lublin. However, as in the case of the Grand Duchy of Lithuania, this legal parity effectively favoured the interests of Polish elites, which enjoyed political and economic superiority over their Moldavian counterparts. In the Grand Duchy, access to landownership constituted a constant source of tension throughout the early modern period. Less affluent than their Polish peers, Lithuanian nobles consequently tried to

166   *The Ottomans and Eastern Europe*

prevent them from the ranks of landholders. The Third Lithuanian Statute, adopted in 1588, effectively ignored the realities of the union, aimed at excluding Crown nobility from inheriting or buying landed estates, and for a good reason. The fear of being marginalized by wealthier Poles fuelled much of Lithuanian regionalism, which on several occasions led to deep institutional crises within the Commonwealth.[69] Given that Moldavian boyars wielded even fewer resources than the Lithuanians, this stipulation carried considerable risks for the survival of the local elite.

This brings us to the motives that drove the incorporation plans. Most scholars addressing the topic highlighted the Commonwealth's geopolitical interests in the region. According to Dariusz Skorupa and Dariusz Milewski, Zamoyski's goal was to improve border security against the Crimean Tatars and the Sublime Porte by cutting the land route from Crimea to the Ottoman lands.[70] However, this seems unlikely and incorporating Moldavia would hardly reduce the threat. Annexing Moldavia would actually *extend* the already long steppe border with Crimean and Ottoman lands, thus exposing the Commonwealth to the attacks. Given that the Polish-Lithuanian army was already spread thin, it was hardly capable of providing additional security to an even longer stretch of the open frontier. Moreover, the annexation would almost certainly result in Ottoman military response, dragging the Commonwealth into a full-scale conflict. Thus, annexing Moldavia would likely spark an open conflict with the Sublime Porte, which most Polish-Lithuanian nobles, including Zamoyski, hoped to prevent.

Instead, the main rationale for these incorporation plans seems to lay in economic resources of the principality rather than geopolitical concerns. As Cristian Bobicescu demonstrated, beginning in 1595 the future colonization of Moldavia by the Polish nobility was a widely discussed matter within Zamoyski's entourage. In correspondence between members of the faction and in diplomatic reports from Poland-Lithuania, we find frequent references to the concept of redistributing the land among 'men of merit', particularly soldiers.[71] In this sense, it would constitute a remedy to the growing number of landless nobles in the late sixteenth century, while also benefiting the magnates and middle gentry.[72]

While one would expect such plan to garner universal support, the following *Sejm* showed considerable opposition against the *Hetman*'s actions, accusing him of pursuing his own political interests rather than upholding those of the Commonwealth.[73] Moreover, there is little evidence that Zamoyski was particularly concerned about the plight of landless brethren, which had little political clout and was not the constituency the chancellor was hoping to attract. One would also hardly expect Zamoyski to promote the interests of his adversaries among the magnates. The annexation of Moldavia and subsequent redistribution of land was not meant to profit all nobility in an equal manner, but instead was intended to satisfy the demands of Zamoyski's own men.

That this was the case is suggested by the circumstances in which Ieremia Movilă performed his oath in 1595. The act itself took place in Zamoyski's tent, with few people in attendance, including the chancellor himself, Stanisław Żółkiewski and Jan Szczęsny Herburt.[74] Whereas the presence of Zamoyski and his second-in-command, Żółkiewski, is easy to explain given their military and official seniority, Herburt's is not. His only official position was that of *starosta* of Mostys'ka, which put him well below other participants of the campaign. In short, his participation on such a momentous and secretive occasion does not correspond to his relatively modest rank in institutional hierarchies.

However, once we look at Herburt's position within Zamoyski's faction, his puzzling presence in the tent becomes understandable. A relative of the chancellor, Herburt was his client since the beginning of his political career and even dedicated a Latin eulogy to his patron.[75] Apart from putting his literary talents in Zamoyski's service, Herburt was also a career soldier and an important political operative at the Vyšnja dietine, where his family had considerable political influence. In this sense, he was the embodiment of Zamoyski's constituency in the region, to whose interests the chancellor had to appeal. At the same time, this group was also hit the hardest by the magnate's conflict with the king. When Sigismund III cut off Zamoyski's backers from appointments and the stream of patronage resources dried up, careers of the magnate's clients came to a halt.[76] In Herburt's case, his repeated failures at career advancement were exacerbated by his financial woes. Nonetheless, he remained steadfast in supporting his patron, hoping that the tables would turn in his favour.

From the perspective of Herburt and his likes, the Moldavian campaign offered the prospects of breaking the stranglehold. As a victorious commander, Zamoyski would exert considerable sway over the redistribution of Moldavian estates in the case of planned incorporation. Having suffered the brunt of factional conflict and demonstrated his loyalty, Herburt – along with other clients in a similar position – clearly felt entitled to a reward in the form of landholdings and offices in the principality. By including the incorporation clause into Movilă's oath and involving Herburt in the event, Zamoyski made a concession to his core constituency, offering them a prospect of partaking in the benefits from the conquest.[77] In the following years, Herburt continued to support the chancellor, while at the same time insisting on the annexation of the principality.

168   *The Ottomans and Eastern Europe*

By declaring his will to annex Moldavia, Zamoyski made a commitment that his Ruthenian clients would be soon rewarded, thus reinforcing their loyalty. However, the oath carried considerable risk for the cohesion of his cross-border faction. Quite naturally, Ieremia Movilă and Moldavian boyars were far from enthralled by the prospect of having to give up their political power and landed estates to Zamoyski's Polish clients. Instead, they opted for the preservation of Moldavia as a dependent principality. Since the interests of 'incorporationist' and 'autonomist' currents within the faction were irreconcilable, the rift between them was bound to grow wider. Eventually, this would force Zamoyski into a difficult position of prioritizing one pressure group over another, thus running the risk of alienating a large chunk of his patronage network.

The contradictory interests of these two groups came to light at the *Sejm* of 1597. Overall, the proceedings seem like a victory for Zamoyski, who managed to humiliate his adversary, Prince Kostjantyn-Vasyl Ostroz'kyj, and his clients remained active during the debates. Still, several public appearances suggest a growing tension among the chancellor's men. The Moldavian embassy, comprising representatives of all estates, asked the king to confirm their privileges, including the boyars' exclusive rights to hold land and offices of Moldavia.[78] This clearly contravened the demands of Zamoyski's Polish clients and was ultimately rejected by the king. At the same time, Herburt who made his appearance at the *Sejm* as a representative of the army, delivered an impassioned speech in defence of his brothers-in-arms and demanded rewards for their service. The tone was extremely harsh, and thinly veiled warnings bordered on the crime of *lese majesté*:

> It is my hope that it won't come to what happened to a Turkish emperor Basoktis [*sic!*]. Soldiers asked him to promote one of their own to the rank of pasha, but he refused their demands and showed no gratitude for their knightly service. Thus, [disgruntled], they decided to kill him and send his head to King Matthias.[79]

It is unclear whether Herburt acted on his own or consulted the speech with Zamoyski. If the king conceded and rewarded Herburt and other soldiers, the upcoming clash within Zamoyski's faction could be alleviated by bringing more resources to the patronage network. The fact that Herburt supported the chancellor's agenda at Vyšnja and the following year was sent to Istanbul as the grand ambassador suggests that he was not acting against Zamoyski. Nonetheless, the harsh tone of his speech indicates that his patience was wearing thin. However, the king did not give in, and the frustrated chancellor remarked that his pleas were as effective as 'throwing beans against the wall'.[80] Some clients began to abandon him, and the tensions within the faction continued to mount.[81]

Annexing Moldavia 169

Herburt's mission to the Porte epitomized this escalation. Its central goal was to secure Ottoman recognition of Polish–Lithuanian rights to Moldavia, a necessary step to consolidate the gains. For the mission to succeed, Herburt was instructed to coordinate his efforts with Ieremia Movilă. Rather than working together, the two engaged in constant squabbles and exchanged snubs, and the mission failed short of its stated goal.[82] Herburt's relationship with his patron also cooled, particularly when he left the estates leased from Zamoyski just before the harvest without notifying the chancellor, which disrupted fieldworks.[83]

Soon, new developments upset the balance of power in the region and accelerated the conflict. In 1599 Wallachian voivode Michael the Brave invaded Transylvania and defeated Prince András Báthory (1598–9), Zamoyski's relative, taking control of the principality. In May the following year, Michael invaded Moldavia and quickly ousted Ieremia Movilă.[84] The latter fled to the border castle of Hotin and immediately called Zamoyski for help. By September 1600 the chancellor entered Moldavia for the second time and quickly restored Movilă's rule. Seeing this as an opportune moment to extend his influence, Zamoyski moved south into Wallachia, defeating Michael in the battle of Bucov and putting Ieremia's brother, Simion, as the new voivode there.[85]

From the military point of view, the campaign was another resounding success, even if Simion's rule in Wallachia turned out to be short-lived.[86] However, in the backstage, the Zamoyski–Movilă faction seemed to unravel. When the troops established a camp near Suceava, the only Moldavian fortress to mount any resistance, the chancellor demanded that Ieremia fulfil his obligation to carry out the incorporation.[87] The voivode flatly rejected the request, and infuriated Zamoyski began to consider replacing him with a more malleable candidate. However, there seemed to be no suitable candidate and eventually, the chancellor renounced his plans. Instead, he drew up a new oath of allegiance, sworn by both Ieremia and Simion Movilă.[88] It omitted any references to incorporation, instead opting for annual payments to the royal treasury and a contribution to the upkeep of Polish–Lithuanian forces stationed in the principalities. The clause regarding land grants to well-deserving people was included, but the final say would belong to the voivode rather than the king, effectively rendering the whole issue moot and privileging Moldavian boyars with noble *indigenatus*.[89]

This new arrangement marked a victory for the Movilăs and left Herburt's camp empty-handed. While Zamoyski managed to hold to the Moldavian–Wallachian section of his patronage network, this came at the cost. Disillusioned with the patron who failed to protect his interests, Herburt increasingly distanced himself from the chancellor. This sense of betrayal seems to have been widespread among the soldiers, who in 1601 refused to follow orders until the arrears were paid. Unable to procure the money from the royal treasury, Zamoyski was forced to earmark his own resources to pacify his subordinates. At the same time, in January 1603 Herburt, until that point a loyal agent of the chancellor, flatly refused to attend to his patron's interests at the upcoming dietine, claiming that he was 'too busy' with his own matters.[90] He launched a last-ditch attempt to bring incorporation plans to fruition, this time on his home turf in Ruthenia. During a dietine in Vyšnja, he laid out a plan to annex Moldavia and Wallachia, claiming that they rightfully belonged to the Commonwealth by historical precedent and the right of conquest.[91] The land was to be distributed between deserving noblemen, who would also take over newly created offices. The fact that none of Zamoyski's other agents at the dietine supported the motion shows that Herburt was acting alone and ultimately failed in his efforts.

In a somewhat paradoxical manner, two militarily successful campaigns left Zamoyski's faction weaker and more divided than it had been before. The chancellor lost at least one of his key clients, while his vacillating position regarding Ieremia Movilă cooled the relationship between them. This somewhat surprising result illustrates the difficulties in managing cross-border networks and the inherent problems connected with Polish–Lithuanian nobility's focus on landholding and fixed capital. Since land could not be multiplied, the rivalry between 'incorporationists' and 'autonomists' was effectively a zero-sum game between Polish–Lithuanian and Moldavian sections of Zamoyski's clientele.

This irreconcilable conflict put the chancellor in an impossible position, stuck between two opposing visions of his faction's 'moral economy'. On the one hand, Herburt and his supporters considered themselves entitled to partake in the windfall produced by the conquest of Moldavia and Wallachia. After all, they had remained loyal to Zamoyski and shared his hardships, when the king reduced the flow of patronage resources to a trickle. When the prospect of reward presented itself, it seemed obvious to them that their interests would take precedence. However, this would require side-lining the Moldavian section of the patronage network, as Ieremia Movilă and the boyars were unwilling to concede. As the principality's local elite, they considered themselves rightful masters of the country and its resources, which they did not want to relinquish in order to satisfy Zamoyski's Polish clients. While facilitating the exchange of resources, the cross-border nature of the faction ultimately worked against any annexation plans.

In many respects, Zamoyski's intervention may seem like a state affair. The magnate justified his decision by invoking his duties as an official of the Crown and during his military campaigns relied on the standing army. However, this should not detract us from the fact that the whole affair was driven by factional concerns, and state resources were deployed to keep the chancellor's faction together rather than pursuit geopolitical goals. While the main impulse came from the conflict within the Polish–Lithuanian arena, it quickly spilled beyond its boundaries and throughout Zamoyski's cross-border faction. It was ultimately the cross-border factional aspect that both informed the magnate's strategy and ultimately put him into an impossible situation of satisfying mutually exclusive expectations of his clientele.

The king and the poet: Sobieski's failure in Moldavia

The year 1672 brought a sudden shift in the balance of power between Poland–Lithuania and the Ottoman Empire. In summer, a massive Ottoman army led by Mehmed IV and Köprülü Ahmed Pasha marched north into the Polish–Lithuanian province of Podolia. The war took the Commonwealth off guard. The country stumbled towards a civil war between the supporters of King Michael I (1669–73) and his opponents; many nobles did not believe the news of an impending invasion, considering it a ploy against the monarch. The fortress of Kam'janec', the key to Polish–Lithuanian defence system, surrendered after just a week of siege. The conditions imposed by the Porte were harsh: in the Treaty of Bučač in October 1672, the Commonwealth had to cede control over Podolia and Right-Bank Ukraine and agree to pay an annual *harac* to the Porte.[92]

The humiliation of Bučač united the nobility and muted internal disputes. The *Sejm* rejected the treaty and voted new taxes to finance a renewed military effort. In the campaign of 1673, the Polish–Lithuanian army led by Crown Grand *Hetman* Jan Sobieski was able to recoup some losses and score a major victory in the battle of Hotin (10–11 November 1673).[93] This success fell short of re-establishing control over Podolia. However, it gave a huge boost to Sobieski's popularity and King Michael's death on the eve of the battle paved the way for the magnate's election as the new ruler. Having ascended the throne as John III (1674–96), Sobieski continued the war against the Porte for three more years. Ultimately, the treaty of Žuravna (1676) brought an end to the hostilities. The Commonwealth failed to reconquer the provinces it had lost in 1672 but was freed from the humiliating obligation to pay tribute to the Ottomans.[94]

The following two decades saw the resurgence of factional interests in the Danubian principalities, driven by Sobieski's dynastic plans. This represents a peculiar case in that John III – the leader of the faction – was at the same time the ruler of the Polish–Lithuanian Commonwealth; thus, it may be argued that the king's Moldavian–Wallachian designs were an outgrowth of state-driven policy. However, there are reasons that favour a faction-oriented reading of his actions. Ascending the throne did not mean that Sobieski was above the fray of factional politics. The elective character of the monarchy and the balance of power were exacerbated by Sobieski's position as a magnate-turned-ruler. Despite his military achievements, Sobieski's encountered considerable opposition among the magnates, as many were jealous to see him ascending the throne. Unlike his predecessor, who had been either monarchs elsewhere, or at least scions of ruling dynasties, Sobieski had no prestigious dynastic lineage that would set him apart from the Commonwealth's elite. To rise above the polarized political landscape and enhance his prestige, he had to bring in new resources and put his reign and his family's position on a stronger footing.

This he hoped to accomplish by establishing dynastic rule in one of the polities adjacent to Poland–Lithuania. Initially, his plan involved an alliance with Sweden and France to take control of Ducal Prussia, a former satellite of the Commonwealth to which it had to renounce its rights in 1657.[95] French diplomacy was also to assist Polish–Lithuanian efforts to renegotiate the treaty of Žuravna. His hopes were dashed on both accounts. Louis XIV opted for an alliance with Elector Friedrich Wilhelm and abandoned his support for Sobieski's plans altogether. In turn, the Porte refused to discuss any territorial changes. Disillusioned, John III began to shift his strategy, moving towards an alliance with the Habsburgs and a new war against the Ottoman Empire. Moldavia and Wallachia rather than Ducal Prussia would thus become the intended power base of the Sobieski family.

Sobieski seemed well-positioned to bring those plans to the fruition. As a major landholder in the Ukraine and a former Crown grand *hetman*, he had intimate knowledge of regional affairs and knew at least some Ottoman Turkish and Romanian languages. Moreover, during the battle of Hotin, a number of Moldavian boyars, including Voivode Ştefan Petriceicu, abandoned the Ottoman camp and took up residence in the Commonwealth.[96] The king quickly established himself as the émigrés' patron, providing them with employment in the army and supporting their efforts to secure Polish noble titles.[97] Finally, his plans to reconquer Podolia and Ukraine enjoyed the support of the vocal lobby of exiles from the lost palatinates, who hoped to return to their estates.[98]

The key figure in this plan matter was Miron Costin, one of the wealthiest and most influential Moldavian boyars of the second half of the seventeenth century. A son of a one-time Polish–Lithuanian candidate to the throne, Iancu Costin, Miron grew up in Podolia and had deep ties with the Polish–Lithuanian elite. While his father was illiterate, Costin received a thorough education in the Jesuit college in Bar before returning to Moldavia in the 1650s. There, he quickly became one of the central political figures, holding the highest-ranking office of the grand *logofăt* (chancellor). His move to Moldavia did not mean breaking off ties with the Polish–Lithuanian elites; on the contrary, he maintained frequent correspondence with Sobieski and one of his closest associates, Marek Matczyński.[99] Although he did not side with Petriceicu upon the latter's defection to the Commonwealth, he has been widely considered by historians as a leader of the pro-Polish party in Moldavia and was expected to play a pivotal role in Sobieski's designs for the principality.

Polish–Ottoman hostilities resumed in 1683. Having signed a military alliance with Emperor Leopold I, Sobieski led an expedition to relieve Vienna and his troops were instrumental in lifting the siege. At the same time, a secondary front opened in Moldavia and Ottoman-controlled Ukraine. In November a Polish raid led by Crown Field *Hetman* Andrzej Potocki captured incumbent voivode Gheorghe Duca and his entourage, installing Ștefan Petriceicu in Iași. The captives, including Miron Costin, were transported to the Commonwealth, where Duca soon passed away.[100]

Given Miron Costin's ties to Sobieski and his presumed standpoint as the Polish-Lithuanian sympathizer, it has been argued that Costin had been in cahoots with the king and orchestrated Duca's capture.[101] However, there is no evidence to support this claim, and the captive boyar was imprisoned along with others in Potocki's residence. Only subsequently was he transported to the royal residence at Javoriv, where he met the king in person. The meeting took place in a friendly atmosphere and Costin was moved to Dašava, where he enjoyed relative freedom of movement.[102]

This preferential treatment was partly the result of Costin's long-standing ties to the king's close advisor, Marek Matczyński, and did not necessarily mean that the boyar had been acting as the king's agent in Moldavia. Nonetheless, Sobieski clearly hoped to co-opt Costin in order to expand his base in the principality. The short reign of Petriceicu in 1683–4 clearly demonstrated that the voivode failed to muster sufficient support, and Costin's political clout made him an important ally for the future, as well as the focal point for Sobieski's sympathizers among the boyars.[103]

Initially, these hopes seemed well-founded. On 25 July 1684 boyars assembled in Žovkva presented the king with a memorandum laying out the

174   *The Ottomans and Eastern Europe*

future status of the principality. According to this project, after the Ottomans were ousted from Moldavia, the principality would join the Polish–Lithuanian Commonwealth and the boyars would receive the same status as the nobility under the authority of the Polish monarch.[104] It is unclear on whose initiative the memorandum was drawn up. By this point, Moldavian emigration in the Commonwealth included three distinct groups.[105] The first one comprised petty boyars, who came and went depending on the military and political situation in Moldavia and had only limited political influence. The second group consisted of 'old émigrés', who defected to the Polish–Lithuanian camp with Petriceicu back in 1673. While initially this group counted up to a thousand individuals, its numbers dwindled throughout the 1670s.[106] Finally, another group included high-ranking officials taken by Potocki in 1684; while they held considerable sway in Moldavian politics, their move to Poland–Lithuania was involuntary and did not necessarily indicate their political sympathies.

As Lidia Vlasova pointed out, it was the latter group behind the memorandum. The document ignored the interests of the voivode altogether, which would have been unlikely if the initiative came from Petriceicu's backers.[107] Instead, it focused on the interests of high-ranking boyars and seems to indicate the growing position of this group – and Miron Costin personally – in Sobieski's patronage network and political designs. The proposed arrangement did not necessarily erase Moldavia's political identity; instead, the project envisioned the inclusion of Moldavia into the composite monarchy on par with the Polish Crown and the Grand Duchy of Lithuania, with the latter explicitly mentioned as the blueprint for the principality's future status.

Equally important, however, is what was missing from the project, namely landownership rights. As I have mentioned in the previous section, the control of landed estates had been a particularly contentious issue within Zamoyski's faction and encountered considerable opposition in Moldavia. Given the centrality of this topic, its omission from the memorandum is telling and illustrates the boyar's resolve to retain control of the principality's resources. The Moldavian elite were ready to give up on the institution of the voivode, but they were clearly unwilling to relinquish monopoly on landholding. Nonetheless, for John III the memorandum seemed to promise the boyars' support for his plans and showed the path forward.

By December 1684, Costin appealed to the king, requesting his permission to return to Moldavia. According to the boyar, his prolonged sojourn in Poland–Lithuania cast doubts on his loyalty and posed a grave danger to his relatives, who remained in Moldavia. As proof, he presented the king with a letter from his brother Velicico:

> We wonder why, being in this free and safe country and surrounded by people not prone to unfounded suspicions, you have not sent us any news regarding your fortunes and your health. It made us think that you have rejected Moldavia as your homeland. The voivode himself, after such a long time without any news, decided to summon you and assure you of his good dispositions towards you [...] and I second that with my brotherly plea. For the love of God, if you have decided not to return, please change your mind and reject that thought, because it would bring death upon us and your own children. It is my understanding that His Majesty, being of sound mind and with a great heart, who has been the lord and patron of our family for so long, would not prohibit you to come here.[108]

However, it seems that the letter, rather than by Velicico, was authored or at least heavily edited by Miron Costin. It bears the stylistic characteristics of the latter's writing style, and it seems to be intended for John III rather than the boyar himself. By this point, Costin was already pleading to the king for permission to leave, and the focus of the whole letter was the declaration of the family's loyalty to their patron and the eulogy of Sobieski. The strategy worked, as Costin was soon let go for Moldavia, promising to become a pillar in Sobieski's Moldavian designs.

Throughout the year 1685, Costin maintained intensive correspondence with the king, mediating between him and the new ruler Constantin Cantemir (1685–93). His ascension to the throne was itself a product of cross-border patronage. According to Ion Neculce, the incumbent ruler of Wallachia, Șerban Cantacuzino (r. 1678–88), utilized his own connections at the Porte to promote relatively poor and effectively illiterate Cantemir as a means to establish control over Moldavia and settle scores with the Ruset family, influential in the principalities and at the imperial centre.[109] Cantemir, while enforcing orders coming from the Porte, seemed open to Sobieski's overtures. However, the negotiations soon collapsed and in 1686 Sobieski organized a major expedition meant to bring Moldavia to the fold. In July 1686 a thirty-thousand-strong Polish–Lithuanian army entered the principality, and the king issued a proclamation encouraging Moldavians to join his side.[110] At the same time, he dispatched letters to Miron and Velicico Costins, ordering them to foment unrest among Cantemir's troops. By mid-August, the royal army entered Iași, while the voivode withdrew with his troops and treasury towards the Ottoman border. Entering the capital, Sobieski was allegedly received enthusiastically by the inhabitants and greeted by a delegation of boyars led by Metropolitan Dosoftei.[111] Both Costins were absent from the crowd; rather than joining the king, they retreated with the voivode.[112]

176   *The Ottomans and Eastern Europe*

Soon, Sobieski's position in the principalities deteriorated. Moldavian forces, supported by Ottoman and Tatar troops, mounted stiff resistance and the hopes that boyars would flock to the Polish–Lithuanian camp did not materialize. The king's hopes for Cantemir's defection also proved futile. Harsh terrain, terrible weather and disease took their toll on Sobieski's troops. To make matters worse, a fire consumed much of Iași, destroying warehouses and leaving the army without necessary supplies. The campaign, which consumed large sums of money and war materiel ended in a humiliating retreat. No major objective was accomplished, and all Sobieski was able to wrest was control of few minor fortresses in the north of the country.

Most importantly, however, Miron Costin had a hand in this disappointing outcome. Although most scholars have generally claimed that he tried to assist Polish–Lithuanian efforts, Lidia Vlasova rightly pointed out that there is no evidence to support the thesis.[113] While the boyar exchanged correspondence with Sobieski, he failed to contribute in any substantial way to improve the prospect of victory. Even if we assume that he remained in Cantemir's camp as a part of the plan to gather intelligence for the king, there is no doubt that he adopted a wait-and-see standpoint, which proved fatal for royal plans and sat uneasily with Costin's image as the leader of a pro-Polish faction.

Sobieski was clearly disappointed with the campaign and the lack of boyar support. While he maintained contact with Miron Costin, he also changed his policy regarding Moldavia. He no longer seemed focused on swaying the Moldavian elite, but rather consolidating the gains and harnessing resources for the war effort. This took the form of the colonization plans pursued primarily by Crown Grand *Hetman* Jan Stanisław Jabłonowski.[114] The landholdings in the territories controlled by Polish forces were to be seized and redistributed among deserving soldiers. Some concessions were made to Moldavian boyars, who had decisively sided with the king, such as Constantin Turcul, appointed the *starosta* of Cernăuți.[115] However, overall, this shift towards colonization demonstrated Sobieski's growing disillusionment with his Moldavian clients. In turn, both Miron Costin and his brother loyally performed their official duties as Cantemir's officials. Velicico, commanding Moldavian troops, actively tried to dislodge Polish garrisons in northern Moldavia, while at the same time corresponding with Polish commanders.[116]

In 1691 John III made the last attempt to take control of Moldavia and install his son, Jakub, in the principality.[117] In comparison with the major campaign of 1686, the new expedition was a much more modest affair and unfolded in the atmosphere of growing indifference of the nobility. In August the small army crossed the Moldavian border, slowly advancing towards Iaşi. The troops were constantly harassed by Crimean Tatars and, more importantly, suffered from hunger and disease. By October 1691 it became clear that there was no support among the boyars for the royal plans and Sobieski decided to pull out from Moldavia. While retreating, the army suffered greatly from bad weather, disease and enemy raids, losing 1,500 men and most of its equipment and artillery.[118] King John III's last campaign turned out to be a sorry affair, and his Moldavian plans never materialized, largely due to the lack of support from the local elite.

However, why was this support lacking? According to Zdzisław Spieralski, by this point, Miron Costin and his faction lost all their influence and were being closely watched by the voivode's agents. In October 1691, Costin sent a letter, in which he begged the king to intervene on his behalf and save him and his brother.[119] Indeed, just two months later Miron and Velicico Costins were killed on the orders of Constantin Cantemir. The context would suggest that the boyars' demise was due to their actions during the 1691 campaign, but it is telling that Sobieski did not even bother to respond to Miron Costin's pleas. As Lidia Vlasova pointed out, the letter seems to have served as an excuse for Costins' inaction and lack of support.[120] Similarly, no Moldavian source draws a connection between the two events. Instead, Costins' death stemmed from the internal struggle for power within the principality.

By the late seventeenth century, the Moldavian political scene was divided into two major factions, led by the Costins and Rusets, respectively. The rivalry between them reached its peak during the reign of Constantin Cantemir. For much of this period, a relative equilibrium between the factions was maintained due to the efforts of Gavriliță Costache, the grand *vornic* of Upper Moldavia and a partisan of the Costins.[121] According to a Moldavian author, Costache's influence with the voivode had been instrumental in reinstating Miron to power after his return to Moldavia in 1685.[122] Cantemir also made plans for marrying his daughter with one of Miron's sons. However, Costache passed away in 1688, depriving the faction of a crucial member with contacts in the Ottoman centre. Costache's death and the demise of Şerban Cantacuzino the same year freed Cantemir from having to take his former patron into account. As a result, he began promoting his relative, Lupu Bogdan; even more importantly, he recalled the Rusets, who had been in exile in the imperial capital.[123] The Costins' influence began to slip away. In 1689 Velicico was replaced by Lupu Bogdan at the helm of Moldavian army, while Iordache Ruset exercised full control of the treasury. This alliance – with Rusets' extensive holdings in Moldavia and a widespread network of familial ties in Istanbul – posed an imminent danger to

178 *The Ottomans and Eastern Europe*

the vestiges of Costins' power.[124] To add insult to injury, Cantemir scrapped the idea of a marital alliance with the boyar family.[125]

As they were losing grip on power, the Costin faction tried to respond. In December 1691, Velicico Costin met with Costache's sons and Ion Pălade at the latter's wedding. They planned to flee to Wallachia, under the protection of Voivode Constantin Brâncoveanu. With his help, they hoped to sway the Porte against the incumbent and secure Velicico's appointment.[126] However, Constantin Cantemir learned of the meeting and immediately ordered its participants arrested and brought to the court. According to Ion Neculce, the voivode personally beheaded Velicico, and only a handful of conspirators managed to evade capture.[127] Ruset and Bogdan also convinced Cantemir to arrest Miron Costin, who had not participated in the meeting and was allegedly unaware of the conspiracy, but this did not save him from death. The Costins' faction was defeated, and the Rusets gained the upper hand.

The conflict between these two factions was often described as an ideological clash between pro-Polish and pro-Ottoman groups within the Moldavian elite. However, there is little to support this thesis, and the gist of the conflict seems to have been a domestic one. First, despite his allegedly pro-Polish stance, Costin did surprisingly little to substantiate this claim. In 1673 he refused to join Ştefan Petriceicu in Polish-Lithuanian exile. In 1684, he remained loyal to Gheorghe Duca and his move to the Commonwealth was an involuntary one. Finally, in 1686–91 he adopted a passive strategy and failed to provide any assistance to Sobieski's war effort. Secondly, calling the likes of Lupu Bogdan as pro-Ottoman partisans is also misleading. Bogdan himself shifted his allegiance several times during the war. In 1684 he backed Ştefan Petriceicu's short-lived reign in Moldavia only to abandon him and join the camp of his relative, Constantin Cantemir. His subsequent actions followed the same pattern. Somewhat ironically, Iordache Ruset and Lupu Bogdan, the leaders of the 'pro-Ottoman' faction and instigators of Miron Costin's death, successfully sought Polish–Lithuanian protection in 1693, when the Porte appointed their enemy, Constantin Duca, as the new voivode.[128]

Sobieski's attempts to establish control over the Danubian principalities have much in common with that of Zamoyski. With a shaky position within the Polish–Lithuanian political arena, he sought to enhance his authority by taking control over Moldavia and Wallachia. As in the other episodes discussed in this chapter, his goal was factional in nature rather than geopolitical, and should be interpreted within a factional key. His patronage over Costin, the king thought, would facilitate the task, given their long-standing relationship that spanned over two decades. However, while Costin was willing to provide some support, there was a limit to his commitment. As long as the interests of the king and the boyar aligned, the cooperation proceeded smoothly. However, Costin was quick to defect as soon as the interests of his patron clashed with his own.

Why did Moldavia and Wallachia survive?

According to Ion Neculce, when Ottoman troops besieged the fortress of Kam'janec' in 1672, Köprülü Ahmed Pasha asked Miron Costin:

> The vizier ordered him to tell the truth [and asked]: 'Do you rejoice that the emperor took Kam'janec'?' Miron replied that he feared to tell the truth. The vizier smiled and began to laugh, telling him not to worry. To this Miron responded: 'We Moldavians are happy that the sultan's domains expand, but we would prefer if it grew in some other direction.'[129]

As the evidence in this chapter has shown, the Moldavians could say the same about the Commonwealth. While eager to establish individual alliances with Ottoman and Polish–Lithuanian elites, they obstructed the attempts to merge the political arenas. They profited from the exchange of resources but were against bringing down the barriers that separated them from their counterparts.

The behaviour of Moldavian boyars casts doubts on the presumed existence of 'pro-Polish' and 'pro-Ottoman' factions. This distinction hinges on the notion of two ideologically opposed, coherent camps, and is often filtered through the nationalist lens, which projects an opposition between pro-Christian 'freedom fighters' and collaborationists profiteering from the 'Turkish yoke'. However, drawing such a clear-cut picture misrepresents the realities on the ground. As Lidia Vlasova pointed out, the boyars were interested first and foremost in their own socio-political position rather than international trends. The allegiances of individual boyars to one party or another were in constant flux, and the goals of each group were basically the same, even if the means they employed differed depending on the circumstances.[130] According to her, throughout the early modern period, the Moldavian revenue-extraction system oscillated between two distinct models: seigneurial-feudal and fiscal-statist. In the former, the surplus from agricultural production was extracted by individual boyars in the form of rents from the demesne, while the latter procured revenue from tax collection in which they boyars partook. According to the author, Moldavia's integration into the Polish–Lithuanian system would strengthen the former tendency, providing

180   *The Ottomans and Eastern Europe*

high-ranking boyars with immunities, while marginalizing those with smaller estates, like the Cantemir family. In turn, the continued allegiance to the Porte would entrench the fiscal-statist model.[131]

Although they adhere to Soviet-style Marxist orthodoxy, Vlasova's arguments are worth our attention, as they provide a link between political developments and a deeper structural background. However, its singular focus on class interests falls short of explaining the divergence among the boyars. If the political orientations were hardwired to economic interests, why would individual allegiances shift so frequently? Moreover, if wealthy boyars, like Miron Costin, had so much to gain from strengthening the *seigneurial-feudal* mode of extraction, why would they steer away from the Polish–Lithuanian bid for power?

Answering these questions leads us away from the Marxist standpoint adopted by Vlasova. As I have demonstrated in previous chapters, actors on each side of the border sought to use patron–client relations to procure resources that would otherwise remain beyond their reach. Their capacity to establish such ties would determine their position, depending on the political conjuncture. For instance, during Constantin Cantemir's reign, Iordache Ruset and Lupu Bogdan profited from their association with the ruler and pursued a 'pro-Ottoman' policy. However, once Constantin Duca took over the throne, they fled to Poland–Lithuania. Would this make them suddenly the leaders of the 'pro-Polish' party? Hardly. Thus, it is more appropriate to see the political landscape of the principalities as shaped by patronage relations and factional rivalries rather than international politics.

The role of personal and factional interests allows us to explain tensions associated with the annexation projects. A radical redrawing of the political map brought to the fore contradictory interests of different cliques within the cross-border patronage network. In Zamoyski–Movilă faction, the annexation attempt unearthed contradictory goals and 'moral economies' of redistribution within the faction, which eventually undid the project and damaged the cohesion of the network. In the Ottoman attempt of 1595, the fragmentation of the imperial elite and the availability of cross-border patronage as a risk-averse solution prompted the grandees to abandon the scheme altogether after a single try. The Ottoman elite could procure financial resources, while boyars could also cut their share of the revenue and secure political support. While not equally remunerative for all actors, it was nonetheless convenient and efficient enough, and the losers in this arrangement lacked the influence necessary to restructure the system.

Thirdly, procuring resources from beyond the pale was one thing; integrating the political arenas was another. Moldavian–Wallachian boyars had no qualms about involving Polish–Lithuanian magnates or Ottoman grandees into internal power struggles, but they dissociated themselves from any annexation attempts. Even if they paid lip service to the idea, they clearly obstructed any steps to carry out such plans. It is not difficult to understand why. Moldavian and Wallachian boyars controlled comparatively meagre resources and could be easily overshadowed by their rivals if the existing barriers were brought down. Thus, by becoming part of Poland–Lithuania, the boyars could only lose. The Lithuanian middle gentry and its anxiety about the influx of new rivals from the Crown serve as a good analogy in this respect.

Finally, the failed annexation attempts elucidate the crucial difference in cross-border patronage of Polish–Lithuanian magnates and Ottoman grandees. Both in 1595–1600 and the 1680s, the elites of the Commonwealth sought to secure control of landed estates and redistribute them among the nobility, in line with the cultural models and patterns of a relatively non-monetized and land-oriented economy dominant in Poland–Lithuania. This stood in stark contrast with the Ottoman approach. Even when the Porte tried to do away with the Danubian principalities, it did not seek the rearrangement of agricultural relations: rather than creating *timars*, Ferhad Pasha and other grandees sought to ensure the flow of cash revenues. This system was far more flexible and more accommodating for boyars' interests, and greatly facilitated the ultimate success of the Ottoman Empire in the struggle for control of the principalities in the seventeenth century, as well as the subsequent integration of Moldavia and Wallachia into the imperial system after the Treaty of Karlowitz.

Figure 6.1 Romanian and Ottoman inscriptions commemorating the construction of a fountain near the St Spiridon Monastery in Iași, 1766.

6

Choosing Ottomans?

In hindsight, the Treaty of Karlowitz, concluded on 26 January 1699, constituted a major watershed in the history of Ottoman presence in Eastern Europe.[1] While the demarcation of the boundaries was not a novel practice for the Ottoman elite, the *'ahdname* issued to the Polish king retained the rhetorical bluster of earlier instruments of peace, much changed in the regional political landscape.[2] The treaty marked the end of Polish–Ottoman rivalry in the Danubian principalities and the Commonwealth's general withdrawal from the active policy in the region. In the following years, the ravages of the Great Northern War (1700–1721) effectively knocked out Poland–Lithuania, reducing it to an object of diplomatic schemes. Rather than to Warsaw, Moldavian and Wallachian boyars began to look to the courts of Vienna and Saint Petersburg for alternatives to the Ottoman rule.[3]

Even though the Ottoman Empire emerged from the war with major territorial losses and tarnished prestige, it managed to hold to the Danubian principalities and even enhance its hegemony in the region. By 1714, the Ottomans established a permanent garrison in Moldavian Hotin, and the principalities themselves entered what came to be known as 'the Phanariot period'.[4] Polish–Lithuanian political patronage over Moldavian boyars all but ceased, although border exchanges with Ottoman officials of Hotin and elites of the principality continued to flourish.[5] Thus, by the early eighteenth century, over a century of Polish–Ottoman struggles in the Lower Danube region concluded with the Ottoman victory. In the following decades, Moldavia and Wallachia became even more integrated into the imperial fabric of the 'Well-Protected Domains' until the second half of the century, when growing Russian threat undermined Ottoman hegemony in the region. According to this model, the final outcome was a product of a geopolitical rivalry, and ultimately boiled down to the balance of military power between the Porte and the Commonwealth.

However, once we zoom in at the course of events throughout the seventeenth century, the state is conspicuously missing as the moving force. Rather than a game of geopolitical chess, what we find instead is a complex fabric of individual actors, banding together in cross-border factions to harness necessary resources and achieve their goals. Many of those who partook in these networks of patronage were office-holders, and on occasions the political competition escalated into a full-scale war between the states. Nonetheless, – as I have argued throughout the book – the logic that drove the political life and informed the actions of its participants was not that of the state, but rather of cross-border factionalism.

Throughout the seventeenth century, Polish–Lithuanian nobles, Ottoman officials and Moldavian–Wallachian boyars inhabited a highly competitive environment, characterized by fierce rivalry for political and economic resources and the growing importance of factional politics. The rise of the factions, itself a response to the changing socio-economic conditions, subverted political hierarchies, weakening the position of the rulers, while empowering leaders of vast patronage networks. Despite structural differences between arenas, the process was general throughout the region, with the emerging patronage networks wielding considerable political, economic and military resources, which they could deploy to prevail over rival groupings or even to challenge the ruler.

While most studies have focused on the process within the bounds of a single polity, the expansion of factions – as I have demonstrated throughout the study – straddled political boundaries in the region, with important consequences for the shape of Eastern European politics. By extending their reach beyond the pale and forming cross-border patronage networks, Polish–Lithuanian nobles, Ottoman officials and Moldavian–Wallachian boyars were able to access resources that they would otherwise be unable to tap. As shown in Chapter 2, in order to do so, they repurposed their toolkits of faction-building, selecting appropriate tools and adapting them to the specific requirements of cross-border patronage. In the process, some methods of providing trust – such as Ottoman practice of political slavery – were discarded, others recalibrated. While the resulting toolkits were hardly novel in their content, their successful adaptation and deployment proves considerable flexibility and adaptability on part of their users.

Once successfully established, cross-border patronage enabled the exchange of resources between members of the faction and, consequently, their transfer across individual arenas. As the analysis in Chapter 3 demonstrates, these consisted of extremely diverse and seemingly incompatible items, ranging from watermelons to considerable sums of cash, to tens of thousands of soldiers. What gave them relevance was their role in the political, social and economic logic of

Choosing Ottomans? 185

faction and political competition. Calling on political support, military force, financial resources and intelligence of one's allies on the other side of the border brought a competitive advantage and frequently tilted the balance within the arena. This was particularly the case of Moldavia and Wallachia, as comparatively meagre resources that the local elite wielded could be overwhelmed by Polish–Lithuanian or Ottoman powerholders. However, this does not mean that Moldavian–Wallachian input did not feature prominently in factional strategies. They played a key role in furnishing information, managing the flow of communication, and contributed to the upkeep of their patrons' political machines, in many respects providing resources that would be otherwise difficult to obtain. Finally, a separate category of gifts served the purpose of maintaining the patronage network and expressing its members' continued commitment to the political enterprise.

The different ways in which Moldavian boyars were expected to provide economic resources exhibits a crucial difference between Polish–Lithuanian and Ottoman modes of cross-border patronage. The latter, operating under conditions of a monetized economy, were primarily interested in extracting liquid cash, which they could subsequently deploy to financing their political household. In contrast, the magnates of the Polish–Moldavian borderland generally sought to secure landed estates and pastures within the principality. This preference, dictated by both the structure of the Commonwealth's economy and the nobility's cultural ideal, had far-reaching consequences. Not only was it more cumbersome to handle than moveable wealth, but also could be obtained only at the expense of local Moldavian elite. As a result, the push for annexation of the Danubian principalities was much more pronounced than among Ottoman grandees, content with financial windfall from the 'shadow *iltizam*' arrangements.

The proliferation of cross-border patronage testifies clearly that they proved a reliable mechanism of problem-solving and resource-procurement, eventually producing a geography of power different from that dictated by the state. At the same time, as more actors jumped the bandwagon, the growing extent of factional politics produced unintended effects. Crucially, the fierceness of political rivalry within individual arenas and the importance of cross-border ties in the calculus of power had an important consequence: by strengthening ties between the arenas, it weakened the bonds within them, making it more difficult to enforce cooperation between individual actors. Moreover, the increasing entanglement meant that factional struggles quickly spilled between the arenas. As I have demonstrated in Chapter 4, many conflicts that have been usually interpreted as manifestations of geopolitical rivalry in the region, were in fact clashes between cross-border political networks, driven by their interests rather than alleged state interests. In such instances, individual actors picked sides not based on their political allegiance to a specific ruler or polity but rather a specific cross-border faction. Although this frequently involved what we may call state resources, state interest played little role in the lead-up and development of such conflicts.

However, competition over resources did not take place only between distinct factions, but also within them. Far-flung factions that brought together numerous individuals and groups, each with their own vested interests and different concepts of how the spoils should be divided, were bound to create tensions. The latter sometimes escalated into an open conflict and the breakup of the faction into two or more hostile camps. It is telling of the strength and importance of cross-border ties that the split usually occurred not along boundaries of the arenas, but rather across them, again suggesting that factional allegiance took precedence over the political allegiance to a specific ruler. A particularly critical point in such networks' lifetime was the moment of generational change: since the members of a factional edifice were tied personally to the patron, whose role was to harmonize their often-conflicting interests, his death often triggered a struggle for power between his closest subordinates. Some factions – such as that of Köprülüs and their Moldavian–Wallachian clients – survived, while others disintegrated in the succession conflict.

Similar dynamics played out in the Ottoman and Polish–Lithuanian attempts to annex Moldavia and Wallachia, analysed in Chapter 5. These ultimately unsuccessful ventures have been interpreted by historians as reflections of geopolitical rivalry between the Commonwealth and the Porte, but a closer examination of the events suggests a different story. The conditions in which they were undertaken, and their ultimate failure subscribed to the logic of cross-border factionalism, while also demonstrating its limits. Most of these attempts were not defeated by enemy forces, but rather by inter- and intra-factional struggle within the camp. In 1595, there was little cooperation among Ottoman officials to carry out the annexation of the principalities; instead, key figures at the Porte actively sabotaged the expedition to remove their personal rivals from power. Moreover, after the campaign failed, the likes of Koca Sinan Pasha and his successor quickly abandoned the venture altogether, reverting to cross-border patronage as a less risky and efficient enough method to procure resources from the principalities. The lack of cohesion within the arena and factional bonds between Ottoman grandees and Moldavian–Wallachian elites discouraged outright annexation while at the same time providing a viable alternative.

A somewhat similar dynamic played out in the parallel attempt carried out by Jan Zamoyski. The grand Crown chancellor had engaged in the venture as a response to his conflict with the king, which had deprived him of patronage resources he direly needed to satisfy members of his patronage network, whose patience was running thin. His plans for annexing Moldavia and Wallachia constituted an attempt to escape this situation and provide for his subordinates. However, the military success did not alleviate the tensions within his faction. Instead, it forced him into an impossible position of trying to mediate between two sections of his faction – Moldavian and Polish–Lithuanian – each staking their claim to the principalities' resources they felt entitled to. In effect, Zamoyski's faction was effectively crippled following his Moldavian campaign, as his vacillating position alienated both his Polish–Lithuanian and Moldavian–Wallachian clients.

Finally, Sobieski's attempt to take control of the principalities displayed similar features. Although as a ruler of the Polish–Lithuanian Commonwealth his actions lend themselves to a state-centred interpretation, they followed a similar logic of cross-border patronage, and its goals were set by his own factional interests. Despite his patronage relations with Moldavian elite, his attempt similarly fizzled out, as the boyars failed to flock to the royal camp; even his most prominent client, Miron Costin, provided only limited assistance and never abandoned Voivode Constantin Cantemir's camp to join his patron. This lack of support, as I argued, was due to the fact that Sobieski's plans directly threatened the political, social and economic foundations of the local elite's status, and went beyond what his Moldavian boyars were ready to accept. Ultimately, the failure led the king to a more modest plan of managing Moldavia's resources, engaging in a colonization plan that only further alienated the local elite.

The experiences of the failed annexation attempts suggest a different interpretation of the reasons why, post-1699, the Danubian principalities remained within the orbit of the Sublime Porte. Compared with their Ottoman counterparts, Polish–Lithuanian powerholders failed to develop a viable mechanism of cross-border patronage that would accommodate interests of their Moldavian clients in the long run. While able to mount serious challenges and seemingly coming close to establishing their influence in Moldavia, their efforts ultimately failed to satisfy the boyars' demands for political resources. At the same time, the economic attitude presented by magnates trying to take over the agricultural estates in the principality posed a grave danger for the local elites' ability to remain at the apex of power. Although the latter was eager to draw on the political and military resources of their Polish–Lithuanian patrons, they drew a line in sand with respect to ventures that would undercut their own basis of power.

Several external factors also made Polish–Moldavian cooperation less likely. Whereas in the first half of the seventeenth century, the nobility of the Commonwealth was still multi-confessional, this attitude changed significantly in the aftermath of the 1648 Cossack rebellion. The uprising and subsequent war with Muscovy eroded the position of the Orthodox community, increasingly associated with tsarist sympathizers and marginalized in public life. This growing wave of Catholicization increasingly distanced Polish–Lithuanian nobility from their Moldavian–Wallachian counterparts. Taken together, these factors contributed to the growing rift between the two elites and diminished incentives to establish cross-border ties.

In contrast, the Ottoman mode of patronage proved far more accommodating for boyars' interests and more reliable in delivering coveted spoils. Unlike the magnates of the Commonwealth, Ottoman grandees had no interest in taking over control of the resources that the local elite relied on. The arrangements based on informal cash flows and political cooperation were satisfactory enough for both parties and did not leave Moldavian–Wallachian boyars empty-handed. Moreover, while the fortunes of Orthodox nobility declined in Poland–Lithuania, the situation was starkly different within the Ottoman ecumene. The early eighteenth century saw the culmination of a long process of the ascendancy of Orthodox notables that operated at the interface of the imperial centre and Moldavian–Wallachian periphery. This elite, bound to both arenas by ties of family, blood, patronage and finance, occupied the position of brokers and stabilized the system of cross-border patronage.[6] As such, they provided a crucial link that facilitated further integration into the Ottoman imperial system.

As I demonstrated throughout the present study, state as an actor was prominently absent from these developments. This is not to stay that it was irrelevant: most participants in patronage networks were office-holders, and the resources they deployed in cross-border patronage were drawn from state circuits; finally, it played a crucial role in legitimizing their actions. However, it would be a mistake to claim paramountcy of the state over the sphere of cross-border patronage. Its role within this context should be understood not as a cohesive actor vested with its own agency, but rather as an institutional scaffolding and part of the larger political environment in which actors operated. As I have argued in the introduction, what is often presented as 'a state', is better understood once we disaggregate it into constitutive parts. A significant share of resources flowing through cross-border patronage networks originated from state circuits and the actors' status as office-holders; however, the way they deployed them was driven by their role as faction members rather than state officials. Moreover, the relationship between state circuits and cross-border patronage was by no means parasitical. While the latter fed partly on the resources provided by the former, the reverse was also true. For instance, money obtained from Moldavian–Wallachian clients contributed to the upkeep of Ottoman *kapıs*, which in turn provided military force for large-scale campaigns. Thus, one should think of the geography of early modern polities and that of cross-border patronage as parallel – and in many instances – rather than mutually exclusive. The coexistence of alternative geographies of power provided early modern elites with multiple options, and the fact that they so often chose factional interest over state interest testifies to the importance of the former for their political activity.

What is more, the co-existence of multiple circuits enhanced the position of the powerholders vis-à-vis the ruler. This is best demonstrated in the case of one of the most important aspects of state power, legitimacy. As the examples I presented throughout the book show, although it constituted a crucial and sought-after resource, it did not suffice to enforce the rule will or enforce cooperation between members of different factions. Rather than being deployed by the ruler in a top-down manner, it was always negotiated and often used as a rubber stamp to recognize the outcome of factional conflict that had already played out. Particularly instructive in this respect is the attitude of Abaza Mehmed Pasha, who openly defied orders by supporting Matei Basarab and saw his actions rubber-stamped by Murad IV. Under conditions defined by the rise of factionalism the rulers themselves were not above the fray. Thus, they often had no choice but to side with the winner, thus legitimizing the outcome, or risk dethronement. It is not by accident that the period under discussion witnessed two civil wars in the Commonwealth, frequent revolts in Moldavia and Wallachia and a full half of incumbent Ottoman sultans faced deposition.

As I have sought to demonstrate throughout the present study, the rise of faction in Poland–Lithuania, the Ottoman Empire and the Danubian principalities was not only parallel, but also intertwined within the larger geography of power that straddled political boundaries and brought together actors of different backgrounds in joint political ventures. While facilitating transfer of resources, it also contributed to the growing entanglement between conflicts playing out in different arenas. Despite holding official posts and claiming to serve their rulers, powerholders partaking in cross-border patronage were driven by factional logic, showing more enthusiasm in bringing down personal rivals rather than supporting war effort or engaging enemy forces. Polish–Lithuanian, Moldavian–Wallachian and Ottoman powerholders were quick to dissociate themselves or even derail enterprises that collided with their personal, familial and factional interests. What modern historians – influenced by the modern concepts of statehood – would consider state interest was not at the top of the elites' list of priorities. When factional interests clashed with those of the state, the former usually gained the upper hand.

In this sense, they were not different from other early modern elites around the world. As Bartolomé Yun Casalilla pointed out, biological and social reproduction of elite households and retaining control over resources was a more pressing concern than state service per se.[7] In a society, in which power and authority continued to be inextricably tied with the person of its holder, this should come as no surprise. For Ottoman dignitaries, Polish–Lithuanian magnates and Moldavian–Wallachian boyars, the polity they inhabited constituted a joint enterprise, meant to safeguard their interest and allow their social reproduction.[8] This was a common thread in other polities as well. In a fascinating study of Dutch *regents*, Julia Adams pointed out how familial interests of the elite profoundly shaped the very structure of the United Provinces, since 'corporate elites acquired pieces of the nascent state, in some cases selling them or passing them on to descendants'.[9] This familial compact was responsible for the extraordinary success of the Dutch polity throughout the seventeenth century, but the same mechanisms led to its unravelling as *regent* families were reluctant to give up their share of power necessary to overhaul the system, thus prioritizing social reproduction over the very survival of the state. In arguably the most radical example of this kind, considerable share of Chinese gentry preferred to let the Ming Empire die rather than surrender their symbolic capital.[10] Against this background, the rampant cross-border factionalism of three Eastern European elites by no means seems an outlier.

In traditional historiographies on Poland–Lithuania, the Ottoman Empire and the Danubian principalities, the eighteenth century is presented in many respects as a period of decline, a depiction that only relatively recently was overcome by a new wave of historiography. Much of the blame for this alleged decline used to be placed with the elites of respective polities, accused of short-sightedness, self-interest and egoism. However, this approach stems from the confusion over principal motives that informed the elites' political behaviour of the seventeenth century. Polish–Lithuanian nobles, Ottoman officials, and Moldavian–Wallachian boyars were not so much interested in the state as such, but rather in the continued preservation of the socio-political system that allowed them to thrive. In achieving this goal, they had multiple options: relying on state networks was one of them, as was cross-border patronage. Both coexisted and produced important changes during events and the very structure of seventeenth-century Eastern European politics. From their perspective, state was not the ultimate goal – as has often been for modern historians – but rather one circuit of power among many overlapping ones.

Notes

Introduction

1   Agnieszka Biedrzycka (ed.), *Korespondencja Stanisława Koniecpolskiego hetmana wielkiego koronnego, 1632–1646* (Cracow, 2005), pp. 565–78.

2   Kemal Beydilli, *Die Polnischen Königswahlen und Interregnen von 1572 und 1576 im Lichte osmanischer Archivalien: Ein Beitrag zur Geschichte der osmanischen Machtspolitik* (Munich, 1976).

3   See Victor Ostapchuk, 'The Ottoman Black Sea frontier and the relations of the Porte with the Polish-Lithuanian Commonwealth and Muscovy, 1622–1628' (PhD diss., Harvard University, 1989).

4   To name only a few: Ilona Czamańska, 'Mołdawia i Wołoszczyzna w stosunkach polsko-tureckich XV–XVIII w', *Balcanica Posnaniensia* 4 (1989), pp. 301–12; Zdzisław Spieralski, *Awantury mołdawskie* (Warsaw, 1967); Veniamin Ciobanu, *La cumpănă de veacuri: Ţările Române în contextul politicii poloneze la sfârşitul secolului al XVI-lea şi începutul secolului al XVII-lea* (Iaşi, 1991); Veniamin Ciobanu, *Politică şi diplomaţie în secolul al XVII-lea: Ţările Române în raporturile polono-otomano-habsburgice (1601–1634)* (Bucharest, 1994); Tahsin Gemil, 'La Moldavie dans les traités de paix ottomano-polonais du XIXᵉ siècle (1621–1672)', *Revue Roumaine d'Histoire* 12/4 (1973), pp. 687–714; Tahsin Gemil, *Ţările Române în contextul politic internaţional (1621–1672)* (Bucharest, 1979); İ. Metin Kunt, '17. yüzyılda Osmanlı kuzey politikası üzerine bir yorum', *Boğaziçi Üniversitesi Dergisi. Hümaniter Bilimler – Humanities* 4–5 (1976–1977), pp. 111–16.

5   Hillard von Thiessen, *Diplomatie und Patronage: Die spanisch-römischen Beziehungen 1605–1621 in akteurszentrierter Perspektive* (Epfendorf, 2010), p. 15.

6   Daniel H. Nexon, *The Struggle for Power in Early Modern Europe: Religious Conflict, Dynastic Empires, and International Change* (Princeton, NJ, 2009), pp. 20–1.

7   For the concept of methodological nationalism, see Andreas Wimmer and Nina Glick Schiller, 'Methodological nationalism and beyond: nation-state building, migration and the social sciences', *Global Networks* 2/4 (2002), pp. 301–31.

8   Jeremy Black, *Kings, Nobles and Commoners: States and Societies in Early Modern Europe – A Revisionist History* (London, 2004).

9   Timothy Mitchell, 'The limits of the state: beyond statist approaches and their critics', *American Political Science Review* 85/1 (1991), p. 95; Bartolomé Yun Casalilla, 'Introducción: entre el imperio colonial y la monarquía compuesta. Élites

192 *Notes*

     y territorios en la Monarquía Hispánica', in Bartolomé Yun Casalilla (ed.), *Las redes del imperio: Élites sociales en la articulación de la Monarquía Hispánica* (Madrid, 2009), pp. 11–35.

10   Antonio M. Hespanha, 'The legal patchwork of empires', *Rechtsgeschichte* 22 (2014), p. 303; Wolfgang Reinhard, 'Introduction: power elites, state servants, ruling classes and the growth of state power', in Wolfgang Reinhard (ed.), *Power Elites and State Building* (Oxford, 1996), p. 7; Robert Descimon, 'Power elites and the prince: the state as enterprise', in Wolfgang Reinhard (ed.), *Power Elites and State Building* (Oxford, 1996), pp. 101–21; Guy Rowlands, *The Dynastic State and the Army under Louis XIV: Royal Service and Private Interest, 1661–1701* (Cambridge, 2002).

11   André Holenstein, 'Empowering interactions: looking at statebuilding from below', in Wim Blockmans, André Holenstein and Jon Mathieu (eds), *Empowering Interactions: Political Cultures and the Emergence of the State in Europe, 1300–1900* (Aldershot, 2009), p. 6.

12   Dariusz Kołodziejczyk, 'What is inside and what is outside? Tributary states in Ottoman politics', in Gábor Kármán and Lovro Kunčević (eds), *The European Tributary States of the Ottoman Empire in the Sixteenth–Seventeenth Centuries* (Leiden – Boston, 2013), pp. 421–32.

13   Orest Subtelny, *Domination of Eastern Europe: Native Nobilities and Foreign Absolutism, 1500–1715* (Kingston, 1986), p. 56.

14   For instance, see Perry Anderson, *Lineages of the Absolutist State* (London, 1974), pp. 297–8.

15   On this topic, see particularly Radu G. Păun, 'La circulation des pouvoirs dans les Pays Roumains au XIXe siècle: repères pour un modèle théorique', *New Europe College Yearbook* 6 (1998–1999), pp. 264–9 and 294–5.

16   See Michael G. Müller and Cornelius Torp, 'Conceptualising transnational spaces in history', *European Review of History* 16/5 (2009), p. 611.

17   The literature on the topic of patronage in the Ottoman Empire, Poland–Lithuania and the Danubian principalities is vast, consisting of both sweeping overviews and in-depth studies of individual factions or regions. For the rise of grandee households among the Ottoman elite, the most important studies include Carter V. Findley, 'Political culture and the great households', in Suraiya Faroqhi (ed.), *The Cambridge History of Turkey*, vol. 3 (Cambridge, 2006), pp. 65–80; Jane Hathaway, *The Politics of Households in Ottoman Egypt: The Rise of Qazdağlıs* (Cambridge, 1997); Günhan Börekçi, 'Factions and favorites at the courts of Sultan Ahmed I (r. 1603–1617) and his immediate predecessors' (PhD diss., Ohio State University, 2010); Michael Nizri, *Ottoman High Politics and the Ulema Household* (Basingstoke, 2014). For Poland–Lithuania, see Antoni Mączak, *Klientela: Nieformalne systemy władzy w Polsce i Europie XVI–XVIII w.* (Warsaw, 1994); Antoni Mączak, 'The structure of power in the Commonwealth of the sixteenth and seventeenth centuries', in J. K. Fedorowicz (ed.), *A Republic of Nobles: Studies in*

Polish History to 1864 (Cambridge, 1982), pp. 109–34; Wojciech Tygielski, *Politics of Patronage in Renaissance Poland: Chancellor Jan Zamoyski, His Supporters and the Political Map of Poland, 1572–1605* (Warsaw, 1990); Urszula Augustyniak, *Dwór i klientela Krzysztofa Radziwiłła, 1585–1640: Mechanizmy patronatu* (Warsaw, 2001). For the Danubian principalities, the most important study is Radu G. Păun, 'Pouvoirs, offices et patronage dans la Principauté de Moldavie au XIXe siècle: l'aristocratie roumaine et la pénétration gréco-levantine' (PhD diss., L'École des Hautes Études en Sciences Sociales, 2003). See also Ştefan S. Gorovei, 'Clanuri, familii, autorități, puteri (Moldova, secolele XV–XVII)', *Arhiva Genealogică* 1/1–2 (1994), pp. 87–93.

18 See, for instance, Gintautas Sliesoriūnas, 'Walka stronnictw w przededniu i podczas wojny domowej na Litwie XVII/XVIII wieku', in Jerzy Urwanowicz, Ewa Dubas-Urwanowicz and Piotr Guzowski (eds), *Władza i prestiż: Magnateria Rzeczypospolitej w XVI–XVIII wieku* (Białystok, 2003), pp. 231–42; Lidia Vlasova, 'Dva napravlenija vnešnej politiki Moldavii i ix prelomlenie v ee vzaimootnošneijax s Pol'šej v 80–90-e gody XVII v.', in B. A. Rybakov (ed.), *Rossija, Pol'ša i Pričernomor'e v XV–XVIII v.* (Moscow, 1979), p. 341.

19 E. Natalie Rothman, *Brokering empire: trans-imperial subjects between Venice and Istanbul* (Ithaca, NY – London, 2012); Radu G. Păun, 'Some remarks about the historical origins of the "Phanariot phenomenon" in Moldavia and Wallachia (16th–19th centuries)', in Gelina Harlaftis and Radu G. Păun (eds), *Greeks in Romania in the nineteenth century* (Athens, 2013), pp. 47–94; Radu G. Păun, '"Well-born of the polis": the Ottoman conquest and the reconstruction of the Greek Orthodox elites under Ottoman rule', in Robert Born and Sabine Jagodzinski (eds), *Türkenkriege und Adelskultur in Ostmitteleuropa vom 16.-18. Jahrhundert* (Leipzig, 2014), pp. 59–85; Noel Malcolm, *Agents of Empire: Knights, Pirates, Jesuits and Spies in the Sixteenth-century Mediterranean World* (Oxford – New York, 2015). I would like to thank Radu Păun for bringing the latter book to my attention.

20 Palmira Brummett, 'Placing the Ottomans in the Mediterranean world: the question of notables and households', *Osmanlı Araştırmaları* 36 (2010), p. 81.

21 The metaphor of 'lopsided friendship' was first coined by Julian A. Pitt-Rivers, *The People of the Sierra* (London, 1954) p. 140.

22 Jane Hathaway, 'The household: an alternative framework for the military society of eighteenth-century Ottoman Egypt', *Oriente Moderno* 18/1 (1999), p. 62.

23 Mączak, *Klientela*, pp. 18–19.

24 Ibid., 119.

25 On this topic, see Dariusz Kołodziejczyk, 'Permeable frontiers: contacts between Polish and Turkish-Tatar elites in the early modern era', in Björn Forsén and Mika Hakkarainen (eds), *Foreign Drums Beating: Transnational Experiences in Early Modern Europe* (Helsinki, 2017), pp. 153–68. I would like to thank Dariusz Kołodziejczyk with providing me with a copy of the study.

26 Sharon Kettering, *Patrons, Brokers, and Clients in Seventeenth-Century France* (New York, 1986), pp. 3–4; Wolfgang Reinhard, 'Oligarchische Verflechtung und Konfession in oberdeutschen Städten', in Antoni Mączak and Elisabeth Müller-Luckner (eds), *Klientelsysteme im Europa der Früher Neuzeit* (Munich, 1988), p. 50.

27 Georg Flemming, a Saxon bureaucrat turned Lithuanian grand treasurer, provides an instructive example in this respect. Upon his appointment to Lithuania by King Augustus III in 1746, Flemming set out to establish a royal faction in the Grand Duchy. His bureaucratic approach to the task at hand, however, alienated many of potential clients. According to the contemporaries, Flemming recruited clients, assigned them landholdings leases, put the names on the rolls and sent them away. He barely knew his noble clientele and did not even bother to remember their names, summoning them only to vote at the dietines. Although the nobles welcomed economic resources he provided, they nonetheless considered Flemming's bureaucratic style insulting, thus hampering the efficiency of his political machine, see Mączak, *Klientela*, p. 11.

28 Javier Auyero, *Poor People's Politics: Peronist Survival Networks and the Legacy of Evita* (Durham, NC, 2001), p. 174.

29 Robert R. Kaufman, 'The patron-client concept and macro-politics: prospects and problems', *Comparative Studies in Society and History* 16/3 (1974), pp. 290–1.

30 Sharon Kettering, 'The historical development of political clientelism', *Journal of Interdisciplinary History* 18/3 (1988), p. 425.

31 Michael J. Braddick, *State Formation in Early Modern England, c. 1550–1700* (Cambridge, 2004), p. 9; Karen Barkey, *Empire of Difference: The Ottomans in Comparative Perspective* (Cambridge, 2008); Kerry Ward, *Networks of Empire: Forced Migration in the Dutch East India Company* (Cambridge, 2009), p. 6.

32 Ronald S. Burt, *Brokerage and Closure: An Introduction to Social Capital* (Oxford, 2005), p. 4.

33 Sebouh D. Aslanian, *From the Indian Ocean to the Mediterranean: The Global Trade Networks of Armenian Merchants from New Julfa* (Berkeley, CA, 2011), p. 14.

34 Claire Lemercier, 'Formale Methoden der Netzwerkanalyse in den Geschichtswissenschaften: Warum und Wie?', *Österreichische Zeitschrift für Geschichtswissenschaften* 23/1 (2012), p. 21.

35 Frederick G. Bailey, *Stratagems and Spoils: A Social Anthropology of Politics*, revised edition (Boulder, 2001), p. 147. For an updated concept of the arena, see also Daniel Cefaï, 'Qu'est-ce qu'une arene publique', in Daniel Cefaï and Isaac Joseph (eds), *L'heritage du pragmatisme: conflits d'urbanité et épreuves de civisme* (La Tour d'Aigues, 2001), pp. 51–81. I would like to thank Radu Păun for bringing this study to my attention.

36 Jane Hathaway, *A Tale of Two Factions: Myth, Memory, and Identity in Ottoman Egypt and Yemen* (Albany, 2003), p. 4; Rhoads Murphey, *Exploring Ottoman Sovereignty: Tradition, Image and Practice in the Ottoman Imperial Household, 1400–1800* (London, 2008), pp. 149–50.

Chapter 1

1   M. G. Safargaliev, *Raspad Zolotoj Ordy* (Saransk, 1960); Alan W. Fisher, *The Crimean Tatars* (Stanford, 1987), p. 7.

2   Brian L. Davies, *Warfare, State and Society on the Black Sea Steppe, 1500–1700* (London – New York, 2007), pp. 1–2.

3   Ibid., p. 11; Brian J. Boeck, *Imperial Boundaries: Cossack Communities and Empire-Building in the Age of Peter the Great* (Cambridge, 2009), pp. 61–4.

4   Jerzy Wyrozumski, 'Węgry i sprawa Rusi halicko-włodzimierskiej za Kazimierza Wielkiego', in Krystyna Zielińska-Melkowska (ed.), *Europa Środkowa i Wschodnia w polityce Piastów* (Toruń, 1996), pp. 111–20.

5   Halil İnalcık, 'Yeni vesikalara göre Kırım hanlığının Osmanlı tabiliğine girmesi ve ahidname meselesi', *Belleten* 8/30 (1944), pp. 185–229; Fisher, *The Crimean Tatars*, pp. 11–12; Dariusz Kołodziejczyk, *The Crimean Khanate and Poland-Lithuania: International Diplomacy on the European Periphery (15th–18th Century): A Study of Peace Treaties Followed by Annotated Documents* (Leiden – Boston, 2011), p. 22.

6   Carl M. Kortepeter, *Ottoman Imperialism during the Reformation: Europe and the Caucasus* (London – New York, 1972), p. 14; Kołodziejczyk, *The Crimean Khanate and Poland-Lithuania*, p. 185.

7   Mária Ivanics, 'The military co-operation of the Crimean Khanate with the Ottoman Empire in the sixteenth and seventeenth centuries', in Gábor Kármán and Lovro Kunčević (eds), *The European Tributary States of the Ottoman Empire in the Sixteenth–Seventeenth Centuries* (Leiden – Boston, 2013), pp. 275–300.

8   Mikhail Kizilov, 'Slave trade in the early modern Crimea from the perspective of Christian, Muslim, and Jewish sources', *Journal of Early Modern History* 11/1 (2007), p. 2.

9   Dariusz Kołodziejczyk, 'Slave hunting and slave redemption as a business enterprise: the northern Black Sea region in the sixteenth to seventeenth centuries', *Oriente Moderno* 86/1 (2006), p. 151.

10   Davies, *Warfare, State and Society*, pp. 9–10.

11   Victor Ostapchuk, 'The Ottoman Black Sea frontier and the relations of the Porte with the Polish–Lithuanian Commonwealth and Muscovy, 1622–1628' (PhD diss., Harvard University, 1989), p. 4.

12   Davies, *Warfare, State and Society*, p. 115.

13   Marian Coman, *Putere și teritoriu: Țara Românească medievală (secolele XIV–XVI)* (Iași, 2013), pp. 307–8. See also Ștefan S. Gorovei, *Întemeierea Moldovei: Probleme controversate* (Iași, 1997).

14   Dennis Deletant, 'Moldavia between Hungary and Poland, 1347–1412', *The Slavonic and East European Review* 64/2 (1986), p. 203.

15   Ilona Czamańska, *Mołdawia i Wołoszczyzna wobec Polski, Węgier i Turcji w XIV i XV wieku* (Poznań, 1996), p. 54; Liviu Pilat, 'De la Liov la Colomeea: observații

196   *Notes*

privind ceremonialul depunerii omagiului de către domnii moldoveni', *Analele Putnei* 4/1 (2008), pp. 133–52.

16   Czamańska, *Mołdawia i Wołoszczyzna wobec Polski*, p. 292.

17   Andrei Pippidi, 'Moldavie et Pologne: la fin de la vassalité', *Acta Poloniae Historica* 83 (2001), pp. 59–78.

18   Cristian A. Bobicescu, 'Unia, inkorporacja czy lenno? Kilka uwag o stosunkach Mołdawii z Rzecząpospolitą podczas panowania Jeremiego Mohiły (1595–1606)', in Bogusław Dybaś, Paweł Hanczewski and Tomasz Kempa (eds), *Rzeczpospolita w XVI—XVIII wieku: Państwo czy wspólnota?* (Toruń, 2007), p. 222.

19   Viorel Panaite, *Război, comerț și pace în islam: țările române și dreptul otoman al popoarelor*, second edition (Iași, 2013), pp. 294–7.

20   Ibid., p. 296; Tahsin Gemil, *Romanians and Ottomans in the XIVth–XVIth Centuries*, trans. Remus Bejan and Paul Sanders (Bucharest, 2009), p. 190; Czamańska, *Mołdawia i Wołoszczyzna wobec Polski*, p. 120.

21   Halil İnalcık, 'The question of the closing of the Black Sea under the Ottomans', *Archeion Pontou* 35 (1979), pp. 74–111.

22   Gemil, *Romanians and Ottomans*, p. 56; Ion Chirtoagă, *Sud-Estul Moldovei și stânga Nistrului (1484–1699): Expansiunea și dominația turco-tatară* (Bucharest, 1999), pp. 56–7.

23   Panaite, *Pace, război și comerț*, pp. 399–412; Czamańska, *Mołdawia i Wołoszczyzna wobec Polski*, p. 323; Mihai Maxim, *Țările Române și Înalta Poartă: Cadrul juridic al relațiilor româno-otomane în evul mediu* (Bucharest, 1993), p. 54.

24   Mihai Berza, 'Haraciul Moldovei și Țării Românești în sec. XV–XIX', *Studii și Materiale de Istorie Medie* 2 (1957), pp. 7–47; Mihai Maxim, 'Recherches sur les circonstances de la majoration du *Kharadj* de la Moldavie entre les années 1538–1574', in Mihai Maxim, *L'Empire Ottoman au nord du Danube et l'autonomie des Principautés Roumaines au XVIᵉ siècle* (Istanbul, 1999), pp. 185–214.

25   On this topic, see Radu G. Păun, 'Conquered by the (s)word: governing the tributary principalities of Wallachia and Moldavia (16th–17th centuries)', in Robert Born and Marek Dziewulski (eds), *The Ottoman Orient in Renaissance Culture* (Cracow, 2015), pp. 24–9; Cf Mihai Maxim, 'Țările Române și Imperiul otoman', in Virgil Cândea (ed.), *Istoria românilor*, vol. 5, second edition (Bucharest, 2012), pp. 818–9.

26   Ioan D. Condurachi, *Soli și agenți ai domnilor Moldovei la Poartă în secolul al XVII-lea* (Bucharest, 1920); Aurel H. Golimas, *Despre capuchehăile Moldovei și poruncile Porții către Moldova până la 1829* (Iași, 1943); Ion Matei, *Reprezentanții diplomatici (capuchehăi) al Țării Românești la Poarta otomană*, ed. Tudor Teotoi and Nagy Pienaru (Bucharest, 2008); Viorel Panaite, 'Reprezentanța diplomatică a Țării Românesti la Poarta Otomană în epoca lui Constantin Brâncoveanu', *Revista de Istorie* 41/9 (1988), pp. 877–94. For the political role of Ottoman *kapı kethüda*s, see Michael Nizri, 'Rethinking center-periphery communication in the Ottoman

Empire: the *kapı kethüdası*', *Journal of the Economic and Social History of the Orient* 59/3 (2016), pp. 473–98.

27 Maxim, *Țările Române și Înalta Poartă*, p. 40.

28 Viorel Panaite, 'The voivodes of the Danubian Principalities – as *haracgüzarlar* of the Ottoman sultans', in Kemal H. Karpat and Robert W. Zens (eds), *Ottoman Borderlands: Issues, Personalities and Political Changes* (Madison, 2003), pp. 59–78; Panaite, *Război, pace și comerț*, p. 177.

29 Davies, *Warfare, State and Society*, p. 193; Victor Ostapchuk, 'The human landscape of the Ottoman Black Sea in the face of the Cossack naval raids', *Oriente Moderno* 20/1 (2001), p. 34.

30 Caroline Finkel and Victor Ostapchuk, 'Outpost of empire: an appraisal of Ottoman building registers as sources for the archeology and construction of the Black Sea fortress of Özi', *Muqarnas* 22 (2005), p. 157.

31 Baki Tezcan, 'Khotin 1621, or how the Poles changed the course of Ottoman history', *Acta Orientalia Academiae Scientiarum Hungaricae* 62/2 (2009), p. 192.

32 See, for instance, the remark by Paul of Aleppo (Bulus b. Makariyos al-Halabi): 'The voivode sent a mission to the pasha of Silistre, Siyavuş. [Siyavuş Pasha] oversees the rulers of Moldavia and Wallachia, and no complaint arrives to Istanbul without his consent', Paul of Aleppo, *Jurnal de călătorie în Moldova și Valahia*, ed. Ioana Feodorov (Bucharest, 2014), p. 274.

33 Scholars generally interpreted such instances, and particularly the reign of the Movilă dynasty (1595–1611), as periods of Polish–Ottoman condominium, see Ștefan S. Gorovei, 'O lămurire: domnia ereditară a familiei Movilă', *Revista de istorie* 28/7 (1975), pp. 1091–4. However, the instruments of peace issued in 1595 and 1598 do not provide any indications that the Porte envisioned any further Polish–Lithuanian involvement in Moldavian affairs, and merely granted hereditary rule to the Movilăs, see Dariusz Kołodziejczyk, *Ottoman-Polish diplomatic relations (15ᵗʰ–18ᵗʰ century): an annotated edition of* 'ahdname*s and other documents* (Leiden – Boston, 2000), pp. 298–302 and 317. That no power-sharing agreement was in place can be also seen in the case of Miron Barnovschi, see Dariusz Milewski, *Mołdawia między Polską a Turcją: hospodar Miron Barnowski i jego polityka (1626–1629)* (Oświęcim, 2014), pp. 192–3. Thus, rather than a 'condominium', the term 'polyvassalage' proposed by Ukrainian historian Taras Čuxlib seems more appropriate, see Taras V. Čuxlib, *Kozaky i monarxy: Mižnarodni vidnosyny rannʹomodernoji ukrajinsʹkoji deržavy, 1648–1721* (Kyiv, 2009), p. 22; Victor Ostapchuk, 'Cossack Ukraine in and out of Ottoman orbit, 1648–1681', in Gábor Kármán and Lovro Kunčević (eds), *The European Tributary States of the Ottoman Empire in the Sixteenth-Seventeenth Centuries* (Leiden – Boston, 2013), p. 151.

34 Janusz Wojtasik, 'Uwagi Księcia Krzysztofa Zbaraskiego, posła wielkiego do Turcji z 1622 r. – o państwie otomańskim i jego siłach zbrojnych', *Studia i Materiały do Historii Wojskowości* 7/1 (1961), pp. 333–4.

35 Cemal Kafadar, 'The question of Ottoman decline', *Harvard Middle Eastern and Islamic Review* 4/1–2 (1997–1998), pp. 30–75; Caroline Finkel, '"The treacherous cleverness of hindsight": myths of Ottoman decay', in Gerald McLean (ed.), *Re-orienting the Renaissance* (London, 2005), pp. 148–74.

36 Baki Tezcan, *The Second Ottoman Empire: Political and Social Transformation in the Early Modern World* (Cambridge, 2010), p. 238.

37 Ibid., pp. 81–2.

38 Rifa'at A. Abou-El-Haj, *Formation of the Modern State: The Ottoman Empire, Sixteenth to Eighteenth Centuries*, second edition (Syracuse, 2005), p. 59.

39 Tezcan, *The Second Ottoman Empire*, p. 11.

40 Ariel Salzmann, 'An ancien régime revisited: "privatization" and political economy in the eighteenth-century Ottoman Empire', *Politics and Society* 21/4 (1993), pp. 398–9; Michael Ursinus, 'The transformation of the Ottoman fiscal regime, *c.* 1600–1850', in Christine Woodhead (ed.), *The Ottoman World* (London – New York, 2012), pp. 424–5.

41 Tezcan, *The Second Ottoman Empire*, p. 179.

42 Ibid., pp. 35–7.

43 Leslie Peirce, *The Imperial Harem: Women and Sovereignty in the Ottoman Empire* (Oxford, 1993), p. 102. As Günhan Börekçi pointed out, the lapse of fratricide at the beginning of the seventeenth century was closely connected with the biological crisis of the dynasty, see Günhan Börekçi, 'Factions and favorites at the courts of Sultan Ahmed I (r. 1603–1617) and his immediate predecessors' (PhD diss., Ohio State University, 2010), p. 81. However, these exceptions subsequently translated into a new dynastic principle, Tezcan, *The Second Ottoman Empire*, p. 63.

44 Ibid., p. 199; Börekçi, 'Factions and favorites', p. 48.

45 Karen Barkey, 'In different times: scheduling and social control in the Ottoman Empire, 1550 to 1650', *Comparative Studies in Society and History* 38/3 (1996), pp. 460–1.

46 Karen Barkey, *Bandits and Bureaucrats: The Ottoman Route to State Centralization* (Ithaca, 1994), p. 80.

47 İ. Metin Kunt, *The Sultan's Servants: Transformation of the Ottoman Provincial Government, 1550–1650* (New York, 1983), p. 97.

48 İ. Metin Kunt, 'Derviş Mehmed Paşa, vezir and entrepreneur: a study in Ottoman political-economic theory and practice', *Turcica* 9/1 (1977), p. 212.

49 Tezcan, *The Second Ottoman Empire*, pp. 143–4.

50 Suraiya Faroqhi, 'Seeking wisdom in China: an attempt to make sense of the Celali rebellions', in Rudolf Vesely and Eduard Gombár (eds), *Zafar Nama: Memorial Volume to Felix Tauer* (Prague, 1994), pp. 101–24; Barkey, *Bandits and Bureaucrats*, pp. 185–6.

51 Mustafa Akdağ, *Celâlî İsyanları, 1550–1603* (Ankara, 1963); Sam White, *The Climate of Rebellion in the Early Modern Ottoman Empire* (Cambridge, 2011), p. 74; Oktay Özel, *The Collapse of Rural Order in Ottoman Anatolia: Amasya, 1576–1643* (Leiden – New York, 2016).

Notes

52 Barkey, *Bandits and Bureaucrats*, p. 239; Marios Hadjianastasis, 'Crossing the line in the sand: regional officials, monopolisation of state power and "rebellion". The case of Mehmed Ağa Boyacıoğlu in Cyprus, 1685–1690', *Turkish Historical Review* 2/2 (2011), p. 158; Stefan Winter, *The Shiites of Lebanon under Ottoman Rule, 1516–1788* (Cambridge, 2010), p. 109.

53 Antoni Mączak, 'Jedyna i nieporównywalna? Kwestia odrębności Rzeczypospolitej w Europie XVI-XVII wieku', *Kwartalnik Historyczny* 100/4 (1993), pp. 121–36; Adam Manikowski, 'Was the seventeenth-century Commonwealth an anomaly among other European states?', *Odrodzenie i Reformacja w Polsce* special issue (2014), pp. 27–39.

54 For a recent and comprehensive account of the making of the Commonwealth, see Robert I. Frost, *The Oxford History of Poland-Lithuania*, vol. 1 (Oxford – New York, 2015).

55 Antoni Mączak, 'Export of grain and the problem of distribution of national income in the years 1550–1650', *Acta Poloniae Historica* 18 (1968), pp. 75–98.

56 *Volumina legum*, vol. 2 (Saint Petersburg, 1859), pp. 133–4 and 152.

57 Jolanta Choińska-Mika, *Między społeczeństwem szlacheckim a władzą: Problemy komunikacji społeczności lokalne – władza w epoce Jana Kazimierza* (Warsaw, 2002), p. 7. For the political concepts of the Polish–Lithuanian nobility, see Anna Grześkowiak-Krwawicz, *Queen Liberty: The Concept of Freedom in the Polish-Lithuanian Commonwealth*, trans. Daniel J. Sax (Leiden – Boston, 2012).

58 Jan Dzięgielewski, 'Fakcje a funkcjonowanie sejmu Rzeczypospolitej w końcu XVI i w XVII wieku', *Barok* 18/1 (2011), p. 169; Edward Opaliński, *Sejm Srebrnego Wieku, 1587–1652: Między głosowaniem większościowym a liberum veto* (Warsaw, 2001).

59 Antoni Mączak, 'The structure of power in the Commonwealth of the sixteenth and seventeenth centuries', in J. K. Fedorowicz (ed.), *A Republic of Nobles: Studies in Polish History to 1864* (Cambridge, 1982), p. 121.

60 On Polish–Lithuanian fiscal apparatus, see Anna Filipczak-Kocur, 'Poland-Lithuania before Partition', in Richard Bonney (ed.), *The Rise of the Fiscal State in Europe, c. 1200–1815* (Oxford, 1999), pp. 443–79.

61 Frank E. Sysyn, *Between Poland and the Ukraine: The Dilemma of Adam Kysil, 1600–1653* (Cambridge, MA, 1985), pp. 21–2. See also Teresa Chynczewska-Hennel, *Świadomość narodowa szlachty ukraińskiej i Kozaczyzny od schyłku XVI do połowy XVII w.* (Warsaw, 1985).

62 Natalja Jakovenko, *Ukrajins'ka šljaxta z kincja XIV do seredyny XVII st. (Volyn' i Central'na Ukrajina)*, second edition (Kyiv, 2008), p. 80.

63 Henryk Litwin, 'Fakcje magnackie na Kijowszczyźnie 1569–1648', in Jerzy Urwanowicz, Ewa Dubas-Urwanowicz and Piotr Guzowski (eds), *Władza i prestiż: Magnateria Rzeczypospolitej w XVI–XVIII wieku* (Białystok, 2003), p. 52.

64 Karol Mazur, *W stronę integracji z Koroną: Sejmiki Wołynia i Ukrainy w latach 1569–1648* (Warsaw, 2006); Henryk Litwin, *Równi do równych: kijowska*

200   *Notes*

reprezentacja sejmowa, 1569–1648 (Warsaw, 2009); Sysyn, *Between Poland and the Ukraine*, pp. 21–2; Wojciech Sokołowski, *Politycy schyłku Złotego Wieku: Małopolscy przywódcy szlachty i parlamentarzyści w latach 1574–1605* (Warsaw, 1997), pp. 27–8.

65 Sysyn, *Between Poland and the Ukraine*, pp. 109–10; Jarosław Stolicki, *Egzulanci podolscy (1672–1699): Znaczenie uchodźców z Podola w życiu politycznym Rzeczypospolitej* (Cracow, 1994), p. 6.

66 Tomasz Kempa, *Konstanty Wasyl Ostrogski (ok. 1524/1525–1608), wojewoda kijowski i marszałek ziemi wołyńskiej* (Toruń, 1997), p. 189.

67 Dariusz Kołodziejczyk, 'Ottoman Podillja: The Eyalet of Kam'janec', 1672–1699', *Harvard Ukrainian Studies* 16/1–2 (1992), pp. 87–8.

68 Barbara Skinner, 'Khmelnytsky's shadow: the confessional legacy', in Karin Friedrich and Barbara M. Pendzich (eds), *Citizenship and Identity in a Multinational Commonwealth: Poland-Lithuania in Context, 1550–1772* (Leiden – Boston, 2009), pp. 149–70; Henryk Litwin, 'Catholicization among the Ruthenian nobility and assimilation processes in the Ukraine during the years 1569–1648', *Acta Poloniae Historica* 55 (1987), pp. 82–3.

69 On the Union of Brest', see Borys A. Gudziak, *Crisis and Reform: The Kyivan Metropolitanate, the Patriarchate of Constantinople, and the Genesis of the Union of Brest* (Cambridge MA, 2001).

70 Maurycy Horn, 'Chronologia i zasięg najazdów tatarskich na ziemie Rzeczypospolitej Polskiej w latach 1600–1647', *Studia i Materiały do Historii Wojskowości* 8/1 (1962), p. 70.

71 Jan Wimmer, *Wojsko polskie w drugiej połowie XVII wieku* (Warsaw, 1965), p. 22. For instance, among 19,000-strong army assembled against the Tatars in 1619, private troops constituted almost three-fourths, see Przemysław Gawron, *Hetman koronny w systemie ustrojowym Rzeczypospolitej w latach 1581–1646* (Warsaw, 2010), p. 125.

72 On the role of Byzantine models, see Andrei Pippidi, *Tradiția politică bizantină în Țările Române în secolele XVI–XVIII*, second edition (Bucharest, 2001).

73 On the role and structure of the princely council, see Nicolae Stoicescu, *Sfatul domnesc și marii dregători din Țara Românească și Moldova: Sec. XIV–XVII* (Bucharest, 1968); Cornelius R. Zach, *Staat und Staatsträger in der Walachei und Moldau im 17. Jahrhundert* (Munich, 1992).

74 For the summary of the debate, see Ștefan Aftodor, *Boierimea în Țara Românească: Aspecte politice și social-economice (1601–1654)* (Brăila, 2014), pp. 19–28.

75 Paul Cernovodeanu, 'Mobility and traditionalism: the evolution of the boyar class in the Romanian Principalities in the 18th century', *Revue des Études Sud-Est Européennes* 24/3 (1986), pp. 249–57; Neagu Djuvara, 'Les grand boïars ont-ils constitué dans les principautés roumaines une veritable oligarchie institutionelle et héréditaire?', *Südost-Forschungen* 76 (1987), pp. 1–55; Cristina Codarcea, 'Rapports

de pouvoir et strategie de gouvernement dans la Valachie du XVIIe siècle', *New Europe College Yearbook* 1 (1996–1997), pp. 131–2; Cristina Codarcea, *Société et pouvoir (1601–1654): entre la coutume et la loi* (Bucharest, 2002), pp. 182–6; Radu G. Păun, 'Pouvoirs, offices et patronage dans la Principauté de Moldavie au XVIIe siècle: l'aristocratie roumaine et la penetration gréco-levantine' (PhD diss., École des Hautes Études en Sciences Sociales, 2003), pp. 107–76.

76 Bogdan Murgescu, *România și Europa: Acumularea decalajelor economice (1500–2010)* (Iași, 2012), pp. 37–40.

77 Bogdan Murgescu, 'The "modernization" of the Romanian Principalities during the 16th–17th centuries: patterns, distortions, prospects', in Marian Dygo, Sławomir Gawlas and Hieronim Grala (eds), *Modernizacja struktur władzy w warunkach opóźnienia: Europa Środkowa i Wschodnia na przełomie średniowiecza i czasów nowożytnych* (Warsaw, 1999), pp. 173–84.

78 Păun, 'Pouvoirs, offices et patronage', pp. 173–6; Constantin Rezachevici, 'Populație și economie în Țara Românească și Moldova', in Virgil Cândea (ed.), *Istoria românilor*, vol. 5, second edition (Bucharest, 2012), p. 409.

79 Codarcea, *Société et pouvoir*, pp. 54–140.

80 Petre P. Panaitescu, *Începuturile și biruința scrisului în limba română* (Bucharest, 1965), p. 94.

81 Radu G. Păun, 'Les grands officiers d'origine gréco-levantine en Moldavie au XVIIe siècle: Offices, carrièrs et stratègies de pouvoir', *Revue des Études Sud-Est Européennes* 45/1–4 (2007), p. 170.

82 Andrei Pippidi, 'Phanare, phanariotes, phanariotisme', *Revue des Études Sud-Est Européennes* 13/2 (1975), p. 234; Lidia Cotovanu, '"Chasing away the Greeks": the prince-state and the undesired foreigners (Wallachia and Moldavia between the 16th and 18th centuries)', in Olga Katsiardē-Hering and Maria A. Stassinopoulou (eds), *Across the Danube: Southeastern Europeans and Their Travelling Identities (17th–19th C.)* (Leiden – Boston, 2017), pp. 215–52.

83 Radu G. Păun, 'Some observations on the historical origins of the "Phanariot phenomenon" in Moldavia and Wallachia', in Gelina Harlaftis and Radu G. Păun (eds), *Greeks in Romania in the nineteenth century* (Athens, 2013), p. 46.

84 Mączak, 'The structure of power', pp. 127–8.

85 Carter V. Findley, 'Political culture and the great households', in Suraiya Faroqhi (ed.), *The Cambridge History of Turkey*, vol. 3 (Cambridge, 2006), pp. 65–6.

86 Constantin Rezachevici, 'Moldova de la Ghiculești la fanarioți', in Virgil Cândea (ed.), *Istoria românilor*, vol. 5, second edition (Bucharest, 2012), pp. 276–7.

87 Findley, 'Political culture', p. 75.

88 Rifa'at A. Abou-El-Haj, 'The Ottoman vezir and pașa households, 1683–1703: a preliminary report', *Journal of the American Oriental Society* 94/4 (1974), p. 439.

202   *Notes*

89 Zofia Zielińska, 'Magnaten und Adel im politischen Landleben Polen-Litauens des 18. Jahrhunderts', in Antoni Mączak and Elisabeth Müller-Luckner (eds), *Klientelsysteme im Europa der Früher Neuzeit* (Munich, 1988), pp. 203–10.
90 İ. Metin Kunt, *The Sultan's Servants: The Transformation of Ottoman Provincial Government, 1550–1650* (New York, 1983), p. 64.
91 See, for instance, recent study by Oktay Özel, *The Collapse of Rural Order in Ottoman Anatolia: Amasya 1576–1643* (Leiden – Boston, 2016).
92 Kunt, 'Derviş Mehmed Paşa', p. 202.
93 Ariel Salzmann, *Tocqueville in the Ottoman Empire: Rival Paths to the Modern State* (Leiden – Boston, 2004), p. 119.
94 Damaschin Mioc, 'Despre modul de impunere şi percepere a birului în Ţara Romînească pînă la 1632', *Studii şi Materiale de Istorie Medie* 2 (1957), pp. 110–11.
95 Urszula Augustyniak, *Dwór i klientela Krzysztofa Radziwiłła, 1585–1640: Mechanizmy patronatu* (Warsaw, 2001), pp. 68–9; Andrzej Rachuba, 'Hegemonia Sapiehów na Litwie jako przejaw skrajnej dominacji magnaterii w życiu kraju', in Jerzy Urwanowicz, Ewa Dubas-Urwanowicz and Piotr Guzowski (eds), *Władza i prestiż: Magnateria Rzeczypospolitej w XVI-XVIII wieku* (Białystok, 2003), pp. 226–7.
96 Jane Hathaway, *The Politics of Households in Ottoman Egypt: The Rise of Qazdağlıs* (Cambridge, 1997), pp. 17–20.
97 Wimmer, *Wojsko polskie*, p. 22; Findley, 'Political culture', p. 76.
98 The phenomenon was marginal in the case of Moldavian–Wallachian elites due to their negligible military potential.
99 See Özgür Kolçak, 'XVII. yüzyıl askerî gelimişi ve Osmanlılar: 1660–64 Osmanlı-Avusturya savaşları' (PhD diss., Istanbul University, 2012), pp. 104–24.

Chapter 2

1 Günhan Börekçi, 'Factions and favorites at the courts of Sultan Ahmed I (r. 1603–1617) and his immediate predecessors' (PhD diss., Ohio State University, 2010), p. 186.
2 Charles Tilly, *Trust and Rule* (Cambridge, 2005), p. 4.
3 Ronald S. Burt, *Brokerage and Closure: An Introduction to Social Capital* (Oxford, 2005), p. 95.
4 Ibid., p. 97.
5 Jane Hathaway, 'The household: an alternative framework for the military society of eighteenth-century Ottoman Egypt', *Oriente Moderno* 18/1 (1999), p. 63.
6 Julia Adams, 'The familial state: elite family practices and state-making in the early modern Netherlands', *Theory and Society* 23/2 (1994), pp. 510–2; Guy

Rowlands, *The Dynastic State and the Army under Louis XIV: Royal Service and Private Interest, 1661–1701* (Cambridge, 2002), pp. 12–17; Urszula Augustyniak, 'Znaczenie więzów krwi w systemach nieformalnych w Rzeczypospolitej pierwszej połowy XVII wieku na przykładzie klienteli Radziwiłłów birżanskich', in Stanisław Bylina (ed.), *Kultura staropolska – kultura europejska* (Warsaw, 1997), pp. 205–10; Ştefan S. Gorovei, 'Clanuri, familii, autorități, puteri (Moldova, secolele XV–XVII)', *Arhiva Genealogică* 1/1–2 (1994), pp. 87–93; Radu G. Păun, 'Pouvoirs, offices et patronage dans la Principauté de Moldavie au XVIIe siècle: l'aristocratie roumaine et la penetration gréco-levantine' (PhD diss., L'École des Hautes Études en Sciences Sociales, 2003).

7   Pavel V. Sovetov, *Issledovanie po istorii feodalizma v Moldavii: očerki istorii zemlevladenija*, vol. 1 (Chişinău, 1974), pp. 20–1; Paul Păltânea, 'Familia cronicarului Miron Costin şi risipirea moşiilor prin descendenți: partea a 2-a', *Arhiva Genealogică* 5/1–2 (1998), pp. 87–106. There were differences in the pattern of inheritance between Wallachia and Moldavia, most importantly regarding women's right to inherit landed property, see Maria Magdalena Székely, 'Structuri de familie în societatea medievală moldovenească', *Arhiva Genealogică* 4/1–2 (1997), pp. 59–117; Constanța Ghițulescu, 'Familie şi societate în Ţara Românească (secolul al XVII-lea)', *Studii şi Materiale de Istorie Medie* 20 (2002), pp. 80–97.

8   On family entails in Poland–Lithuania, see Teresa Zielińska, 'Ordynacje w dawnej Polsce', *Przegląd Historyczny* 68/1 (1977), pp. 17–30; Mariusz Kowalski, *Księstwa Rzeczpospolitej: państwo magnackie jako region polityczny* (Warsaw, 2013), p. 162.

9   On the role of pious foundations in safeguarding familial wealth, see Amy Singer, *Constructing Ottoman Beneficence: An Imperial Soup Kitchen in Jerusalem* (Albany, 2002), pp. 30–2.

10 Karl K. Barbir, 'One marker of Ottomanism: confiscation of Ottoman officials' estates', in Karl K. Barbir and Baki Tezcan (eds), *Identity and Identity Formation in the Ottoman World: A Volume Essays in Honor of Norman Itzkowitz* (Madison, 2007), pp. 135–45. The fortunes of Moldavian and Wallachian voivodes, whom the Ottomans saw as servants of the Porte, were also subject to confiscation; see Mihai Maxim, 'The institution of müsadere (confiscation) in the Ottoman–Romanian relations', in Mihai Maxim, *Romano-Ottomanica: Essays & Documents from the Turkish Archives* (Istanbul, 2001), pp. 173–200.

11 Rifa'at A. Abou-El-Haj, *Formation of the Modern State: The Ottoman Empire, Sixteenth to Eighteenth Centuries*, second edition (Syracuse, 2005), pp. 47–8.

12 İ. Metin Kunt, 'Kulların kulları', *Boğaziçi Üniversitesi Dergisi. Hümaniter Bilimler – Humanities* 3 (1975), pp. 27–42; Carter V. Findley, 'Political culture and the great households', in Suraiya Faroqhi (ed.), *The Cambridge History of Turkey*, vol. 3 (Cambridge, 2006), pp. 66–7.

13 Paul G. Forand, 'The relation of the slave and the client to the master or patron in medieval Islam', *International Journal of Middle East Studies* 2 (1971), p. 66.

204   *Notes*

14 Jane Hathaway, *The Politics of Households in Ottoman Egypt: The Rise of Qazdağlıs* (Cambridge, 1997), p. 109.

15 Leslie Peirce, *The Imperial Harem: Women and Sovereignty in the Ottoman Empire* (Oxford, 1993), p. 119.

16 Ibid., p. 248; Baki Tezcan, 'The question of regency in Ottoman dynasty: the case of the early reign of Ahmed I', *Archivum Ottomanicum* 25 (2008), pp. 185–98.

17 Peirce, *The Imperial Harem*, pp. 146–9.

18 Hathaway, *The Politics of Households*, pp. 119–20.

19 For more on this topic, see Michał Wasiucionek, 'Danube-hopping: conversion, jurisdiction and spatiality between the Ottoman Empire and the Danubian principalities in the seventeenth century', in Claire Norton (ed.), *Conversion and Islam in the Early Modern Mediterranean* (London – New York, 2017), pp. 77–99.

20 Mihai Maxim, 'New Turkish documents concerning Michael the Brave and his time', in Mihai Maxim, *L'Empire Ottoman au nord du Danube et l'autonomie des Principautés Roumaines au XVIᵉ siècle* (Istanbul, 1999), p. 131.

21 Bucharest, Direcţia Arhivelor Naţionale – Instituţie Centrală [hereafter: DANIC], M-rea Radu Vodă xxxix/9.

22 DANIC, M-rea Radu Vodă xxxix/12.

23 Another case, brought to the Imperial Council in 1659, involved a certain 'Ali, a Wallachian boyar, who had fled to Istanbul and converted to Islam to escape punishment for embezzling the money from the voivodal treasury. However, after several years of living as a Muslim and marrying a certain Ayşe, he sold all her property and ran away to Moldavia, where he returned to the Orthodox Church. Destitute, Ayşe appealed to the *divan*. In response a *ferman* was sent to Voivode Gheorghe Ghica ordering 'Ali's arrest, see Istanbul, Başbakanlık Osmanlı Arşivi [hereafter: BOA], Mühimme Defterleri [MD] 93/79. See also Wasiucionek, 'Danube-hopping', pp. 77–8.

24 See *Documente privitoare la istoria românilor, culese de Eudoxiu de Hurmuzaki* [hereafter: Hurmuzaki] (Bucharest, 1893), Suppl. i/1, p. 144.

25 Constantin Grecescu and Dan Simonescu (eds), *Istoria Ţării Româneşti, 1290–1690: Letopiseţul Cantacuzinesc* (Bucharest, 1960), p. 53.

26 Selanikî Mustafa Efendi, *Tarih-i Selânikî*, vol. 1, ed. Mehmet İpşirli (Ankara, 1989), p. 239; Halil Sahillioğlu (ed.), *Koca Sinan Paşa'nın Telhisleri* (Istanbul, 2004), p. 183.

27 Cristian Luca, *Ţările Române şi Veneţia în secolul al XVII-lea: Din relaţiile politico-diplomatice, comerciale şi culturale ale Ţării Româneşti şi ale Moldovei cu Serenissima* (Bucharest, 2007), pp. 62–3; Radu vornicul Popescu, *Istoriile domnilor Ţării Romîneşti*, ed. Constantin Grecescu (Bucharest, 1963), p. 67.

28 Ibid., p. 63; Virgil Cândea, 'Letopiseţul Ţării Româneşti (1292–1664) în versiunea arabă a lui Macarie Zaim', *Studii. Revistă de Istorie* 23/4 (1970), p. 689; Matei al Mirelor (Matthew of Myra) 'Mathaiou istoria tis Ungro-Vlachias', in Alexandru Papiu Ilarian (ed.), *Tesauru de monumente istorice pentru România*, vol. 1

(Bucharest, 1862), p. 336; Grecescu and Simonescu (eds), *Istoria Țării Românești*, p. 53; Noel Malcolm, *Agents of Empire: Knights, Corsairs, Jesuits and Spies in the Sixteenth-Century Mediterranean World* (Oxford–New York, 2015), p. 377.

29 On Bruttis' ties to Koca Sinan Pasha and Mihnea's family, see Malcolm, *Agents of Empire*, pp. 220 and 261–77.

30 Hurmuzaki, vol. 13, p. 104.

31 Dan Simonescu, 'Le chroniquer Matthieu de Myre et une traduction ignorée de son "Histoire"', *Revue des Études Sud-Est Européennes* 4/1–2 (1966), p. 109.

32 Hurmuzaki, Suppl. ii/1, p. 411.

33 On this conflict, see Constantin Rezachevici, 'Bătălia de la Gura Nișcovului (august 1601): contribuții privind istoria Țării Românești în epoca lui Mihai Viteazul și activitatea militară a lui Radu Șerban înaintea domniei', *Studii. Revistă de Istorie* 24/6 (1971), pp. 1143–57; Veniamin Ciobanu, *Politică și diplomație în secolul al XVII-lea: Țările Române în raporturile polono-otomano-habsburgice (1601–1634)* (Bucharest, 1994), pp. 110–1.

34 Ștefan Andreescu, 'Radu Mihnea Corvin, domn al Moldovei și Țării Românești', in Ștefan Andreescu, *Restitutio Daciae*, vol. 2 (Bucharest, 1989), p. 49.

35 Nicolae Iorga, 'Frații pagâni ai lui Radu Mihnea', *Revista Istorică* 10/4–6 (1924), p. 81.

36 Sever Zotta, 'Doi frați ai lui Radu Mihnea V.V. călugăriți în Moldova', *Revista Arhivelor* 1 (1924), pp. 136–7.

37 Andreescu, 'Radu Mihnea Corvin (II)', p. 130. It is likely that Mustafa was Mihnea II's eldest son, also named Radu, born in 1584, see Valentin Constantinov, 'Din istoria Basarabilor: interpretări cu privire la cronica de la Bucovăț', *Cercetări Istorice* 30–31 (2011–2012), pp. 91–2.

38 See, for instance, Agnieszka Biedrzycka (ed.), *Korespondencja Stanisława Koniecpolskiego hetmana wielkiego koronnego, 1632–1646* (Cracow, 2005), p. 512. Stanisław Koniecpolski's anonymous informant clearly despised the pretenders, describing them as dogs and claiming that 'there are scores of those bastards' in the Ottoman capital.

39 Such ties of fictive kinship were also widespread between Ottoman officials and Hungarian magnates, on this topic see János B. Szabó, 'Prince György Rákoczi I of Transylvania and the elite of Ottoman Hungary, 1630–1636', in Gábor Kármán (ed.), *Tributaries and Peripheries of the Ottoman Empire* (Leiden–Boston, forthcoming). I would like to thank János B. Szabó and Gábor Kármán for providing me with a copy of the paper.

40 Hurmuzaki, Suppl. i/1, p. 141.

41 Anna Filipczak-Kocur (ed.), *Korespondencja Krzysztofa księcia Zbaraskiego koniuszego koronnego 1612–1627* (Opole, 2015), p. 116.

42 Veniamin Ciobanu, *La cumpănă de veacuri: Țările Române în contextul politicii poloneze la sfârșitul secolului al XVI-lea și începutul secolului al XVII-lea* (Iași, 1991),

206 *Notes*

p. 151; Dariusz Milewski, 'Polskie oczekiwania i polityka wobec obsady tronu mołdawskiego w okresie pochocimskim 1621–1624', *Saeculum Christianum* 20 (2013), pp. 99–108.

43 Gábor Kármán, 'The networks of a Wallachian pretender in Constantinople: the contacts of the future Voivode Mihail Radu 1654–1657', in Gábor Kármán and Radu G. Păun (eds), *Europe and the 'Ottoman World': Exchanges and Conflicts (Sixteenth and Seventeenth Centuries)* (Istanbul, 2013), pp. 136–8.

44 Kármán, 'The networks of a Wallachian pretender', p. 138. The relationship between Atike Sultan and Turhan Hatice was very close, since the former had been taking care of the future *valide sultan* at the beginning of her career in the harem, see Peirce, *The Imperial Harem*, p. 236; Ahmed Resmi Efendi, *Hamîletü'l Kübera*, ed. Ahmed Nezihi Turan (Istanbul, 2000), p. 56.

45 The appointment took place on 22 *rebiülevvel* 1067/8 January 1658, see DANIC, Documente Istorice, dxcv/118, vol. 1, f. 132; Radu G. Păun, 'Enemies within: networks of influence and the military revolts against Ottoman power (Moldavia and Wallachia, sixteenth–seventeenth centuries)', in Gábor Kármán and Lovro Kunčević (eds), *The European Tributary States of the Ottoman Empire in the Sixteenth and Seventeenth Centuries* (Leiden–Boston, 2013), p. 218.

46 Evliyâ Çelebi, *Günümüz Türkçesiyle Evliyâ Çelebi Seyahatnâmesi*, ed. Seyit A. Kahraman and Yücel Dağlı, vol. v/2 (Istanbul, 2007), p. 398. See also Păun, 'Enemies within', pp. 223–6.

47 N. C. Bejenaru, *Ştefan Tomşa II (1611–1616, 1621–1623) şi rivalitatea turco-polonă pentru Moldova* (Iaşi, 1926), p. 40.

48 See Popescu, *Istoriile domnilor*, pp. 121–5.

49 Iaşi, Sediul Judeţean Arhivelor Naţionale [hereafter: SJAN–Iaşi], M-rea Galata ii/4. On Mihnea III's attempts to enhance his legitimacy, see Radu G. Păun, '*Si deus nobiscum, quis contra nos?* Mihnea III: note de teologie politică', in Ovidiu Cristea and Gheorghe Lazăr (eds), *Naţional şi universal în istoria românilor: Studii oferite prof. dr. Şerban Papacostea cu ocazia împlinirii a 70 de ani* (Bucharest, 1998), pp. 69–99; Andrei Pippidi, *Tradiţia politică bizantină în Ţările Române în secolele XVI–XVIII*, second edition (Bucharest, 2001), pp. 306–13.

50 Aurel Iacob, *Ţara Moldovei în vremea lui Ştefan Tomşa al II-lea* (Brăila, 2010), pp. 89–92.

51 Henryk Litwin, 'Catholicization among the Ruthenian nobility and assimilation processes in the Ukraine during the years 1569–1648', *Acta Poloniae Historica* 55 (1987), pp. 76–7.

52 Hurmuzaki Suppl. ii/1, p. 193.

53 Individual members of the family ruled Moldavia (Alexandru Movilă, 1615–16; Moise Movilă, 1630–1 and 1633–4) and Wallachia (Gavril Movilă, 1618–20) after 1611, but their position was a far cry from the one they had enjoyed prior to 1611.

54 A. Mesrobeanu, 'Rolul politic al Movileștilor până în domnia lui Ieremia Vodă', *Cercetări Istorice* 1 (1925), pp. 177–89; Ștefan S. Gorovei, 'Pe marginea unei filiații incerte: Maria Movilă – fiica lui Petru Rareș', *Cercetări Istorice* 11 (1980), pp. 325–80; Ion C. Miclescu-Prăjescu, 'Noi date privind înscaunarea Movileștilor', *Arhiva Genealogică* 4/1–2 (1997), pp. 159–78; Ion C. Miclescu-Prăjescu, 'New data regarding the installation of Movilă princes', *The Slavonic and East European Review* 49/115 (1971), pp. 214–34.

55 Constantin Rezachevici, 'Dimensiunea polonă a activității lui Ieremia Movilă in lumina izvoarelor vremii', in *Movileștii: Istorie și spiritualitate românească*, vol. 2 (Sucevița, 2006), pp. 253–4; Ilona Czamańska, 'Caracterul legăturilor lui Jan Zamoyski cu Movileștii', *Arhiva Genealogică* 3/3–4 (1996), pp. 307–12; Cristian A. Bobicescu, 'Pe marginea raporturilor lui Jan Zamoyski cu Moldova și Țara Românească', *Studii și Materiale de Istorie Medie* 20 (2002), pp. 201–6; Michał Wasiucionek, 'Kanclerz i hospodar – klientelizm nietypowy? Na marginesie stosunków Jana Zamoyskiego z Jeremim Mohyłą', *Wschodni Rocznik Humanistyczny* 6 (2009), pp. 65–72.

56 Jerzy Michta, 'Nobilitacja i indygenat w szlacheckiej Rzeczypospolitej', *Annales Universitatis Mariae Curie-Skłodowska* 45 (1990), p. 359.

57 Zygmunt Wdowiszewski, *Regesty przywilejów indygenatu w Polsce* (Buenos Aires–Paris, 1971), p. 25; Ilona Czamańska, 'Rumuńska imigracja polityczna w Polsce XVII wieku', *Balcanica Posnaniensia* 6 (1993), p. 7.

58 Szymon Okolski, *Orbis Polonus*, vol. 2 (Cracow, 1643), p. 229; Kasper Niesiecki, *Herbarz polski*, vol. 6, ed. J. N. Bobrowicz (Leipzig, 1845), pp. 448–9; Ștefan S. Gorovei, 'Steme moldovenești augmentate în Polonia', *Arhiva Genealogică* 2/1–2 (1995), pp. 307–9.

59 It also facilitated Movilă's acquisition of landed estates in Poland–Lithuania, see Tatiana Cojocaru, 'When did Ieremia Movilă acquire Uście estate?', *Revue Roumaine d'Histoire* 52/1–4 (2013), pp. 15–9.

60 Zamoyski's death in early June 1605 disrupted the system, which became clear with regard to the last group of Moldavians to receive *indigenatus* in 1607, promoted at the behest of Ieremia Movilă. While the privileges were ultimately granted by the *Sejm*, they also triggered vehement protests among the nobility, who pointed out that they lacked the necessary recommendation by provincial dietines, see Cristian A. Bobicescu, 'Câteva observații pe marginea unor izvoare inedite cu privire la relațiile dintre Polonia și Moldova sub Movilești', in Stanislava Iachimovschi and Elżbieta Wieruszewska-Calistru (eds), *Relacje polsko-rumuńskie w historii i kulturze* (Suceava, 2010), p. 110.

61 Warsaw, Archiwum Główne Akt Dawnych [hereafter: AGAD], Archiwum Zamoyskich 262/4; Ilona Czamańska, *Wiśniowieccy: Monografia rodu* (Poznań, 2007), p. 115; Constantin Rezachevici, 'Principii Dimitrie Wiśniowiecki și Michal

Korybut şi înrudirile lor cu Bogdănești și Movilești: lămurirea unor confuzii istorice', *Arhiva Genealogică* 3/3–4 (1996), pp. 313–21.

62 AGAD, Archiwum Zamoyskich 262/5.

63 Czamańska, *Wiśniowieccy*, p. 121.

64 Zdzisław Spieralski, *Awantury mołdawskie* (Warsaw, 1967), p. 158.

65 Marian Wolski, *Potoccy herbu Pilawa do początku XVII wieku: Studium genealogiczno-własnościowe* (Cracow, 2013), pp. 287–8.

66 Charles de Joppencourt, 'Histoire des troubles de Moldauie', in A. Papiu Ilarian (ed.), *Tesauru de monumente istorice pentru România*, vol. 2 (Bucharest, 1864), p. 56.

67 Ştefan S. Gorovei, 'Doamna Elisabeta Movilă: contribuţii pentru o biografie nescrisă', in *Movileştii: istorie și spiritualitate românească*, vol. 2 (Suceava, 2006), pp. 273–302.

68 Dariusz Milewski, *Mołdawia między Polską a Turcją: Hospodar Miron Barnowski i jego polityka (1626–1629)* (Oświęcim, 2014), p. 39.

69 Milewski, *Mołdawia między Polską a Turcją*, pp. 90–2.

70 On Miron Barnovschi's origin, see Ştefan S. Gorovei, 'Neamul lui Miron vodă Barnovschi', in *Dragomirna: istorie, tezaur, ctitori* (Dragomirna, 2014), pp. 299–311; idem, '"Din Purice-Movilă" şi "Barnovschi-Moghilă": două explicaţii (nu numai) genealogice', *Arhiva Genealogică* 5/3–4 (1998), pp. 327–32.

71 AGAD, Archiwum Publiczne Potockich, MS 36, p. 9; Stanisław Kobierzycki, *Historia Władysława, królewicza polskiego i szwedzkiego*, ed. Janusz Byliński and Włodzimierz Kaczorowski (Wrocław, 2005), pp. 328 and 366.

72 Alper Başer, 'Bucak Tatarları (1550–1700)' (PhD diss., Afyon Kocatepe University, 2010), p. 107.

73 Milewski, *Mołdawia między Polską a Turcją*, pp. 77–93.

74 AGAD, Metryka Koronna, MS 177, ff. 15–16v.; Cracow, Jagiellonian University Library, MS 7, ff. 408–408v; Milewski, *Mołdawia między Polską a Turcją*, p. 181–3; Dariusz Milewski, 'The granting of Polish indygenat to the Moldavian voyevode Miron Barnovski', *Medieval and Early Modern Studies for Central and Eastern Europe* 3 (2011), pp. 117–49.

75 Hurmuzaki, Suppl. i/1, p. 230. On this topic, see Milewski, *Mołdawia między Polską a Turcją*, pp. 89–93; Ştefan S. Gorovei, 'Neamul lui Miron vodă Barnovschi', in *Dragomirna: istorie, tezaur, ctitori* (Dragomirna, 2014), p. 341, fn. 5; Valentin Constantinov, *Ţara Moldovei în cadrul relaţiilor internaţionale (1611–1634)* (Iaşi, 2014), p. 257; Ilona Czamańska, 'Miron Barnowski i jego rodzina w relacjach z Polakami', in Elżbieta Wieruszewska-Calistru and Stanislava Iachimovschi (eds), *Wielowiekowe bogactwo polsko-rumuńskich związków historycznych i kulturowych* (Suceava, 2014), p. 82.

76 Milewski, *Mołdawia między Polską a Turcją*, pp. 278–89.

77 Ibid., pp. 55–6.

78 Hurmuzaki, vol. iv/2, p. 505. See also Antal Beke and Samu Barabás (eds), *I. Rákóczy György és a Porta: Levelek és okiratok* (Budapest, 1888), p. 480; Miron Costin, *Letopiseţul Ţării Moldovei dela Aron Vodă încoace*, ed. Petre P. Panaitescu (Bucharest, 1943), p. 108.

79 Ion Eremia, *Relaţiile externe ale lui Vasile Lupu (1634–1653): Contribuţii la istoria diplomaţiei moldoveneşti în secolul al XVII-lea* (Chişinău, 1999), p. 102.

80 Hurmuzaki, vol. iv/2, p. 505.

81 Niccolò Barsi, *Le voyage de Niccolò Barsi en Moldavie*, ed. Constantin C. Giurescu (Bucharest, 1925), p. 51.

82 Çelebi, *Evliyâ Çelebi Seyahatnâmesi*, vol. v/2, p. 480.

83 Barsi, *Le voyage*, p. 51.

84 Çelebi, *Evliyâ Çelebi Seyahatnâmesi*, vol. v/2, p. 480.

85 Barsi, *Le voyage*, p. 45.

86 Paul of Aleppo, *Jurnal de călătorie în Moldova şi Valahia*, ed. Ioana Feodorov (Bucharest, 2014), p. 488. See also János B. Szabó and Balázs Sudár, "'Independens fejedelem az Portán kívül": II. Rákóczi György oszmán kapcsolatai. Esettanulmány az Erdélyi Fejedelmség és az Oszmán Birodalom viszonyának történetéhez. 2. rész', *Századok* 147 (2013), p. 949. I would like to thank Gábor Kármán for providing me with the reference.

87 Çelebi, *Evliyâ Çelebi Seyahatnâmesi*, vol. v/2, p. 480.

88 Biedrzycka (ed.), *Korespondencja Stanisława Koniecpolskiego*, p. 551. In October 1639, Transylvanian agents in Istanbul reported that Sultan Murad IV himself was displeased with the khan for agreeing to the marriage, see Beke and Barabás (eds), *I. Rákóczy György és a Porta*, p. 483. I would like to thank Gábor Kármán for bringing this source to my attention and providing me with a translation from Hungarian.

89 Mehmed İpşirli, 'Derviş Mehmed Paşa', *Türkiye Diyanet Vakfı İslam Ansiklopedisi*, vol. 9 (Istanbul, 1994), p. 193.

90 İ. Metin Kunt, 'Derviş Mehmed Paşa, vezir and entrepreneur: a study in Ottoman political-economic theory and practice', *Turcica* 9/1 (1977), p. 197; Mehmed Süreyya, *Sicill-i Osmanî*, ed. Seyit A. Kahraman, vol. 2 (Istanbul, 1996), p. 416.

91 See, for instance, Istanbul Topkapı Sarayı Müzesi Arşivi [hereafter: TSMA] E.524/73 and 6019/1; Hurmuzaki, vol. iv/2, p. 500.

92 İ. Metin Kunt, 'Ethnic-regional (*cins*) solidarity in the seventeenth-century Ottoman establishment', *International Journal of Middle East Studies* 5/3 (1974), pp. 233–9.

93 Ibid., pp. 234–5.

94 Ibid., p. 237.

95 Norman Itzkowitz, 'Eighteenth century Ottoman realities', *Studia Islamica* 16 (1962), pp. 84–7.

96 Baki Tezcan, 'Ethnicity, race, religion, and social class: Ottoman markers of difference', in Christine Woodhead (ed.), *The Ottoman World* (London–New York, 2012), pp. 166–7.

97 William H. McNeill, 'Hypotheses concerning possible ethnic role changes in the Ottoman Empire in the seventeenth century', in Osman Okyar and Halil İnalcık (eds), *Türkiye'nin Sosyal ve Ekonomik Tarihi (1071–1920)* (Ankara, 1980), pp. 127–8.

98 Aleksandar Matkovski, 'Prilog pitanju devširme', *Prilozi za Orijentalnu Filologiju* 14–15 (1969), pp. 276–7.

99 Antonis Anastasopoulos, 'Albanians in the eighteenth-century Ottoman Balkans', in Elias Kolovos (ed.), *The Ottoman Empire, the Balkans, the Greek Lands: Towards a Social and Economic History. Studies in Honor of John C. Alexander* (Istanbul, 2007), pp. 38–9.

100 Kunt, 'Ethnic-regional (*cins*) solidarity', pp. 238–9.

101 Sergiu Bacalov, 'Boierimea Țării Moldovei la mijlocul secolului al XVII-lea – începutul secolului al XVIII-lea (studiu istorico-genealogic)' (PhD diss., Moldavian Academy of Sciences, 2012), p. 133; Ștefan S. Gorovei, 'Vechi însemnări genealogice ale familiei Abaza', *Arhiva Genealogică* 1/1–2 (1994), p. 168. At the same time, there are indications that common ethnic–regional origin from Caucasus brought some boyars and Ottoman officials together, see Ion Neculce, *Opere: Letopisețul Țării Moldovei și O samă de cuvinte*, ed. Gabriel Ștrempel (Bucharest, 1982), pp. 346–7.

102 By the 1630s, the 'Greco-Levantines' occupied almost a half of all seats in the Moldavian princely council, although the ratio varied widely depending on the incumbent voivode, see Radu G. Păun, 'Les grands officiers d'origine gréco-levantine en Moldavie au XVIIᵉ siècle: Offices, carrièrs et stratègies de pouvoir', *Revue des Études Sud-Est Européennes* 45/1–4 (2007), p. 155; Păun, 'Povoirs, offices et patronage', pp. 424–35.

103 Bogdan Murgescu, '"Fanarioți" și "pământeni": religie și etnicitate în definirea identităților în Țările Române și în Imperiul Otoman', in Bogdan Murgescu, *Țările Române între Imperiul Otoman și Europa creștină* (Iași, 2012), p. 57.

104 Nikos Panou, 'Greek-Romanian symbiotic patterns in the early modern period: history, mentalities, institutions (I)', *The Historical Review* 3 (2006), p. 78. See also Neculce, *Opere*, pp. 299–300.

105 Lidia Cotovanu, '"Chasing away the Greeks": the prince-state and the undesired foreigners (Wallachia and Moldavia between the 16th and 18th centuries)', in Olga Katsiardē-Hering and Maria A. Stassinopoulou (eds), *Across the Danube: Southeastern Europeans and Their Travelling Identities (17th–19th C.)* (Leiden–Boston, 2017), pp. 218–23.

106 On the rebellion, see Aurel H. Golimas, *Diplomatul Constantin Batiște Vevelli Rettimiotul și revoluția Moldovei din primavara anului 1633* (Iași, 1943).

Notes

211

107 Costin, *Letopisețul Țării Moldovei*, p. 81.

108 Cotovanu, "'Chasing away the Greeks'", p. 218.

109 Lidia Cotovanu, 'Le diocèse de Dryinoupolis et ses bienfaiteurs de Valachie et de Moldavie: Solidarités de famille et traits identitaires multiples (XVIᵉ–XVIIᵉ siècles)', in Petronel Zahariuc (ed.), *Contribuții privitoare la istoria relațiilor dintre Țările Române și bisericile răsăritene în secolele XIV–XIX* (Iași, 2009), pp. 219–360; Lidia Cotovanu, 'Autour des attaches epirotes du futur prince de Moldavie Constantin Duca (XVIIᵉ siècle)', in Cristian Luca and Ionel Cândea (eds), *Studia Varia in Honorem Professoris Ștefan Ștefănescu Octogenarii* (Bucharest, 2009), pp. 465–88.

110 John V. A. Fine, *When Ethnicity Did Not Matter in the Balkans: A Study of Identity in Prenationalist Croatia, Dalmatia, and Slavonia in the Medieval and Early-Modern Periods* (Ann Arbor, 2005); Robert Dankoff, *An Intimate Life of an Ottoman Statesman: Melek Ahmed Paşa (1588–1662) as Portrayed in Evliya Çelebi's Book of Travel (Seyahat-name)* (Albany, 1991), pp. 8–9.

111 Tezcan, 'Ethnicity, race, religion', p. 163.

112 Illustrative in this respect is the phenomenon of late-eighteenth-century warlords, such as Cezzar Ahmed, Osman Pasvanoğlu or Mehmed Ali 'turning Albanian' in order to appeal to Albanian troops, see Virginia H. Aksan, *Ottoman Wars, 1700–1870: An Empire Besieged* (London, 2007), pp. 220, 230 and 306–7.

113 Constantin Șerban, *Vasile Lupu, domn al Moldovei (1634–1653)* (Bucharest, 1991), p. 26.

114 Franz Babinger, 'Originea și sfârșitul lui Vasile Lupu', *Analele Academiei Române. Memoriile Secțiunii Istorice*, Seria III, 19 (1936), pp. 65–83.

115 Ioan Bianu and Nerva Hodoș (eds), *Bibliografia românească veche*, vol. 1 (Bucharest, 1903), p. 308; Dimitrie Cantemir, *Descrierea Moldovei*, ed. Gheorghe Guțu (Bucharest, 1973), p. 71.

116 Ibid., p. 71; Costin, *Letopisețul Țării Moldovei*, p. 191; Hurmuzaki, vol. 13, p. 338; Neculce, *Opere*, p. 187.

117 Çelebi, *Evliyâ Çelebi Seyahatnâmesi*, vol. v/2, p. 474.

118 Costin, *Letopisețul Țării Moldovei*, p. 191. See also Cantemir, *Descrierea Moldovei*, p. 142.

119 Paul Cernovodeanu, 'Știri privitoare la Gheorghe Ghica vodă al Moldovei (1658–9) și familia sa (I)', *Anuarul Institutului de Istorie și Arheologie 'A.D. Xenopol'* 19 (1982), pp. 333–4.

120 Mihai ban Cantacuzino, *Genealogia Cantacuzinilor*, ed. Nicolae Iorga (Bucharest, 1902).

121 Cantemir, *Descrierea Moldovei*, p. 142.

122 He was grand *șetrar* (responsible for approvization of the court, 1638–41), grand *medelnicer* (1643), *stolnic* (1647) and finally the grand *vornic* of Upper Moldavia (1647–52), see Stoicescu, *Dicționar*, p. 403.

212 *Notes*

123 Cernovodeanu, 'Ştiri privitoare la Gheorghe Ghica (I)', p. 336.

124 Costin, *Letopiseţul Ţării Moldovei*, p. 192. His presence in Istanbul is confirmed in Ottoman sources, see BOA, İbnülemin, Maliye 24/2268 and 2269.

125 Costin, *Letopiseţul Ţării Moldovei*, p. 192.

126 Neculce, *Opere*, pp. 187–8.

127 In Neculce's account, Köprülü Mehmed Pasha appears as being roughly the same age, or even younger than Gheorghe Ghica. However, by 1658 Gheorghe Ghica's age was estimated by contemporaries at around 60 years, while the grand vizier was already an octogenarian. Cf Christine Philliou, *Biography of an Empire: Governing Ottomans in an Age of Revolution* (Berkeley–Los Angeles, 2011), p. 16; Petronel Zahariuc, *Ţara Moldovei în vremea lui Gheorghe Ştefan voievod (1653–1658)* (Iaşi, 2003), p. 115.

128 Cernovodeanu, 'Ştiri privitoare la Gheorghe Ghica (I)', p. 333.

129 Nikoussios, who managed a considerable chunk of the Köprülüs' political network and acted as protector of both the younger Ghica and Constantin Cantacuzino, see Radu G. Păun, '"Well-born of the Polis"', p. 81, fn. 61; Hurmuzaki, vol. 14/1, pp. 206–9; imitrie Cantemir, *Vita Constantini Cantemyrii, cognomento Senis, Moldaviae principis*, ed. Dan Sluşanschi and Ilieş Câmpeanu (Bucharest, 1996), p. 81. On Panagiotis Nikoussios, see Damien Janos, 'Panaiotis Nicousios and Alexander Mavrocordatos: the rise of the Phanariots and the office Grand Dragoman in the Ottoman administration in the second half of the seventeenth century', *Archivum Ottomanicum* 23 (2005), pp. 177–96.

130 Axinte Uricariul, *Cronica paralelă a Ţării Româneşti şi a Moldovei*, ed. Gabriel Ştrempel, vol. 1 (Bucharest, 1993), pp. 84–7.

131 Osmânzade Ahmed Taîb, *Hadîkat ül-Vüzerâ*, vol. 1 (Istanbul, 1271/1854–5), p. 104.

132 Coşkun Yılmaz (ed.), *İstanbul Kadi Sicilleri Bâb Mâhkemesi 3 Numaralı Sicil (H. 1077/M. 1666–1667)* (Istanbul, 2011), p. 678; Muhammed F. Çalışır, 'A virtuous grand vizier: politics and patronage in the Ottoman Empire during the grand vizierate of Fazıl Ahmed Pasha (1661–1676)' (PhD diss., Georgetown University, 2016), pp. 21–3.

133 Kunt, 'Ethnic-regional (*cins*) solidarity', pp. 236–7.

134 Ibid.; Semayi Eyice, 'Mimar Kasım hakkında', *Belleten* 43/172 (1979), p. 786. Cf. Çalışır, 'A virtuous grand vizier', pp. 21–3.

135 On the reign of Mihnea III, see Lia Lehr, 'Mihnea al III-lea', *Studii. Revistă de Istorie* 26/6 (1973), pp. 1161–78.

136 Abdurrahman Sağırlı, 'Mehmed b. Mehmed er-Rûmî (Edirneli)'nin Nuhbetü't-Tevârih ve'l-ahbâr'ı ve Târih-i Âl-i Osman'ı: Metinleri, Tahlilleri', vol. 2 (PhD diss., Istanbul University, 2000), p. 59; Tülin Ülgen, 'Tabanı-yassı Mehmed Paşa' (MA thesis, Istanbul University, 1962), p. 1–2; Süreyya, *Sicill-i Osmanî*, vol. 4, p. 1075.

Notes 213

137 Mustafa Naima, *Tarih*, vol. 3 (Istanbul, 1283/1866–67), pp. 104–5. See also Mehmed Halife, *Tarih-i Gılmani*, TSMK Revan MS 1306, ff. 7 and 11, where the author describes both officials as Albanians.

138 Gheorghe Ghibănescu (ed.), *Surete și izvoade*, vol. 7 (Iași, 1926), pp. 133–4.

139 Çalışır, 'A virtuous grand vizier', p. 23.

140 See Păun, '"Well-born of the Polis"', p. 81.

141 Constantin C. Giurescu (ed.), *Letopisețul Țării Moldovei dela Istratie Dabija până la domnia a doua a lui Antioh Cantemir* (Bucharest, 1913), p. 56.

142 Anton Maria del Chiaro, *Istoria delle moderne rivoluzioni della Valachia: con la descrizione del paese, natura, costume, riti e religione degi abitanti*, ed. Nicolae Iorga (Bucharest, 1914), p. 127.

143 Hurmuzaki, vol. 13, p. 338; see also Defterdar Sarı Mehmed Paşa, *Zübde-î Vekayiât*, ed. Abdülkadir Özcan (Ankara, 1995), p. 828.

144 Cotovanu, 'Autour des attaches epirotes', pp. 465–88.

145 Păun, '"Well-born of the Polis"', p. 81.

146 Ibid.; Constantin A. Stoide, 'Prima domnie moldovenească a lui Gheorghe Duca vodă', *Revista istorică română* 15/1 (1945), pp. 26–42.

147 Viktor Dam'jan, 'Kazacko-moldavskie otnošenja v period pravlenija moldavskogo gospodarja Georgija Duki (1678–1683)', *Ukrajina v Central'no-Sxidnoj Jevropi* 8 (2008), pp. 92–104.

148 Urszula Augustyniak, 'Klientelizm w wojsku litewskim pierwszej połowy XVII wieku: Problemy dyskusyjne', in Ewa Dubas-Urwanowicz and Jerzy Urwanowicz (eds), *Patron i dwór: Magnateria Rzeczypospolitej w XVI–XVIII wieku* (Warsaw, 2006), pp. 19–20; Baki Tezcan, *The Second Ottoman Empire: Political and Social Transformation in the Early Modern World* (Cambridge, 2010), pp. 182–3; Constantin Rezachevici, 'Fenomene de criza social-politică în Țara Românească în veacul al XVII-lea (I)', *Studii și Materiale de Istorie Medie* 9 (1978), pp. 81–3.

149 Mustafa Akdağ, *Celâlî İsyanları, 1550–1603* (Ankara, 1963); Halil İnalcık, 'Military and fiscal transformation of the Ottoman Empire, 1600–1700', *Archivum Ottomanicum* 6 (1980), pp. 304–11; Karen Barkey, *Bandits and Bureaucrats: The Ottoman Route to State Centralization* (Ithaca, 1994), pp. 164–75; Sam White, *The Climate of Rebellion in the Early Modern Ottoman Empire* (Cambridge, 2011), pp. 163–86.

150 Tezcan, *The Second Ottoman Empire*, pp. 141–5.

151 White, *The Climate of Rebellion*, pp. 187–226; Oktay Özel, 'The reign of violence: the *celalis, c.* 1550–1700', in Christine Woodhead (ed.), *The Ottoman World* (London–New York, 2012), pp. 184–204.

152 Barkey, *Bandits and Bureaucrats*, pp. 196–7.

153 Ibid., 211–3; Marios Hadjianastasis, 'Crossing the line in the sand: regional officials, monopolisation of state power and "rebellion". The case of Mehmed Ağa Boyacıoğlu in Cyprus, 1685–1690', *Turkish Historical Review* 2/2 (2011),

214 *Notes*

pp. 155–76; Stefan Winter, *The Shiites of Lebanon under Ottoman Rule, 1516–1788* (Cambrige, 2010), p. 111.

154 Süreyya, *Sicill-i Osmanî*, vol. 4, p. 1230; Baki Tezcan, 'Searching for Osman: a reassessment of the deposition of the Ottoman sultan Osman II (1618–1622)' (PhD diss., Princeton University, 2001), pp. 96–7; Börekçi, 'Factions and favorites', p. 248.

155 Hasan Bey-zade Ahmed Paşa, *Hasan Bey-zade tarihi*, ed. Şevki N. Aykut, vol. 3 (Ankara, 2004), p. 866; Sağırlı, 'Mehmed b. Mehmed er-Rumî', vol. 2, p. 32.

156 Barkey, *Bandits and Bureaucrats*, p. 166; Tezcan, *The Second Ottoman Empire*, pp. 148–9.

157 Andrei Veress (ed.), *Documente privitoare la istoria Ardealului, Moldovei şi Ţării-Româneşti*, vol. 8 (Bucharest, 1935), p. 239. The Hungarian plural form *kazulok* (sing. *kazul*) is a corrupted and truncated form of *kızılbaş*. In another letter from this period, Voivode Radu Mihnea referred to Shah Abbas I as *kazul passa*, ibid., p. 234. See also, Hurmuzaki, vol. iv/1, p. 463. For Tomşa's marriage, see Ştefan S. Gorovei, 'Genealogia familiei domnitoare Tomşa', *Revista Arhivelor* 33/3 (1971), pp. 375–90.

158 Hurmuzaki, Suppl. i/1, p. 140.

159 Iacob, *Ţara Moldovei*, pp. 72–3.

160 See, for instance, Hurmuzaki, vol. iv/2, p. 461; Bejenaru, *Ştefan Tomşa II*, p. 13.

161 Caroline Finkel, 'French mercenaries in the Habsburg–Ottoman war of 1593–1606: the desertion of the Papa garrison to the Ottomans in 1600', *Bulletin of the School of Oriental and African Studies* 55/3 (1992), pp. 451–71.

162 In a letter sent in January 1616, Dutch ambassador Cornelius Haga claimed that, in appointing Tomşa, the *kaymakam* was acting alone and against the wishes of Nasuh Pasha, Amsterdam, University Library, Hs. Diederichs 9 U. However, there are reasons to doubt Haga's reliability in this respect. At the end of 1611, when the appointment took place, Haga was absent from Istanbul, arriving to the Ottoman capital only in April the following year. His most likely sources of information on these events were the English representative at the Porte, Thomas Glover, and his protégé and Tomşa's main rival, Ştefan Bogdan, with whom he remained in touch. The latter's failed bid for the throne and subsequent conversion resulted in a huge embarrassment for Glover and the English court, and it seems likely that they adopted a 'sore loser' attitude, blaming conspiracy and trying to undermine Tomşa's legitimacy. The date of Haga's letter also suggests that the Dutch ambassador, busy negotiating with the Porte, did not consider Moldavian affairs his priority, see Bülent Arı, 'The first Dutch ambassador in Istanbul: Cornelius Haga and the Dutch capitulations of 1612' (PhD diss., Bilkent University, 2003), pp. 83, 106. On English, and particularly Glover's, involvement with Ştefan Bogdan and his failed bid for the throne, see Ludovic Demény and Paul Cernovodeanu, *Relaţiile politice ale Angliei cu Moldova, Ţara Românească şi*

Transilvania în secolele XVI–XVIII (Bucharest, 1974), pp. 45–56; Laura Coulter, 'An examination of the status and activities of the English ambassadors to the Ottoman Porte in the late sixteenth and early seventeenth centuries', *Revue des Études Sud-Est Européennes* 28/1-4 (1990), pp. 67–9; Laura Coulter, 'The involvement of the English Crown and its embassy in Constantinople with pretenders to the throne of the principality of Moldavia between the years 1583 and 1620, with particular reference to the pretender Ştefan Bogdan between 1590 and 1612' (PhD diss., University of London, 1993).

163 Milewski, 'Polskie oczekiwania', *passim.*

164 Börekçi, 'Factions and favorites', p. 248.

165 Barkey, *Bandits and Bureaucrats*, p. 166.

166 Nuh Arslantaş and Yaron Ben Haen (eds), *Anonim Bir İbranice Kroniğe Göre 1622-1624 Yıllarında Osmanlı Devleti ve İstanbul: Neşir-Tercüme* (Ankara, 2013), p. 48; Gabriel Piterberg, 'The alleged rebellion of Abaza Mehmed Paşa: historiography and the Ottoman state in the seventeenth century', *International Journal of Turkish Studies* 8/1-2 (2002), pp. 22–3.

167 Tezcan, *The Second Ottoman Empire*, p. 167.

168 Hrand D. Andreasyan 'Abaza Mehmed Paşa', *Tarih Dergisi* 22 (1968), pp. 131–4; Barkey, *Bandits and Bureaucrats*, p. 223; Gabriel Piterberg, 'The alleged rebellion of Abaza Mehmed Paşa: historiography and the Ottoman state in the seventeenth century', in Jane Hathaway (ed.), *Mutiny and Rebellion in the Ottoman Empire* (Madison, 2009), pp. 13–24; Arslantaş and Ben Haen (eds), *Anonim Bir İbranice Kroniğe*, pp. 53–4.

169 Barkey, *Bandits and Bureaucrats*, pp. 224–5.

170 Popescu, *Istoriile domnilor*, pp. 93–4; Nicolae Stoicescu, *Matei Basarab* (Bucharest, 1988), pp. 11–12.

171 Valentin A. Georgescu, 'Hrisovul din 15 iunie 1631 al lui Leon vodă Tomşa în Ţara Românească şi problema "cărţilor de libertăţi"', *Revista de Istorie* 29/7 (1976), pp. 1018–29.

172 Stoicescu, *Matei Basarab*, pp. 16–18.

173 Ibid., p. 14.

174 Damaschin Mioc, Saşa Caracaş and Constantin Bălan (eds), *Documenta Romaniae Historica. Seria B. Ţara Românească*, vol. 24 (Bucharest, 1974), pp. 283–4.

175 Grecescu and Simonescu (eds), *Istoria Ţării Româneşti*, p. 98.

176 Ibid., p. 94; Stoicescu, *Matei Basarab*, p. 23.

177 Paul Cernovodeanu, 'Campania de înscaunare a lui Matei Basarab (august-septembrie 1632)', *Anuarul Institutului de Istorie şi Arheologie din Iaşi* 24/1 (1987), pp. 311–7; Stoicescu, *Matei Basarab*, pp. 22–8.

178 Paul Cernovodeanu, 'Noi precizării privitoare la bătălia câştigată de Matei Basarab în împrejurimile Bucureştilor', *Anuarul Institutului de Istorie şi Arheologie din Iaşi* 22/2 (1985), pp. 623–9.

216 *Notes*

179 Hurmuzaki, vol. iv/2, p. 460.
180 Grecescu and Simonescu (eds) *Istoria Țării Românești*, pp. 104–5. On Curt Çelebi, see Condurachi, *Soli și agenți*, p. 27; Nicolae Iorga, '"Coconul" lui Radu Mihnea și capuchehaiaua Curt Celebi', *Revista istorică* 18/4–6 (1932), pp. 97–102; Constantin A. Stoide, *Curt Celebi* (Iași, 1936); Păun, 'Pouvoirs, offices et patronage', pp. 326–30.
181 Costin, *Letopisețul Țării Moldovei*, p. 92, spelled *cirac*.
182 The role of priest Ignatie in negotiations between Abaza Mehmed Pasha and Matei Basarab suggests the governor's reliance on local Christian notables and their expertise. Ignatie, who came from a prominent family of Niğbolu and knew Turkish, was well-suited to act as a go-between in brokering the alliance. He was subsequently rewarded by Matei Basarab with the positions of the Bishop of Râmnic and the metropolitan seat, see Ștefan Andreescu, 'Popa Ignatie din Nicopol, episcop de Râmnic și mitropolit al Țării Românești: o identificare', *Revista istorică* 20/5–6 (2009), pp. 413–7. I would like to thank Radu Păun for bringing this study to my attention.
183 Aurel H. Golimas, *Diplomatul Constantin Batişte Vevelli, passim.*
184 Czamańska, 'Rumuńska imigracja polityczna', p. 14.
185 Costin, *Letopisețul Țării Moldovei*, pp. 84–5.
186 Biedrzycka (ed.), *Korespondencja Stanisława Koniecpolskiego*, p. 116.
187 Hurmuzaki, Suppl. i/1, p. 467.
188 Ibid.
189 Costin, *Letopisețul Țării Moldovei*, pp. 84–5.
190 Biedrzycka (ed.), *Korespondencja Stanisława Koniecpolskiego*, pp. 153, 155–6, 159, 169–70; Stanisław Oświęcim, *Stanisława Oświęcima dyaryusz, 1643–1651*, ed. Wiktor Czerman (Cracow, 1907), p. 56. On the war, see Leszek Podhorodecki, 'Wojna polsko-turecka 1633–1634 r.', *Studia i Materiały do Historii Wojskowości* 20 (1976), pp. 27–72.
191 Costin, *Letopisețul Țării Moldovei*, p. 84.
192 See, for instance, Hathaway, *The Politics of Households*, pp. 143–7.

Chapter 3

1 Nan Lin, *Social Capital: A Theory of Social Structure and Action* (Cambridge, 2001), pp. 190–1.
2 Bartolomé Yun Casalilla, 'Reading sources throughout P. Bourdieu and Cyert and March: aristocratic patrimonies vs. commercial enterprises in Europe (*c.* 1550–1650)', in Francesco Ammannati (ed.), *Dove va la storia economica? Metodi e prospettive secc. XIII–XVIII* (Florence, 2011), pp. 327–32.

Notes

3   Ilie Corfus (ed.), *Documente privitoare la istoria României culese din arhivele polone: Secolul al XVI-lea* (Bucharest, 1979), pp. 381–2; Dariusz Kołodziejczyk, *Ottoman-Polish Diplomatic Relations (15th–18th Century): An Annotated Edition of 'Ahdnames and Other Documents* (Leiden – Boston, 2000), p. 317; Ştefan S. Gorovei, 'O lămurire: domnia ereditară a Movileştilor', *Revista de istorie* 28/7 (1975), pp. 1091–4.

4   On Catargi, see Nicolae Stoicescu, *Dicţionar al marilor dregători din Ţara Românească şi Moldova (sec. XIV–XVII)* (Bucharest, 1971), p. 369.

5   Agnieszka Biedrzycka (ed.), *Korespondencja Stanisława Koniecpolskiego hetmana wielkiego koronnego, 1632–1646* (Cracow, 2005), pp. 265–6.

6   Ibid., p. 266.

7   Ibid., pp. 268–9.

8   Sefik Peksevgen, 'Secrecy, information control and power building in the Ottoman Empire, 1566–1603' (PhD diss., McGill University, 2004), p. 177; Pál Fodor, 'Sultan, imperial council, grand vizier: changes in the Ottoman ruling elite and the formation of the grand vizier telhis', *Acta Orientalia Academiae Scientiarum Hungaricae* 47/1–2 (1994), pp. 67–85.

9   Miron Costin, *Letopiseţul Ţării Moldovei dela Aron Vodă încoace*, ed. Petre P. Panaitescu (Bucharest, 1943), p. 99.

10   Hurmuzaki, vol. iv/2, p. 500; Andrei Veress (ed.), *Documente privitoare la istoria Ardealului, Moldovei şi Ţării-Româneşti* vol. 9 (Bucharest, 1935), pp. 8, 184–5.

11   Mehmed Süreyya, *Sicill-i Osmanî*, ed. Seyit A. Kahraman, vol. 3 (Istanbul, 1996), p. 761.

12   Klaus Röhrborn, 'Die Emanzipation der Finanzbürokratie im osmanischen Reich (Ende des 16. Jahrhunderts)', *Zeitschrift der Deutschen Morgenländischen Gesellschaft* 122 (1972), pp. 118–39.

13   Baki Tezcan, *The Second Ottoman Empire: Political and Social Transformation in the Early Modern World* (Cambridge, 2010), p. 190.

14   Biedrzycka (ed.), *Korespondencja Stanisława Koniecpolskiego*, p. 523.

15   Ibid., p. 523.

16   Hurmuzaki, vol. iv/2, p. 452.

17   Biedrzycka (ed.), *Korespondencja Stanisława Koniecpolskiego*, p. 523; İsazade, *İsazade Tarihi: Metin ve Tahlil*, ed. Ziya Yılmazer (Istanbul, 1996), p. 60.

18   TSMA E.704/24; Hurmuzaki, vol. iv/2, p. 498. On Silahdar Mustafa Pasha, who – despite his enormous wealth and political influence – was largely neglected in Ottoman narrative sources, see Hedda Reindl-Kiel, *Leisure, Pleasure and Duty: The Daily Life of Silahdar Mustafa, éminence grise in the Final Years of Murad IV (1635–1640)* (Berlin, 2016), particularly pp. 20–1. I would like to thank Hedda Reindl-Kiel for providing me with a copy of her book.

19   Biedrzycka (ed.), *Korespondencja Stanisława Koniecpolskiego*, p. 459.

218 *Notes*

20 Hurmuzaki, vol. iv/2, p. 474.

21 TSMA E.5645, E.5073; On this increase, see also Aurel Decei, 'Relațiile lui Vasile Lupu și Matei Basarab cu Poarta în lumina unor documente turcești inedite', *Anuarul Institutului de Istorie și Arheologie – Cluj* 15 (1972), pp. 64–8; Tahsin Gemil, 'Date noi privind haraciul Țărilor Române în secolul al XVII-lea', *Revista de Istorie* 30/8 (1977), p. 1444.

22 Ibid., p. 1444.

23 In this sense, it would constitute an attempt to reverse the trend of grandees siphoning the funds from the inner treasury, see Tezcan, *The Second Ottoman Empire*, p. 182.

24 Stoicescu, *Dicționar*, pp. 135–6; Maria M. Bonchiș-Gheorghe, 'Elite politice în secolul al XVII-lea: Familia Cantacuzino' (PhD diss., University of Bucharest, 2003), pp. 70–5.

25 Radu G. Păun, '"Well-born of the Polis": the Ottoman conquest and the reconstruction of the Greek Orthodox elites under Ottoman rule', in Robert Born and Sabine Jagodzinski (eds), *Türkenkriege und Adelskultur in Osmitteleuropa vom 16.-18. Jahrhundert* (Leipzig, 2014), pp. 64–6; Mircea C. Soreanu, 'Țările Române și Imperiul otoman în perioada guvernării marilor viziri din familia Köprülü (1656–1710)' (PhD diss., University of Bucharest, 1998), pp. 201–2. For the bond between Ghica and Nikoussios, see also Dimitrie Cantemir, *Vita Constantini Cantemyrii, cognomento Senis, Moldaviae principis*, ed. Dan Slușanschi and Ilieș Câmpeanu (Bucharest, 1996), pp. 78–80.

26 Mihai ban Cantacuzino, *Genealogia Cantacuzinilor*, ed. Nicolae Iorga (Bucharest, 1902), pp. 86–9.

27 Constantin Grecescu and Dan Simonescu (eds), *Istoria Țării Românești, 1290–1690: Letopisețul Cantacuzinesc* (Bucharest, 1960), p. 146; Radu vornicul Popescu, *Istoriile domnilor Țării Românești*, ed. Constantin Grecescu (Bucharest, 1963), pp. 130–1.

28 Ibid., p. 149; 'Poveste de jale asupra uciderii postelnicului Constantin Cantacuzino (20 decembrie 1663)', in Dan Simonescu (ed.), *Cronici și povestirii românești versificate (sec. XVI–XVIII)* (Bucharest, 1967), pp. 35–48.

29 Radu vornicul Popescu, *Istoriile domnilor Țării Romînești*, ed. Constantin Grecescu (Bucharest, 1963), p. 126. See also 'Kaisariou Daponte Chronographos', in Constantin Erbiceanu (ed.), *Cronicarii greci carii au scris despre români în epoca fanariotă* (Bucharest, 1888), p. 14. The latter chronicle, although traditionally attributed to Kaisarios Dapontes, was in fact a work of Dimitrios Ramadanis, see Machi Païzi-Apostolopoulou, 'Dimitrios Ramadanis: enas istoriographos tou 18ou aiona se aphaneia', *O Eranistis* 20 (1995), pp. 20–35; Machi Païzi-Apostolopoulou, 'To cheirographo tou "Chronographou tou Daponte" kai i lusi enos ainigmatos: to chph Kuriazi tis Gennadeiou', *O Eranistis* 24 (2003), pp. 85–94. I would like to thank Radu Păun for bringing this to my attention.

Notes

30 Ion Ionaşcu, 'Din politica internă şi externă a Ţării Româneşti în domnia lui Antonie Vodă din Popeşti (1669–1672)', in Nicolae I. Simache (ed.), *Pagini din trecutul istoric al judeţului Prahova* (Ploieşti, 1971), pp. 19–20; Constantin Rezachevici, 'Fenomene de criza social-politică în Ţara Românească în veacul al XVII-lea (II)', *Studii şi Materiale de Istorie Medie* 14 (1996), pp. 114–5.

31 Popescu, *Istoriile domnilor*, p. 143.

32 See the discussion 'Problema organizării statelor ca "regim boieresc" în Ţara Românească şi Moldova', *Revista de Istorie* 32/5 (1979), pp. 941–56.

33 See, for instance, Rezachevici, 'Fenomene de criza (II)', p. 53.

34 David Parrott, *The Business of War: Military Enterprise and Military Revolution in Early Modern Europe* (Cambridge – New York, 2012), p. 8.

35 For the evolution of the office, see Przemysław Gawron, *Hetman koronny w systemie ustrojowym Rzeczypospolitej w latach 1581–1646* (Warsaw, 2010); Przemysław Gawron, 'Relacje pomiędzy dowódcami wojsk państwowych i prywatnych w I połowie XVII wieku: wybrane przykłady', in Karol Łopatecki and Wojciech Walczak (eds), *Nad społeczeństwem staropolskim* (Białystok, 2007), pp. 231–47.

36 Sometimes, however, some magnates requested the *hetman*'s opinion, not only due to their role as commanders of royal troops, but also political actors in their own right. For instance, in 1632 the palatine of Kyiv, Tomasz Zamoyski requested *Hetman* Stanisław Koniecpolski's opinion on providing troops to Miron Barnovschi, who sought to recapture the throne of Moldavia, AGAD, Archiwum Zamoyskich, 890. Since both were among the most powerful faction leaders in the region, it seems that Zamoyski did not want to alienate the *hetman*, see Henryk Litwin, 'Fakcje magnackie na Kijowszczyźnie 1569–1648', in Jerzy Urwanowicz, Ewa Dubas-Urwanowicz and Piotr Guzowski (eds), *Władza i prestiż: Magnateria Rzeczypospolitej w XVI–XVIII wieku* (Białystok, 2003), pp. 62–3; Dariusz Milewski, *Mołdawia między Polską a Turcją: Hospodar Miron Barnowski i jego polityka (1626–1629)* (Oświęcim, 2014), pp. 278–9.

37 AGAD, Archiwum Radziwiłłów, vi/2/48, f. 12.

38 Ibid., ff. 20–1.

39 Ilona Czamańska, 'Rumuńska imigracja polityczna w Polsce XVII wieku', *Balcanica Posnaniensia* 6 (1993), pp. 8–9; Tahsin Gemil, *Ţările Române în contextul politic internaţional (1621–1672)* (Bucharest, 1979), p. 39; Dariusz Skorupa, *Stosunki polsko-tatarskie, 1595–1623* (Warsaw, 2004), pp. 189–91; Zdzisław Spieralski, *Awantury mołdawskie* (Warsaw, 1967), p. 163.

40 Dariusz Skorupa, 'Bitwa pod Bukowem 20 października 1600 r.', in Mirosław Nagielski (ed.), *Staropolska sztuka wojenna XVI–XVIII wieku: Prace ofiarowane Profesorowi Jaremie Maciszewskiemu* (Warsaw, 2002), p. 22; Dariusz Milewski, 'A campaign of the Great Hetman Jan Zamoyski in Moldavia (1595). Part I. Politico-diplomatic and military preliminaries', *Codrul Cosminului* 18/2 (2012), p. 285.

220 *Notes*

41 Ryszard Majewski, *Cecora: rok 1620* (Warsaw, 1970), p. 222.

42 Ahmed Nedim, *Sahaif ül-Ahbar* (Istanbul, 1285/1868), pp. 115–8; İsazade, *İsazade Tarihi*, pp. 45–6; Silahdâr Mehmed Agha, *Silahdar Tarihi*, vol. 2 (Istanbul, 1928), pp. 114–6.

43 Ibid., vol. 1, p. 118.

44 Carl M. Kortepeter, *Ottoman Imperialism during the Reformation: Europe and the Caucasus* (London – New York, 1972), p. 145; Ion Chirtoagă, *Sud-Estul Moldovei și stânga Nistrului (1484–1699): Expansiunea și dominația turco-tatară* (Bucharest, 1999), p. 124.

45 Costin, *Letopisețul Țării Moldovei*, p. 194.

46 Ronald S. Burt, *Brokerage and Closure: An Introduction to Social Capital* (Oxford, 2005), pp. 3–4.

47 Mihai Maxim, *Țările Române și Înalta Poartă: Cadrul juridic al relațiilor românootomane în evul mediu* (Bucharest, 1993), p. 182.

48 Bogdan Murgescu, 'Balances of trade and payments between the Ottoman Empire and Central Europe (16th–18th centuries)', in Simonetta Cavaciocchi (ed.), *Relazioni economiche tra Europa e mondo islamico, secc. XIII–XVIII* (Florence, 2007), pp. 962–4.

49 Viorel Panaite, 'The voivodes of the Danubian principalities – as *haracgüzarlar* of the Ottoman sultans', in Kemal H. Karpat and Robert W. Zens (eds), *Ottoman Borderlands: Issues, Personalities and Political Changes* (Madison, 2003), pp. 59–78.

50 On this topic, see Viorel Panaite, *Război, pace și comerț în Islam: Țările române și dreptul otoman al popoarelor* (Iași, 2013), pp. 400–3.

51 Ibid., p. 404–5; Bogdan Murgescu, *România și Europa: Acumularea decalajelor economice (1500–2010)* (Iași, 2012), pp. 34–5.

52 Mihai Berza, 'Haraciul Moldovei și Țării Românești în sec. XV–XIX', *Studii și Materiale de Istorie Medie* 2 (1957), pp. 27–30; Mihai Maxim, 'Haraciul Moldovei și Țării Românești în ultimul sfert al veacului XVI', *Studii și Materiale de Istorie Medie* 12 (1994), pp. 44–5.

53 Murgescu, *România și Europa*, p. 39.

54 Mihai Maxim, 'Recherches sur les circonstances de la majoration du *kharadj* de la Moldavie entre les années 1538–1574', in Mihai Maxim, *L'Empire Ottoman au nord du Danube et l'autonomie des Principautés Roumaines au XVIᵉ siècle* (Istanbul, 1999), pp. 185–214; Mihai Maxim, 'Circonstances de la majoration du *kharadj* payé par la Valachie à l'Empire ottoman durant la période 1540–1575', in Mihai Maxim, *L'Empire Ottoman au nord du Danube et l'autonomie des Principautés Roumaines au XVIᵉ siècle* (Istanbul, 1999), pp. 215–30.

55 Bogdan Murgescu, 'Câteva observații pe marginea datoriilor domnilor Țării Românești și Moldovei în 1594', *Revista Istorică* 6/3–4 (1995), pp. 243–53; Mihai Maxim, 'Les relations roumano-ottomanes entre 1574 et 1594', in Mihai Maxim,

L'Empire Ottoman au nord du Danube et l'autonomie des Principautés Roumaines au XVIᵉ siècle (Istanbul, 1999), pp. 125–6; Păun, '"Well-born of the Polis"', pp. 60–2 and 8; Ion Caproșu, *O istorie a Moldovei prin relațiile de credit până la mijlocul secolului al XVIII-lea* (Iași, 1989), pp. 47–67. We know little about Muslim creditors of voivodes, but apparently many of them were Janissaries, providing further evidence on the relationship between the socio-economic changes in the Ottoman Empire and the evolution of Ottoman–Moldavian–Wallachian relations, see, for instance, BOA, MD 85/542; Selanikî Mustafa Efendi, *Tarih-i Selânikî*, vol. 1, ed. Mehmet İpşirli (Ankara, 1989), pp. 409–10.

56 Gemil, 'Date noi', pp. 1437–8; Berza, 'Haraciul Moldovei și Țării Românești', p. 17.

57 Tahsin Gemil, *Țările Române în contextul politic internațional (1621–1672)* (Bucharest, 1979), pp. 14–5. This tendency began already in the 1590s, see Murgescu, *România și Europa*, p. 34. On *pișkeș*, see Ann Lambton, 'Pīshkash: present or tribute?', *Bulletin of the School of Oriental and African Studies* 57/1 (1994), pp. 145–58; Tim Stanley, 'Ottoman gift exchange: royal give and take', *Muqarnas* 27 (2010), pp. 189–207; Hedda Reindl-Kiel, 'Power and submission: gifting at royal circumcision festivals in the Ottoman Empire (16th–18th centuries)', *Turcica* 41 (2009), pp. 37–88.

58 Dragoș Ungureanu, 'Constantin Brâncoveanu și Înalta Poartă: Relații financiaro-vasalice în lumina Condicii visteriei', http://www.cimec.ro/istorie/Condica-vistieriei-tarii-romanestiBrancoveanu/dl.asp?filename=Ungureanu-Dragos_Constantin-Brancoveanu-si-Inalta-Poarta-Relatii-financiarovasalice-in-lumina-Condicii-vistieriei.pdf (accessed 20 May 2014), p. 9.

59 Gemil, 'Date noi', p. 1437.

60 On this topic, see Linda T. Darling, 'Ottoman fiscal administration: decline or adaptation?', *Journal of European Economic History* 26/1 (1997), pp. 166–72; Mehmet Genç, 'Osmanlı maliyesinde malikane sistemi', in Osman Okyar and Halil İnalcık (eds), *Türkiye'nin Sosyal ve Ekonomik Tarihi (1071–1920)* (Ankara, 1980), p. 236.

61 In his study on the topic, Tahsin Gemil juxtaposed the Danubian principalities and Dubrovnik, claiming that the *harac* of the republic increased during the seventeenth century. However, as Vesna Miović-Perić has shown, this was not the case, and Dubrovnik's *harac* remained stable, amounting to 12,500 ducats annually, although the exchange rate was subject to some dispute between Ottoman authorities and Ragusan agents, see Vesna Miović-Perić, 'Turske priznanice u uplaćenom Dubrovačkom haraču', *Anali Dubrovnik* 42 (2004), pp. 53–77.

62 Molly Greene, *A Shared World: Christians and Muslims in the Early Modern Mediterranean* (Princeton, NJ, 2002), pp. 27–8; Özgür Kolçak, 'Köprülü ambitions in Transylvania: consolidation of Ottoman power and transfer of royal estates', paper presented at the conference Ottoman Archeology in Romania: Challenges, Realities, Perspectives in Bucharest, 20–21 October 2017.

63 İ. Metin Kunt, 'Derviş Mehmed Paşa, vezir and entrepreneur: a study in Ottoman political-economic theory and practice', *Turcica* 9/1 (1977), p. 202; Jane Hathaway, *The Politics of Households in Ottoman Egypt: The Rise of Qazdağlıs* (Cambridge, 1997), p. 25.

64 Şevket Pamuk, 'The evolution of fiscal institutions in the Ottoman Empire, 1500–1914', in Bartolomé Yun Casalilla and Patrick K. O'Brien (eds), *The Rise of Fiscal States: A Global History, 1500–1914* (New York, 2012), pp. 317–8; Michael Ursinus, 'The transformation of the Ottoman fiscal regime, *c.* 1600–1850', in Christine Woodhead (ed.), *The Ottoman World* (London – New York, 2012), pp. 423–7; Linda T. Darling, *Revenue-Raising and Legitimacy: Tax Collection and Finance Administration in Ottoman Empire, 1560–1660* (Leiden – Boston, 1996), pp. 119–60.

65 On the legal framework of *iltizam*, see Murat Çizakça, *A Comparative Evolution of Business Partnerships: The Islamic World and Europe, with Specific Reference to the Ottoman Archives* (Leiden – Boston, 1996), pp. 140–1.

66 Ibid., pp. 146–7; Darling, *Revenue-Raising and Legitimacy*, pp. 159–60; Ariel Salzmann, *Tocqueville in the Ottoman Empire: Rival Paths to the Modern State* (Leiden – Boston, 2004), p. 106; Michael Nizri, *Ottoman High Politics and the Ulema Household* (Basingstoke, 2014), p. 166.

67 Tom Papademetriou, *Render unto the Sultan: Power, Authority, and the Greek Orthodox Church in the Early Ottoman Centuries* (Oxford, 2015), p. 117. The same argument has been presented earlier in Paraskevas Konortas, *Les rapports juridiques et politiques entre le Patriarcat de Constantinople et l'administration ottoman de 1453 à 1600 (d'après les documents grecs et ottomans)* (PhD diss., University of Paris I, 1985), which I have been unable to consult. I would like to thank Radu Păun for bringing this work to my attention.

68 For this argument, see Păun, '"Well-born of the Polis"', p. 61; Păun, 'Pouvoirs, offices et patronage', pp. 281–302.

69 Çizakça, *A Comparative Evolution*, pp. 143–5, 158.

70 Panaite, 'The voivodes of the Danubian principalities', p. 64; On the dual character of the voivodes' position, see Radu G. Păun, 'La construction de l'état moderne et le sud-est de l'Europe: Quelques réflexions méthodologiques', *Revue des Études Sud-Est Européennes* 35/3–4 (1997), p. 223.

71 Çizakça, *A Comparative Evolution*, pp. 147–8.

72 Unfortunately, the inventories listing property confiscated from Tabanıyassı Mehmed Pasha following his execution in December 1639 are heavily deteriorated and does not provide information on the topic, BOA, Ali Emiri, 7/718, 721.

73 Biedrzycka (ed.), *Korespondencja Stanisława Koniecpolskiego*, p. 574; Vecihi Hasan Çelebi, *Tarih-i Vecihi*, TSMK Revan MS 1153, ff. 18–9.

74 Ungureanu, 'Constantin Brâncoveanu și Înalta Poartă', p. 9; DANIC, Manuscrise MS 126, p. 109; Dinu C. Giurescu, 'Anatefterul: Condica de porunci a visteriei lui

Notes   223

Constantin Brîncoveanu', *Studii și Materiale de Istorie Medie* 5 (1962), pp. 420, 429, 438. On the term *plocon*, see Alexandru Constantinescu, 'Ploconul', *Studii și Materiale de Istorie Medie* 5 (1973), pp. 217–24.

75 See, for instance, Hurmuzaki, vol. iv/2, p. 500.

76 Evliyâ Çelebi, *Günümüz Türkçesiyle Evliyâ Çelebi Seyahatnâmesi*, vol. v/2, ed. Seyit A. Kahraman and Yücel Dağlı (Istanbul, 2007), p. 464.

77 Dariusz Kołodziejczyk, *Podole pod panowaniem tureckim: Ejalet kamieniecki 1672–1699* (Warszawa, 1994), p. 56.

78 Mehmet İnbaşı, *Ukrayna'da Osmanlılar: Kamaniçe Seferi ve Organizasyonu (1672)* (Istanbul, 2004), p. 301; Halime Doğru, *Lehistan'da bir Osmanlı Sultanı: IV. Mehmed'in Kamaniçe–Hotin Seferi ve Bir Masraf Defteri* (Istanbul, 2007); Mustafa N. Türkmen, 'Kamaniçe seferinin lojistik hazırlıkları' (PhD diss., Ankara University, 2002).

79 Bogdan Murgescu, 'The Ottoman military demand and the Romanian market: a case study: 1672', *Revue des Études Sud-Est Européennes* 25/4 (1987), p. 312.

80 Ion Neculce, *Opere: Letopisețul Țării Moldovei și O samă de cuvinte*, ed. Gabriel Ştrempel (Bucharest, 1982), pp. 216–8.

81 Eugeniusz Barwiński (ed.), *Dyaryusze sejmowe r. 1597* (Cracow, 1907), p. 343.

82 Claudio Rangoni, *Relacja o Królestwie Polskim z 1604 roku*, ed. Janusz Byliński and Włodzimierz Kaczorowski (Opole, 2013), p. 159.

83 See, for instance, Hurmuzaki, Suppl. ii/1, p. 532.

84 AGAD, Archiwum Radziwiłłów, vi/2/48, f. 12.

85 Hurmuzaki, Suppl. ii/2, p. 611.

86 Corfus (ed.), *Documente – XVII*, p. 57.

87 Marta Kupczewska, 'Działalność polityczno-wojskowa Jana, Jakuba i Stefana Potockich w okresie kampanii smoleńskiej', *Białostockie Teki Historyczne* 8 (2010), pp. 27–46.

88 Corfus (ed.), *Documente – XVII*, p. 282.

89 On the Polish oriental trade, Andrzej Dziubiński, *Na szlakach Orientu: handel między Polską a Imperium Osmańskim w XVI–XVIII wieku* (Wrocław, 1998); Dariusz Kołodziejczyk, 'The export of silver coin through the Polish–Ottoman border and the problem of the balance of trade', *Turcica* 28 (1996), pp. 105–16; Władimir Szłapinskij, 'Współoddziaływanie rynków pieniężnych: Województwo ruskie a Turcja, Mołdawia i Wołoszczyzna', *Wiadomości Numizmatyczne* 44/1 (2000), pp. 26–7.

90 Jolanta Choińska-Mika, *Sejmiki mazowieckie w dobie Wazów* (Warsaw, 1998), p. 12.

91 Andrzej Rachuba, 'Hegemonia Sapiehów na Litwie jako przejaw skrajnej dominacji magnaterii w życiu kraju', in Jerzy Urwanowicz, Ewa Dubas-Urwanowicz and Piotr Guzowski (eds), *Władza i prestiż: Magnateria Rzeczypospolitej w XVI–XVIII wieku* (Białystok, 2003), pp. 219–20.

224 *Notes*

92 Stanisław Makowiecki, *Relacyja Kamieńca wziętego przez Turków w roku 1672*, ed. Piotr Borek (Cracow, 2008), p. 172.

93 For a masterful account of political communication and the strategies of leaking in early modern Venice, see Filippo de Vivo, *Information and Communication in Venice: Rethinking Early Modern Politics* (Oxford, 2007).

94 Arndt Brendecke, 'Informing the council: central institutions and local knowledge in the Spanish Empire', in Willem P. Blockmans, André Holenstein and Jon Mathieu (eds), *Empowering Interactions: Political Cultures and the Emergence of the State in Europe, 1300–1900* (Aldershot, 2009), p. 240.

95 Vivo, *Information and Communication*, p. 13.

96 Peksevgen, 'Secrecy', p. 119.

97 Jolanta Choińska-Mika, *Między społeczeństwem szlacheckim a władzą: Problemy komunikacji społeczności lokalne – władza w epoce Jana Kazimierza* (Warsaw, 2002), p. 127.

98 Neculce, *Opere*, pp. 360–1.

99 See Biedrzycka (ed.), *Korespondencja Stanisława Koniecpolskiego*, pp. 290, 605.

100 See Ionel-Claudiu Dumitrescu, 'Activităţi informative româneşti în serviciul Porţii otomane (secolele XVI–XVII)', *Anuarul Institutului de Istorie şi Arheologie 'A.D. Xenopol'* 35 (1998), p. 43.

101 Corfus (ed.), *Documente – XVII*, p. 106; Irena Sułkowska, 'Noi documente privind relaţiile romîno-polone în perioada 1589–1622', *Studii. Revistă de Istorie* 12/6 (1959), p. 94.

102 Hurmuzaki, Suppl. i/1, p. 343.

103 Constantin Grecescu and Dan Simonescu (eds), *Cronica anonimă a Moldovei, 1661–1729: Pseudo-Amiras* (Bucharest, 1975), pp. 43–4.

104 Mustafa Naima, *Tarih-i Naima*, vol. 3 (Istanbul, 1283/1866–67), p. 403.

105 TSMA E.5645 and E.5073; Biedrzycka (ed.), *Korespondencja Stanisława Koniecpolskiego*, p. 460.

106 On this topic, see Michał Wasiucionek, 'Diplomacy, power, and ceremonial entry: Polish–Lithuanian grand embassies in Moldavia in the seventeenth century', *Acta Poloniae Historica* 105 (2012), pp. 55–83.

107 Biedrzycka (ed.), *Korespondencja Stanisława Koniecpolskiego*, p. 290.

108 Ibid., pp. 312, 324.

109 Tomasz Kempa, 'Konflikt między kanclerzem Jan Zamoyskim a książętami Ostrogskimi i jego wpływ na sytuację wewnętrzną i zewnętrzną Rzeczypospolitej w końcu XVI wieku', *Socium: Al'manax Social'noj Istorji* 9 (2010), pp. 85–7.

110 Ştefan Andreescu, 'Exarhul patriarhal Nichifor Dascălul, cneazul Constantin Vasile de Ostrog şi Mihai Viteazul', in Ştefan Andreescu, *Restitutio Daciae*, vol. 3 (Bucharest, 1997), pp. 81–5.

111 Hurmuzaki, Suppl. ii/1, p. 389.

Notes

225

112 *Akty otnosjaščiesja k istorii Zapadnoj Rossii (Saint Petersburg, 1851)*, pp. 163; Eugeniusz Barwiński (ed.), *Dyaryusze sejmowe r. 1597* (Cracow, 1907), p. 122.

113 Tomasz Kempa, 'Proces Nicefora na sejmie w Warszawie w 1597 roku', in Zbigniew Karpus, Tomasz Kempa and Dorota Michaluk (eds), *Europa Orientalis: Polska i jej wschodni sąsiedzi od średniowiecza po współczesność* (Toruń, 1996), p. 156.

114 Barwiński (ed.), *Dyaryusze sejmowe r. 1597*, pp. 103–4.

115 Kempa, 'Konflikt', p. 163.

116 Ibid., pp. 87–8.

117 Emrah S. Gürkan, 'Fooling the Sultan: information, decision-making and the "Mediterranean Faction" (1585–1587)', *Osmanlı Araştırmaları* 45 (2015), p. 91.

118 Corfus (ed.), *Documente – XVII*, p. 155.

119 Ibid., pp. 130–1.

120 See, for instance, Sharon Kettering, 'Gift-giving and patronage in early modern France', *French History* 2/2 (1988), pp. 131–51; Ilana Krausman Ben-Amos, *The Culture of Giving: Informal Support and Gift-Exchange in Early Modern England* (Cambridge, 2008); Irma Thoen, *Strategic Affection? Gift-Exchange in Seventeenth-Century Holland* (Amsterdam, 2007).

121 On this topic see also, Cristian A. Bobicescu, 'Daruri și solidarități în raporturile polono-lituaniano-moldovenești în perioada lui Ieremia Movilă: considerații preliminare', in Karina Stempel-Gancarczyk and Elżbieta Wieruszewska-Calistru (eds), *Historia i dzień dzisiejszy relacji polsko-rumuńskich* (Suceava, 2017), pp. 22–39.

122 Hedda Reindl-Kiel, 'Bread for the followers, silver vessels for the lord: the system of distribution and redistribution in the Ottoman Empire (16th–18th centuries)', *Osmanlı Araştırmaları* 43 (2013), pp. 93–104.

123 Radu vornicul Popescu, *Istoriile domnilor Țării Romînești*, ed. Constantin Grecescu (Bucharest, 1963), p. 126.

124 Urszula Augustyniak, *Dwór i klientela Krzysztofa Radziwiłła, 1585–1640: Mechanizmy patronatu* (Warsaw, 2001), p. 109.

125 Nicolae Iorga, 'Doamna lui Ieremia Movilă', *Analele Academiei Române. Memoriile Secțiunii Istorice*, Seria II, 32 (1910), p. 1068.

126 Gheorghe Pungă, 'Contribuții la biografia marelui logofăt Luca Stroici', *Arhiva Genealogică* 1/1–2 (1994), pp. 183 and 192–3; Cristian A. Bobicescu, 'Luca Stroici între Ieremia Movilă și Jan Zamoyski', paper presented at the scientific session of the Nicolae Lorga Institute of History in Bucharest, 2002. For the Stroici family, see also Maria Magdalena Székely, 'Contribuții la genealogia familiei Stroici', *Arhiva Genealogică* 1/1–2 (1994), pp. 249–53; Maria Magdalena Székely, 'Noi contribuții la genealogia familiei Stroici', *Arhiva Genealogică* 2/1–2 (1995), pp. 65–77.

226 *Notes*

127 See, for instance, Hurmuzaki, Suppl. ii/1, pp. 368, 416, 433, 435, 445–6, 447, 449, 460, 471, 520, 549, 594; Ibid. Suppl. ii/2, 267. His and Ieremia Movilă's style closely reflect the one employed in Polish–Lithuanian correspondence, see Bobicescu, 'Daruri și solidarități', p. 29.

128 Hurmuzaki, Suppl. ii/1, p. 435.

129 Sułkowska, 'Noi documente', p. 94.

130 Franciszek Pułaski (ed.), *Źródła do poselstwa Jana Gnińskiego wojewody chełmińskiego do Turcyi w latach 1677–1678* (Cracow, 1907), p. 219; Lidia Vlasova, *Moldavsko-pol'skie političeskie svjazi v poslednej četverti XVII v. – načale XVIII v.* (Chișinău, 1980), pp. 31–3.

131 Zofia Zielińska, 'Magnaten und Adel im politischen Landleben Polen-Litauens des 18. Jahrhunderts', in Antoni Mączak and Elisabeth Müller-Luckner (eds), *Klientelsysteme im Europa der Früher Neuzeit* (Munich, 1988), p. 208.

Chapter 4

1 See, for instance, Veniamin Ciobanu, *La cumpănă de veacuri: Țările Române în contextul politicii poloneze la sfârșitul secolului al XVI-lea și începutul secolului al XVII-lea* (Iași, 1991), p. 9.

2 Michael J. Braddick, 'Administrative performance: the representation of political authority in early modern England', in Michael J. Braddick and John Walter (eds), *Negotiating Power in Early Modern Society: Order, Hierarchy, and Subordination in Britain and Ireland* (Cambridge, 2001), p. 185.

3 Halil Sahillioğlu (ed.), *Koca Sinan Paşa'nın Telhisleri* (Istanbul, 2004), pp. 122–3.

4 James C. Scott, 'Patron–client politics and political change in Southeast Asia', *American Political Science Review* 66/1 (1972), p. 97; For quasi-groups, see Robert R. Kaufman, 'The patron-client concept and macro-politics: prospects and problems', *Comparative Studies in Society and History* 16/3 (1974), p. 297; Adrian C. Meyer, 'The significance of quasi-groups in the study of complex societies', in Michael Banton (ed.), *Social anthropology of complex societies* (London – New York, 1966), pp. 97–121.

5 Constantin Rezachevici, 'Domnia lui Matei Basarab – un factor de stabilitate', in Virgil Cândea et al. (eds), *Istoria românilor*, vol. 5, second edition (Bucharest, 2012), pp. 121–2; Nicolae Stoicescu, *Matei Basarab* (Bucharest, 1988), p. 132.

6 Tahsin Gemil, *Țările Române în contextul politic internațional (1621–1672)* (Bucharest, 1979), p. 129; V. Motogna, 'Epoca lui Matei Basarab și Vasile Lupu', *Cercetării Istorice* 13–16 (1940), pp. 453–513.

7 Constantin Șerban, *Vasile Lupu, domn al Moldovei (1634–1653)* (Bucharest, 1991), pp. 21–6; Ion Eremia, *Relațiile externe ale lui Vasile Lupu (1634–1653): Contribuții la istoria diplomației moldovenești în secolul al XVII-lea* (Chișinău, 1999), p. 11.

Notes

8   On the relationship between Rákóczy and Matei Basarab, see Ion Sîrbu, *Mateiu-Vodă Basarabas auswärtige Beziehungen, 1632-1654* (Leipzig, 1899). For a detailed analysis of Rákóczy's stance in the conflict, see János B. Szabó, 'Prince György Rákoczi I of Transylvania and the elite of Ottoman Hungary, 1630-1636', in Gábor Kármán (ed.), *Tributaries and Peripheries of the Ottoman Empire* (Leiden – Boston, forthcoming).

9   Miron Costin, *Letopisețul Țării Moldovei dela Aron Vodă încoace*, ed. Petre P. Panaitescu (Bucharest, 1943), p. 84. Cf. Eremia, *Relațiile externe*, pp. 44–8.

10 Nicolae Stoicescu, *Dicționar al marilor dregători din Țara Românească și Moldova (sec. XIV–XVII)* (Bucharest, 1971), pp. 369–71. On the role of Catargi family in the conflict, see Motogna, 'Epoca lui Matei Basarab', p. 473; Șerban, *Vasile Lupu*, p. 128; Stoicescu, *Matei Basarab*, p. 140.

11 Ibid., p. 130.

12 Costin, *Letopisețul Țării Moldovei*, pp. 114–15; Stoicescu, *Matei Basarab*, p. 146; Șerban, *Vasile Lupu*, p. 128; Eremia, *Relațiile externe*, pp. 57–8.

13 Gemil, *Țările Române în contextul politic*, p. 129; Șerban, *Vasile Lupu*, p. 122; Dumitru Năstase, 'Imperial claims in the Romanian principalities from the fourteenth to the seventeenth centuries: new contributions', in Lowell Clucas (ed.), *The Byzantine Legacy in Eastern Europe* (Boulder, 1988), p. 206.

14 For this topic, see Ștefan Andreescu, 'Radu Mihnea Corvin, domn al Moldovei și Țării Românești', in Ștefan Andreescu, *Restitutio Daciae*, vol. 2 (Bucharest, 1989), pp. 40–1.

15 Andrei Veress (ed.), *Documente privitoare la istoria Ardealului, Moldovei și Țării-Românești*, vol. 9 (Bucharest, 1935), pp. 8, 184–5. On Zülfikar Agha and his political role, see Gábor Kármán, *A Seventeenth-Century Odyssey in East Central Europe: The Life of Jakab Harsányi Nagy* (Leiden – Boston, 2016), pp. 74–83; Gábor Kármán, 'Zülfikár aga portai főtolmács', *Aetas* 31/3 (2016), pp. 54–76.

16 It is worth noting that İbrahim Efendi also maintained frequent correspondence with Matei's ally, Transylvanian prince György Rákoczi I, see Szábo, 'Prince György Rákoczi'.

17 Agnieszka Biedrzycka (ed.), *Korespondencja Stanisława Koniecpolskiego hetmana wielkiego koronnego, 1632-1646* (Cracow, 2005), p. 459; Hurmuzaki, vol. iv/2, p. 500.

18 Costin, *Letopisețul Țării Moldovei*, p. 99.

19 Biedrzycka (ed.), *Korespondencja Stanisława Koniecpolskiego*, pp. 311–12.

20 Ibid., p. 459.

21 Tülin Ülgen, 'Tabanı-yassı Mehmed Paşa' (MA thesis, Istanbul University 1962), p. 4; Mehmed Süreyya, *Sicill-i Osmanî*, ed. Seyit A. Kahraman, vol. 3 (Istanbul, 1996), pp. 104–5.

22 Alper Başer, 'Bucak Tatarları (1550–1700)' (PhD diss., Afyon Kocatepe University, 2010), pp. 122–5; Dariusz Kołodziejczyk, *The Crimean Khanate and Poland-Lithuania: International Diplomacy on the European Periphery (15th–18th Century):*

228 *Notes*

A Study of Peace Treaties Followed by Annotated Documents (Leiden – Boston, 2011), p. 130.

23 Hurmuzaki, vol. iv/2, p. 462.

24 Costin, *Letopisețul Țării Moldovei*, p. 102.

25 Ibid.

26 Biedrzycka (ed.), *Korespondencja Stanisława Koniecpolskiego*, p. 433.

27 Hurmuzaki, vol. iv/2, p. 500.

28 See, for instance, TSMA, E.524/15.

29 TSMA, E.2584/2, 5, 8; E. 524/73.

30 Ibid., pp. 512–13; Hurmuzaki vol. iv/2, p. 464.

31 Hurmuzaki, vol. iv/2, pp. 506–7.

32 Constantin Velichi, 'Vasile Lupu ca domn al Moldovei și al Țării Românești', *Revista Istorică* 22/4–6 (1936), pp. 101–2.

33 Paul Cernovodeanu, 'Știri privitoare la Gheorghe Ghica vodă al Moldovei (1658–9) și familia sa (I)', *Anuarul Institutului de Istorie și Arheologie 'A.D. Xenopol'* 19 (1982), p. 336.

34 Hurmuzaki, vol. iv/2, pp. 506–7.

35 Costin, *Letopisețul Țării Moldovei*, p. 104; Mustafa Naima, *Tarih-i Naima*, vol. 3 (Istanbul, 1281–4/1864), p. 403; Gemil, *Țările Române în contextul politic*, p. 105.

36 Biedrzycka (ed.), *Korespondencja Stanisława Koniecpolskiego*, p. 561; Hurmuzaki, vol. iv/2, p. 485.

37 TSMA, E.5645.

38 Biedrzycka (ed.), *Korespondencja Stanisława Koniecpolskiego*, p. 566.

39 TSMA, E.5073; Eudoxiu de Hurmuzaki (ed.), *Fragmente zur Geschichte der Rumänen*, vol. 3 (Bucharest, 1881), p. 142.

40 Ibid., p. 566.

41 Costin, *Letopisețul Țării Moldovei*, p. 107.

42 Ibid., p. 108; Constantin C. Giurescu, 'Uciderea veziuriului Mohamed Tabani Buiuc, sprijinătorul lui Vasile Lupu', *Revista Istorică* 12/3 (1926), p. 102; Biedrzycka (ed.), *Korespondencja Stanisława Koniecpolskiego*, p. 566.

43 Veress (ed.), *Documente*, vol. 9, p. 65.

44 Biedrzycka (ed.), *Korespondencja Stanisława Koniecpolskiego*, p. 566.

45 Ibid., p. 579.

46 Adam Przyboś (ed.), *Wielka legacja Wojciecha Miaskowskiego do Turcji w 1640 r.* (Warsaw, 1985), pp. 45–7; Eduard Baidaus, *Politica și diplomația Moldovei în timpul domniei lui Vasile Lupu: Relațiile politice cu Republica Nobiliară Polonă și Rusia Moscovită în anii 1634–1653* (Chișinău, 1998), p. 22.

47 Hurmuzaki, vol. iv/2, p. 489.

48 Naima, *Tarih-i Naima*, vol. 4, pp. 51–2; Hedda Reindl-Kiel, *Leisure, Pleasure and Duty: The Daily Life of Silahdar Mustafa, Éminence Grise in the Final Years of Murad IV (1635–1640)* (Berlin, 2016), pp. 23–8.

Notes

49 Veress (ed.), *Documente*, vol. 10, pp. 139–41; Hurmuzaki, *Fragmente*, vol. 3, p. 167.

50 Caroline Finkel, *Osman's Dream: The History of the Ottoman Empire* (London, 2003), pp. 223–6.

51 Eremia, *Relațiile externe*, pp. 136–7; Baidaus, *Politica și diplomația*, pp. 45–6.

52 See, for instance, Gemil, *Țările Române în contextul politic*, p. 105–6.

53 Vecihi, *Tarih-i Vecihi*, TSMK MS Revan 1306, ff. 18–19.

54 Naima, *Tarih-i Naima*, vol. 3, pp. 399–404.

55 Cristian A. Bobicescu, 'Pe marginea raporturilor lui Jan Zamoyski cu Moldova și Țara Românească', *Studii și Materiale de Istorie Medie* 20 (2002), pp. 201–4.

56 Violetta Urbaniak, *Zamoyszczycy bez Zamoyskiego: Studium dekompozycji ugrupowania politycznego* (Warsaw, 1995), p. 36.

57 Jerzy Besala, *Stanisław Żółkiewski* (Warsaw, 1988), p. 178.

58 Urbaniak, *Zamoyszczycy*, p. 57.

59 Henryk Litwin, 'Fakcje magnackie na Kijowszczyźnie 1569–1648', in Jerzy Urwanowicz, Ewa Dubas-Urwanowicz and Piotr Guzowski (eds), *Władza i prestiż: Magnateria Rzeczypospolitej w XVI–XVIII wieku* (Białystok, 2003), p. 57.

60 Besala, *Stanisław Żółkiewski*, p. 18.

61 Ștefan S. Gorovei, 'O lămurire: domnia ereditară a familiei Movilă', *Revista de istorie* 28/7 (1975), pp. 1091–4; Ciobanu, *La cumpănă de veacuri*, p. 175.

62 Vasile Lungu, 'Mihăilaș Vodă Movilă și Moldova în anul 1607', *Cercetări Istorice* 8/1 (1932), pp. 2–3; Veniamin Ciobanu, 'Succesiunea domnească a Movileștilor–un litigiu politic internațional', *Anuarul Institutului de Istorie și Arheologie 'A.D. Xenopol'* 25/1 (1988), p. 283; Veniamin Ciobanu, *Politică și diplomație în secolul al XVII-lea: Țările Române în raporturile polono-otomano-habsburgice (1601–1634)* (Bucharest, 1994), pp. 76–7; Zdzisław Spieralski, *Awantury mołdawskie* (Warsaw, 1967), pp. 159–60.

63 Nicolae Iorga, 'Doamna lui Ieremia Movilă', *Analele Academiei Române. Memoriile Secțiunii Istorice*, Seria II, 32 (1910), pp. 1019–77. Nicolae Iorga mistakenly identified Elizabeta's origins, claiming that she was a member of the Hungarian Csomortányi family, ibid., p. 1020–1, a mistake repeated subsequently by some historians. For Elizabeta's origin, see Sever Zotta, 'Doamna Elisaveta a lui Ieremia Movilă a fost fiica lui Gheorghe pârcălab de Hotin', *Arhiva Genealogică* 2 (1913), pp. 178–80; Ștefan S. Gorovei, 'Doamna Elisabeta Movilă: contribuții pentru o biografie nescrisă', in *Movileștii: istorie și spiritualitate românească*, vol. 2 (Suceava, 2006), pp. 274–7.

64 See Teodor Bălan (ed.), *Documente bucovinene*, vol. 1 (Cernăuți, 1933), p. 169.

65 Dumitru Ciurea, 'Despre Ieremia Movilă și situația politică a Moldovei la sfârșitul sec. XVI și începutul sec. XVII', in *Movileștii: istorie și spiritualitate românească*, vol. 1 (Suceava, 2006), pp. 109–11; Ciobanu, *Politică și diplomație*, p. 32; Ștefan Andreescu, '"Movileștii" în Țara Românească', in Ștefan Andreescu, *Restitutio Daciae*, vol. 2 (Bucharest, 1989), pp. 7–34.

230   *Notes*

66   Ilie Corfus (ed.), *Documente privitoare la istoria României culese din arhivele polone: Secolul al* XVII-lea (Bucharest, 1983), p. 46.

67   Cengiz Orhonlu (ed.), *Telhisler (1597–1606)* (Istanbul, 1970), p. 119; Cristina Rotman-Bulgaru, 'Relațiile Moldovei cu Imperiul otoman la începutul secolului al XVII-lea', *Revista de Istorie* 26/5 (1976), p. 694; Ciobanu, *Politică și diplomație*, p. 75.

68   Ciobanu, 'Succesiunea domnească', p. 283.

69   Cracow, Czartoryski Library MS 100, p. 267.

70   Wojciech Sokołowski, *Politycy schyłku Złotego Wieku: Małopolscy przywódcy szlachty i parlamentarzyści w latach 1574–1605* (Warsaw, 1997), p. 140; Barbara Janiszewska-Mincer, *Rzeczpospolita Polska w latach 1600–1603: narastanie konfliktu między Zygmuntem III Wazą a stanami* (Bydgoszcz, 1984), p. 107.

71   Sokołowski, *Politycy schyłku Złotego Wieku*, pp. 26–7.

72   Lungu, 'Mihăilaș Vodă Movilă', pp. 2–3.

73   Corfus (ed.), *Documente–XVII*, p. 46.

74   Ilie Corfus (ed.), *Documente polone privitoare la istoria României: secolele al XVI-lea și al XVII* (Bucharest, 2001), p. 150.

75   Samuel Maskiewicz, 'Dyaryusz Samuela Maskiewicza', in Julian U. Niemcewicz (ed.), *Zbiór pamiętników o dawnej Polszcze* (Leipzig, 1839), p. 249.

76   Corfus (ed.), *Documente –XVII*, pp. 46–7.

77   Lungu, 'Mihăilaș Vodă Movilă', p. 15.

78   Spieralski, *Awantury mołdawskie*, pp. 159–60; Ciobanu, 'Succesiunea domnească', pp. 281–2.

79   Corfus (ed.), *Documente–XVII*, p. 46.

80   Alfons Bruening, '"Voevodych zemli moldavskoi"… : Peter Mohyla's youth and political heritage', *Socium: Al'manax Socjal'noj Istorii* 4 (2004), p. 22.

81   Stoicescu, *Dicționar*, p. 307.

82   Ciobanu, 'Succesiunea domnească', p. 57. See also, Ilona Czamańska, 'Rumuńska imigracja polityczna w Polsce XVII wieku', *Balcanica Posnaniensia* 6 (1993), p. 8.

83   Marta Kupczewska, 'Działalność polityczno-wojskowa Jana, Jakuba i Stefana Potockich w okresie kampanii smoleńskiej', *Białostockie Teki Historyczne* 8 (2010), pp. 27–46.

84   Corfus (ed.), *Documente –XVII*, p. 57.

85   Ibid., p. 58.

86   Maria Magdalena Székely, 'Neamul lui Nestor Ureche', *Anuarul Institutului de Istorie 'A.D. Xenopol'* 30 (1993), pp. 653–70; Maria Magdalena Székely, 'Structura domeniului boieresc: Nestor Ureche și proprietățile lui', *Revista istorică* 9/3–4 (1998), pp. 153–68. See also Ștefan S. Gorovei, '"Nepoții Balicăi, săminţenia Movileștilor"', *Arhiva Genealogică* 1/3–4 (1994), pp. 123–33.

87   Ibid., p. 57.

Notes

88 Spieralski, *Awantury mołdawskie*, p. 160.

89 Dariusz Skorupa, *Stosunki polsko-tatarskie, 1595–1623* (Warsaw, 2004), pp. 168–70; August Bielowski (ed.), *Pisma Stanisława Żółkiewskiego, kanclerza koronnego i hetmana* (L'viv, 1861), p. 411.

90 Paweł Piasecki, *Kronika Pawła Piaseckiego biskupa przemyślskiego*, ed. Antoni Chrząszczewski (Cracow, 1870), pp. 251–2; Skorupa, *Stosunki polsko-tatarskie*, p. 171; Constantin Rezachevici, 'Bătălia de la "Cornul lui Sas" (3/13 iulie 1612): o reconstituire', *Studii şi Materiale de Istorie Militară* 9 (1976), pp. 59–70; Constantin Rezachevici, 'Din nou despre bătălia de la Cornul lui Sas', *Anuarul Institutului de Istorie şi Arheologie 'A.D. Xenopol'* 35/2 (1988), pp. 501–3.

91 Stockholm, Riksarkivet, Extranea, 105; Hurmuzaki, Suppl. i/1, pp. 158–9; Corfus (ed.), *Documente – XVI şi XVII*, pp. 210–3; Hurmuzaki, Suppl. ii/2, p. 380.

92 Cracow, Czartoryski Library MS 108, pp. 189–92; Cracow, State Archive, Archiwum Sanguszków 423, pl. 8, pp. 11–14; Aurel H. Golimas, *Luptă decisivă de la Tătareni şi capitularea darabanilor deasupra Tăuteştilor, 22 decembrie 1615* (Iaşi, 1935), p. 9; Skorupa, *Stosunki polsko-tatarskie*, pp. 189–91; Ilona Czamańska, 'Kampania mołdawska księcia Samuela Koreckiego 1615–1616 r.', in Robert Majzner (ed.), *Si vis pacem, para bellum: bezpieczeństwo i polityka Polski* (Częstochowa – Włocławek, 2013), p. 130.

93 Jakub Pszonka, *Pamiętnik*, ed. Janusz Byliński and Włodzimierz Kaczorowski (Opole, 2014), pp. 85–6.

94 Charles de Joppencourt, 'Histoire des troubles de Moldauie', in A. Papiu Ilarian (ed.), *Tesauru de monumente istorice pentru România*, vol. 2 (Bucharest, 1864), p. 66; Piasecki, *Kronika*, p. 259; Golimas, *Luptă decisivă de la Tătareni*, pp. 9–11; Czamańska, 'Kampania mołdawska', p. 132; Besala, *Stanisław Żółkiewski*, pp. 304–5.

95 Bielowski (ed.), *Pisma Stanisława Żółkiewskiego*, p. 243; Władysław Syrokomla, *Przyczynki do historii wojny domowej w Polsce (Samuel Korecki, Adam Tarło, Bogusław Radziwiłł)* (Vilnius, 1858), p. 19.

96 Antoni Prochaska (ed.), *Akta grodzkie i ziemskie z czasów Rzeczypospolitej Polskiej z archiwum tak zwanego Bernardyńskiego we Lwowie*, vol. 21 (L'viv, 1911), p. 151.

97 Bielowski (ed.), *Pisma Stanisława Żółkiewskiego*, p. 243.

98 Wojciech Hejnosz (ed.), *Akta grodzkie i ziemskie z czasów Rzeczypospolitej Polskiej z archiwum tak zwanego Bernardyńskiego we Lwowie*, vol. 24 (L'viv, 1935), p. 21.

99 Veress (ed.), *Documente*, vol. 9, p. 58; Hurmuzaki, Suppl. ii/2, p. 391.

100 Syrokomla, *Przyczynki do historii wojny domowej*, p. 23.

101 Iuliu Peksa, 'Zólkiewski şi expediţia doamnei Elisabeta Movilă în Moldova în anii 1615–1616', *Revista Istorică* 14/1 (1928), p. 46; Jerzy Urwanowicz, 'Stanisław Żółkiewski w życiu publicznym: wybory – zachowania – poglądy', *Barok* 18/1 (2001), pp. 223–35.

102   Zbigniew Ossoliński, *Pamiętnik*, ed. Józef Długosz (Warsaw, 1983), pp. 68–9.

103   Prochaska (ed.), *Akta grodzkie i ziemskie z czasów Rzeczypospolitej Polskiej z archiwum tak zwanego Bernardyńskiego we Lwowie*, vol. 21, p. 151.

104   Besala, *Stanisław Żółkiewski*, pp. 306–7.

105   Amsterdam Universiteitsbibliotheek, Hs. Diederichs 9 U.

106   Bielowski (ed.), *Pisma Stanisława Żółkiewskiego*, pp. 555–8; Ciobanu, *Politică și diplomație*, p. 173.

107   Korec'kyj cut the bars and climbed down a rope he had smuggled to his cell. He stayed two months in hiding before securing a passport from the Ecumenical Patriarch and, dressed as a monk, he embarked on a westbound merchant vessel. En route to Naples, the ship was attacked by corsairs, but the crew managed to repel the attackers. From Naples, the prince went to Rome and was received by Pope Paul V. He eventually returned to Poland–Lithuania via Vienna in the summer of 1618. Several different accounts circulated about Korec'kyj's adventures, undoubtedly mixing reality with fiction, but their wide circulation testifies the popularity of the magnate in the Commonwealth and beyond.

108   Maskiewicz, 'Dyaryusz Samuela Maskiewicza', p. 301; Skorupa, *Stosunki polsko-tatarskie*, p. 214.

109   Piasecki, *Kronika*, p. 279; Ryszard Majewski, *Cecora: rok 1620* (Warsaw, 1970), p. 77.

110   Czamańska, 'Kampania mołdawska', p. 139.

111   İ. Metin Kunt, 'Naima, Köprülü and the grand vizierate', *Boğaziçi Üniversitesi Dergisi. Hümaniter Bilimler–Humanities* 1 (1973), pp. 60–1.

112   Finkel, *Osman's Dream*, pp. 252–63.

113   Rifa'at A. Abou-El-Haj, *The 1703 Rebellion and the Structure of Ottoman Politics* (Leiden, 1984), p. 43.

114   For the thesis of a *ghazi* revival under Mehmed IV, see Marc D. Baer, *Honored by the Glory of Islam: Conversion and Conquest in Ottoman Empire* (Oxford, 2007). As reviewers pointed out, by highlighting the symbolic aspect of Mehmed IV's activity, the author overemphasized the political role of the sultan, see Merlijn Olnon's review in *Bibliotheca Orientalis* 68/3–4 (2011), pp. 415–16.

115   See, for instance, Yasir Yılmaz, 'Grand vizieral authority revisited: Köprülüs' legacy and Kara Mustafa Paşa', *Mediterranean Historical Review* 31/1 (2016), pp. 21–42.

116   'Kaisariou Daponte Chronographos', in Constantin Erbiceanu (ed.), *Cronicarii greci carii au scris despre români în epoca fanariotă* (Bucharest, 1888), p. 9.

117   It is possible that these efforts led İsazade to mistakenly claim that Grigore Ghica replaced his father as the voivode of Moldavia in 1659, see İsazade, *İsazade Tarihi: Metin ve Tahlil*, ed. Ziya Yılmazer (Istanbul, 1996), p. 60.

118   Constantin Grecescu and Dan Simonescu (eds), *Istoria Țării Românești, 1290–1690: Letopisețul Cantacuzinesc* (Bucharest, 1960), p. 166.

Notes

233

119 Radu vornicul Popescu, *Istoriile domnilor Țării Romînești*, ed. Constantin Grecescu (Bucharest, 1963), p. 126.

120 Constantin I. Andreescu and Constantin A. Stoide, *Ștefăniță Lupu, domn al Moldovei (1659–1661)* (Bucharest, 1938), p. 117.

121 Cernovodeanu, 'Știri privitoare la Gheorghe Ghica (I)', p. 346.

122 Radu G. Păun, '"Well-born of the Polis": the Ottoman conquest and the reconstruction of the Greek Orthodox elites under Ottoman rule', in Robert Born and Sabine Jagodzinski (eds), *Türkenkriege und Adelskultur in Osmitteleuropa vom 16.-18. Jahrhundert* (Leipzig, 2014), pp. 64–6.

123 Yılmaz, 'Grand vizieral authority revisited', pp. 33–4.

124 Özgün D. Yoldaşlar, 'The realization of Mehmed IV's *ghazi* title at the campaign of Kamaniçe' (MA thesis, Sabancı University, 2013), pp. 55–60; Yılmaz, 'Grand vizieral authority revisited', pp. 22 and 31.

125 For instance, in January 1669, the grand vizier was genuinely surprised to learn that the Venetian ambassador had been imprisoned and sent to Chania, and had to ask the detainee about the details of his mission. The diplomat's presence in Crete was a major inconvenience for Ahmed Pasha, because the soldiers came to believe that the Venetian's presence on the island was to surrender Candia, making them less inclined to risk their life during the siege, Abubekir S. Yücel, 'Mühürdar Hasan Ağa'nın Cevâhirü't-Tevârih'i' (PhD diss., Erciyes University, 1996), pp. 354–61; Yoldaşlar, 'The realization', pp. 67–70.

126 On Cantacuzinos' rivals, known in historiography as the 'Băleni–Leurdeni faction', see Spiridon Cristocea, *Din trecutul marii boierimii muntene: Marele-vornic Stroe Leurdeanu* (Brăila, 2011), pp. 223–6; Constantin Rezachevici, 'Fenomene de criza social-politică în Țara Românească în veacul al XVII-lea (II)', *Studii și Materiale de Istorie Medie* 14 (1996), p. 106.

127 Grecescu and Simonescu (eds), *Istoria Țării Românești*, p. 149.

128 Dimitrios Ramadanis, 'Kaisariou Daponte Chronographos', in Constantin Erbiceanu (ed.), *Cronicarii greci carii au scris despre români in epoca fanariotă* (Bucharest, 1888), p. 14.

129 Gemil, *Țările Române în contextul politic*, pp. 192–3.

130 Ibid., p. 193; Yücel, 'Mühürdar Hasan Ağa'nın Cevâhirü't-Tevârih'i', p. 279; Özgür Kolçak, 'XVII. yüzyıl askerî gelimişi ve Osmanlılar: 1660–64 Osmanlı-Avusturya savaşları' (PhD diss., Istanbul University, 2012), pp. 215–17.

131 Andrei Veress, 'Pribegia lui Gligorașcu vodă prin Ungaria și aiurea (1664–1672)', *Analele Academiei Române. Memoriile Secțiunii Istorice*, Seria III, 2 (1924), pp. 286–90; Cristian Luca, *Țările Române și Veneția în secolul al XVII-lea: Din relațiile politico-diplomatice, comerciale și culturale ale Țării Românești și ale Moldovei cu Serenissima* (Bucharest, 2007), pp. 137–9; Cristian Luca, 'Il soggiorno veneziano del principe Gregorio I Ghica e della sua famiglia (1671–1672)', *Studia Historica, Adriatica ac Danubiana* 3/1-2 (2010), pp. 92–4.

234 Notes

132 Hurmuzaki, *Fragmente*, vol. 3, pp. 327–8; Luca, *Țările Române și Veneția*, p. 138.

133 Constantin C. Giurescu (ed.), *Letopisețul Țării Moldovei dela Istratie Dabija până la domnia a doua a lui Antioh Cantemir* (Bucharest, 1913), pp. 54–5; Nicolae Iorga, *Studii și documente cu privire la istoria românilor*, vol. 4 (Bucharest, 1902), p. 258.

134 Popescu, *Istoriile domnilor*, p. 133.

135 Hurmuzaki, *Fragmente*, vol. 3, p. 327; Mircea C. Soreanu, 'Țările Române și Imperiul otoman în perioada guvernării marilor viziri din familia Köprülü (1656–1710)' (PhD diss., University of Bucharest, 1998), p. 203.

136 Dan Simonescu (ed.), *Cronica anonimă a Moldovei, 1661–1729: Pseudo-Amiras* (Bucharest, 1975), p. 43.

137 Ibid., p. 44; Ion Neculce, *Opere: Letopisețul Țării Moldovei și O samă de cuvinte*, ed. Gabriel Ștrempel (Bucharest, 1982), pp. 206–7; 'Kaisariou Daponte Chronographos', p. 12; Gemil, *Țările Române în contextul politic*, p. 198; Soreanu, 'Țările Române și Imperiul otoman', pp. 209–10.

138 Hurmuzaki, *Fragmente*, vol. 3, p. 276; Ion Ionașcu, 'Din politica internă și externă a Țării Românești în domnia lui Antonie Vodă din Popești (1669–1672)', in Nicolae I. Simache (ed.), *Pagini din trecutul istoric al județului Prahova* (Ploiești, 1971), p. 20. See also, Hurmuzaki, vol. 9/1, p. 256.

139 Yoldaşlar, 'The realization', pp. 69–70.

140 Merlijn Olnon, '"A most agreeable and pleasant creature?" Merzifonlu Kara Mustafa Paşa in the correspondence of Justinus Colyer', *Oriente Moderno* 22/3 (2003), p. 656.

141 Antoine Galland, *Le voyage à Smyrne: un manuscript d'Antoine Galland (1678)*, ed. Frédéric Bauden (Paris, 2000), pp. 170–1.

142 Luca, 'Il soggiorno veneziano', pp. 94–6; Popescu, *Istoriile domnilor*, pp. 144–5.

143 Popescu, *Istoriile domnilor*, p. 145; Soreanu, 'Țările Române și Imperiul otoman', p. 206.

144 Grecescu and Simonescu (eds), *Istoria Țării Românești*, p. 168.

145 Neculce, *Opere*, p. 230–1.

146 Olnon, 'A most agreeable and pleasant creature', p. 657.

147 It is indicative that, whereas Kara Mustafa Pasha hosted members of the Cantacuzino family following their flight from Wallachia, Nikoussios provided accommodation for Grigore Ghica when the latter returned to the imperial capital in 1672, see 'Kaisariou Daponte Chronografos', p. 14; Luca, 'Il soggiorno veneziano', p. 94.

148 Popescu, *Istoriile domnilor*, pp. 158–61; Grecescu and Simonescu (eds), *Istoria Țării Românești*, p. 169.

149 Ibid., pp. 172–3.

Notes 235

Chapter 5

1   Lucian Boia, *History and Myth in Romanian Consciousness*, trans. James Christian
    Brown (Budapest – New York, 2003), p. 79.

2   See, for instance, Mihai Maxim, 'Le statut des Pays Roumaines envers le Porte
    ottomane au XVIᵉ–XIXᵉ siècles', in Mihai Maxim, *Romano-Ottomanica: Essays &*
    Documents from the Turkish Archives (Istanbul, 2001), pp. 23–46; Ștefan S. Gorovei
    and Maria M. Székely, 'Old questions, old clichés. New approaches, new results?
    The case of Moldavia', in Oliver J. Schmitt (ed.), *The Ottoman Conquest of the*
    Balkans: Interpretations and Research Debates (Vienna, 2016), pp. 209–42.

3   Constantin Giurescu, *Capitulațiile Moldovei cu Poarta otomană: Studiu istoric*
    (Bucharest, 1908).

4   Mihai Maxim, *Țările Române și Înalta Poartă: Cadrul juridic al relațiilor româno-*
    otomane în evul mediu (Bucharest, 1993), p. 52.

5   Sándor Papp, 'The system of autonomous Muslim and Christian communities,
    churches, and states in the Ottoman Empire', in Gábor Kármán and Lovro Kunčević
    (eds), *The European Tributary States of the Ottoman Empire in the Sixteenth–*
    Seventeenth Centuries (Leiden – Boston, 2013), p. 417.

6   Viorel Panaite, 'The legal and political status of Wallachia and Moldavia in relation
    to the Ottoman Porte', in Gábor Kármán and Lovro Kunčević (eds), *The European*
    Tributary States of the Ottoman Empire in the Sixteenth–Seventeenth Centuries
    (Leiden – Boston, 2013), pp. 9–42; Viorel Panaite, *Război, pace și comerț în Islam:*
    Țările române și dreptul otoman al popoarelor, second edition (Iași, 2013).

7   On this evolution, see Viorel Panaite, 'The re'ayas of the tributary-protected
    principalities: the sixteenth through eighteenth centuries', in Kemal H. Karpat
    and Robert W. Zens (eds), *Ottoman Borderlands: Issues, Personalities and Political*
    Changes (Madison, 2003), pp. 79–104.

8   Halil İnalcık, 'Ottoman methods of conquest', *Studia Islamica* 2 (1954), pp. 103–29.

9   Petre P. Panaitescu, 'De ce n-au cucerit turcii Țările Române?', in Petre P.
    Panaitescu, *Interpretări românești: Studii de istorie economică și socială*, second
    edition (Bucharest, 1994), pp. 111–18.

10 Ibid., pp. 112–13.

11 Ibid., pp. 117–18.

12 Maxim, *Țările Române și Înalta Poartă*, pp. 130–1.

13 Ibid.

14 See, for instance, Hurmuzaki, Suppl. ii/2, p. 415; Andrei Veress (ed.), *Documente*
    privitoare la istoria Ardealului, Moldovei și Țării-Românești, vol. 10 (Bucharest,
    1935), p. 266.

15 İ. Metin Kunt, '17. yüzyılda Osmanlı kuzey politikası üzerine bir yorum', *Boğaziçi*
    Üniversitesi Dergisi. Hümaniter Bilimler – Humanities 4–5 (1976–1977), p. 115;

236 *Notes*

Tahsin Gemil, *Țările Române în contextul politic internațional (1621–1672)* (Bucharest, 1979), p. 41; Maxim, *Țările Române și Înalta Poartă*, p. 52.

16 Constantin Grecescu and Dan Simonescu (eds), *Istoria Țării Românești, 1290–1690: Letopisețul Cantacuzinesc* (Bucharest, 1960), pp. 145–6.

17 Halil Sahillioğlu (ed.), *Koca Sinan Paşa'nın Telhisleri* (Istanbul, 2004), p. 226; Mustafa Naima, *Tarih-i Naima*, vol. 1 (Istanbul, 1281/1864), p. 101.

18 The details of his campaign in Yemen have been narrated in the chronicle of Qutb al-Din al-Nawrahali al-Makki, see Clive Smith (ed.), *Lightning over Yemen: A History of the Ottoman Campaign (1569–71)* (London – New York, 2002).

19 Giancarlo Casale, *The Ottoman Age of Exploration* (Oxford, 2010), p. 156.

20 Baki Tezcan, *The Second Ottoman Empire: Political and Social Transformation in the Early Modern World* (Cambridge, 2010), pp. 99–100.

21 Günhan Börekçi, 'Factions and favorites at the courts of Sultan Ahmed I (r. 1603–1617) and his immediate predecessors' (PhD diss., Ohio State University, 2010), p. 197.

22 Ibid., p. 16.

23 Mihai Maxim, '*Voyvodalık* ou *beğlerbeğlik*? La politique ottomane envers la Moldavie et la Valachie (november 1594 – février 1596) à la lumière des nouveaux documents turcs', in Mihai Maxim, *Romano-Ottomanica: Essays & Documents from the Turkish Archives* (Istanbul, 2001), p. 164; Selanikî Mustafa Efendi, *Tarih-i Selânikî*, ed. Mehmet İpşirli, vol. 2 (Ankara, 1989), p. 410.

24 Maxim, '*Voyvodalık* ou *beğlerbeğlik*?', p. 166.

25 Rhoads Murphey, *Exploring Ottoman Sovereignty: Tradition, Image and Practice in the Ottoman Imperial Household, 1400–1800* (London, 2008), p. 131.

26 İbrahim Peçevi, *Tarih-i Peçevi*, vol. 2 (Istanbul, 1283/1866), p. 135.

27 Murphey, *Exploring Ottoman Sovereignty*, pp. 131–2.

28 Naima, *Tarih-i Naima*, p. 101.

29 Selanikî, *Tarih-i Selânikî*, vol. 2, pp. 464–5.

30 Maxim, '*Voyvodalık* ou *beğlerbeğlik*?', pp. 167–8. See also Salih Özbaran, 'Some notes on the salyâne system in the Ottoman provinces as organised in Arabia in the sixteenth century', *Osmanlı Araştırmaları* 6 (1986), pp. 39–40.

31 Tezcan, *The Second Ottoman Empire*, p. 22.

32 Ibid., pp. 181–2.

33 Kâtib Çelebi, *Fezleke*, vol. 1 (Istanbul, 1286/1869–70), p. 50.

34 Selanikî, *Tarih-i Selânikî*, vol. 2, p. 474.

35 Rhoads Murphey, *Ottoman Warfare, 1500–1700* (London, 1999), p. 140; Nezihi Aykut, 'Damad İbrahim Paşa', *İstanbul Üniversitesi Tarih Enstitüsü Dergisi* 15 (1997), p. 218.

36 During his career in the Caucasus, Ca'fer Pasha had been associated with Özdemiroğlu Osman Pasha.

Notes
237

37 BOA, Bab-ı Asafi, Nişancı, Tahvil Kalemi 1141, p. 87.

38 Carl M. Kortepeter, *Ottoman Imperialism during the Reformation: Europe and the Caucasus* (London – New York, 1972), p. 145; Ion Chirtoagă, *Sud-Estul Moldovei și stângă Nistrului (1484–1699): Expansiunea și dominația turco-tatară* (Bucharest, 1999), p. 124.

39 Reinhold Heidenstein, 'Vitae Joannis Zamoysci', in Adam Działyński (ed.), *Collectanea Vitam Resque Gestas Joannis Zamoyscii Magni Cancellarii et Summi Ducis Reipublicae Polonae* (Poznań, 1861), p. 121.

40 Dariusz Kołodziejczyk, *Ottoman-Polish Diplomatic Relations (15th–18th Century): An Annotated Edition of 'Ahdnames and Other Documents* (Leiden – Boston, 2000), pp. 126–7.

41 Hurmuzaki, Suppl. ii/1, pp. 355–7.

42 AGAD, Dział Turecki, 484/809 and 278/516.

43 Selanikî, *Tarih-i Selânikî*, vol. 2, p. 554; Ziya Yılmazer (ed.), *Topçular Kâtibi ʿAbdülkâdir (Kadrî) Efendi Tarihi (Metin ve Tahlîl)*, vol. 1 (Ankara, 2003), p. 68–9.

44 Selanikî, *Tarih-i Selânikî*, vol. 2, p. 565; Veress (ed.), *Documente*, vol. 5, pp. 50–1; Ştefan Andreescu, 'O "pace prefăcută" la Dunărea de Jos: tratativele transilvano-muntene cu Poarta din anii 1597–1598', in Ştefan Andreescu, *Restitutio Daciae*, vol. 3 (Bucharest, 1997), pp. 176–7; Maxim, '*Voyvodalık* ou *beğlerbeğlik*?', p. 172.

45 BOA, Maliyeden Müddever Defterleri 5240, p. 106; Maxim, '*Voyvodalık* ou *beğlerbeğlik*?', p. 170.

46 İbrahim Peçevi, *Tarih-i Peçevi*, vol. 1 (Istanbul, 1283/1866), pp. 27–8; on this episode, see Tezcan, *The Second Ottoman Empire*, pp. 97–8.

47 Stanisław Kobierzycki, *Historia Władysława, królewicza polskiego i szwedzkiego*, ed. Janusz Byliński and Włodzimierz Kaczorowski (Wrocław, 2005), p. 33.

48 Wojciech Sokołowski, *Politycy schyłku Złotego Wieku: Małopolscy przywódcy szlachty i parlamentarzyści w latach 1574–1605* (Warsaw, 1997), pp. 127–8.

49 Wojciech Tygielski, 'A faction which could not lose', in Antoni Mączak and Elisabeth Müller-Luckner (eds), *Klientelsysteme im Europa der Früher Neuzeit* (Munich, 1988), pp. 192–3.

50 Sokołowski, *Politycy schyłku Złotego Wieku*, p. 19. See also Wojciech Tygielski, *Listy – ludzie – władza: Patronat Jana Zamoyskiego w świetle korespondencji* (Warsaw, 2007), pp. 397–407.

51 Przemysław Gawron, *Hetman koronny w systemie ustrojowym Rzeczypospolitej w latach 1581–1646* (Warsaw, 2010), p. 109.

52 Sokołowski, *Politycy schyłku Złotego Wieku*, p. 19.

53 Mariusz Kowalski, *Księstwa Rzeczpospolitej: państwo magnackie jako region polityczny* (Warsaw, 2013), p. 287.

54 Tygielski, 'A faction which could not lose', *passim*.

55 Sokołowski, *Politycy schyłku Złotego Wieku*, p. 173.

Notes

56 Henryk Wisner, *Zygmunt III Waza* (Warsaw, 2006), pp. 61–5.

57 Sokołowski, *Politycy schyłku Złotego Wieku*, p. 25.

58 Ibid.; Wojciech Tygielski, 'W poszukiwaniu patrona', *Przegląd Historyczny* 78/2 (1987), p. 205.

59 Veniamin Ciobanu, *La cumpănă de veacuri: Țările Române în contextul politicii poloneze la sfârșitul secolului al XVI-lea și începutul secolului al XVII-lea* (Iași, 1991), p. 105.

60 Dariusz Skorupa, *Stosunki polsko-tatarskie, 1595–1623* (Warsaw, 2004), p. 61.

61 An indicative example of the degree of control Zamoyski exercised in this respect is the episode from 1600, when royal envoy Andrzej Taranowski was detained by the chancellor's men, who suspected him of secret dealings with the Wallachian voivode, Michael the Brave, AGAD, Archiwum Zamoyskich 701.

62 Przemysław Gawron, 'Jan Zamoyski, kanclerz i hetman wielki koronny, wobec zmagań turecko-habsburskich w latach 1593–1605/6', in Ryszard Skowron (ed.), *Polska wobec wielkich konfliktów w Europie nowożytnej: Z dziejów dyplomacji i stosunków międzynarodowych w XV–XVIII wieku* (Cracow, 2009), pp. 34–5.

63 Józef Jasnowski, 'Dwie relacje z wyprawy Zamoyskiego pod Cecorę w 1595 r.', *Przegląd Historyczno-Wojskowy* 10/2 (1938), p. 243; Dumitru Ciurea, 'Despre Ieremia Movilă și situația politică a Moldovei la sfârșitul sec. XVI și începutul sec. XVII', in *Movileștii: Istorie și spiritualitate românească*, vol. 1 (Sucevița, 2006), pp. 102–3; Cristian A. Bobicescu, 'Între integrare și păstrarea autonomiei: modelul polonez și controlul domnilor în Moldova și Țara Românească la cumpăna secolelor XVI–XVII', in *Movileștii: Istorie și spiritualitate românească*, vol. 2 (Sucevița, 2006), pp. 230–1; Zdzisław Spieralski, *Awantury mołdawskie* (Warsaw, 1967), pp. 146–7; Dariusz Milewski, 'A campaign of the Great Hetman Jan Zamoyski in Moldavia (1595). Part I. Politico-diplomatic and military preliminaries', *Codrul Cosminului* 18/2 (2012), pp. 284–5; Skorupa, *Stosunki polsko-tatarskie*, pp. 63–4.

64 Kołodziejczyk, *Ottoman-Polish Diplomatic Relations*, pp. 126–7.

65 Hurmuzaki, Suppl. ii/1, pp. 344–5.

66 Constantin Rezachevici, 'Politica internă și externă a Țărilor Române în primele decenii ale secolului al XVII-lea', *Revista de Istorie* 38/1 (1985), pp. 12–15; Bobicescu, 'Între integrare și păstrarea autonomiei', p. 231.

67 Hurmuzaki, Suppl. ii/1, pp. 344.

68 On Royal Prussia, see Karin Friedrich, *The Other Prussia: Royal Prussia, Poland and Liberty, 1569–1772* (Cambridge, 2000).

69 Zbigniew Wójcik, 'The separatist tendencies in the Grand Duchy of Lithuania in the 17th century', *Acta Poloniae Historica* 69 (1994), pp. 58–9.

70 Dariusz Skorupa, 'Bitwa pod Bukowem 20 października 1600 r.', in Mirosław Nagielski (ed.), *Staropolska sztuka wojenna XVI–XVIII wieku: Prace ofiarowane Profesorowi Jaremie Maciszewskiemu* (Warsaw, 2002), p. 36; Milewski, 'A campaign of the Great Hetman (I)', p. 285.

71 Cristian A. Bobicescu, 'Tyranny and colonization: preliminary considerations about the colonization plans of Moldavia during the time of Jan Zamoyski', *Revue des Études Sud-Est Européennes* 54/1–4 (2016), pp. 99–118.

72 Bobicescu, 'Între integrare și păstrarea autonomiei', p. 232.

73 'Postulata dwu województw: poznańskiego i kaliskiego, z którymi słali do Króla J. Mci do Warszawy anno 1596' in Eugeniusz Barwiński (ed.), *Dyaryusze sejmowe r. 1597* (Cracow, 1907), p. 343.

74 Bobicescu, 'Tyranny and colonization', p. 111.

75 Ludwika Szczerbicka, 'Jan Szczęsny Herburt – zarys monografii', in Kazimierz Budzyk (ed.), *Ze studiów nad literaturą staropolską* (Wrocław, 1957), pp. 208–13.

76 Ibid., pp. 213–7; Tygielski, *Listy – ludzie – władza*, p. 97.

77 Cristian A. Bobicescu, 'Pe marginea raporturilor lui Jan Zamoyski cu Moldova și Țara Românească', *Studii și Materiale de Istorie Medie* 20 (2002), pp. 201–6.

78 Bobicescu, 'Între integrare și păstrarea autonomiei', pp. 233–4.

79 Eugeniusz Barwiński (ed.), *Dyaryusze sejmowe r. 1597* (Cracow, 1907), p. 89.

80 Tygielski, *Listy – ludzie – władza*, p. 418.

81 Sokołowski, *Politycy schyłku Złotego Wieku*, p. 16.

82 Petre P. Panaitescu (ed.), *Documente privitoare la istoria lui Mihai Viteazul* (Bucharest, 1936), pp. 53–6 and 70–4.

83 Tygielski, *Listy – ludzie – władza*, p. 355.

84 Constantin Cihodaru, 'Campania lui Mihai Viteazul în Moldova (mai–iunie 1600)', *Cercetări Istorice* 1 (1970), pp. 131–45.

85 Skorupa, *Stosunki polsko-tatarskie*, pp. 17–43.

86 Ciobanu, *La cumpănă de veacuri*, p. 287.

87 Veress (ed.), *Documente*, vol. 6, p. 242–3; Ilie Corfus, *Mihai Viteazul și poloni* (Bucharest, 1937), pp. 383–4.

88 Hurmuzaki, Suppl. ii/1, pp. 642–3.

89 Bobicescu, 'Tyranny and colonization', p. 115.

90 AGAD, Archiwum Zamoyskich 190.

91 Hurmuzaki, Suppl. ii/1, pp. 490–502; Bobicescu, 'Pe marginea raporturilor', pp. 201–6; Bobicescu, 'Tyranny and colonization', p. 114.

92 Dariusz Kołodziejczyk, *Podole pod panowaniem tureckim: Ejalet kamieniecki 1672–1699* (Warszawa, 1994), pp. 63–4; Marek Wagner, *Wojna polsko-turecka, 1672–1676*, vol. 1 (Zabrze, 2009), p. 292.

93 Ibid., p. 382; Kołodziejczyk, *Podole pod panowaniem tureckim*, pp. 76–7; Janusz Woliński, 'Po Chocimie 1673-1674', in Janusz Woliński, *Z dziejów wojen polsko-tureckich* (Warsaw, 1983), pp. 60–89.

94 Kołodziejczyk, *Ottoman-Polish Diplomatic Relations*, pp. 520–7; Janusz Woliński, 'Żórawno', in Janusz Woliński, *Z dziejów wojen polsko-tureckich* (Warsaw, 1983), pp. 163–81.

240   *Notes*

95   Kazimierz Piwarski, 'Polityka bałtycka Jana III w latach 1675–1679', in Oskar
Halecki (ed.), *Księga pamiątkowa ku czci Profesora Dra Wacława Sobieskiego*
(Cracow, 1932), pp. 153–86; Janusz Woliński, 'Sprawa pruska i traktat jaworowski',
Przegląd Historyczno-Wojskowy 30/1 (1932), pp. 1–32.

96   Ioan Moga, *Rivalitatea polono-austriacă și orientarea politică a Țărilor Române la
sfârșitul secolului al XVII-lea* (Cluj, 1933), p. 37–41.

97   Marek Wagner, 'Mołdawianie i Serbowie w służbie Jana III Sobieskiego', in
Marek Wagner, *W cieniu szukamy jasności chwały: studia z dziejów panowania
Jana III Sobieskiego* (Siedlce, 2002), pp. 116–23. For two published diplomas
– issued in February 1676, see Costin Feneșan, 'Diplomele de indigenat ale
boierilor Grigore Hăbășescu și Gheorghe Hâjdau', *Arhiva Genealogică* 4/1–2
(1997), pp. 101–6.

98   On this topic, see Jarosław Stolicki, *Egzulanci podolscy (1672–1699): Znaczenie
uchodźców z Podola w życiu politycznym Rzeczypospolitej* (Cracow, 1994). On the
cooperation between Moldavian and Podolian exiles, see Jarosław Stolicki (ed.),
Akta sejmiku podolskiego in hostico, 1672–1698 (Cracow, 2002), pp. 26, 84.

99   Ilie Corfus, 'O nouă scrisoare a lui Miron Costin', *Studii. Revistă de Istorie* 24/2
(1971), pp. 237–52.

100   Moga, *Rivalitatea polono-austriacă*, p. 102.

101   Spieralski, *Awantury mołdawskie*, pp. 198–9.

102   Czesław Chowaniec, *Miron Costin en Pologne: Contributions à l'année 1684–1685*
(Cluj, 1931), pp. 3–4; Moga, *Rivalitatea polono-austriacă*, pp. 103–7.

103   Lidia Vlasova, *Moldavsko-pol'skie političeskie svjazi v poslednej četverti XVII v. –
načale XVIII v.* (Chișinău, 1980), p. 37.

104   Hurmuzaki, Suppl. ii/3, pp. 152–3; Moga, *Rivalitatea polono-austriacă*, p. 115;
Vlasova, *Moldavsko-pol'skie političeskie svjazi*, p. 37.

105   Ibid., pp. 17–19.

106   Ilona Czamańska, 'Rumuńska imigracja polityczna w Polsce XVII wieku',
Balcanica Posnaniensia 6 (1993), p. 18.

107   Vlasova, *Moldavsko-pol'skie političeskie svjazi*, p. 37. Cf. Chowaniec, *Miron Costin
en Pologne*, p. 5.

108   Ibid., p. 9.

109   Neculce, *Opere: Letopisețul Țării Moldovei și O samă de cuvinte*, ed. Gabriel
Ștrempel (Bucharest, 1982), pp. 294–5.

110   Czesław Chowaniec, 'Wyprawa Sobieskiego do Mołdawii', *Przegląd Historyczno-
Wojskowy* 4/2 (1931), pp. 1–117.

111   On Dosoftei, see Tatiana Cojocaru, 'Metropolita suczawski Dosoftei (1624–1693) a
Rzeczpospolita', *Balcanica Posnaniensia* 13 (2003), pp. 243–4.

112   Moga, *Rivalitatea polono-austriacă*, pp. 147–50.

113   Vlasova, *Moldavsko-pol'skie političeskie svjazi*, p. 105.

Notes 241

114 Marek Wagner, 'Konflikt polsko-mołdawski w latach 1695–1696', in Marek Wagner, *W cieniu szukamy jasności chwały: studia z dziejów panowania Jana III Sobieskiego* (Siedlce, 2002), p. 124; Marek Wagner, 'Pogranicze polsko-mołdawskie w końcu XVII wieku', in Krzysztof Mikulski and Agnieszka Zielińska-Nowicka (eds), *Etniczne, kulturowe i religijne pogranicza Rzeczypospolitej w XVI–XVIII wieku* (Toruń, 2006), pp. 40–1.

115 Mariusz Kaczka, 'The gentry of the Polish–Ottoman borderlands: the case of the Moldavian-Polish family of Turkuł/Turculeţ', *Acta Poloniae Historica* 104 (2011), pp. 129–50.

116 Neculce, *Opere*, pp. 305–6.

117 Przemysław Smolarek, *Kampania mołdawska Jana III roku 1691* (Oświęcim, 2015); Marek Wagner, *Stanisław Jabłonowski (1634–1702): polityk i dowódca*, vol. 2 (Siedlce, 1997), pp. 66–74.

118 Moga, *Rivalitatea polono-austriacă*, pp. 186–95.

119 Kazimierz Sarnecki, *Pamiętniki z czasów Jana Sobieskiego: diariusz i relacje z l. 1691–1696*, ed. Janusz Woliński (Wrocław, 1958), p. 347; Spieralski, *Awantury mołdawskie*, p. 204.

120 Vlasova, *Moldavsko-pol'skie političeskie svjazi*, p. 105.

121 Nicolae Stoicescu, *Dicţionar al marilor dregători din Ţara Românească şi Moldova (sec. XIV–XVII)* (Bucharest, 1971), pp. 380–2. On Costache's political alliances, see Radu G. Păun, 'Pouvoirs, offices et patronage dans la Principauté de Moldavie au XVIIᵉ siècle: l'aristocratie roumaine et la pénétration gréco-levantine' (PhD diss., École des Hautes Études en Sciences Sociales, 2003), p. 178. See also, Neculce, *Opere*, pp. 305.

122 Vlasova, *Moldavsko-pol'skie političeskie svjazi*, p. 81.

123 Neculce, *Opere*, pp. 317–19.

124 On the career and political role of the Ruset family, see Radu Rosetti, *Familia Rosetti: coborâtorii moldoveni ai lui Lascaris Rousaitos*, vol. 1 (Bucharest, 1938), pp. 26–33; Păun, 'Pouvoirs, offices et patronage', pp. 336–45.

125 Ibid., p. 105.

126 Dimitrie Cantemir, *Vita Constantini Cantemyrii, cognomento Senis, Moldaviae principis*, ed. Dan Sluşanschi and Ilieş Câmpeanu (Bucharest, 1996), pp. 178–82.

127 Neculce, *Opere*, pp. 333–43.

128 In a rather amusing episode, Constantin Duca sent a messenger from Istanbul, ordering the boyars to detain Iordache Ruset and Lupu Bogdan. The letters were handed over to Grand *Comis* Ştefan Cerchezul who, being illiterate, passed them to the incriminated officials. Learning about their contents, they immediately took flight under Polish–Lithuanian protection, see Nestor Camariano and Ariadna Camariano-Cioran (eds), *Cronica Ghiculeştilor: Istoria Moldovei între anii 1695–1754* (Bucharest, 1965), pp. 8–10.

242   *Notes*

129   Neculce, *Opere*, p. 221.

130   Vlasova, *Moldavsko-poľskie političeskie svjazi*, pp. 14–16.

131   Ibid., p. 12.

Chapter 6

1   For Polish–Lithuanian and Ottoman instruments of peace, see Dariusz Kołodziejczyk, *Ottoman-Polish Diplomatic Relations (15ᵗʰ–18ᵗʰCentury): An Annotated Edition of* 'Ahdname*s and Other Documents* (Leiden – Boston, 2000), pp. 581–625.

2   According to a well-known argument, proposed by Rifa'at A. Abou-El-Haj in 1969, the Treaty of Karlowitz and the boundary demarcation that followed was the first instance when the Porte recognized the principles of linear boundary and inviolability of territorial sovereignty, and thus put an end to the *ghaza* tradition, see Rifa'at A. Abou-El-Haj, 'The formal closure of the Ottoman frontier in Europe: 1699–1703', *Journal of the American Oriental Society* 89/3 (1969), pp. 468–70. This argument has been since revised by Dariusz Kołodziejczyk, 'Between universalistic claims and reality: Ottoman frontiers in the early modern period', in Christine Woodhead (ed.), *The Ottoman World* (London – New York, 2012), pp. 210–1.

3   Virginia H. Aksan, *Ottoman Wars, 1700–1870: An Empire Besieged* (London, 2013), pp. 28–9.

4   Ibid., p. 29.

5   Particularly interesting from this perspective is the archive of Ilyas Kolçak Pasha, the Ottoman governor of Hotin during the 1730s. Seized along with its owner by Russian troops in 1739, it is currently held in Moscow and Černihiv, and remains virtually untapped. However, the documents analysed by Dariusz Kołodziejczyk and Mariusz Kaczka – who, at the moment of writing, are preparing the edition of its contents – indicate considerable continuity with the practices of cross-border sociability from the earlier period, see Dariusz Kołodziejczyk, 'A man, a woman and livestock crossing the borders of the *Dar al-Islam*: a glimpse into everyday life of the *sancak* of Hotin in the early 18th century', paper presented at the 23rd Symposium of the Comité International des Études Pré-Ottomanes et Ottomanes, Sofia, 11–15 September 2018; Mariusz Kaczka, 'Networking across *Dar al-Islam*: Ilyash Colceag Pasha of Hotin and his Polish network', paper presented at the 23rd Symposium of the Comité International des Études Pré-Ottomanes et Ottomanes, Sofia, 11–15 September 2018.

6   On this process of *Verflechtung*, see particularly Radu G. Păun, 'Some observations on the historical origins of the "Phanariot phenomenon" in Moldavia and Wallachia', in Gelina Harlaftis and Radu G. Păun (eds), *Greeks in Romania in the*

Nineteenth Century (Athens, 2013), pp. 43–90; Radu G. Păun, "'Well-born of the Polis": the Ottoman conquest and the reconstruction of the Greek Orthodox elites under Ottoman rule (15th -17th centuries)', in Robert Born and Sabine Jagodzinski (eds), *Türkenkriege und Adelskultur in Ostmitteleuropa* (Leipzig, 2014), pp. 59–85.

7   Bartolomé Yun Casalilla, 'Reading sources throughout P. Bourdieu and Cyert and March: aristocratic patrimonies vs. commercial enterprises in Europe (*c.* 1550–1650)', in Francesco Ammannati (ed.), *Dove va la storia economica? Metodi e prospettive secc. XIII–XVIII* (Florence, 2011), p. 332.

8   For the Danubian principalities, see Radu G. Păun, 'La circulation des pouvoirs dans les Pays Roumaines au XVIIe siècle: repères pour un modèle theorique', *New Europe College Yearbook* 6 (1998–9), pp. 265–310.

9   Julia Adams, 'The familial state: elite family practices and state-making in the early modern Netherlands', *Theory and Society* 23/2 (1994), p. 508.

10   Harry Miller, *State versus gentry in late Ming China, 1572–1644* (Basingstoke, 2009).

Bibliography

Unpublished Sources

Amsterdam, University Library
Hs. Diederichs 9 U.

Bucharest, Direcția Arhivelor Naționale – Instituție Centrală (DANIC)
Documente Istorice, dxcv/118.
M-rea Radu Vodă xxxix/9, 12.
Manuscrise MS 126.

Cracow, Jagiellonian University Library
MS 7.

Cracow, Czartoryski Library
MS 100, 108.

Cracow, State Archive
Archiwum Sanguszków 423.

Iași, Sediul Județean Arhivelor Naționale – Iași (SJAN – Iași)
M-rea Galata ii/4.

Istanbul, Başbakanlık Osmanlı Arşivi (BOA)
Ali Emiri 7/718, 721.
Bab-ı Asafi, Nişancı, Tahvil Kalemi 1141.
İbnülemin, Maliye 24/2268, 2269.
Mühimme Defterleri 85, 93.
Maliyeden Müddever Defterleri 5240.

Istanbul, Topkapı Sarayı Müzesi Arşivi (TSMA)
E. 524/15, 73; 2584/2, 5, 8; 5073; 5645.

Istanbul, Topkapı Sarayı Müzesi Kütüphanesi (TSMK)
Mehmed Halife, *Tarih-i Gılmani*, Revan MS 1306.
Vecihi Hasan Çelebi, *Tarih-i Vecihi*, Revan MS 1153.

Stockholm, Riksarkivet
Extranea, Polen, 105.

Warsaw, Archiwum Główne Akt Dawnych (AGAD)
Archiwum Publiczne Potockich, MS 36.

Bibliography 245

Archiwum Zamoyskich, 190, 262, 701, 890.
Dział Turecki, 484/809, 278/516.
Metryka Koronna, 177.

Published Primary Sources

Anon., 'Poveste de jale asupra uciderii postelnicului Constantin Cantacuzino (20 decembrie 1663)', in Dan Simonescu (ed.), *Cronici și povestiri românești versificate (sec. XVI–XVIII)* (Bucharest, 1967), pp. 35–48.

Akty otnosjaščiesja k istorii Zapadnoj Rossii (Saint Petersburg, 1851).

Arslantaş, Nuh and Yaron Ben Haen (eds), *Anonim Bir İbranice Kroniğe Göre 1622–1624 Yıllarında Osmanlı Devleti ve İstanbul: Neşir – Tercüme* (Ankara, 2013).

Axinte, Uricariul, *Cronica paralelă a Țării Românești și a Moldovei*, 2 vols, ed. Gabriel Ștrempel (Bucharest, 1993).

Barsi, Niccolò, *Le voyage de Niccolò Barsi en Moldavie*, ed. Constantin C. Giurescu (Bucharest, 1925).

Bălan, Teodor (ed.), *Documente bucovinene*, vol. 1 (Cernăuți, 1933).

Barwiński, Eugeniusz (ed.), *Dyaryusze sejmowe r. 1597* (Cracow, 1907).

Beke Antal and Samu Barabás (eds), *I. Rákóczy György és a Porta: Levelek és okiratok* (Budapest, 1888).

Bianu, Ioan and Nerva Hodoș (eds), *Bibliografia românească veche*, vol. 1 (Bucharest, 1903).

Biedrzycka, Agnieszka (ed.), *Korespondencja Stanisława Koniecpolskiego hetmana wielkiego koronnego, 1632–1646* (Cracow, 2005).

Bielowski, August (ed.), *Pisma Stanisława Żółkiewskiego, kanclerza koronnego i hetmana* (L'viv, 1861).

Camariano, Nestor and Ariadna Camariano-Cioran (eds), *Cronica Ghiculeștilor: Istoria Moldovei între anii 1695–1754* (Bucharest, 1965).

Cândea, Virgil, 'Letopisețul Țării Românești (1292–1664) în versiunea arabă a lui Macarie Zaim', *Studii. Revistă de Istorie* 23/4 (1970), pp. 673–92.

Cantacuzino, Mihai ban, *Genealogia Cantacuzinilor*, ed. Nicolae Iorga (Bucharest, 1902).

Cantemir, Dimitrie, *Descrierea Moldovei*, ed. Gheorghe Guțu (Bucharest, 1973).

Cantemir, Dimitrie, *Vita Constantini Cantemyrii, cognomento Senis, Moldaviae principis*, ed. Dan Slușanschi and Ilieș Câmpeanu (Bucharest, 1996).

Chiaro, Anton Maria del, *Istoria delle moderne rivoluzioni della Valachia: con la descrizione del paese, natura, costume, riti e religione degli abitanti*, ed. Nicolae Iorga (Bucharest, 1914).

Corfus, Ilie, *Mihai Viteazul și polonii* (Bucharest, 1937).

Corfus, Ilie, 'O nouă scrisoare a lui Miron Costin', *Studii. Revistă de Istorie* 24/2 (1971), pp. 237–52.

246   *Bibliography*

Corfus, Ilie (ed.), *Documente privitoare la istoria României culese din arhivele polone: Secolul al XVI-lea* (Bucharest, 1979).

Corfus, Ilie (ed.), *Documente privitoare la istoria României culese din arhivele polone: Secolul al XVII-lea* (Bucharest, 1983).

Corfus, Ilie (ed.), *Documente polone privitoare la istoria României: secolele al XVI-lea şi al XVII-lea* (Bucharest, 2001).

Costin, Miron, *Letopiseţul Ţării Moldovei dela Aron Vodă încoace*, ed. Petre P. Panaitescu (Bucharest, 1943).

Defterdar Sarı Mehmed Paşa, *Zübde-î Vekayiât*, ed. Abdülkadir Özcan (Ankara, 1995).

Documente privitoare la istoria românilor, culese de Eudoxiu de Hurmuzaki, 22 vols (Bucharest, 1878–1942).

Efendi, Ahmed Resmi, *Hamîletü'l Kübera*, ed. Ahmed Nezihi Turan (Istanbul, 2000).

Evliyâ Çelebi, *Günümüz Türkçesiyle Evliyâ Çelebi Seyahatnâmesi*, ed. Seyit A. Kahraman and Yücel Dağlı (Istanbul, 2007).

Feneşan, Costin, 'Diplomele de indigenat ale boierilor Grigore Hăbăşescu şi Gheorghe Hâjdau', *Arhiva Genealogică* 4/1–2 (1997), pp. 93–109.

Filipczak-Kocur, Anna (ed.), *Korespondencja Krzysztofa księcia Zbaraskiego koniuszego koronnego 1612–1627* (Opole, 2015).

Galland, Antoine, *Le voyage à Smyrne: un manuscrit d'Antoine Galland (1678)*, ed. Frédéric Bauden (Paris, 2000).

Ghibănescu, Gheorghe (ed.), *Surete şi izvoade*, vol. 7 (Iaşi, 1926).

Giurescu, Constantin C. (ed.), *Letopiseţul Ţării Moldovei dela Istratie Dabija până la domnia a doua a lui Antioh Cantemir* (Bucharest, 1913).

Giurescu, Constantin C. (ed.), 'Uciderea veziuriului Mohamed Tabani Buiuc, sprijinătorul lui Vasile Lupu', *Revista Istorică* 12/3 (1926), pp. 98–103.

Giurescu, Dinu C., 'Anatefterul: Condica de porunci a visteriei lui Constantin Brîncoveanu', *Studii şi Materiale de Istorie Medie* 5 (1962), pp. 351–493.

Grecescu, Constantin and Dan Simonescu (eds), *Istoria Ţării Româneşti, 1290–1690: Letopiseţul Cantacuzinesc* (Bucharest, 1960).

Hasan Bey-zade Ahmed Paşa, *Hasan Bey-zade Tarihi*, 3 vols, ed. Şevki N. Aykut (Ankara, 2004).

Heidenstein, Reinhold, 'Vitae Joannis Zamoysci', in Adam Działyński (ed.), *Collectanea Vitam Resque Gestas Joannis Zamoyscii Magni Cancellarii et Summi Ducis Reipublicae Polonae* (Poznań, 1861).

Hurmuzaki, Eudoxiu de (ed.), *Fragmente zur Geschichte der Rumänen*, 5 vols (Bucharest, 1878–1883).

İbrahim Peçevi, *Tarih-i Peçevi*, 2 vols (Istanbul, 1283/1866).

Iorga, Nicolae, *Studii şi documente cu privire la istoria românilor*, vol. 4 (Bucharest, 1902).

İsazade, *İsazade Tarihi: Metin ve Tahlil*, ed. Ziya Yılmazer (Istanbul, 1996).

Jasnowski, Józef, 'Dwie relacje z wyprawy Zamoyskiego pod Cecorę w 1595 r', *Przegląd Historyczno-Wojskowy* 10/2 (1938), pp. 239–50.

Bibliography

Joppencourt, Charles de, 'Histoire des troubles de Moldauie', in A. Papiu Ilarian (ed.), *Tesauru de monumente istorice pentru România*, vol. 2 (Bucharest, 1864), pp. 5–136.

Kâtib Çelebi, *Fezleke*, 2 vols (Istanbul, 1286–7/1869–70).

Kobierzycki, Stanisław, *Historia Władysława, królewicza polskiego i szwedzkiego*, ed. Janusz Byliński and Włodzimierz Kaczorowski (Wrocław, 2005).

Kołodziejczyk, Dariusz, *Ottoman-Polish Diplomatic Relations (15th–18th Century): An Annotated Edition of* 'Ahdnames *and Other Documents* (Leiden – Boston, 2000).

Makowiecki, Stanisław, *Relacyja Kamieńca wziętego przez Turków w roku 1672*, ed. Piotr Borek (Cracow, 2008).

Maskiewicz, Samuel, 'Dyaryusz Samuela Maskiewicza', in Julian U. Niemcewicz (ed.), *Zbiór pamiętników o dawnej Polszcze*, vol. 2 (Leipzig, 1839), pp. 243–304.

Matei al Mirelor (Matthew of Myra), 'Mathaiou istoria tis Ungro-Vlachias', in Alexandru Papiu Ilarian (ed.), *Tesauru de monumente istorice pentru România*, vol. 1 (Bucharest, 1862), pp. 327–84.

Maxim, Mihai, 'New Turkish documents concerning Michael the Brave and his time', in Mihai Maxim, *L'Empire Ottoman au nord du Danube et l'autonomie des Principautés Roumains au XVIe siècle* (Istanbul, 1999), pp. 126–57.

Mioc Damaschin, Saşa Caracaş and Constantin Bălan (eds), *Documenta Romaniae Historica. Seria B. Ţara Românească*, vol. 24 (Bucharest, 1974).

Mustafa Naima, *Tarih-i Naima*, 6 vols (Istanbul, 1281–3/1864–6).

Neculce, Ion, *Opere: Letopiseţul Ţării Moldovei şi O samă de cuvinte*, ed. Gabriel Ştrempel (Bucharest, 1982).

Nedim, Ahmed, *Sahaif ül-Ahbar* (Istanbul, 1285/1868).

Niesiecki, Kasper, *Herbarz polski*, vol. 6, ed. J.N. Bobrowicz (Leipzig, 1845).

Okolski, Szymon, *Orbis Polonus*, 2 vols (Cracow, 1641–3).

Orhonlu, Cengiz (ed.), *Telhisler (1597–1606)* (Istanbul, 1970).

Osmânzade Ahmed Taîb, *Hadıkat ül-Vüzerâ*, 2 vols (Istanbul, 1271/1854–5).

Oświęcim, Stanisław *Stanisława Oświęcima dyaryusz, 1643–1651*, ed. Wiktor Czerman (Cracow, 1907).

Panaitescu, Petre P. (ed.), *Documente privitoare la istoria lui Mihai Viteazul* (Bucharest, 1936).

Paul of Aleppo, *Jurnal de călătorie în Moldova şi Valahia*, ed. Ioana Feodorov (Bucharest, 2014).

Piasecki, Paweł, *Kronika Pawła Piaseckiego biskupa przemyślskiego*, ed. Antoni Chrząszczewski (Cracow, 1870).

Popescu, Radu vornicul, *Istoriile domnilor Ţării Romîneşti*, ed. Constantin Grecescu (Bucharest, 1963).

Przyboś, Adam (ed.), *Wielka legacja Wojciecha Miaskowskiego do Turcji w 1640 r.* (Warsaw, 1985).

Pszonka, Jakub, *Pamiętnik*, ed. Janusz Byliński and Włodzimierz Kaczorowski (Opole, 2014).

Pułaski, Franciszek (ed.), *Źródła do poselstwa Jana Gnińskiego wojewody chełmińskiego do Turcyi w latach 1677–1678* (Cracow, 1907).

248   *Bibliography*

Rangoni, Claudio, *Relacja o Królestwie Polskim z 1604 roku*, ed. Janusz Byliński and Włodzimierz Kaczorowski (Opole, 2013).

[Ramadanis, Dimitrios], 'Kaisariou Daponte Chronographos', in Constantin Erbiceanu (ed.), *Cronicarii greci carii au scris despre români în epoca fanariotă* (Bucharest, 1888), pp. 1–63.

Sağırlı, Abdurrahman, 'Mehmed b. Mehmed er-Rûmî (Edirneli)'nin Nuhbetü't-Tevârih ve'l-ahbâr'ı ve Târih-i Âl-i Osman'ı: Metinleri, Tahlilleri', 2 vols (PhD diss., Istanbul University, 2000).

Sahillioğlu, Halil (ed.), *Koca Sinan Paşa'nın Telhisleri* (Istanbul, 2004).

Sarnecki, Kazimierz, *Pamiętniki z czasów Jana Sobieskiego: diariusz i relacje z l. 1691–1696*, ed. Janusz Woliński (Wrocław, 1958).

Selanikî Mustafa Efendi, *Tarih-i Selânikî*, 2 vols, ed. Mehmet İpşirli (Ankara, 1989).

Silahdâr Mehmed Agha, *Silahdar Tarihi*, 2 vols (Istanbul, 1928).

Simonescu, Dan (ed.), *Cronica anonimă a Moldovei, 1661–1729: Pseudo-Amiras* (Bucharest, 1975).

Smith, Clive (ed.), *Lightning over Yemen: A History of the Ottoman Campaign 1569–71* (London – New York, 2002).

Stolicki, Jarosław (ed.), *Akta sejmiku podolskiego in hostico, 1672–1698* (Cracow, 2002).

Sułkowska, Irena, 'Noi documente privind relaţiile romîno-polone în perioada 1589–1622', *Studii. Revistă de Istorie* 12/6 (1959), pp. 91–100.

Syrokomla, Władysław, *Przyczynki do historii wojny domowej w Polsce (Samuel Korecki, Adam Tarło, Bogusław Radziwiłł)* (Vilnius, 1858).

Veress, Andrei (ed.), *Documente privitoare la istoria Ardealului, Moldovei și Ţării-Românești*, vols 5–10 (Bucharest, 1932–8).

Wdowiszewski, Zygmunt, *Regesty przywilejów indygenatu w Polsce* (Buenos Aires – Paris, 1971).

Wojtasik, Janusz, 'Uwagi Księcia Krzysztofa Zbaraskiego, posła wielkiego do Turcji z 1622 r. – o państwie otomańskim i jego siłach zbrojnych', *Studia i Materiały do Historii Wojskowości* 7/1 (1961), pp. 333–46.

Yılmaz, Coşkun (ed.), *İstanbul Kadi Sicilleri Bâb Mâhkemesi 3 Numaralı Sicil (H. 1077/M. 1666–1667)* (Istanbul, 2011).

Yılmazer, Ziya (ed.), *Topçular Kâtibi 'Abdülkâdir (Kadrî) Efendi Tarihi (Metin ve Tahlîl)*, 2 vols (Ankara, 2003).

Yücel, Abubekir S., 'Mühürdar Hasan Ağa'nın Cevâhirü't-Tevârih'I' (PhD diss., Erciyes University, 1996).

Secondary Sources

Abou-El-Haj, Rifa'at A., 'The formal closure of the Ottoman frontier in Europe: 1699–1703', *Journal of the American Oriental Society* 89/3 (1969), pp. 467–75.

Bibliography

Abou-El-Haj, Rifa'at A., 'The Ottoman Vezir and Paşa households 1683–1703: a preliminary report', *Journal of the American Oriental Society* 94/4 (1974), pp. 438–47.

Abou-El-Haj, Rifa'at A., *The 1703 Rebellion and the Structure of Ottoman Politics* (Leiden, 1984).

Abou-El-Haj, Rifa'at A., *Formation of the Modern State: The Ottoman Empire, Sixteenth to Eighteenth Centuries*, second edition (Syracuse, 2005).

Adams, Julia, 'The familial state: elite family practices and state-making in the early modern Netherlands', *Theory and Society* 23/2 (1994), pp. 505–39.

Aftodor, Ştefan, *Boierimea în Ţara Românească: Aspecte politice şi social-economice (1601–1654)* (Brăila, 2014).

Akdağ, Mustafa, *Celâlî İsyanları, 1550–1603* (Ankara, 1963).

Aksan, Virginia, *Ottoman Wars, 1700–1870: An Empire Besieged* (London, 2013).

Anastasopoulos, Antonis, 'Albanians in the eighteenth-century Ottoman Balkans', in Elias Kolovos (ed.), *The Ottoman Empire, the Balkans, the Greek Lands: Towards a Social and Economic History. Studies in Honor of John C. Alexander* (Istanbul, 2007), pp. 37–47.

Anderson, Perry, *Lineages of the Absolutist State* (London, 1974).

Andreasyan, Hrand D., 'Abaza Mehmed Paşa', *Tarih Dergisi* 22 (1968), pp. 131–42.

Andreescu, Constantin I. and Constantin A. Stoide, *Ştefăniţă Lupu, domn al Moldovei (1659–1661)* (Bucharest, 1938).

Andreescu, Ştefan, '"Movileştii" în Ţara Românească', in Ştefan Andreescu, *Restitutio Daciae*, vol. 2 (Bucharest, 1989), pp. 7–34.

Andreescu, Ştefan, 'Radu Mihnea Corvin, domn al Moldovei şi Ţării Româneşti', in Ştefan Andreescu, *Restitutio Daciae*, vol. 2 (Bucharest, 1989), pp. 35–84.

Andreescu, Ştefan, 'Exarhul patriarhal Nichifor Dascălul, Cneazul Constantin Vasile de Ostrog şi Mihai Viteazul', in Ştefan Andreescu, *Restitutio Daciae*, vol. 3 (Bucharest, 1997), pp. 81–113.

Andreescu, Ştefan, 'O "pace prefăcută" la Dunărea de Jos: tratativele transilvano-muntene cu Poarta din anii 1597–1598', in Ştefan Andreescu, *Restitutio Daciae*, vol. 3 (Bucharest, 1997), pp. 175–225.

Andreescu, Ştefan, 'Popa Ignatie din Nicopol, episcop de Râmnic şi mitropolit al Ţării Româneşti: o identificare', *Revista istorică* 20/5–6 (2009), pp. 413–7.

Arı, Bülent, 'The first Dutch ambassador in Istanbul: Cornelius Haga and the Dutch capitulations of 1612' (PhD diss., Bilkent University, 2003).

Aslanian, Sebouh D., *From the Indian Ocean to the Mediterranean: The Global Trade Networks of Armenian Merchants from New Julfa* (Berkeley, 2011).

Augustyniak, Urszula, 'Znaczenie więzów krwi w systemach nieformalnych w Rzeczypospolitej pierwszej połowy XVII wieku na przykładzie klienteli Radziwiłłów birżanskich', in Stanisław Bylina (ed.), *Kultura staropolska – kultura europejska* (Warsaw, 1997), pp. 205–10.

Augustyniak, Urszula, *Dwór i klientela Krzysztofa Radziwiłła, 1585–1640: Mechanizmy patronatu* (Warsaw, 2001).

250 Bibliography

Augustyniak, Urszula, 'Specyfika patronatu magnackiego w Wielkim Księstwie Litewskim w XVII wieku: Problemy badawcze', *Kwartalnik Historyczny* 109/1 (2002), pp. 97–110.

Augustyniak, Urszula, 'Klientelizm w wojsku litewskim pierwszej połowy XVII wieku: Problemy dyskusyjne', in Ewa Dubas-Urwanowicz and Jerzy Urwanowicz (eds), *Patron i dwór: Magnateria Rzeczypospolitej w XVI–XVIII wieku* (Warsaw, 2006), pp. 11–21.

Auyero, Javier, *Poor People's Politics: Peronist Survival Networks and the Legacy of Evita* (Durham, 2001).

Aykut, Nezihi, 'Damad İbrahim Paşa', *İstanbul Üniversitesi Tarih Enstitüsü Dergisi* 15 (1997), pp. 197–219.

Babinger, Franz, 'Originea şi sfârşitul lui Vasile Lupu', *Analele Academiei Române. Memoriile Secţiunii Istorice*, Seria III, 19 (1936), pp. 65–83.

Bacalov, Sergiu, 'Boierimea Ţării Moldovei la mijlocul secolului al XVII-lea – începutul secolului al XVIII-lea (studiu istorico-genealogic)' (PhD diss., Moldavian Academy of Sciences, 2012).

Baer, Marc D., *Honored by the Glory of Islam: Conversion and Conquest in Ottoman Empire* (Oxford, 2007).

Baidaus, Eduard, *Politica şi diplomaţia Moldovei în timpul domniei lui Vasile Lupu: Relaţiile politice cu Republica Nobiliară Polonă şi Rusia Moscovită în anii 1634–1653* (Chişinău, 1998).

Bailey, Frederick G., *Stratagems and Spoils: A Social Anthropology of Politics*, revised edition (Boulder, 2001).

Barbir, Karl K., 'One marker of Ottomanism: confiscation of Ottoman officials' estates', in Karl K. Barbir and Baki Tezcan (eds), *Identity and Identity Formation in the Ottoman World: A Volume of Essays in Honor of Norman Itzkowitz* (Madison, 2007), pp. 135–45.

Barkey, Karen, *Bandits and Bureaucrats: The Ottoman Route to State Centralization* (Ithaca, 1994).

Barkey, Karen, 'In different times: scheduling and social control in the Ottoman Empire, 1550 to 1650', *Comparative Studies in Society and History* 38/3 (1996), pp. 460–85.

Barkey, Karen, *Empire of Difference: The Ottomans in Comparative Perspective* (Cambridge, 2008).

Başer, Alper, 'Bucak Tatarları (1550–1700)' (PhD diss., Afyon Kocatepe University, 2010).

Bejenaru, N. C., *Ştefan Tomşa II (1611–1616, 1621–1623) şi rivalitatea turco-polonă pentru Moldova* (Iaşi, 1926).

Berza, Mihai, 'Haraciul Moldovei şi Ţării Româneşti în sec. XV–XIX', *Studii şi Materiale de Istorie Medie* 2 (1957), pp. 7–47.

Besala, Jerzy, *Stanisław Żółkiewski* (Warsaw, 1988).

Beydilli, Kemal, *Die Polnischen Königswahlen und Interregnen von 1572 und 1576 im Lichte osmanischer Archivalien: Ein Beitrag zur Geschichte der osmanischen Machtspolitik* (Munich, 1976).

Bibliography

Black, Jeremy, *Kings, Nobles and Commoners: States and Societies in Early Modern Europe – A Revisionist History* (London, 2004).

Bobicescu, Cristian A., 'Luca Stroici între Ieremia Movilă și Jan Zamoyski', paper presented at the scientific session of the Nicolae Iorga Institute of History in Bucharest, 2002.

Bobicescu, Cristian A., 'Pe marginea raporturilor lui Jan Zamoyski cu Moldova și Țara Românească', *Studii și Materiale de Istorie Medie* 20 (2002), pp. 201–6.

Bobicescu, Cristian A., 'Unia, inkorporacja czy lenno? Kilka uwag o stosunkach Mołdawii z Rzecząpospolitą podczas panowania Jeremiego Mohiły (1595–1606)', in Bogusław Dybaś, Paweł Hanczewski and Tomasz Kempa (eds), *Rzeczpospolita w XVI—XVIII wieku: Państwo czy wspólnota?* (Toruń, 2007), pp. 219–39.

Bobicescu, Cristian A., 'Câteva observații pe marginea unor izvoare inedite cu privire la relațiile dintre Polonia și Moldova sub Movilești', in Stanislava Iachimovschi and Elżbieta Wieruszewska-Calistru (eds), *Relacje polsko-rumuńskie w historii i kulturze* (Suceava, 2010), pp. 108–14.

Bobicescu, Cristian A., 'Tyranny and colonization: preliminary considerations about the colonization plans of Moldavia during the time of Jan Zamoyski', *Revue des Études Sud-Est Européennes* 54/1–4 (2016), pp. 99–118.

Bobicescu, Cristian A., 'Daruri și solidarități în raporturile polono-lituaniano-moldovenești în perioada lui Ieremia Movilă: considerații preliminare', in Karina Stempel-Gancarczyk and Elżbieta Wieruszewska-Calistru (eds), *Historia i dzień dzisiejszy relacji polsko-rumuńskich* (Suceava, 2017), pp. 22–39.

Boeck, Brian J., *Imperial Boundaries: Cossack Communities and Empire-Building in the Age of Peter the Great* (Cambridge, 2009).

Boia, Lucian, *History and Myth in Romanian Consciousness*, trans. James Christian Brown (Budapest – New York, 2001).

Bonchiș-Gheorghe, Maria M., 'Elite politice în secolul al XVII-lea: familia Cantacuzino' (PhD diss., University of Bucharest, 2003).

Börekçi, Günhan, 'Factions and favorites at the courts of Sultan Ahmed I (r. 1603–1617) and his immediate predecessors' (PhD diss., Ohio State University, 2010).

Braddick, Michael J., 'Administrative performance: the representation of political authority in early modern England', in Michael J. Braddick and John Walter (eds), *Negotiating Power in Early Modern Society: Order, Hierarchy, and Subordination in Britain and Ireland* (Cambridge, 2001), pp. 166–87.

Braddick, Michael J., *State Formation in Early Modern England, c. 1550–1700* (Cambridge, 2004).

Brendecke, Arndt, 'Informing the council: central institutions and local knowledge in the Spanish Empire', in Willem P. Blockmans, André Holenstein and Jon Mathieu (eds), *Empowering Interactions: Political Cultures and the Emergence of the State in Europe, 1300–1900* (Aldershot, 2009), pp. 235–52.

Bruening, Alfons, '"Voevodych zemli moldavskoi" … : Peter Mohyla's youth and political heritage', *Socium: Al'manax Socjal'noj Istorii* 4 (2004), pp. 19–25.

252 *Bibliography*

Brummett, Palmira, 'Placing the Ottomans in the Mediterranean world: the question of notables and households', *Osmanlı Araştırmaları* 36 (2010), pp. 75–94.

Burt, Ronald S., *Brokerage and Closure: An Introduction to Social Capital* (Oxford, 2005).

Çalışır, Muhammed F., 'A virtuous grand vizier: politics and patronage in the Ottoman Empire during the grand vizierate of Fazıl Ahmed Pasha (1661–1676)' (PhD diss., Georgetown University, 2016).

Caproşu, Ion, *O istorie a Moldovei prin relaţiile de credit până la mijlocul secolului al XVIII-lea* (Iaşi, 1989).

Casale, Giancarlo, *The Ottoman Age of Exploration* (Oxford, 2010).

Cefaï, Daniel, 'Qu'est-ce qu'une arene publique', in Daniel Cefaï and Isaac Joseph (eds), *L'heritage du pragmatisme: conflits d'urbanité et épreuves de civisme* (La Tour d'Aigues, 2001), pp. 51–81.

Cernovodeanu, Paul, 'Ştiri privitoare la Gheorghe Ghica vodă al Moldovei (1658–9) şi familia sa (I)', *Anuarul Institutului de Istorie şi Arheologie "A.D. Xenopol"* 19 (1982), pp. 333–52.

Cernovodeanu, Paul, 'Noi precizării privitoare la bătălia câştigată de Matei Basarab în împrejurimile Bucureştilor', *Anuarul Institutului de Istorie şi Arheologie din Iaşi* 22/2 (1985), pp. 623–9.

Cernovodeanu, Paul, 'Mobility and traditionalism: the evolution of the boyar class in the Romanian principalities in the 18th century', *Revue des Études Sud-Est Européennes* 24/3 (1986), pp. 249–57.

Cernovodeanu, Paul, 'Campania de înscaunare a lui Matei Basarab (august–septembrie 1632)', *Anuarul Institutului de Istorie şi Arheologie din Iaşi* 24/1 (1987), pp. 311–7.

Chirtoagă, Ion, *Sud-Estul Moldovei şi stângă Nistrului (1484–1699): Expansiunea şi dominaţia turco-tatară* (Bucharest, 1999).

Choińska-Mika, Jolanta, *Sejmiki mazowieckie w dobie Wazów* (Warsaw, 1998).

Choińska-Mika, Jolanta, *Między społeczeństwem szlacheckim a władzą: Problemy komunikacji społeczności lokalne – władza w epoce Jana Kazimierza* (Warsaw, 2002).

Chowaniec, Czesław, *Miron Costin en Pologne: Contributions à l'année 1684–1685* (Cluj, 1931).

Chowaniec, Czesław, 'Wyprawa Sobieskiego do Mołdawii', *Przegląd Historyczno-Wojskowy* 4/2 (1931), pp. 1–117.

Chynczewska-Hennel, Teresa, *Świadomość narodowa szlachty ukraińskiej i Kozaczyzny od schyłku XVI do połowy XVII w.* (Warsaw, 1985).

Cihodaru, Constantin, 'Campania lui Mihai Viteazul în Moldova (mai–iunie 1600)', *Cercetări Istorice* 1 (1970), pp. 131–45.

Ciobanu, Veniamin, 'Succesiunea domnească a Movileştilor – un litigiu politic internaţional', *Anuarul Institutului de Istorie şi Arheologie 'A.D. Xenopol'* 25/1 (1988), pp. 281–91.

Ciobanu, Veniamin, *La cumpănă de veacuri: Ţările Române în contextul politicii poloneze la sfârşitul secolului al XVI-lea şi începutul secolului al XVII-lea* (Iaşi, 1991).

Ciobanu, Veniamin, *Politică și diplomație în secolul al XVII-lea: Țările Române în raporturile polono-otomano-habsburgice (1601-1634)* (Bucharest, 1994).

Ciurea, Dumitru, 'Despre Ieremia Movilă și situația politică a Moldovei la sfârșitul sec. XVI și începutul sec. XVII', in *Movileștii: Istorie și spiritualitate românească*, vol. 1 (Sucevița, 2006), pp. 101–14.

Çizakça, Murat, *A Comparative Evolution of Business Partnerships: The Islamic World and Europe, with Specific Reference to the Ottoman Archives* (Leiden – Boston, 1996).

Codarcea, Cristina, 'Rapports de pouvoir et strategie de gouvernement dans la Valachie du XVIIᵉ siècle', *New Europe College Yearbook* 1 (1996–1997), pp. 131–50.

Codarcea, Cristina, *Société et pouvoir en Valachie (1601-1654): entre la coutume et la loi* (Bucharest, 2002).

Cojocaru, Tatiana, 'Metropolita suczawski Dosoftei (1624–1693) a Rzeczpospolita', *Balcanica Posnaniensia* 13 (2003), pp. 235–51.

Cojocaru, Tatiana, 'When did Ieremia Movilă acquire Uście estate?', *Revue Roumaine d'Histoire* 52/1–4 (2013), pp. 15–20.

Coman, Marian, *Putere și teritoriu: Țara Românească medievală (secolele XIV–XVI)* (Iași, 2013).

Condurachi, Ioan D., *Soli și agenți ai domnilor Moldovei la Poartă în secolul al XVII-lea* (Bucharest, 1920).

Constantinescu, Alexandru, 'Ploconul', *Studii și Materiale de Istorie Medie* 5 (1973), pp. 217–24.

Constantinov, Valentin, 'Din istoria Basarabilor: interpretări cu privire la cronica de la Bucovăț', *Cercetări Istorice* 30–31 (2011–2012), pp. 83–92.

Constantinov, Valentin, *Țara Moldovei în cadrul relațiilor internaționale (1611–1634)* (Iași, 2014).

Cotovanu, Lidia, 'Autour des attaches epirotes du futur prince de Moldavie Constantin Duca (XVIIᵉ siècle)', in Cristian Luca and Ionel Cândea (eds), *Studia varia in honorem Professoris Ștefan Ștefănescu octogenarii* (Bucharest, 2009), pp. 465–88.

Cotovanu, Lidia, 'Le diocèse de Dryinoupolis et ses bienfaiteurs de Valachie et de Moldavie: Solidarités de famille et traits identitaires multiples (XVIᵉ–XVIIᵉ siècles)', in Petronel Zahariuc (ed.), *Contribuții privitoare la istoria relațiilor dintre Țările Române și bisericile răsăritene în secolele XIV–XIX* (Iași, 2009), pp. 219–360.

Cotovanu, Lidia, '"Chasing away the Greeks": the prince-state and the undesired foreigners (Wallachia and Moldavia between the 16th and 18th centuries)', in Olga Katsiardē-Hering and Maria A. Stassinopoulou (eds), *Across the Danube: Southeastern Europeans and Their Travelling Identities (17th–19th C.)* (Leiden – Boston, 2017), pp. 215–52.

Coulter, Laura, 'An examination of the status and activities of the English ambassadors to the Ottoman Porte in the late sixteenth and early seventeenth centuries', *Revue des Études Sud-Est Européennes* 28/1–4 (1990), pp. 57–88.

Coulter, Laura, 'The involvement of the English Crown and its embassy in Constantinople with pretenders to the throne of the principality of Moldavia

254 Bibliography

between the years 1583 and 1620, with particular reference to the pretender Ştefan Bogdan between 1590 and 1612', (PhD diss., University of London, 1993).

Cristocea, Spiridon, *Din trecutul marii boierimii muntene: Marele-vornic Stroe Leurdeanu* (Brăila, 2011).

Čuxlib, Taras V., *Kozaky i monarxy: Mižnarodni vidnosyny rann'omodernoji Ukrajins'koji deržavy, 1648–1721* (Kyiv, 2009).

Czamańska, Ilona, 'Mołdawia i Wołoszczyzna w stosunkach polsko-tureckich XV–XVIII w.', *Balcanica Posnaniensia* 4 (1989), pp. 301–12.

Czamańska, Ilona, 'Rumuńska imigracja polityczna w Polsce XVII wieku', *Balcanica Posnaniensia* 6 (1993), pp. 5–22.

Czamańska, Ilona, 'Caracterul legăturilor lui Jan Zamoyski cu Movileştii', *Arhiva Genealogică* 3/3–4 (1996), pp. 307–12.

Czamańska, Ilona, *Mołdawia i Wołoszczyzna wobec Polski, Węgier i Turcji w XIV i XV wieku* (Poznań, 1996).

Czamańska, Ilona, *Wiśniowieccy: Monografia rodu* (Poznań, 2007).

Czamańska, Ilona, 'Kampania mołdawska księcia Samuela Koreckiego 1615–1616 r.', in Robert Majzner (ed.), *Si vis pacem, para bellum: bezpieczeństwo i polityka Polski* (Częstochowa – Włocławek, 2013), pp. 125–40.

Czamańska, Ilona, 'Miron Barnowski i jego rodzina w relacjach z Polakami', in Elżbieta Wieruszewska-Calistru and Stanislava Iachimovschi (eds), *Wielowiekowe bogactwo polsko-rumuńskich związków historycznych i kulturowych* (Suceava, 2014), pp. 79–89.

Dam'jan, Viktor, 'Kazacko-moldavskie otnošenja v period pravlenija moldavskogo gospodarja Georgija Duki (1678–1683)', *Ukrajina v Central'no-Sxidnoj Jevropi* 8 (2008), pp. 92–104.

Dankoff, Robert, *An Intimate Life of an Ottoman Statesman: Melek Ahmed Paşa (1588–1662) as Portrayed in Evliya Çelebi's Book of Travel (Seyahat-name)* (Albany, 1991).

Darling, Linda T., *Revenue-Raising and Legitimacy: Tax Collection and Finance Administration in Ottoman* Empire, *1560–1660* (Leiden – Boston, 1996).

Darling, Linda T., 'Ottoman fiscal administration: decline or adaptation?' *Journal of European Economic History* 26/1 (1997), pp. 157–79.

Davies, Brian L., *Warfare, State and Society on the Black Sea Steppe, 1500–1700* (London – New York, 2007).

Decei, Aurel, 'Relaţiile lui Vasile Lupu şi Matei Basarab cu Poarta în lumina unor documente turceşti inedite', *Anuarul Institutului de Istorie şi Arheologie – Cluj* 15 (1972), pp. 49–84.

Deletant, Dennis, 'Moldavia between Hungary and Poland, 1347–1412', *The Slavonic and East European Review* 64/2 (1986), pp. 189–211.

Demény, Ludovic and Paul Cernovodeanu, *Relaţiile politice ale Angliei cu Moldova, Ţara Românească şi Transilvania în secolele XVI–XVIII* (Bucharest, 1974).

Descimon, Robert, 'Power elites and the prince: the state as enterprise', in Wolfgang Reinhard (ed.), *Power Elites and State Building* (Oxford, 1996), pp. 101–21.

Bibliography

Djuvara, Neagu, 'Les grand boïars ont-ils constitué dans les principautés roumaines une veritable oligarchie institutionelle et héréditaire?' *Südost-Forschungen* 76 (1987), pp. 1–55.

Doğru, Halime, *Lehistan'da bir Osmanlı Sultanı: IV. Mehmed'in Kamaniçe–Hotin Seferi ve Bir Masraf Defteri* (Istanbul, 2007).

Dumitrescu, Ionel-Claudiu, 'Activități informative românești în serviciul Porții otomane (secolele XVI–XVII)', *Anuarul Institutului de Istorie şi Arheologie 'A.D. Xenopol'* 35 (1998), pp. 37–60.

Dzięgielewski, Jan, 'Fakcje a funkcjonowanie sejmu Rzeczypospolitej w końcu XVI i w XVII wieku', *Barok* 18/1 (2011), pp. 155–70.

Dziubiński, Andrzej, *Na szlakach Orientu: handel między Polską a Imperium Osmańskim w XVI–XVIII wieku* (Wrocław, 1998).

Eremia, Ion, *Relaţiile externe ale lui Vasile Lupu (1634–1653): Contribuţii la istoria diplomaţiei moldoveneşti în secolul al XVII-lea* (Chişinău, 1999).

Eyice, Semayi, 'Mimar Kasım hakkında', *Belleten* 43/172 (1979), pp. 767–808.

Faroqhi, Suraiya, 'Seeking wisdom in China: an attempt to make sense of the Celali rebellions', in Rudolf Vesely and Eduard Gombár (eds), *Zafar Nama: Memorial Volume to Felix Tauer* (Prague, 1994), pp. 101–24.

Filipczak-Kocur, Anna, 'Poland-Lithuania before partition', in Richard Bonney (ed.), *The Rise of the Fiscal State in Europe, c. 1200–1815* (Oxford, 1999), pp. 443–79.

Findley, Carter V., 'Political culture and the great households', in Suraiya Faroqhi (ed.), *The Cambridge History of Turkey*, vol. 3 (Cambridge, 2006), pp. 65–80.

Fine, John v.A., *When Ethnicity Did Not Matter in the Balkans: A Study of Identity in Prenationalist Croatia, Dalmatia, and Slavonia in the Medieval and Early-Modern Periods* (Ann Arbor, 2005).

Finkel, Caroline, 'French mercenaries in the Habsburg–Ottoman war of 1593–1606: the desertion of the Papa garrison to the Ottomans in 1600', *Bulletin of the School of Oriental and African Studies* 55/3 (1992), pp. 451–71.

Finkel, Caroline, *Osman's Dream: The History of the Ottoman Empire* (London, 2003).

Finkel, Caroline, '"The treacherous cleverness of hindsight": myths of Ottoman decay', in Gerald McLean (ed.), *Re-orienting the Renaissance* (London, 2005), pp. 148–74.

Finkel, Caroline and Victor Ostapchuk, 'Outpost of empire: an appraisal of Ottoman building registers as sources for the archeology and construction of the Black Sea fortress of Özi', *Muqarnas* 22 (2005), pp. 150–88.

Fisher, Alan W., *The Crimean Tatars* (Stanford, 1987).

Fodor, Pál, 'Sultan, imperial council, grand vizier: changes in the Ottoman ruling elite and the formation of the grand vizier telhis', *Acta Orientalia Academiae Scientiarum Hungaricae* 47/1–2 (1994), pp. 67–85.

Forand, Paul G., 'The relation of the slave and the client to the master or patron in medieval Islam', *International Journal of Middle East Studies* 2 (1971), pp. 59–66.

Friedrich, Karin, *The Other Prussia: Royal Prussia, Poland and Liberty, 1569–1772* (Cambridge, 2000).

256   *Bibliography*

Frost, Robert I., *The Oxford History of Poland-Lithuania*, vol. 1 (Oxford – New York, 2015).

Gawron, Przemysław, 'Relacje pomiędzy dowódcami wojsk państwowych i prywatnych w I połowie XVII wieku: wybrane przykłady', in Karol Łopatecki and Wojciech Walczak (eds), *Nad społeczeństwem staropolskim* (Białystok, 2007), pp. 231–47.

Gawron, Przemysław, 'Jan Zamoyski, kanclerz i hetman wielki koronny, wobec zmagań turecko-habsburskich w latach 1593–1605/6', in Ryszard Skowron (ed.), *Polska wobec wielkich konfliktów w Europie nowożytnej: Z dziejów dyplomacji i stosunków międzynarodowych w XV–XVIII wieku* (Cracow, 2009), pp. 23–47.

Gawron, Przemysław, *Hetman koronny w systemie ustrojowym Rzeczypospolitej w latach 1581–1646* (Warsaw, 2010).

Gemil, Tahsin, 'La Moldavie dans les traités de paix ottomano-polonais du XVIIᵉ siècle (1621–1672)', *Revue Roumaine d'Histoire* 12/4 (1973), pp. 687–714.

Gemil, Tahsin, 'Date noi privind haraciul Țărilor Române în secolul al XVII-lea', *Revista de Istorie* 30/8 (1977), pp. 1433–46.

Gemil, Tahsin, *Țările Române în contextul politic internațional (1621–1672)* (Bucharest, 1979).

Gemil, Tahsin, *Romanians and Ottomans in the XIVth–XVIth Centuries*, trans. Remus Bejan and Paul Sanders (Bucharest, 2009).

Genç, Mehmet, 'Osmanlı maliyesinde malikane sistemi', in Osman Okyar and Halil İnalcık (eds), *Türkiye'nin Sosyal ve Ekonomik Tarihi (1071–1920)* (Ankara, 1980), pp. 231–91.

Georgescu, Valentin A., 'Hrisovul din 15 iunie 1631 al lui Leon vodă Tomșa în Țara Românească și problema "cărților de libertăți"', *Revista de Istorie* 29/7 (1976), pp. 1018–29.

Ghițulescu, Constanța, 'Familie și societate în Țara Românească (secolul al XVII-lea)', *Studii și Materiale de Istorie Medie* 20 (2002), pp. 80–97.

Giurescu, Constantin, *Capitulațiile Moldovei cu Poarta otomană: Studiu istoric* (Bucharest, 1908).

Golimas, Aurel H., *Luptă decisivă de la Tătareni și capitularea darabanilor deasupra Tăuteștilor, 22 decembrie 1615* (Iași, 1935).

Golimas, Aurel H., *Despre capuchehăile Moldovei și poruncile Porții către Moldova până la 1829* (Iași, 1943).

Golimas, Aurel H., *Diplomatul Constantin Batiște Vevelli Rettimiotul și revoluția Moldovei din primavara anului 1633* (Iași, 1943).

Gorovei, Ștefan S., 'Genealogia familiei domnitoare Tomșa', *Revista Arhivelor* 33/3 (1971), pp. 375–90.

Gorovei, Ștefan S., 'O lămurire: domnia ereditară a familiei Movilă', *Revista de istorie* 28/7 (1975), pp. 1091–4.

Gorovei, Ștefan S., 'Pe marginea unei filiații incerte: Maria Movilă – fiica lui Petru Rareș', *Cercetări Istorice* 11 (1980), pp. 325–80.

Gorovei, Ștefan S., 'Clanuri, familii, autorități, puteri (Moldova, secolele XV–XVII)', *Arhiva Genealogică* 1/1–2 (1994), pp. 87–93.

Gorovei, Ştefan S., "'Nepoţii Balicăi, săminţenia Movileştilor'", *Arhiva Genealogică* 1/3–4 (1994), pp. 123–33.

Gorovei, Ştefan S., 'Vechi însemnări genealogice ale familiei Abaza', *Arhiva Genealogică* 1/1–2 (1994), pp. 163–70.

Gorovei, Ştefan S., 'Steme moldoveneşti augmentate în Polonia', *Arhiva Genealogică* 2/1–2 (1995), pp. 307–9.

Gorovei, Ştefan S., *Întemeierea Moldovei: Probleme controversate* (Iaşi, 1997).

Gorovei, Ştefan S., "'Din Purice-Movilă" şi "Barnovschi-Moghilă": două explicaţii (nu numai) genealogice', *Arhiva Genealogică* 5/3–4 (1998), pp. 327–32.

Gorovei, Ştefan S., 'Doamna Elisabeta Movilă: contribuţii pentru o biografie nescrisă', in *Movileştii: istorie şi spiritualitate românească*, vol. 2 (Suceviţa, 2006), pp. 273–302.

Gorovei, Ştefan S., 'Neamul lui Miron vodă Barnovschi', in *Dragomirna: istorie, tezaur, ctitori* (Dragomirna, 2014), pp. 299–312.

Gorovei, Ştefan S., and Maria M. Székely, 'Old questions, old clichés. New Approaches, new Results? The case of Moldavia', in Oliver J. Schmitt (ed.), *The Ottoman Conquest of the Balkans: Interpretations and Research Debates* (Vienna, 2016), pp. 209–42.

Greene, Molly, *A Shared World: Christians and Muslims in the Early Modern Mediterranean* (Princeton, 2002).

Grześkowiak-Krwawicz, Anna, *Queen Liberty: The Concept of Freedom in the Polish-Lithuanian Commonwealth*, trans. Daniel J. Sax (Leiden – Boston, 2012).

Gudziak, Borys A., *Crisis and Reform: The Kyivan Metropolitanate, the Patriarchate of Constantinople, and the Genesis of the Union of Brest* (Cambridge, MA, 2001).

Gürkan, Emrah S., 'Fooling the Sultan: information, decision-making and the "Mediterranean Faction" (1585–1587)', *Osmanlı Araştırmaları* 45 (2015), pp. 57–96.

Hadjianastasis, Marios, 'Crossing the line in the sand: regional officials, monopolisation of state power and "rebellion". The case of Mehmed Ağa Boyacıoğlu in Cyprus, 1685–1690', *Turkish Historical Review* 2/2 (2011), pp. 155–76.

Hathaway, Jane, *The Politics of Households in Ottoman Egypt: The Rise of Qazdağlıs* (Cambridge, 1997).

Hathaway, Jane, 'The household: an alternative framework for the military society of eighteenth-century Ottoman Egypt', *Oriente Moderno* 18/1 (1999), pp. 57–66.

Hathaway, Jane, *A Tale of Two Factions: Myth, Memory, and Identity in Ottoman Egypt and Yemen* (Albany, 2003).

Hespanha, Antonio M., 'The legal patchwork of empires', *Rechtsgeschichte* 22 (2014), pp. 303–14.

Holenstein, André, 'Introduction: Empowering interactions: looking at statebuilding from below', in Wim Blockmans, André Holenstein and Jon Mathieu (eds), *Empowering Interactions: Political Cultures and the Emergence of the State in Europe, 1300–1900* (Aldershot, 2009), pp. 1–34.

Horn, Maurycy, 'Chronologia i zasięg najazdów tatarskich na ziemie Rzeczypospolitej Polskiej w latach 1600–1647', *Studia i Materiały do Historii Wojskowości* 8/1 (1962), pp. 3–71.

Iacob, Aurel, *Țara Moldovei în vremea lui Ștefan Tomșa al II-lea* (Brăila, 2010).

Ionașcu, Ion, 'Din politica internă și externă a Țării Românești în domnia lui Antonie Vodă din Popești (1669–1672)', in Nicolae I. Simache (ed.), *Pagini din trecutul istoric al județului Prahova* (Ploiești, 1971), pp. 7–31.

Iorga, Nicolae, 'Doamna lui Ieremia Movilă', *Analele Academiei Române. Memoriile Secțiuni Istorice*. Seria II, 32 (1910), pp. 1019–78.

Iorga, Nicolae, 'Frații pagâni ai lui Radu Mihnea', *Revista Istorică* 10/4–6 (1924), pp. 81–3.

Iorga, Nicolae, '"Coconul" lui Radu Mihnea și capuchehaiaua Curt Celebi', *Revista istorică* 18/4–6 (1932), pp. 97–102.

Itzkowitz, Norman, 'Eighteenth century Ottoman realities', *Studia Islamica* 16 (1962), pp. 73–94.

Ivanics, Mária, 'The military co-operation of the Crimean Khanate with the Ottoman Empire in the sixteenth and seventeenth centuries', in Gábor Kármán and Lovro Kunčević (eds), *The European Tributary States of the Ottoman Empire in the Sixteenth–Seventeenth Centuries* (Leiden – Boston, 2013), pp. 275–300.

İnalcık, Halil, 'Yeni vesikalara göre Kırım hanlığının Osmanlı tabiliğine girmesi ve ahidname meselesi', *Belleten* 8/30 (1944), pp. 185–229.

İnalcık, Halil, 'Ottoman methods of conquest', *Studia Islamica* 2 (1954), pp. 103–29.

İnalcık, Halil, 'The question of the closing of the Black Sea under the Ottomans', *Archeion Pontou* 35 (1979), pp. 74–111.

İnalcık, Halil, 'Military and fiscal transformation of the Ottoman Empire, 1600–1700', *Archivum Ottomanicum* 6 (1980), pp. 283–337.

İnbaşı, Mehmet, *Ukrayna'da Osmanlılar: Kamaniçe Seferi ve Organizasyonu (1672)* (Istanbul, 2004).

Jakovenko, Natalja, *Ukrajins'ka šljaxta z kincja XIV do seredyny XVII st. (Volyn' i Central'na Ukrajina)*, second edition (Kyiv, 2008).

Janiszewska-Mincer, Barbara, *Rzeczpospolita Polska w latach 1600–1603: narastanie konfliktu między Zygmuntem III Wazą a stanami* (Bydgoszcz, 1984).

Janos, Damien, 'Panaiotis Nicousios and Alexander Mavrocordatos: the rise of the Phanariots and the office Grand Dragoman in the Ottoman administration in the second half of the seventeenth century', *Archivum Ottomanicum* 23 (2005), pp. 177–96.

Kaczka, Mariusz, 'The gentry of the Polish–Ottoman borderlands: the case of the Moldavian-Polish family of Turkuł/Turculeț', *Acta Poloniae Historica* 104 (2011), pp. 129–50.

Kaczka, Mariusz, 'Networking across *Dar al-Islam*: Ilyash Colceag Pasha of Hotin and his Polish network', paper presented at the 23rd Symposium of the Comité International des Études Pré-Ottomanes et Ottomanes, Sofia, 11–15 September 2018.

Kafadar, Cemal, 'The question of Ottoman decline', *Harvard Middle Eastern and Islamic Review* 4/1–2 (1997–1998), pp. 30–75.

Kármán, Gábor, 'The networks of a Wallachian pretender in Constantinople: the contacts of the future Voivode Mihail Radu 1654–1657', in Gábor Kármán and Radu G. Păun (eds), *Europe and the 'Ottoman World': Exchanges and Conflicts (Sixteenth and Seventeenth Centuries)* (Istanbul, 2013), pp. 119–39.

Kármán, Gábor, *A Seventeenth-Century Odyssey in East Central Europe: The Life of Jakab Harsányi Nagy* (Leiden – Boston, 2016).

Kármán, Gábor, 'Zülfikár aga portai főtolmács', *Aetas* 31/3 (2016), pp. 54–76.

Kaufman, Robert R., 'The patron-client concept and macro-politics: prospects and problems', *Comparative Studies in Society and History* 16/3 (1974), pp. 284–308.

Kempa, Tomasz, 'Proces Nicefora na sejmie w Warszawie w 1597 roku', in Zbigniew Karpus, Tomasz Kempa and Dorota Michaluk (eds), *Europa Orientalis: Polska i jej wschodni sąsiedzi od średniowiecza po współczesność* (Toruń, 1996), pp. 145–68.

Kempa, Tomasz, *Konstanty Wasyl Ostrogski (ok. 1524/5–1608) wojewoda kijowski i marszałek ziemi wołyńskiej* (Toruń, 1997).

Kempa, Tomasz, 'Konflikt między kanclerzem Jan Zamoyskim a książętami Ostrogskimi i jego wpływ na sytuację wewnętrzną i zewnętrzną Rzeczypospolitej w końcu XVI wieku', *Socium: Al'manax social'noj istorji* 9 (2010), pp. 67–96.

Kettering, Sharon, *Patrons, Brokers, and Clients in Seventeenth-Century France* (New York, 1986).

Kettering, Sharon, 'Gift-giving and patronage in early modern France', *French History* 2/2 (1988), pp. 131–51.

Kettering, Sharon, 'The historical development of political clientelism', *Journal of Interdisciplinary History* 18/3 (1988), pp. 419–47.

Kizilov, Mikhail, 'Slave trade in the early modern Crimea from the perspective of Christian, Muslim, and Jewish sources', *Journal of Early Modern History* 11/1 (2007), pp. 1–31.

Kolçak, Özgür, 'XVII. yüzyıl askerî gelimişi ve Osmanlılar: 1660–64 Osmanlı-Avusturya savaşları' (PhD diss., Istanbul University, 2012).

Kolçak, Özgür, 'Köprülü ambitions in Transylvania: consolidation of Ottoman power and transfer of royal estates', paper presented at the conference Ottoman Archeology in Romania: Challenges, Realities, Perspectives in Bucharest, 20–21 October 2017.

Kołodziejczyk, Dariusz, 'Ottoman Podillja: The Eyalet of Kam" janec", 1672–1699', *Harvard Ukrainian Studies* 16/1–2 (1992), pp. 87–101.

Kołodziejczyk, Dariusz, *Podole pod panowaniem tureckim: Ejalet kamieniecki 1672–1699* (Warszawa, 1994).

Kołodziejczyk, Dariusz, 'The export of silver coin through the Polish–Ottoman border and the problem of the balance of trade', *Turcica* 28 (1996), pp. 105–16.

Kołodziejczyk, Dariusz, 'Slave hunting and slave redemption as a business enterprise: the northern Black Sea region in the sixteenth to seventeenth centuries', *Oriente Moderno* 86/1 (2006), pp. 149–59.

Kołodziejczyk, Dariusz, *The Crimean Khanate and Poland-Lithuania: International Diplomacy on the European Periphery (15th–18th Century): A Study of Peace Treaties Followed by Annotated Documents* (Leiden – Boston, 2011).

Bibliography

Kołodziejczyk, Dariusz, 'Between universalistic claims and reality: Ottoman frontiers in the early modern period', in Christine Woodhead (ed.), *The Ottoman World* (London – New York, 2012), pp. 205–19.

Kołodziejczyk, Dariusz, 'What is inside and what is outside? Tributary states in Ottoman politics', in Gábor Kármán and Lovro Kunčević (eds), *The European Tributary States of the Ottoman Empire in the Sixteenth–Seventeenth Centuries* (Leiden – Boston, 2013), pp. 421–32.

Kołodziejczyk, Dariusz, 'Permeable frontiers: contacts between Polish and Turkish-Tatar elites in the early modern era', in Björn Forsén and Mika Hakkarainen (eds), *Foreign Drums Beating: Transnational Experiences in Early Modern Europe* (Helsinki, 2017), pp. 153–68.

Kołodziejczyk, Dariusz, 'A man, a woman and livestock crossing the borders of the *Dar al-Islam*: a glimpse into everyday life of the *sancak* of Hotin in the early 18th century', paper presented at the 23rd Symposium of the Comité International des Études Pré-Ottomanes et Ottomanes, Sofia, 11–15 September 2018.

Kortepeter, Carl M., *Ottoman Imperialism during the Reformation: Europe and the Caucasus* (London – New York, 1972).

Kowalski, Mariusz, *Księstwa Rzeczpospolitej: państwo magnackie jako region polityczny* (Warsaw, 2013).

Krausman Ben-Amos, Ilana, *The Culture of Giving: Informal Support and Gift-Exchange in Early Modern England* (Cambridge, 2008).

Kunt İ. Metin, 'Naima, Köprülü and the grand vizierate', *Boğaziçi Üniversitesi Dergisi. Hümaniter Bilimler – Humanities* 1 (1973), pp. 57–64.

Kunt İ. Metin, 'Ethnic-regional (*cins*) solidarity in the seventeenth-century Ottoman establishment', *International Journal of Middle East Studies* 5/3 (1974), pp. 233–9.

Kunt, İ. Metin, 'Kulların kulları', *Boğaziçi Üniversitesi Dergisi. Hümaniter Bilimler – Humanities* 3 (1975), pp. 27–42.

Kunt, İ. Metin, '17. yüzyılda Osmanlı kuzey politikası üzerine bir yorum', *Boğaziçi Üniversitesi Dergisi. Hümaniter Bilimler – Humanities* 4–5 (1976–1977), pp. 111–6.

Kunt, İ. Metin, 'Derviş Mehmed Paşa, vezir and entrepreneur: a study in Ottoman political-economic theory and practice', *Turcica* 9/1 (1977), pp. 197–214.

Kunt, İ. Metin, *The Sultan's Servants: The Transformation of Ottoman Provincial Government, 1550–1650* (New York, 1983).

Kupczewska, Marta, 'Działalność polityczno-wojskowa Jana, Jakuba i Stefana Potockich w okresie kampanii smoleńskiej', *Białostockie Teki Historyczne* 8 (2010), pp. 27–46.

Lambton, Ann, 'Pīshkash: present or tribute?', *Bulletin of the School of Oriental and African Studies* 57/1 (1994), pp. 145–58.

Lehr, Lia, 'Mihnea al III-lea', *Studii. Revistă de Istorie* 26/6 (1973), pp. 1161–78.

Lemercier, Claire, 'Formale Methoden der Netzwerkanalyse in den Geschichtswissenschaften: Warum und Wie?', *Österreichische Zeitschrift für Geschichtswissenschaften* 23/1 (2012), pp. 16–41.

Lin, Nan, *Social Capital: A Theory of Social Structure and Action* (Cambridge, 2001).

Litwin, Henryk, 'Catholicization among the Ruthenian nobility and assimilation processes in the Ukraine during the years 1569–1648', *Acta Poloniae Historica* 55 (1987), pp. 57–83.

Litwin, Henryk, 'Fakcje magnackie na Kijowszczyźnie 1569–1648', in Jerzy Urwanowicz, Ewa Dubas-Urwanowicz and Piotr Guzowski (eds), *Władza i prestiż: Magnateria Rzeczypospolitej w XVI–XVIII wieku* (Białystok, 2003), pp. 47–70.

Litwin, Henryk, *Równi do równych: kijowska reprezentacja sejmowa, 1569–1648* (Warsaw, 2009).

Luca, Cristian, *Ţările Române şi Veneţia în secolul al XVII-lea: Din relaţiile politico-diplomatice, comerciale şi culturale ale Ţării Româneşti şi ale Moldovei cu Serenissima* (Bucharest, 2007).

Luca, Cristian, 'Il soggiorno veneziano del principe Gregorio I Ghica e della sua famiglia (1671–1672)', *Studia Historica, Adriatica ac Danubiana* 3/1–2 (2010), pp. 92–103.

Lungu, Vasile, 'Mihăilaş Vodă Movilă şi Moldova în anul 1607', *Cercetări Istorice* 8/1 (1932), pp. 1–15.

Mączak, Antoni, 'Export of grain and the problem of distribution of national income in the years 1550–1650', *Acta Poloniae Historica* 18 (1968), pp. 75–98.

Mączak, Antoni, 'The structure of power in the Commonwealth of the sixteenth and seventeenth centuries', in J. K. Fedorowicz (ed.), *A Republic of Nobles: Studies in Polish History to 1864* (Cambridge, 1982), pp. 109–34.

Mączak, Antoni, 'Jedyna i nieporównywalna? Kwestia odrębności Rzeczypospolitej w Europie XVI–XVII wieku', *Kwartalnik Historyczny* 100/4 (1993), pp. 121–36.

Mączak, Antoni, *Klientela: Nieformalne systemy władzy w Polsce i Europie XVI–XVIII w.* (Warsaw, 1994).

Majewski, Ryszard, *Cecora: rok 1620* (Warsaw, 1970).

Malcolm, Noel, *Agents of Empire: Knights, Pirates, Jesuits and Spies in the Sixteenth-Century Mediterranean World* (Oxford – New York, 2015).

Manikowski, Adam, 'Was the seventeenth-century Commonwealth an anomaly among other European states?' *Odrodzenie i Reformacja w Polsce* special issue (2014), pp. 27–39.

Matei, Ion, *Reprezentanţii diplomatici (capuchehăi) al Ţării Româneşti la Poarta otomană*, ed. Tudor Teotoi and Nagy Pienaru (Bucharest, 2008).

Matkovski, Aleksandar, 'Prilog pitanju devširme', *Prilozi za Orijentalnu Filologiju* 14–15 (1969), pp. 273–309.

Maxim, Mihai, *Ţările Române şi Înalta Poartă: Cadrul juridic al relaţiilor româno-otomane în evul mediu* (Bucharest, 1993).

Maxim, Mihai, 'Haraciul Moldovei şi Ţării Româneşti în ultimul sfert al veacului XVI', *Studii şi Materiale de Istorie Medie* 12 (1994), pp. 3–46.

Maxim, Mihai, 'Circonstances de la majoration du *Kharadj* payé par la Valachie à l'Empire ottoman durant la période 1540–1575', in Mihai Maxim, *L'Empire Ottoman au nord du Danube et l'autonomie des Principautés Roumains au XVIe siècle* (Istanbul, 1999), pp. 215–30.

262 *Bibliography*

Maxim, Mihai, 'Les relations roumano-ottomanes entre 1574 et 1594', in Mihai Maxim, *L'Empire Ottoman au nord du Danube et l'autonomie des Principautés Roumains au XVIᵉ siècle* (Istanbul, 1999), pp. 109–28.

Maxim, Mihai, 'Recherches sur les circonstances de la majoration du *Kharadj* de la Moldavie entre les années 1538–1574', in Mihai Maxim, *L'Empire Ottoman au nord du Danube et l'autonomie des Principautés Roumains au XVIᵉ siècle* (Istanbul, 1999), pp. 185–214.

Maxim, Mihai, 'Le statut des Pays Roumains envers le Porte Ottoman au XVIᵉ–XIXᵉ siècles', in Mihai Maxim, *Romano-Ottomanica: Essays & Documents from the Turkish Archives* (Istanbul, 2001), pp. 23–46.

Maxim, Mihai, 'The institution of *müsadere* (confiscation) in the Ottoman–Romanian relations', in Mihai Maxim, *Romano-Ottomanica: Essays & Documents from the Turkish Archives* (Istanbul, 2001), pp. 173–200.

Maxim, Mihai, '*Voyvodalık* ou *beğlerbeğlik*? La politique ottomane envers la Moldavie et la Valachie (november 1594 – février 1596) à la lumière des nouveaux documents turcs', in Mihai Maxim, *Romano-Ottomanica: Essays & Documents from the Turkish Archives* (Istanbul, 2001), pp. 163–72.

Maxim, Mihai, 'Țările Române și Imperiul otoman', in Virgil Cândea (ed.), *Istoria românilor*, vol. 5 (Bucharest, 2012), pp. 811–72.

Mazur, Karol, *W stronę integracji z Koroną: Sejmiki Wołynia i Ukrainy w latach 1569–1648* (Warsaw, 2006).

McNeill, William H., 'Hypotheses concerning possible ethnic role changes in the Ottoman Empire in the seventeenth century', in Osman Okyar and Halil İnalcık (eds), *Türkiye'nin Sosyal ve Ekonomik Tarihi (1071–1920)* (Ankara, 1980), pp. 127–9.

Mesrobeanu, A., 'Rolul politic al Movileștilor până în domnia lui Ieremia Vodă', *Cercetări Istorice* 1 (1925), pp. 177–89.

Meyer, Adrian C., 'The significance of quasi-groups in the study of complex societies', in Michael Banton (ed.), *Social Anthropology of Complex Societies* (London – New York, 1966), pp. 97–121.

Michta, Jerzy, 'Nobilitacja i indygenat w szlacheckiej Rzeczypospolitej', *Annales Universitatis Mariae Curie-Skłodowska* 45 (1990), pp. 353–69.

Miclescu-Prăjescu, Ion C., 'New data regarding the installation of Movilă princes', *The Slavonic and East European Review* 49 (1971), pp. 214–34.

Miclescu-Prăjescu, Ion C., 'Noi date privind înscaunarea Movileștilor', *Arhiva Genealogică* 3/1–2 (1997), pp. 159–78.

Milewski, Dariusz, 'The granting of Polish indygenat to the Moldavian voyevode Miron Barnovski', *Medieval and Early Modern Studies for Central and Eastern Europe* 3 (2011), pp. 117–49.

Milewski, Dariusz, 'A campaign of the Great Hetman Jan Zamoyski in Moldavia (1595). Part I. Politico-diplomatic and military preliminaries', *Codrul Cosminului* 18/2 (2012), pp. 261–86.

Bibliography

Milewski, Dariusz, 'Polskie oczekiwania i polityka wobec obsady tronu mołdawskiego w okresie pochocimskim 1621-1624', *Saeculum Christianum* 20 (2013), pp. 99-108.

Milewski, Dariusz, *Mołdawia między Polską a Turcją: Hospodar Miron Barnowski i jego polityka (1626-1629)* (Oświęcim, 2014).

Mioc, Damaschin, 'Despre modul de impunere și percepere a birului în Țara Romînească pînă la 1632', *Studii și Materiale de Istorie Medie* 2 (1957), pp. 49-116.

Miović-Perić, Vesna, 'Turske priznanice u uplaćenom Dubrovačkom haraču', *Anali Dubrovnik* 42 (2004), pp. 53-77.

Mitchell, Timothy, 'The limits of the state: beyond statist approaches and their critics', *American Political Science Review* 85/1 (1991), pp. 77-96.

Moga, Ioan, *Rivalitatea polono-austriacă și orientarea politică a Țărilor Române la sfârșitul secolului al XVII-lea* (Cluj, 1933).

Motogna, V., 'Epoca lui Matei Basarab și Vasile Lupu', *Cercetării Istorice* 13-16 (1940), pp. 453-513.

Murgescu, Bogdan, 'The Ottoman military demand and the Romanian market: a case study: 1672', *Revue des Études Sud-Est Européennes* 25/4 (1987), pp. 306-13.

Murgescu, Bogdan, 'Câteva observații pe marginea datoriilor domnilor Țării Românești și Moldovei în 1594', *Revista Istorică* 6/3-4 (1995), pp. 243-53.

Murgescu, Bogdan, 'The "modernization" of the Romanian principalities during the 16th-17th centuries: patterns, distortions, prospects', in Marian Dygo, Sławomir Gawlas and Hieronim Grala (eds), *Modernizacja struktur władzy w warunkach opóźnienia: Europa Środkowa i Wschodnia na przełomie średniowiecza i czasów nowożytnych* (Warsaw, 1999), pp. 173-84.

Murgescu, Bogdan, 'Balances of trade and payments between the Ottoman Empire and Central Europe (16th -18th centuries)', in Simonetta Cavaciocchi (ed.), *Relazioni economiche tra Europa e mondo islamico, secc. XIII-XVIII* (Florence, 2007), pp. 961-80.

Murgescu, Bogdan, '"Fanarioți" și "pământeni": religie și etnicitate în definirea identităților în Țările Române și în Imperiul Otoman', in Bogdan Murgescu, *Țările Române între Imperiul Otoman și Europa creștină* (Iași, 2012), pp. 53-9.

Murgescu, Bogdan, *România și Europa: Acumularea decalajelor economice (1500-2010)* (Iași, 2012).

Murphey, Rhoads, *Ottoman Warfare, 1500-1700* (London, 1999).

Murphey, Rhoads, *Exploring Ottoman Sovereignty: Tradition, Image and Practice in the Ottoman Imperial Household, 1400-1800* (London, 2008).

Müller, Michael G., and Cornelius Torp, 'Conceptualising transnational spaces in history', *European Review of History* 16/5 (2009), pp. 609-17.

Nexon, Daniel H., *The Struggle for Power in Early Modern Europe: Religious Conflict, Dynastic Empires, and International Change* (Princeton, 2009).

Nizri, Michael, *Ottoman High Politics and the Ulema Household* (Basingstoke, 2014).

Nizri, Michael, 'Rethinking center-periphery communication in the Ottoman Empire: the *kapı kethüdası*', *Journal of the Economic and Social History of the Orient* 59/3 (2016), pp. 473-98.

Olnon, Merlijn, "'A most agreeable and pleasant creature?" Merzifonlu Kara Mustafa Paşa in the correspondence of Justinus Colyer', *Oriente Moderno* 22/3 (2003), pp. 649–69.

Opaliński, Edward, *Sejm Srebrnego Wieku, 1587–1652: Między głosowaniem większościowym a liberum veto* (Warsaw, 2001).

Ostapchuk, Victor, 'The Ottoman Black Sea frontier and the relations of the Porte with the Polish–Lithuanian Commonwealth and Muscovy, 1622–1628' (PhD diss., Harvard University, 1989).

Ostapchuk, Victor, 'The human landscape of the Ottoman Black Sea in the face of the Cossack naval raids', *Oriente Moderno* 20/1 (2001), pp. 23–95.

Ostapchuk, Victor, 'Cossack Ukraine in and out of Ottoman orbit, 1648–1681', in Gábor Kármán and Lovro Kunčević (eds), *The European Tributary States of the Ottoman Empire in the Sixteenth–Seventeenth Centuries* (Leiden – Boston, 2013), pp. 123–52.

Özbaran, Salih, 'Some notes on the salyâne system in the Ottoman provinces as organised in Arabia in the sixteenth century', *Osmanlı Araştırmaları* 6 (1986), pp. 39–45.

Özel, Oktay, 'The reign of violence: the *celalis, c.* 1550–1700', in Christine Woodhead (ed.), *The Ottoman World* (London – New York, 2012), pp. 184–204.

Özel, Oktay, *The Collapse of Rural Order in Ottoman Anatolia: Amasya 1576–1643* (Leiden – Boston, 2016).

Païzi-Apostolopoulou, Machi, 'Dimitrios Ramadanis: enas istoriographos tou 18ou aiona se aphaneia', *O Eranistis* 20 (1995), pp. 20–35.

Païzi-Apostolopoulou, Machi, 'To cheirographo tou "Chronographou tou Daponte" kai i lysi enos ainigmatos: to chph Kyriazi tis Gennadeiou', *O Eranistis* 24 (2003), pp. 85–94.

Păltânea, Paul, 'Familia cronicarului Miron Costin şi risipirea moşiilor prin descendenţi: partea a 2-a', *Arhiva Genealogică* 5/1–2 (1998), pp. 87–106.

Pamuk, Şevket, 'The evolution of fiscal institutions in the Ottoman Empire, 1500–1914', in Bartolomé Yun Casalilla and Patrick K. O'Brien (eds), *The Rise of Fiscal States: A Global History, 1500–1914* (New York, 2012), pp. 304–34.

Panaite, Viorel, 'Reprezentanţa diplomatică a Ţării Românesti la Poarta Otomană în epoca lui Constantin Brâncoveanu', *Revista de Istorie* 41/9 (1988), pp. 877–94.

Panaite, Viorel, 'The re'ayas of the tributary-protected principalities: the sixteenth through eighteenth centuries', in Kemal H. Karpat and Robert W. Zens (eds), *Ottoman Borderlands: Issues, Personalities and Political Changes* (Madison, 2003), pp. 79–104.

Panaite, Viorel, 'The voivodes of the Danubian principalities – as *haracgüzarlar* of the Ottoman sultans', in Kemal H. Karpat and Robert W. Zens (eds), *Ottoman Borderlands: Issues, Personalities and Political Changes* (Madison, 2003), pp. 59–78.

Panaite, Viorel, 'The legal and political status of Wallachia and Moldavia in relation to the Ottoman Porte', in Gábor Kármán and Lovro Kunčević (eds), *The European Tributary States of the Ottoman Empire in the Sixteenth–Seventeenth Centuries* (Leiden – Boston, 2013), pp. 9–42.

Panaite, Viorel, *Război, pace și comerț în Islam: Țările române și dreptul otoman al popoarelor*, second edition (Iași, 2013).

Panaitescu, Petre P., *Începuturile și biruința scrisului în limba română* (Bucharest, 1965).

Panaitescu, Petre P., 'De ce n-au cucerit turcii Țările Române?', in Petre P. Panaitescu, *Interpretări românești: Studii de istorie economică și socială*, second edition (Bucharest, 1994), pp. 111–8.

Panou, Nikos, 'Greek-Romanian symbiotic patterns in the early modern period: history, mentalities, institutions (I)', *The Historical Review* 3 (2006), pp. 71–110.

Papademetriou, Tom, *Render unto the Sultan: Power, Authority, and the Greek Orthodox Church in the Early Ottoman Centuries* (Oxford, 2015).

Papp, Sándor, 'The system of autonomous Muslim and Christian communities, churches, and states in the Ottoman Empire', in Gábor Kármán and Lovro Kunčević (eds), *The European Tributary States of the Ottoman Empire in the Sixteenth–Seventeenth Centuries* (Leiden – Boston, 2013), pp. 375–429.

Parrott, David, *The Business of War: Military Enterprise and Military Revolution in Early Modern Europe* (Cambridge – New York, 2012).

Păun, Radu G., 'La construction de l'état moderne et le sud-est de l'Europe: Quelques réflexions méthodologiques', *Revue des Études Sud-Est Européennes* 35/3–4 (1997), pp. 213–26.

Păun, Radu G., '*Si deus nobiscum, quis contra nos*? Mihnea III: note de teologie politică', in Ovidiu Cristea and Gheorghe Lazăr (eds), *Național și universal în istoria românilor: Studii oferite prof. dr. Șerban Papacostea cu ocazia împlinirii a 70 de ani* (Bucharest, 1998), pp. 69–99.

Păun, Radu G., 'Pouvoirs, offices et patronage dans la Principauté de Moldavie au XVIIe siècle: l'aristocratie roumaine et la pénétration gréco-levantine' (PhD diss., L'École des Hautes Études en Sciences Sociales, 2003).

Păun, Radu G., 'Les grands officiers d'origine gréco-levantine en Moldavie au XVIIe siècle: Offices, carrièrs et stratègies de pouvoir', *Revue des Études Sud-Est Européennes* 45/1–4 (2007), pp. 153–95.

Păun, Radu G., 'Enemies within: networks of influence and the military revolts against Ottoman power (Moldavia and Wallachia, sixteenth–seventeenth centuries)', in Gábor Kármán and Lovro Kunčević (eds), *The European Tributary States of the Ottoman Empire in the Sixteenth and Seventeenth Centuries* (Leiden – Boston, 2013), pp. 209–51.

Păun, Radu G., 'Some remarks about the historical origins of the "Phanariot phenomenon" in Moldavia and Wallachia (16th–19th centuries)', in Gelina Harlaftis and Radu G. Păun (eds), *Greeks in Romania in the Nineteenth Century* (Athens, 2013), pp. 47–94.

Păun, Radu G., '"Well-born of the Polis": the Ottoman conquest and the reconstruction of the Greek Orthodox elites under Ottoman rule', in Robert Born and Sabine Jagodzinski (eds), *Türkenkriege und Adelskultur in Ostmitteleuropa vom 16.-18. Jahrhundert* (Leipzig, 2014), pp. 59–85.

266 *Bibliography*

Păun, Radu G., 'Conquered by the (s)word: governing the tributary principalities of Wallachia and Moldavia (16th–17th centuries)', in Robert Born and Marek Dziewulski (eds), *The Ottoman Orient in Renaissance Culture* (Cracow, 2015), pp. 19–40.

Peirce, Leslie, *The Imperial Harem: Women and Sovereignty in the Ottoman Empire* (Oxford, 1993).

Peksa, Iuliu, 'Zólkiewski şi expediţia doamnei Elisabeta Movilă în Moldova în anii 1615–1616', *Revista Istorică* 14/1 (1928), pp. 46–53.

Peksevgen, Sefik, 'Secrecy, information control and power building in the Ottoman Empire, 1566–1603' (PhD diss., McGill University, 2004).

Philliou, Christine, *Biography of an Empire: Governing Ottomans in an Age of Revolution* (Berkeley – Los Angeles, 2011).

Pilat, Liviu, 'De la Liov la Colomeea: observaţii privind ceremonialul depunerii omagiului de către domnii moldoveni', *Analele Putnei* 4/1 (2008), pp. 133–52.

Pippidi, Andrei, 'Phanare, phanariotes, phanariotisme', *Revue des Études Sud-Est Européennes* 13/2 (1975), pp. 231–9.

Pippidi, Andrei, 'Moldavie et Pologne: la fin de la vassalité', *Acta Poloniae Historica* 83 (2001), pp. 59–78.

Pippidi, Andrei, *Tradiţia politică bizantină în Ţările Române în secolele XVI–XVIII*, second edition (Bucharest, 2001).

Piterberg, Gabriel, 'The alleged rebellion of Abaza Mehmed Paşa: historiography and the Ottoman state in the seventeenth century', in Jane Hathaway (ed.), *Mutiny and Rebellion in the Ottoman Empire* (Madison, 2009), pp. 13–24.

Pitt-Rivers, Julian A., *The People of the Sierra* (London, 1954).

Piwarski, Kazimierz, 'Polityka bałtycka Jana III w latach 1675–1679', in Oskar Halecki (ed.), *Księga pamiątkowa ku czci Profesora Dra Wacława Sobieskiego* (Cracow, 1932), pp. 153–86.

Podhorodecki, Leszek, 'Wojna polsko-turecka 1633–1634 r.', *Studia i Materiały do Historii Wojskowości* 20 (1976), pp. 27–72.

'Problema organizării statelor ca "regim boieresc" în Ţara Românească şi Moldova', *Revista de Istorie* 32/5 (1979), pp. 941–56.

Pungă, Gheorghe, 'Contribuţii la biografia marelui logofăt Luca Stroici', *Arhiva Genealogică* 1/1–2 (1994), pp. 183–95.

Rachuba, Andrzej, 'Hegemonia Sapiehów na Litwie jako przejaw skrajnej dominacji magnaterii w życiu kraju', in Jerzy Urwanowicz, Ewa Dubas-Urwanowicz and Piotr Guzowski (eds), *Władza i prestiż: Magnateria Rzeczypospolitej w XVI–XVIII wieku* (Białystok, 2003), pp. 205–29.

Reindl-Kiel, Hedda, 'Power and submission: gifting at royal circumcision festivals in the Ottoman Empire (16th–18th centuries)', *Turcica* 41 (2009), pp. 37–88.

Reindl-Kiel, Hedda, 'Bread for the followers, silver vessels for the lord: the system of distribution and redistribution in the Ottoman Empire (16th–18th centuries)', *Osmanlı Araştırmaları* 43 (2013), pp. 93–104.

Reindl-Kiel, Hedda, *Leisure, Pleasure and Duty: The Daily Life of Silahdar Mustafa, Éminence Grise in the Final Years of Murad IV (1635–1640)* (Berlin: EB-Verlag, 2016).

Reinhard, Wolfgang, 'Oligarchische Verflechtung und Konfession in oberdeutschen Städten', in Antoni Mączak and Elisabeth Müller-Luckner (eds), *Klientelsysteme im Europa der Früher Neuzeit* (Munich, 1988), pp. 47–62.

Reinhard, Wolfgang, 'Introduction: Power Elites, State Servants, Ruling Classes and the Growth of State Power', in Wolfgang Reinhard (ed.), *Power Elites and State Building* (Oxford, 1996), pp. 1–18.

Rezachevici, Constantin, 'Bătălia de la Gura Nișcovului (august 1601): contribuții privind istoria Țării Românești în epoca lui Mihai Viteazul și activitatea militară a lui Radu Șerban înaintea domniei', *Studii. Revistă de Istorie* 24/6 (1971), pp. 1143–57.

Rezachevici, Constantin, 'Bătălia de la "Cornul lui Sas" (3/13 iulie 1612): o reconstituire', *Studii și Materiale de Istorie Militară* 9 (1976), pp. 59–70.

Rezachevici, Constantin, 'Fenomene de criza social-politică în Țara Românească în veacul al XVII-lea (I)', *Studii și Materiale de Istorie Medie* 9 (1978), pp. 59–84.

Rezachevici, Constantin, 'Politica internă și externă a Țărilor Române în primele decenii ale secolului al XVII-lea', *Revista de Istorie* 38/1 (1985), pp. 5–29.

Rezachevici, Constantin, 'Din nou despre bătălia de la Cornul lui Sas', *Anuarul Institutului de Istorie și Arheologie "A.D. Xenopol"* 35/2 (1988), pp. 501–3.

Rezachevici, Constantin, 'Fenomene de criza social-politică în Țara Românească în veacul al XVII-lea (II)', *Studii și Materiale de Istorie Medie* 14 (1996), pp. 85–117.

Rezachevici, Constantin, 'Principii Dimitrie Wiśniowiecki și Michal Korybut și înrudirile lor cu Bogdăneștii și Movileștii: lămurirea unor confuzii istorice', *Arhiva Genealogică* 3/3–4 (1996), pp. 313–21.

Rezachevici, Constantin, 'Dimensiunea polonă a activității lui Ieremia Movilă in lumina izvoarelor vremii', *Movileștii: Istorie și spiritualitate românească*, vol. 2 (Sucevița, 2006), pp. 249–62.

Rezachevici, Constantin, 'Domnia lui Matei Basarab – un factor de stabilitate', in Virgil Cândea (ed.), *Istoria românilor*, vol. 5, second edition (Bucharest, 2012), pp. 106–35.

Rezachevici, Constantin, 'Moldova de la Ghiculești la fanarioți', in Virgil Cândea (ed.), *Istoria românilor*, vol. 5, second edition (Bucharest, 2012), pp. 276–340.

Rezachevici, Constantin, 'Populație și economie în Țara Românească și Moldova', in Virgil Cândea (ed.), *Istoria românilor*, vol. 5, second edition (Bucharest, 2012), pp. 389–470.

Röhrborn, Klaus, 'Die Emanzipation der Finanzbürokratie im osmanischen Reich (Ende des 16. Jahrhunderts)', *Zeitschrift der Deutschen Morgenländischen Gesellschaft* 122 (1972), pp. 118–39.

Rosetti, Radu, *Familia Rosetti: coborâtorii moldoveni ai lui Lascaris Rousaitos*, 2 vols (Bucharest, 1938).

Rothman, E. Natalie, *Brokering Empire: Trans-imperial Subjects between Venice and Istanbul* (Ithaca – London, 2012).

Rotman-Bulgaru, Cristina, 'Relațiile Moldovei cu Imperiul otoman la începutul secolului al XVII-lea', *Revista de Istorie* 26/5 (1976), pp. 677–96.

268 *Bibliography*

Rowlands, Guy, *The Dynastic State and the Army under Louis XIV: Royal Service and Private Interest, 1661–1701* (Cambridge, 2002).

Safargaliev, M. G., *Raspad Zolotoj Ordy* (Saransk, 1960).

Salzmann, Ariel, 'An ancien régime revisited: "privatization" and political economy in the eighteenth-century Ottoman Empire', *Politics and Society* 21/4 (1993), pp. 393–423.

Salzmann, Ariel, *Tocqueville in the Ottoman Empire: Rival Paths to the Modern State* (Leiden – Boston, 2004).

Scott, James C., 'Patron–client politics and political change in Southeast Asia', *American Political Science Review* 66/1 (1972), pp. 91–113.

Simonescu, Dan, 'Le chroniquer Matthieu de Myre et une traduction ignorée de son "Histoire"', *Revue des Études Sud-Est Européennes* 4/1–2 (1966), pp. 81–114.

Singer, Amy, *Constructing Ottoman Beneficence: An Imperial Soup Kitchen in Jerusalem* (Albany, 2002).

Sîrbu, Ion, *Mateiu-Vodă Basarabas auswärtige Beziehungen, 1632–1654* (Leipzig, 1899).

Skinner, Barbara, 'Khmelnytsky's shadow: the confessional legacy', in Karin Friedrich and Barbara M. Pendzich (eds), *Citizenship and Identity in a Multinational Commonwealth: Poland-Lithuania in Context, 1550–1772* (Leiden – Boston, 2009), pp. 149–70.

Skorupa, Dariusz, 'Bitwa pod Bukowem 20 października 1600 r.', in Mirosław Nagielski (ed.), *Staropolska sztuka wojenna XVI–XVIII wieku: Prace ofiarowane Profesorowi Jaremie Maciszewskiemu* (Warsaw, 2002), pp. 17–43.

Skorupa, Dariusz, *Stosunki polsko-tatarskie, 1595–1623* (Warsaw, 2004).

Sliesoriūnas, Gintautas, 'Walka stronnictw w przededniu i podczas wojny domowej na Litwie XVII/XVIII wieku', in Jerzy Urwanowicz, Ewa Dubas-Urwanowicz and Piotr Guzowski (eds), *Władza i prestiż: Magnateria Rzeczypospolitej w XVI–XVIII wieku* (Białystok, 2003), pp. 231–42.

Smolarek, Przemysław, *Kampania mołdawska Jana III roku 1691* (Oświęcim, 2015).

Sokołowski, Wojciech, *Politycy schyłku Złotego Wieku: Małopolscy przywódcy szlachty i parlamentarzyści w latach 1574–1605* (Warsaw, 1997).

Soreanu, Mircea C., 'Ţările Române şi Imperiul otoman în perioada guvernării marilor viziri din familia Köprülü (1656–1710)' (PhD diss., University of Bucharest, 1998).

Sovetov, Pavel V., *Issledovanie po istorii feodalizma v Moldavii: očerki istorii zemlevladenija*, 2 vols (Chişinău, 1974).

Spieralski, Zdzisław, *Awantury mołdawskie* (Warsaw, 1967).

Stanley, Tim, 'Ottoman gift exchange: royal give and take', *Muqarnas* 27 (2010), pp. 189–207.

Stoicescu, Nicolae, *Sfatul domnesc şi marii dregători din Ţara Românească şi Moldova: Sec. XIV–XVII* (Bucharest, 1968).

Stoicescu, Nicolae, *Dicţionar al marilor dregători din Ţara Românească şi Moldova (sec. XIV–XVII)* (Bucharest, 1971).

Stoicescu, Nicolae, *Matei Basarab* (Bucharest, 1988).

Stoide, Constantin A., *Curt Celebi* (Iași, 1936).

Stoide, Constantin A., 'Prima domnie moldovenească a lui Gheorghe Duca vodă', *Revista istorică română* 15/1 (1945), pp. 26–42.

Stolicki, Jarosław, *Egzulanci podolscy (1672–1699): Znaczenie uchodźców z Podola w życiu politycznym Rzeczypospolitej* (Cracow, 1994).

Subtelny, Orest, *Domination of Eastern Europe: Native Nobilities and Foreign Absolutism, 1500–1715* (Kingston, 1986).

Süreyya, Mehmed, *Sicill-i Osmanî*, ed. Seyit A. Kahraman (Istanbul, 1996).

Sysyn, Frank E., *Between Poland and the Ukraine: The Dilemma of Adam Kysil', 1600–1653* (Cambridge, MA, 1985).

Szabó, János B., 'Prince György Rákoczi I of Transylvania and the elite of Ottoman Hungary, 1630–1636', in Gábor Kármán (ed.), *Tributaries and Peripheries of the Ottoman Empire* (Leiden – Boston, forthcoming).

Szabó, János B., and Balázs Sudár, '"Independens fejedelem az Portán kívül": II. Rákóczi György oszmán kapcsolatai. Esettanulmány az Erdélyi Fejedelmség és az Oszmán Birodalom viszonyának történetéhez. 2. rész', *Századok* 147 (2013), pp. 931–99.

Szczerbicka, Ludwika, 'Jan Szczęsny Herburt – zarys monografii', in Kazimierz Budzyk (ed.), *Ze studiów nad literaturą staropolską* (Wrocław, 1957), pp. 205–92.

Székely, Maria Magdalena, 'Neamul lui Nestor Ureche', *Anuarul Institutului de Istorie 'A.D. Xenopol'* 30 (1993), pp. 653–70.

Székely, Maria Magdalena, 'Contribuții la genealogia familiei Stroici', *Arhiva Genealogică* 1/1–2 (1994), pp. 249–53.

Székely, Maria Magdalena, 'Noi contribuții la genealogia familiei Stroici', *Arhiva Genealogică* 2/1–2 (1995), pp. 65–77.

Székely, Maria Magdalena, 'Structuri de familie în societatea medieval moldovenească', *Arhiva Genealogică* 4/1–2 (1997), pp. 59–117.

Székely, Maria Magdalena, 'Structura domeniului boieresc: Nestor Ureche și proprietățile lui', *Revista istorică* 9/3–4 (1998), pp. 153–68.

Szłapinskij, Władimir, 'Współoddziaływanie rynków pieniężnych: Województwo ruskie a Turcja, Mołdawia i Wołoszczyzna', *Wiadomości Numizmatyczne* 44/1 (2000), pp. 1–38.

Șerban, Constantin, *Vasile Lupu, domn al Moldovei (1634–1653)* (Bucharest, 1991).

Tezcan, Baki, 'Searching for Osman: a reassessment of the deposition of the Ottoman sultan Osman II (1618–1622)', (PhD diss., Princeton University, 2001).

Tezcan, Baki, 'The question of regency in Ottoman dynasty: the case of the early reign of Ahmed I', *Archivum Ottomanicum* 25 (2008), pp. 185–98.

Tezcan, Baki, 'Khotin 1621, or how the Poles changed the course of Ottoman history', *Acta Orientalia Academiae Scientiarum Hungaricae* 62/2 (2009), pp. 185–98.

Tezcan, Baki, *The Second Ottoman Empire: Political and Social Transformation in the Early Modern World* (Cambridge, 2010).

Bibliography

Tezcan, Baki, 'Ethnicity, race, religion, and social class: Ottoman markers of difference', in Christine Woodhead (ed.), *The Ottoman World* (London – New York, 2012), pp. 159–70.

Thiessen, Hillard von, *Diplomatie und Patronage: Die spanisch-römischen Beziehungen 1605–1621 in akteurszentrierter Perspektive* (Epfendorf, 2010).

Thoen, Irma, *Strategic Affection? Gift-Exchange in Seventeenth-Century Holland* (Amsterdam, 2007).

Tilly, Charles, *Trust and Rule* (Cambridge, 2005).

Türkmen, Mustafa N., 'Kamaniçe seferinin lojistik hazırlıkları', (PhD diss., Ankara University, 2002).

Tygielski, Wojciech, 'W poszukiwaniu patrona', *Przegląd Historyczny* 78/2 (1987), pp. 191–210.

Tygielski, Wojciech, 'A faction which could not lose', in Antoni Mączak and Elisabeth Müller-Luckner (eds), *Klientelsysteme im Europa der Früher Neuzeit* (Munich, 1988), pp. 191–210.

Tygielski, Wojciech, *Politics of Patronage in Renaissance Poland: Chancellor Jan Zamoyski, His Supporters and the Political Map of Poland, 1572–1605* (Warsaw, 1990).

Tygielski, Wojciech, *Listy – ludzie – władza: Patronat Jana Zamoyskiego w świetle korespondencji* (Warsaw, 2007).

Ülgen, Tülin, 'Tabanı-yassı Mehmed Paşa' (MA thesis, Istanbul University, 1962).

Ungureanu, Dragoş, 'Constantin Brâncoveanu şi Înalta Poartă: Relaţii financiaro-vasalice în lumina Condicii visteriei', http://www.cimec.ro/istorie/ Condica-vistieriei-tarii-romanestiBrancoveanu/dl.asp?filename=Ungureanu-Dragos_Constantin-Brancoveanu-si-Inalta-Poarta-Relatii-financiarovasalice-in-lumina-Condicii-vistieriei.pdf [accessed 20 May 2014].

Urbaniak, Violetta, *Zamoyszczycy bez Zamoyskiego: Studium dekompozycji ugrupowania politycznego* (Warsaw, 1995).

Ursinus, Michael, 'The transformation of the Ottoman fiscal regime, *c.* 1600–1850', in Christine Woodhead (ed.), *The Ottoman World* (London – New York, 2012), pp. 423–35.

Urwanowicz, Jerzy, 'Stanisław Żółkiewski w życiu publicznym: wybory – zachowania – poglądy', *Barok* 18/1 (2001), pp. 223–35.

Velichi, Constantin 'Vasile Lupu ca domn al Moldovei şi al Ţării Româneşti', *Revista Istorică* 22/4–6 (1936), pp. 101–3.

Veress, Andrei, 'Pribegia lui Gligoraşcu vodă prin Ungaria şi aiurea (1664–1672)', *Analele Academiei Române. Memoriile Secţiuni Istorice. Seria III*, 2 (1924), pp. 269–336.

Vivo, Filippo de, *Information and Communication in Venice: Rethinking Early Modern Politics* (Oxford, 2007).

Vlasova, Lidia, 'Dva napravlenija vnešnej politiki Moldavii i ix prelomlenie v ee vzaimootnošneijax s Pol'šej v 80–90-e gody XVII v.', in B. A. Rybakov (ed.), *Rossija, Pol'ša i Pričernomor'e v XV–XVIII v.* (Moscow, 1979), pp. 332–43.

Vlasova, Lidia, *Moldavsko-pol'skie političeskie svjazi v poslednej četverti XVII v. – načale XVIII v.* (Chişinău, 1980).

Wagner, Marek, *Stanisław Jabłonowski (1634–1702): Polityk i dowódca*, 2 vols (Siedlce, 1997).

Wagner, Marek, 'Konflikt polsko-mołdawski w latach 1695–1696', in Marek Wagner, *W cieniu szukamy jasności chwały: studia z dziejów panowania Jana III Sobieskiego* (Siedlce, 2002), pp. 124–9.

Wagner, Marek, 'Mołdawianie i Serbowie w służbie Jana III Sobieskiego', in Marek Wagner, *W cieniu szukamy jasności chwały: studia z dziejów panowania Jana III Sobieskiego* (Siedlce, 2002), pp. 116–23.

Wagner, Marek, 'Pogranicze polsko-mołdawskie w końcu XVII wieku', in Krzysztof Mikulski and Agnieszka Zielińska-Nowicka (eds), *Etniczne, kulturowe i religijne pogranicza Rzeczypospolitej w XVI–XVIII wieku* (Toruń, 2006), pp. 38–45.

Wagner, Marek, *Wojna polsko-turecka, 1672–1676*, 2 vols (Zabrze, 2009).

Ward, Kerry, *Networks of Empire: Forced Migration in the Dutch East India Company* (Cambridge, 2009).

Wasiucionek, Michał, 'Kanclerz i hospodar – klientelizm nietypowy? Na marginesie stosunków Jana Zamoyskiego z Jeremim Mohyłą', *Wschodni Rocznik Humanistyczny* 6 (2009), pp. 65–72.

Wasiucionek, Michał, 'Diplomacy, power, and ceremonial entry: Polish–Lithuanian grand embassies in Moldavia in the seventeenth century', *Acta Poloniae Historica* 105 (2012), pp. 55–83.

Wasiucionek, Michał, 'Danube-hopping: conversion, jurisdiction and spatiality between the Ottoman Empire and the Danubian principalities in the seventeenth century', in Claire Norton (ed.), *Conversion and Islam in the Early Modern Mediterranean* (London – New York, 2017), pp. 77–99.

White, Sam, *The Climate of Rebellion in the Early Modern Ottoman Empire* (Cambridge, 2011).

Wimmer, Andreas and Nina Glick Schiller, 'Methodological nationalism and beyond: nation-state building, migration and the social sciences', *Global Networks* 2/4 (2002), pp. 301–31.

Wimmer, Jan, *Wojsko polskie w drugiej połowie XVII wieku* (Warsaw, 1965).

Winter, Stefan, *The Shiites of Lebanon under Ottoman Rule, 1516–1788* (Cambridge, 2010).

Wisner, Henryk, *Zygmunt III Waza*, second edition (Warsaw, 2006).

Woliński, Janusz, 'Sprawa pruska i traktat jaworowski', *Przegląd Historyczno-Wojskowy* 30/1 (1932), pp. 1–32.

Woliński, Janusz, 'Po Chocimie 1673–1674', in Janusz Woliński, *Z dziejów wojen polsko-tureckich* (Warsaw, 1983), pp. 60–89.

Woliński, Janusz, 'Żórawno', in Janusz Woliński, *Z dziejów wojen polsko-tureckich* (Warsaw, 1983), pp. 163–81.

Wolski, Marian, *Potoccy herbu Pilawa do początku XVII wieku: Studium genealogiczno-własnościowe* (Cracow, 2013).

Wójcik, Zbigniew, 'The separatist tendencies in the Grand Duchy of Lithuania in the 17th century', *Acta Poloniae Historica* 69 (1994), pp. 55–62.

Wyrozumski, Jerzy, 'Węgry i sprawa Rusi halicko-włodzimierskiej za Kazimierza Wielkiego', in Krystyna Zielińska-Melkowska (ed.), *Europa Środkowa i Wschodnia w polityce Piastów* (Toruń, 1996), pp. 111–20.

Yılmaz, Yasir, 'Grand vizieral authority revisited: Köprülüs' legacy and Kara Mustafa Paşa', *Mediterranean Historical Review* 31/1 (2016), pp. 21–42.

Yoldaşlar, Özgün D., 'The realization of Mehmed IV's *ghazi* title at the campaign of Kamaniçe' (MA thesis, Sabancı University, 2013).

Yun Casalilla, Bartolomé, 'Introducción: entre el imperio colonial y la monarquía compuesta. Élites y territorios en la Monarquía Hispánica', in Bartolomé Yun Casalilla (ed.), *Las redes del imperio: Élites sociales en la articulación de la Monarquía Hispánica* (Madrid, 2009), pp. 11–35.

Yun Casalilla, Bartolomé, 'Reading sources throughout P. Bourdieu and Cyert and March: aristocratic patrimonies vs. commercial enterprises in Europe (c. 1550–1650)', in Francesco Ammannati (ed.), *Dove va la storia economica? Metodi e prospettive secc. XIII–XVIII* (2011), pp. 325–38.

Zahariuc, Petronel, *Ţara Moldovei în vremea lui Gheorghe ştefan voievod (1653–1658)* (Iaşi, 2003).

Zielińska, Teresa, 'Ordynacje w dawnej Polsce', *Przegląd Historyczny* 68/1 (1977), pp. 17–30.

Zielińska, Zofia, 'Magnaten und Adel im politischen Landleben Polen-Litauens des 18. Jahrhunderts', in Antoni Mączak and Elisabeth Müller-Luckner (eds), *Klientelsysteme im Europa der Früher Neuzeit* (Munich, 1988), pp. 203–10.

Zotta, Sever, 'Doamna Elisaveta a lui Ieremia Movilă a fost fiica lui Gheorghie pârcălab de Hotin', *Arhiva Genealogică* 2 (1913), pp. 178–80.

Zotta, Sever, 'Doi fraţi ai lui Radu Mihnea V.V. călugăriţi în Moldova', *Revista Arhivelor* 1 (1924), pp. 136–41.

Index

Abaza Hasan Pasha 142, 153
Abaza Mehmed Pasha
   career in Anatolia 74, 76
   death 78, 122
   defiance of the Porte 76–7, 92, 189
   Matei Basarab and 75–7, 86–7, 120, 122
   Miron Barnovschi and 77–8
Abbas I of Persia 73, 214 n.157
Adams, Julia 190
'Ahdnames, Moldavian and Wallachian 25, 149–50
Ahmed Bey, governor of Bender 157, 159
Ahmed Pasha, Fazlı 92
Ahmed Pasha, Köprülüzade Fazıl. See Köprülüzade Fazıl Ahmed Pasha
Akkerman 24
Albanians. See also Ethnic-regional solidarities; Duca, Gheorghe; Ghica, Gheorghe; Ghica, Grigore; Kasım Agha; Kemankeş Kara Mustafa Pasha; Köprülü Mehmed Pasha; Köprülüzade Fazıl Ahmed Pasha; Ştefaniţă Lupu; Tabanıyassı Mehmed Pasha; Vasile Lupu
   Arbănaş 62–4
   Arnavud 62–4
   cross-border patronage 65–70
   Ottoman officialdom 60–1
Alexandru (Coconul, son of Radu Mihnea) 121
Alexandru Iliaş, Wallachian and Moldavian voivode 62, 75, 77, 121
Alexandru Movilă. See Movilă, Alexandru
Anatolia
   Abaza Hasan Pasha 142, 153
   Abaza Mehmed Pasha 74, 76–7
   Celali revolts 29, 72, 152, 158
   Nasuh Pasha 72–4
   Ottoman beginnings 24
Antonie of Popeşti 90, 145–6
Apostol. See Kürd Salman Çavuş
Arbanasi 63

Arenas, socio-political (concept)
   cross-border patronage 15
   definition 14
   mobility between 15, 47–52
   resources embedded in 15
   rules of 14–15, 44
Aron, Moldavian voivode 94, 153, 164
Asanis family 36
Atike Sultan, Burnaz, wife of Ken'an Pasha 51, 67, 100, 206 n.44
Augustyniak, Urszula 112
Axinte Uricariul 66

Babinger, Franz 63
Băcioc, Costea 102, 134–6
Bahadur Giray, Crimean khan 58–60, 124–5, 209 n.88
Bahçesaray 58
Bailey, Frederick G. 14
Băleanu-Leurdeanu faction 118, 233 n.126
Balică, Isac 135–6
Balkans 24, 63
Ballarino, Giovanni Battista 87
Baltic grain trade 30, 33, 103
Bar 113, 173
Barkey, Karen 28
Barnovschi, Miron
   Abaza Mehmed Pasha and 77–8
   Barsi, Niccolò 58
   death 77–8, 121
   Kantemir Mirza and 56
   Maksymilian Przerębski and 56
   Matei Basarab and 77–8
   naturalization in Poland–Lithuania 57
   Stanisław Koniecpolski and 219 n.36
   Ştefan Tomşa II and 56
   Tomasz Zamoyski and 219 n.36
Basarabi dynasty in Wallachia 34
Báthory, András 169
Báthory, Stephen 161, 163
Báthory, Zsigmond 153
Bayezid II (Ottoman sultan, 1481–1512) 24

274   *Index*

Bender 157, 159
Bobicescu, Cristian A. 165–6, 207 n.60
Bogdăneşti–Muşatini dynasty in Moldavia 34
Boh river 25
Börekçi, Günhan 43, 198 n.43
Bosnia 60, 61, 74
Bostanzade Mehmed Efendi 155–6
Bozcaada 141
Braclav, Palatinate of 21, 32, 53
Braddick, Michael J. 118
Brăila. *See* İbrail
Brâncoveanu, Constantin. *See* Constantin Brâncoveanu
Brest', Union of (1596) 33, 108–9
brokerage (concept) 12, 44
Brummett, Palmira 10
Brutti family
    and Koca Sinan Pasha 48
    and Mehmed Bey of Niğbolu 48
    and Radu Mıhnea 48
Bučač, Treaty of (1672) 171
Bucak 24, 56, 123
Bucharest 75–6, 112, 142–3, 157
Bucov, battle of (1600) 169
Bulus b. Makariyos al-Halabi. *See* Paul of Aleppo
Burt, Ronald S., 92
Buzăianul, Dumitraşco 145

Ca'fer Pasha 156–7
Caffa. *See* Kefe
Călugăreni, battle of (1595) 157
Canpoladoğlu Ali Pasha 74
Cantacuzino
    Ban Iane 48
    family 89–90, 112, 118, 145, 147
    Postelnic Constantin 66, 89, 142, 144
    Şerban 112, 143–4, 146, 175, 177
Cantemir, Constantin 175, 177–8, 180, 187
Capitulations. *See* '*Ahdname*s, Moldavian and Wallachian
Capuchehaia
    Curt Çelebi 76
    duties 25
    Gheorghe Ghica 64–5, 69, 125, 143
    Moldavian 108
Caragea family 36
Carpathian Mountains 3, 21, 23

Casimir III the Great 21
Catargi family 121, 123
Catargi, Nicolae 85, 121, 126
Caterina Cercheza, wife of Vasile Lupu 58–60, 78, 108, 124
Caucasus 60–1, 74, 210 n.101
Celalis
    political culture 74, 77–8, 120
    rebellions 29, 71, 74, 152
Césy, Philippe de Harlay de 57
Chiaro, Anton Maria del 69
Ciğalazade Sinan Pasha 155
Circassia 57–8
Çizakça, Murat 97
Coci, Lupu. *See* Vasile Lupu
Colonization
    Moldavia 103, 166, 176, 187
    Ukraine 21–2, 32
Coman, Marian 23
Constantin Brâncoveanu 34, 100, 107, 178
Contarini, Alvise 57, 58, 124
Cornul lui Sas, battle of (1612) 102, 137
Cossacks, Zaporozhian
    1648 uprising 3, 23, 32, 188
    formation 9, 22
    Poland-Lithuania and 3, 22–3
    raids against Ottomans 3, 22, 25
Costache, Gavriliţă 177–8
Costin, Iancu 85, 173
Costin, Miron
    Crimean Khanate 92
    death 178
    Gheorghe Ghica 64–5
    John III Sobieski and 113, 173–8, 187
    Marek Matczyński and 113, 173
    Matei Basarab 76
    Miron Barnovschi 78
    Ottoman officialdom 86, 122
    Vasile Lupu 123, 126
Costin, Velicico 175–8
Crete
    province of 107
    war of (1645–69) 96, 107, 141, 145–6, 158
Crimean Khanate
    campaign participation 21, 59, 164, 177
    Kantemir Mirza and 56
    Ottoman Empire and 22, 25, 92, 106
    raiding economy 3, 21–2, 26

Crimean khans 21, 25, 59, 92. *See also*
  Bahadur Giray; Ghazi Giray II;
  Inayet Giray; Mehmed Giray IV
cross-border patronage
  alternative geography of power 3, 5–6,
    8, 184
  problem-solving 12, 36, 40, 185
  resource conversion 82, 88–9, 99
  state circuits and 8–9, 82, 84, 91, 101,
    147, 170–1
  trust networks 43
Curt Çelebi 76
Čuxlib, Taras V. 197 n.33
Cyprus 66
Czamańska, Ilona 140

Dabija, Istratie (Moldavian voivode) 145
Damad Ibrahim Pasha 156–8
Daniłowicz, Jan 138, 139
Danube river 25, 36, 48, 63, 183
Dardanelles 141
Dašava 173
Davies, Brian L. 23
decline narrative 7, 26, 93–4, 101, 151, 190
Deport, Nicolae 106
Derviş Mehmed Pasha 58–9, 108, 124
Devşirme
  Albanians and 60
  phasing out 28, 38, 61
  recruits 68, 72
Dietines (*sejmiki*) 31, 32, 38, 138, 162
Dnieper river 3
Dniester river 164
Dosoftei (metropolitan of Moldavia) 175
Drama 68
Drohojowski, Jan Tomasz 163
Drugănescu, Gheorghe 146
Dubrovnik, Republic of 96, 221 n.61
Duca, Constantin 106, 178, 180
Duca, Gheorghe
  Cantacuzino family and 146
  captivity and death 173, 178
  career 69–70
  Köprülüzade Fazıl Ahmed Pasha and
    70, 100, 107, 145–6
  Merzifonlu Kara Mustafa Pasha and
    70, 107, 145
  Panagiotis Nikoussios and 69, 70,
    144–5

Ducal Prussia 172
Džadyliv 133

Ecnebis 27–8, 38
Ecumenical Patriarchate 97, 109
Edirne 146, 159
Egypt 46, 68, 123, 154–5
Enderun 15, 85, 87–8
Epirus 63–4, 69
Ethnic-regional solidarities. *See also*
  Albanians; Bosnia
  cross-border patronage 63–4, 66–7,
    69–70, 78
  'easterners' and 'westerners' 60–1, 67, 74
  instrumental character 61
  recruitment 60–1
Evliya Çelebi 58, 63
'executionist movement' 30, 161

faction
  command and 90–2
  instrumental character 44, 61
  military mobilization 33–4, 39–40, 91
  'quasi-group' 119
  recruitment 37–8, 44, 50, 71
  revenue-raising 39, 96–7
Ferhad Pasha
  dismissal and death 156–8
  1595 Wallachian campaign and 48,
    155–6, 181
  Koca Sinan Pasha and 154–6, 158
Firlej, Mikołaj 55
Focşani, congress at (1772) 149
France 172

Galaţi 143
Gemil, Tahsin 96, 221 n.61
Ghazi Giray II 92, 157–8, 164–5
Gheorghe Ştefan 64–6
Ghica, Gheorghe (Moldavian and
    Wallachian voivode)
  Albanian identity 64–6
  capuchehaia in Istanbul 64–5, 67, 69, 125
  death 69
  Köprülü Mehmed Pasha and 65–6,
    153, 212 n.127
  Moldavian voivode 65–7
  Vasile Lupu and 64
  Wallachian voivode 67, 142–3

Ghica, Grigore (Wallachian voivode)
  Constantin *Postelnic* Cantacuzino
    and 66, 89, 142, 144. *See also*
    Cantacuzino, Constantin *Postelnic*
  Köprülüzade Fazıl Ahmed Pasha and
    145, 146
  marriage 65
  Panagiotis Nikoussios and 66, 69,
    89, 142, 144, 146–7. *See also*
    Nikoussios, Panagiotis
  Wallachian voivode 67
gifts and gift-giving
  books 113
  garments 112
  horses 112, 143
  letters 83–5
  watermelons 83, 111, 113–14, 184
  wine 102
Giurescu, Constantin 149
Giurgiu. *See* Yergöğü
Glover, Thomas (English ambassador) 214
  n.162
Golden Horde 20–4
Greco-Levantines 36, 38, 61–2, 210 n.102
Gürcü Mehmed Pasha 50, 51, 72, 73, 112
Gürkan, Emrah Safa 110

Habsburgs 3–4, 70, 144, 152–5, 163, 172
Haga, Cornelius (Dutch ambassador) 214
  n.162
Halil Pasha (governor of Özü) 58–9
Halil Pasha (grand vizier) 74
Halyč 21, 138
Haracgüzar 25, 94, 97
Harac, Moldavian–Wallachian 24, 35,
  87–9, 94–8, 171
Hathaway, Jane 44
Hatice Turhan, mother of Mehmed IV 51,
  67, 141, 206 n.44
Herburt, Jan Szczęsny 163, 167–70
Holenstein, André 5
Horn, Maurycy 33
Hotin
  battle of (1673) 146, 171–2
  fortress 91, 102, 109, 111, 169, 183
Hungary, Kingdom of 20–1, 23–4, 34
Hüseyin Pasha, Deli 126
Hüseyin Pasha (governor of Buda) 145
Hüseyin Pasha, Nasuhpaşazade. *See*
  Nasuhpaşazade Hüseyin Pasha

Hüseyin Pasha, Sarı 146
Hüsrev Pasha 67, 74

Iaşi 77, 108, 164, 173, 175–7, 182
Ibrahim Bey governor of Moldavia 157,
  159
Ibrahim Efendi, Ruznameci. *See*
  Ruznameci Ibrahim Efendi
Ibrahim, Ottoman sultan 127–8
Ibrahim Pasha, Damad. *See* Damad
  Ibrahim Pasha
İbrail 125–6
Idris Agha 124
Ignatie the Serb, priest from Niğbolu 75,
  216 n.182
Iliaş Alexandru (Moldavian voivode) 145
Iltizam
  Grandee households and 39–40, 96,
    156
  proliferation of 27, 100, 156
  'shadow *iltizam*' 93, 98–100, 185
İnalcık, Halil 150
Inayet Giray 123
Ioannina 64
Iştoc *Comis* 66

Jabłonowski, Jan Stanisław 176
Jagiellonian dynasty 3–4, 21, 30, 161
Jani (servant of Ostroz'kyj) 109–10
Javoriv 173
John Albert, King of Poland 24
John III Sobieski, King of Poland
  dynastic plans 152, 171–2
  Miron Costin and 113, 173–8
  Moldavian campaign (1686) 175–6
  Moldavian campaign (1691) 176–7

Kam'janec'
  fortress 21
  Ottoman conquest of (1672) 100, 145,
    171, 179
Kantemir Mirza 50, 56, 123
Kara Mustafa Pasha, Merzifonlu
  Cantacuzino family 112, 142–7
  Gheorghe Duca and 70, 107, 145
  Grigore Ghica and 144–6
  Köprülü Mehmed Pasha and 143, 153
  Köprülüzade Fazıl Ahmed Pasha and
    119, 143–5, 147
  Panagiotis Nikoussios and 143–6

Index

Karlowitz, treaty of (1699) 4, 181, 183
Kasım Agha 67
Kefe 25
Kemankeş Kara Mustafa Pasha 67–8, 124, 127–9
Kempa, Tomasz 110
Ke'nan Pasha, Gürcü 51, 108
Kiliye 24
Kızlar ağası 73, 86, 122
Kołodziejczyk, Dariusz 6
Koniecpolski, Stanisław 85, 102, 126, 140
Köprü 64, 143
Köprülü Mehmed Pasha
  Albanian identity 65–7, 70
  Constantin *Postelnic* Cantacuzino and 89
  Fazlı Ahmed Pasha and 92
  Gheorghe Ghica and 65–9, 142, 212 n.127
  grand vizier 67, 141–2
  Merzifonlu Kara Mustafa Pasha and 143, 153
  Mihnea III and 51, 67
Köprülüzade Fazıl Ahmed Pasha
  Albanian network 69–70
  death 70, 146
  Gheorghe Duca and 70, 100–1, 107, 146
  grand vizier 69, 141–2
  Grigore Ghica and 144, 146
  Kam'janec' campaign (1672) 171, 179
  Merzifonlu Kara Mustafa Pasha and 119, 143–5, 147
  Miron Costin and 179
Korec'kyj, Prince Samijlo
  married to Caterina Movilă 55
  campaign in Moldavia (1615–6) 55
  conflict with Stanisław Żółkiewski 137–40
Kruszyński, Jerzy 108, 122
Kunt, İ. Metin 60
Kürd Salman Çavuş 47
Kyiv, Palatinate of 21, 32, 53

Lala Mustafa Pasha 154, 158
Lemercier, Claire 14
Leopold I Habsburg (Holy Roman Emperor) 173
Lewenz, battle of (1664) 144–5
Lin, Nan 81
Lozonschi, Elizabeta 55, 131–2, 135, 138

Lozonschi family 131–5, 140
Lozonschi, Vasile 133, 135
Lublin, Union of (1569) 20–1, 29, 32, 165
Lupu Bogdan 177–8, 180
Lupu, Ion 123, 125
L'viv 19, 21

Macedonia 63
Makowiecki, Stanisław 104
Malbork. *See* Marienburg
Malkara 156
Marienburg 110
Matczyński, Marek 113, 173
Matei Basarab
  Abaza Mehmed Pasha and 75–8, 86, 120, 122
  boyar 75
  political longevity 34, 120
  revolt against Leon Tomşa 75
  Ruznameci Ibrahim Efendi and 86–8, 95, 124
  Silahdar Mustafa Pasha and 86–7, 107, 124–6, 128
  Vasile Lupu and 1, 59, 86, 107, 119–28
  Zülfikar Agha and 86, 122, 124
Matei of Brâncoveni. *See* Matei Basarab
Mavrocordat, Nicolae 66
Maxim, Mihai 94, 151, 155
Mehmed Bey (*sancakbey* of Niğbolu). *See* Mihnea II
Mehmed II Ottoman sultan 24, 27
Mehmed III Ottoman sultan 27, 155
Mehmed IV Ottoman sultan 100, 141–6, 171
Mehmed Giray IV (Crimean Khan) 92, 107, 145
Mehmed Pasha, Derviş. *See* Derviş Mehmed Pasha
Mehmed Pasha, Gürcü. *See* Gürcü Mehmed Pasha
Mehmed Pasha, Köprülü. *See* Köprülü Mehmed Pasha
Mehmed Pasha, Öküz Kara. *See* Öküz Kara Mehmed Pasha
Mehmed Pasha, Sokollu. *See* Sokollu Mehmed Pasha
Mehmed Pasha, Tabanıyassı. *See* Tabanıyassı Mehmed Pasha
Miaskowski, Łukasz 111, 113–14
Miaskowski, Wojciech 127

Michael I, King of Poland 171
Michael the Brave 47–50
  invasion of Moldavia (1600) 169
  invasion of Transylvania (1599) 169
  rebellion against the Ottomans (1594)
    47, 49, 94, 153–4, 158
Mihnea II 48–50, 158
Mihnea III 51–2, 67, 92
Milewski, Dariusz 166
Miović-Perić, Vesna 221 n.61
Mir Şeref Bey 72
Mostar 86
Movilă, Alexandru 138–9
Movilă, Ana 55–6
Movilă, Caterina 55
Movilă, Constantin 102–3, 130–7
Movilă dynasty 52–3, 55–7, 84, 119, 129,
    136–7, 197 n.33
Movilă, Elizabeta. *See* Lozonschi,
  Elizabeta
Movilă, Gavril 137–9
Movilă, Gheorghe 53
Movilă, Ieremia
  death 130
  Jan Zamoyski and (*see* Zamoyski–
    Movilă faction)
  marriage alliances 54–6
  Moldavian voivode 54
  naturalization in Poland–Lithuania
    53–4
  Polish–Lithuanian exile 53
Movilă, Ion 85
Movilă, Marghita-Melania 132–3, 138–9
Movilă, Maria 55, 130
Movilă Mihăilaş 132–4, 140
Movilă, Moise 77–8, 85, 102
Movilă, Regina-Chiajna 54
Movilă, Simion
  in exile in Poland–Lithuania 53
  Moldavian voivode 131–2, 140
  offspring 132–4, 140
  Wallachian voivode 49, 102, 131
Murad III 118, 154, 160
Murad IV
  Abaza Mehmed Pasha and 74–6, 189
  Bahadur Giray and 209 n.88
  Miron Barnovschi and 77
  Ruznameci Ibrahim Efendi and 86–8,
    122

  Silahdar Mustafa Pasha and 86, 124,
    126–7, 129
  Tabanıyassı Mehmed Pasha and 2, 68,
    76, 123
Murgescu, Bogdan 61, 100
Murtaza Pasha 121
Müsadere (confiscation) 2, 45, 126
Muscovy
  Crimean Khanate and 3, 22, 25
  Poland–Lithuania and 21, 70, 103, 134,
    161, 188
  steppe frontier and 20–1
Mustafa (son of Mihnea II) 49
Mustafa II 37
Mustafa Agha, Hacı 68, 72–3, 123
Mustafa Pasha, Kemankeş Kara. *See*
  Kemankeş Kara Mustafa Pasha
Mustafa Pasha, Lala. *See* Lala Mustafa
  Pasha
Mustafa Pasha, Merzifonlu Kara. *See* Kara
  Mustafa Pasha, Merzifonlu
Mustafa Pasha, Silahdar. *See* Silahdar
  Mustafa Pasha

Naima, Mustafa 128, 156
Nasuhpaşazade Hüseyin Pasha 124
Nasuh Pasha 51, 72–4
Neculce, Ion 64–6, 100, 106, 175, 178–9
networks, socio-political (concept)
  boundary specification 13
  definition 12
  shortcomings of 13–14
  social capital and 12
Niğbolu 48, 50, 75–6, 158
Nikeforos Parasios, *protosynkellos* of the
  Ecumenical Patriarchate 109–10
Nikopol. *See* Niğbolu
Nikoussios, Panagiotis
  Gheorghe Duca and 70, 145
  Grigore Ghica and 70, 144–6
  Köprülüzade Fazıl Ahmed Pasha and
    142–7
  Merzifonlu Kara Mustafa Pasha and
    143–6

Ojogeni, battle of (1639) 1, 125–6
Öküz Kara Mehmed Pasha 51, 73
Oltenia 75
Osman Pasha, governor of Damascus 124

Osman II 25, 74, 87
Ossoliński, Hieronim 53
Ostroz'kyj, Prince Kostjantyn-Vasyl' 32, 108–10, 168
Otwinowski, Hieronim 137, 139

Padua 161
Pălade, Ion 178
Panaitescu, Petre P. 35, 150–1
Panaite, Viorel 25, 149
Patronage (concept)
    definition 11–12
    exchange of resources 11
    historiography 10–11
    macro-politics and 12
    patron-client dyad 11
    'quasi-groups' 119
    rhetoric of 11–12
Paul of Aleppo 58, 197 n.32
Păun, Radu G. 36
Peçevi, Ibrahim 155
Peter the Great (Russian emperor) 21
petitions (arz) 106, 125–6, 158
Petriceicu, Ştefan 172–4, 178
Petru I 23
Petru Aron 24
Phanariots 4, 183
    'pre-Phanariots' 36
Pişkeş 94–8
Podolia
    Ottoman conquest of (1672) 96, 104, 171–3
    Palatinate of 21, 32, 55, 111, 132–3
political slavery 6, 26, 28, 38, 44–6, 184
Popescu, Radu 90, 111–12
Potocki, Andrzej 173–4
Potocki family 50, 130, 132, 134
Potocki, Stanisław Rewera 56
Potocki, Stefan
    estates in Moldavia 102–3, 133, 135
    intervention in Moldavia (1607–08) 91, 103, 132
    intervention in Moldavia (1612) 91, 102, 137
    Lozonschi family and 132–6
    marriage to Maria Movilă 55, 130
    payoffs from Moldavia 133
    Sigismund III Vasa and 132–3
    Stanisław Żółkiewski and 134–6

Przerębski, Maksymilian
    marriage to Ana Movilă 55–6
    Miron Barnovschi and 56–7

Radu Iliaş 76–7, 121–2
Radu Leon 145
Radu Mihnea 48–50, 121, 214 n.157
Radu Şerban 49
Radziwiłł, Prince Janusz 91
raiding economy 3, 21–2, 33
Rákóczy, György I 75, 120, 122
Ramadanis, Dimitrios 142, 218 n.29
Rangoni, Claudio 101–2
Re'aya 27, 28
Reindl-Kiel, Hedda 111
Rezachevici, Constantin 165
Romaszkiewicz 1–2
Royal Prussia 165
Rusçuk 77
Ruse. See Rusçuk
Ruset family 36, 70, 175, 177–8
Ruset, Iordache 177–8, 180
Ruthenia, Palatinate of 11, 23, 32, 163, 170
Ruznameci Ibrahim Efendi
    death 87, 124
    Matei Basarab and 87–8, 95, 122, 124
    Murad IV and 86–8, 122
Ryswick, Treaty of (1697) 107

Safavids–Ottoman wars with 51, 70, 72–3, 123
    Baghdad campaign 87, 124, 127
    Revan campaign 123
Safiye Sultan 72, 156
Sancy, Achille de Harlay de, French ambassador to the Porte 50, 72
Sekbans 29, 71–4, 78
Selâniki, Mustafa 155, 158
Sigismund II Augustus, King of Poland 30, 32, 161
Sigismund III Vasa, King of Poland
    Jan Zamoyski and 109, 160–3, 167
    Moldavia and 129, 131, 133
    Stanisław Żółkiewski and 130
    Stefan Potocki and 130, 132, 137
Silahdar Mustafa Pasha
    death 129
    Derviş Mehmed Pasha and 59–60

280 *Index*

Matei Basarab and 86–7, 107, 124–6, 128
Murad IV and 86, 122
Radu Iliaş and 122
revenue from Wallachia 99
Tabanıyassı Mehmed Pasha and 59–60, 126–7
Silistre 25, 49, 57, 75, 157
Sinan Pasha, Koca
  1595 Wallachian campaign and 48, 156–7, 159, 181
  Brutti family and 48
  career in Tunis and Yemen 154
  death 158
  Ferhad Pasha and 118, 154–6
  Ghazi Giray II and 92
  Mehmed Bey of Niğbolu and 48
  Murad III and 118, 154
  Nikeforos Parasios and 109
  Skorupa, Dariusz 166
Snagov, monastery 144
Sobieski, Jakub 176
Sobieski, Jan. *See* John III Sobieski, King of Poland
Sobieski, Marek 130
Sokollu Mehmed Pasha 154, 160
Soroca 111
Spieralski, Zdzisław 177
state (concept)
  as a homogeneous actor 4–6
  weakness in Eastern Europe 6
  as a system of networks 12
State-centered paradigm
  'container model' 4–6, 10
  shortcomings of 5–7
Ştefan Bogdan 154, 214 n.162
Ştefan, governor of Soroca 111
Ştefaniţă Lupu, Moldavian voivode 63, 67, 69, 142, 143
Ştefan Răzvan, Moldavian voivode 164
Ştefan the Deaf (*Surdul*) 154
Stroici, Luca 53–4, 112–13
Stroici, Vasile 133
Subtelny, Orest 6
Süleyman I 24, 26, 141
Sweden 70, 160, 162–4, 172
Swoszowski, Jan 102
Syria 71

Tabanıyassı Mehmed Pasha
  Abaza Mehmed Pasha and 76–8
  Caterina Cercheza and 58–9
  death 2
  revenue from Moldavia 99
  Vasile Lupu and 1, 68, 123–7, 129
Târgovişte 92, 121, 125, 157
Tărnovo, Tsardom of 24
Tatars. *See* Crimean Khanate
Tatar Süleyman 107, 125
Temeşvar 127
Tezcan, Baki 27, 60, 71
Timar system 27–8, 71, 96, 154–6, 159, 181
Tomşa, Leon 75–6, 124
Tomşa, Ştefan II
  Anatolian campaign 51, 72–3
  Gürcü Mehmed Pasha and 50–1, 72–3, 112
  Miron Barnovschi and 56
  Movilă dynasty and 55, 131, 134–5, 137–8
  Nasuh Pasha and 51, 72–4, 78
  Öküz Kara Mehmed Pasha and 51, 73
  toolkit of faction-building 16, 44, 78–9, 184
Transylvania. *See also* Báthory, András; Báthory, Stephen; Báthory, Zsigmond; Rákóczy, György I
  Kingdom of Hungary and 23
  Matei Basarab in 75
  Michael the Brave in 158, 169
  Ottoman Empire and 21, 96
  Ştefan Răzvan and 164
tribute. *See Harac*, Moldavian–Wallachian
Tunis 154
Turcul, Constantin 176
Ţuţora
  battle of (1595) 157, 164
  battle of (1620) 140
Tygielski, Wojciech 161–2

Uhrowiecki, Mikołaj 101, 130
Ukraine
  colonization 21, 32–3
  militarization 33–4
  Ottoman conquest of 78, 171–3
  social structure 32–3

ulema 27
Ureche, Grigore 126
Ureche, Nestor 102, 134–6

Valide sultan 46, 51, 109. *See also* Hatice Turhan, mother of Mehmed IV; Safiye Sultan
Vasile Lupu
  boyar 62, 78
  death 69
  Gheorghe Ghica and 64, 69
  Kemankeş Kara Mustafa Pasha and 69, 124, 127–8
  marriage to Caterina Cercheza 57–60, 78, 108, 124
  political longevity 34, 120
  Tabanıyassı Mehmed Pasha and (*see* Vasile Lupu–Tabanıyassı Mehmed faction)
Vasile Lupu–Tabanıyassı Mehmed faction
  Albanian identity 68–9
  cooperation against Matei Basarab 1, 59, 69, 123–4, 126
Vecihi, Hasan Efendi 107, 128–9
Venetian *bailo* 48, 57–8, 123, 125
Venice, Republic of 48, 57, 70
Vidin, Tsardom of 24
Vienna 70, 144, 151, 173, 183
Vistula basin 33
Vladislav IV (King of Poland) 1, 85, 126
Vlasova, Lidia 174, 176–7, 179–80
Volhynia, Palatinate of 21, 32, 108 (*see also* Ukraine)
Vyšnevec'kyj (Wiśniowiecki), Prince Myxajlo 54–5, 91, 130, 132, 138
Vyšnja, dietine of 167–8, 170

Warsaw 183
Warsaw, Confederation of (1573) 33
Wojkuszycki (servant of Łukasz Miaskowski) 111

Xmel'nyc'kyj, Bohdan 23

Yedikule 102, 126, 139, 140
Yemen 154
Yergöğü 92, 157
Yoldaşlar, Özgün 145
Yun Casalilla, Bartolomé 81, 190

Zamość 162
Zamoyski, Jan
  career 161–3
  Ieremia Movilă (*see* Zamoyski–Movilă faction)
  Jan Szczęsny Herburt and 163–70
  Kostjantyn-Vasyl' Ostroz'kyj and 108–10, 168
  Luca Stroici and 52, 112–13
  Sigismund III and 109, 160–3, 167
Zamoyski, Jerzy (Bishop of Kulm) 130
Zamoyski–Movilă faction
  blueprint 56–7, 157
  coordination 129
  crisis within 54, 169–71, 174, 180, 187
  decomposition 130–2, 140
  formation 53–4
  Luca Stroici and 112–13
  succession struggle 130–2
Zamoyski Tomasz 130
Żółkiewski, Stanisław
  Jan Zamoyski and 130, 163, 167
  Gavril Movilă and 137–9
  Marghita Movilă and 133, 138–9
  Prince Samijlo Korec'kyj and 91, 137–40
  Stefan Potocki and 134–6
Żovkva 173
Zbaraski, Prince Krzysztof 26, 50
Zebrzydowski, Mikołaj 110, 130
Zieliński, Jakub 85
*zimmi*s, Moldavians and Wallachians as 48, 94, 150
Zülfikar Efendi 86, 122, 124
Żuravna, treaty of (1676) 171

Printed in the USA
CPSIA information can be obtained
at www.ICGtesting.com
LVHW010320090324
773943LV00001B/93